˙SALVATION IN HISTORY

SALVATION
IN HISTORY

OSCAR CULLMANN

HARPER & ROW, PUBLISHERS

NEW YORK AND EVANSTON

English translation drafted by Sidney G. Sowers and afterwards
completed by the editorial staff of the SCM Press,
from the German
Heil als Geschichte:
Heilsgeschichtliche Existenz im Neuen Testament
published 1965 by J. C. B. Mohr (Paul Siebeck)
Tübingen

To the Secretariat for Christian Unity

as a token of thanks for the invitation to take part in the Second Vatican Council as a guest and observer,

and as a contribution to the dialogue between Christians of different confessions,

in the faith and hope that even what separates us may contribute to the fluctuating and circuitous progress of salvation history.

CONTENTS

ABBREVIATIONS

ATANT	Abhandlungen zur Theologie des Alten und Neuen Testaments
BZNW	Beihefte zur *Zeitschrift für die neutestamentliche Wissenschaft*
ET	English translation
EvT	*Evangelische Theologie*
JBL	*Journal of Biblical Literature and Exegesis*
KuD	*Kerygma und Dogma*
NovT	*Novum Testamentum*
NTS	*New Testament Studies*
RGG	*Die Religion in Geschichte und Gegenwart*
RHPR	*Revue d'Histoire et de Philosophie religieuses*
TEx	*Theologische Existenz heute*
TLZ	*Theologische Literaturzeitung*
TWNT	*Theologisches Wörterbuch zum Neuen Testament*, ed. G. Kittel
TZ	*Theologische Zeitschrift*
ZNW	*Zeitschrift für die neutestamentliche Wissenschaft und die Kunde der älteren Kirche*
ZTK	*Zeitschrift für Theologie und Kirche*

FOREWORD

THERE WILL BE very different reactions to the attempt to depict the centre of the New Testament faith in a salvation-historical theology. It may seem extremely apposite when we think of the almost limitless recent literature dealing with the problem of history from the theological standpoint. This re-awakened interest in the salvation history of the Bible found expression in an address by Pope Paul VI before the non-Catholic observers at the Second Vatican Council when he said that 'a concrete, historical theology concentrated on salvation history' is the common basis of ecumenical dialogue. As a matter of fact, in the discussion of the Council's schemata between Roman and non-Roman theologians, mutual understanding was continually furthered when both sides spoke the language of salvation history and thought in its categories.

On the other hand, the attempt to present a salvation-historical theology to modern man is thought by many to be outdated. In the first place, such a venture is all too quickly connected with specific so-called 'salvation-historical' constructions of the seventeenth, eighteenth, and nineteenth centuries, already regarded as obsolete because they were tied too closely to the philosophies of their day. Furthermore, among many the phrase 'salvation history' (perhaps not a happy one, but nevertheless difficult to replace) creates the impression of a position which is in the bad sense 'positive', 'pious', 'churchy' or 'uncritical', and which renders inoffensive the true problems of New Testament theology. Finally, such an undertaking is completely at odds with the present attitude of Protestant theologians in Germany, largely dominated by philosophical existentialism and its concept of 'historicity'. In stating the essence of New Testament faith this attitude feels compelled to eliminate all salvation history as a secondary 'objectification' of a 'word-event' which in reality concerns the 'self-understanding' of true existence.

I hope to show here that it is wrong to contrast Christian existence and salvation history, as opposites. Today's popular view of early Christianity, in which salvation history represents an apostasy from the existential understanding of the original *kerygma*, seems to me to

rest upon a false set of alternatives. Certainly the whole New Testament contains the call for the decision of faith and implies a new
understanding of existence. But does not this call rest on the faith
that a divine history has occurred, is occurring, and will go on
occurring, which, while envisaging this faith, is first of all independent
of it and stands over against the believer? Does not faith therefore
mean *aligning our existence with this series of events* hic et nunc? Is such
a faith really nothing but the false striving after a 'security' by which
the true and original relationship of creaturely consciousness towards
God as the creative ground of being is destroyed, a view which is
often bolstered with an appeal to Jeremiah 45? Is the knowledge
about the creatureliness of our existence only possible if we take for
granted that we must acknowledge our ignorance of where we have
come from and where we are going? Does the consciousness that we
have our place in an over-arching series of events really contradict
the awareness of our creatureliness?[1]

Within the framework of these alternatives, which seem false to
me, salvation-historical theology has been accused of resting upon
'static' thinking. I hope to demonstrate that salvation history understood properly, and not as the opposite to an understanding of one's
existence, is rather the boldest expression of the prophetic dynamism
of the Bible, leaving ample room for a *free decision*. The history
which, for lack of a better term, we call salvation history, is not a
'field of graves and dead men',[2] but is most timely in a real sense.
Must salvation history really be dismissed as 'early Catholicism'
for us to get the real structure of the biblical message? Does not the
Bible, on the contrary, cease to be a dead letter when we realize that
we are directly bound to the great events of which it speaks, which
are summed up in Christ and unfold in the present in which we live?
Does not the Bible testify that this relationship must intrude upon us
from somewhere beyond ourselves and cannot at all be realized in
the search for security? Does not the New Testament place us in a
great stream where we are linked to the past and the future, and
from which the 'intermediate period', of which we are a part, gets
its specific meaning? This book proposes to deal with this reality,
which did not relieve New Testament man of making constant

---

[1] See M. Werner, 'Der Gedanke der Heilsgeschichte und die Sinnfrage der
menschlichen Existenz', *Schweizerische Theologische Umschau* 3, 1962, pp. 129ff.

[2] Thus K. G. Steck, *Die Idee der Heilsgeschichte. Hofmann—Schlatter—Cullmann*,
1959, pp. 53f.

decisions, but did bestow deep peace and exuberant joy upon him, and stirred him to missionary activity in the certainty that he was a fellow-worker with Christ in the Church. New Testament man was certain that he was continuing the work God began with the election of the people of Israel for the salvation of mankind, which God fulfilled in Christ, which he unfolds in the present, and which he will complete at the end.

I took the first draft of the present work as a basis for a series of lectures which I delivered in Union Theological Seminary, New York, in 1959. At that time I carried on a thorough debate with Rudolf Bultmann and his pupils. Since then, a good many more studies have appeared on the cluster of problems with which I was dealing. Although these works avoid the unpopular phrase 'salvation history' if at all possible, it is evident that the matter itself is still not nearly so settled as had been thought in Germany when it was being rejected there merely in criticisms of my book *Christ and Time*.

Theological fashions change even more rapidly than the rest. The new debate about the 'historical Jesus' has also allowed the theological question of history in general to emerge, and not just in terms of the 'historicity' of which existentialist philosophy speaks.

I am extremely glad that the first draft of the present book was already finished before the debate about 'Revelation as history' began.[1] Despite the advantages of any working partnership, I do not regard collective thinking, as it is expressed in fashions and their corresponding slogans, as a good thing in our theological enterprise. In this case the general discussion gets bogged down within narrowly confined circles of thinking instead of leading to a deeper level, often becoming a monotonous, collective monologue without any real encounter, and leaving no room for raising new and individual questions.

Since my book now appears at a much later date, I have, of course, taken account of most recent works (not only in the survey of the most recent developments in the history of our problem in Chapter 3 of Part I, but elsewhere, too). I have learned a number of things from them and have reworked the whole original manuscript in the light of them. However, I still regard it as a fortunate circumstance that I worked out my whole approach independently of these most recent publications—even independently of those which stand near to my own views. By this I do not mean to disparage any of

[1] For the relationship between 'revelation history' and 'salvation history', see below pp. 57f., 89ff., 294f.

the research concerned. It seems to me to be in the interest of a fruitful common discussion that the questions raised and the answers given should have a stamp of individuality. Those who do not see the essential problems at just the same points as the dominant schools should not be rejected out of hand and refused a hearing.[1] I hope that it will become clear from the manner of this treatment that I am not at all dependent upon the systematic theologians of earlier centuries mentioned above, with whom I have been associated[2]—even if there may be points of contact between us. I hope it will also be apparent that my own interpretation has been gained purely from my involvement with the New Testament.

This new work builds primarily upon my book *Christ and Time*, written almost twenty years ago, which appeared in a third edition a short time ago. In the earlier work I already characterized salvation and revelation in the New Testament as a history of a special kind. But whereas it was my concern in *Christ and Time* merely to work out the outline of a New Testament salvation history, here every aspect of the content of this history is to be discussed—its origin, its total importance, its relation to eschatology. I shall also set out to differentiate it from the dominant theological and exegetical currents of today, though it will also be clarified at important points in a positive way by the debate which has been stirred up by these currents. Furthermore, the complex character of the contents of this history will also be demonstrated at points where in my earlier treatments some of the problems appeared somewhat oversimplified.

A further note is needed to show more exactly how this new study is related to *Christ and Time*. I really wanted to follow up *Christ and Time* and the *Christology of the New Testament* with an *Eschatology of the New Testament*, thus presenting my conception of the essential features of New Testament theology in a kind of trilogy. But *Christ and Time* was much misunderstood (I have discussed this in an additional chapter to the third edition of the book) and the interpretation of New Testament eschatology dominant today

---

[1] Thus, if I use the favourite terms of present-day New Testament scholarship less often than is customary, or set them in quotation marks (e.g. 'self-understanding', 'speech-event', 'objectifying utterance', 'existentialist' and 'existential', or even terms less laden theologically and philosophically, like 'to take into one's grasp', the transitive 'to hang on', and the intransitive 'to bear'), it ought not to be regarded as a failure to keep up to date. Nor do I mean to assert that my own favourite expressions are perhaps better. I merely wish to ask my readers not to look upon my interpretation of the New Testament as outmoded because of my 'nonconformity' in this respect (a temptation to which students in particular easily succumb).

[2] Chiefly by K. G. Steck, *op. cit.*

is markedly different. So I felt it necessary first of all to clarify my conception of the relation between salvation history and eschatology in the New Testament. Thus *Christ and Time* appears in some way to be a prolegomenon.

In that book I tried to work out the conception of time and history in the salvation history fundamental to the New Testament. That, of course, should not be understood (as is again and again construed to be my opinion) as though the New Testament writers were somehow interested in the *concept* of time or the *concept* of history as such, as though they had reflected about them. In reality, of course, they know only a 'filled' time and a 'filled' history. To understand better the essential features of this unique salvation history which is so strange to us, *in retrospect* I so to speak sifted out of it a conception tacitly assumed by the New Testament writers which I designated 'linear'. It seems to me that only against this temporal background does the tension characteristic of the whole New Testament between 'already' and 'not yet', evincing at the same time the *limitation of a linear conception,* become understandable.

My earlier book was concerned with the contents of this special 'history', but, as I said, it only considered its outline. So some conclusions from *Christ and Time* must of necessity be repeated briefly. But now they are placed in a new perspective in which my aim is no longer to work out an outline, but rather to account for the origin of the salvation-historical perspective, its development in the New Testament books, and its importance for all areas of early Christian faith, thought, and activity.

In this new work I am developing my total conception independently of my critics. I hope that this fact by itself dispels their misunderstanding in seeing the earliest chapters of *Christ and Time* as the main thesis of the book. I hope that it becomes clear that the oversimplifications which were again and again attributed to me may at most be suggested by my writing, but were never in my basic thought. Thus, it was never my opinion that the direction of salvation history excludes lapses because of man's sin before God. Though I still use the figure of the *line* as the general direction for salvation history, it is now important to me to stress that I did not mean a straight line, but a *fluctuating line* which can show wide variation.

The above assumption, wrongly imputed to me, automatically gave rise to another—that in my conception there is only the constant divine plan and no historical contingency in salvation history. As a result it was inferred that I left no room for 'decision'. I am especially concerned to eliminate this error.

Some Catholic critics have accused me of falling into an historical *positivism*, of not having taken *transcendence* into account.[1] I hope that

---

[1] See in particular J. Frisque, *Oscar Cullmann. Une théologie de l'histoire du salut,* 1960, pp. 206ff., and other Catholic critics, particularly of my *Christology of the New Testament,* 1959, 3rd ed. 1963.

this time I shall succeed in checking this misunderstanding, convincing my readers that while the Bible from beginning to the end speaks of God's *activity*, and not the *being* of God the Father, Son, and Holy Spirit, nevertheless a being is revealed *in* this activity *as* an activity. This being may and must be an object of *dogmatic* reflection, but not of *exegetical* exposition.[1]

I have been rebuked by others (cf. especially the theology of Karl Barth) for my great stress upon the *horizontal line of salvation*. These critics say that the crucial thing in the New Testament is the *vertical saving act of* God in Christ—'*senkrecht von oben*' (vertically from above). In what follows I shall try to show that I do not dispute the verticality of the saving event, but that this verticality becomes significant and understandable only on the basis of the horizontal nature of the line of salvation, and that the vertical line, as in a co-ordinate system, derives its meaning from, and is defined by, the basic, horizontal line.

Often in the footnotes I cite my own earlier works. But this does not mean that I am repeating in this book what I said earlier. On the contrary, I wished to leave enough space to continue my previous inquiries, so I have often been content to refer to these works for further support of assertions which I consider important.

Here, more than in earlier works, I have to take issue with opposing notions, including those that were only developed after the first writing of this present study was finished. This is because of the situation in current Protestant theology. Of course I would have preferred to limit myself to deepening my own view without taking these side glances. In any case, I would like to convince my serious partners in dialogue (above all Bultmann himself), who do not seek to place me in ready-made categories in order to dispose of me, that their objections and way of raising questions, departing very much from my own, have caused me to deepen and make more precise my own position. Thus, in this regard I owe them thanks, even when I feel I must take issue with them.

Finally, I must express my thanks to past and present assistants, Heiko Heck, Felix Christ, and Michael Neubauer, for much technical and other help.

OSCAR CULLMANN

Basel
Christmas, 1964

---

[1] The final part of this book contains a survey in which I try to draw out some implications for dogmatics.

TRANSLATOR'S PREFACE

THE GERMAN WORD *Heilsgeschichte* and its adjective *heilsgeschichtlich* always pose problems for the translator. Sometimes the German is left untranslated, as in the English version of Cullmann's *Christology of the New Testament*, but in a book whose very title is *Heil als Geschichte* and in which the concept occurs so often, this expedient was clearly impossible. Nor was it felt desirable to follow the translation adopted in *Christ and Time* and to translate *Heilsgeschichte* as 'redemptive history'. *Heil* is naturally translated as 'salvation', rather than 'redemption', for which German has another word, *Erlösung*, and given that the title of the book should be *Salvation in History* (the change in preposition derives from the author himself), the natural course was to translate *Heilsgeschichte* and *heilsgeschichtlich* as 'salvation history' and 'salvation-historical' respectively. The resultant English is not particularly graceful, nor does it always immediately indicate the full significance of the original German. If, however, the reader remembers what these ciphers represent, he will not go wrong.

A word should be said about the author's use of terminology in his discussion with Bultmann and his pupils. As he himself has already pointed out (p. 14, note 1), he does not use certain words, particularly a number of adjectives, in the same exact way as the existentialist group. For example, the adjectives *'existentiel'* and *'existential'* (usually translated 'existential' and 'existentialist' respectively) are not used with any degree of precision. *'Existentiel'* occurs rarely, and *'existential'* at times does duty for both 'existential' and 'existentialist'; in addition, Cullmann uses a third adjective *'existentialistisch'*, which takes over some of the significance of the more usual *'existential'*. All this means that the translation often has to depart from current practice to represent the author's meaning accurately.

At some places the biblical quotations follow the author's own translations. Where he uses the translations of the *Zürcher Bibel*, I have quoted from the *Revised Standard Version* unless there was a definite reason not to.

I should like to express my thanks to Professor Cullmann, Dr

Shirley Guthrie and Dr Joseph Burgess for many helpful suggestions. The editorial staff of the SCM Press have also been invaluable in bringing the manuscript to its final form.

SIDNEY SOWERS

Knoxville College

I

PROLEGOMENA

1. THE PROBLEM OF SALVATION HISTORY

IN THE PRESENT study, we are striving for nothing less than an answer to the old question 'WHAT IS CHRISTIANITY?' That means, however, that our object is the study of the nature of the *New Testament* message. Whether, and to what degree, the life and faith of the later Christian Church up to the present can be considered as a means of comprehending the New Testament is a problem in itself, and we will discuss it in due course. But in any case, it is our aim to find out what constitutes the *common* essence, according to the witness of the New Testament, that is fundamental as an impulse to the different expressions of the early Christian proclamation in the various New Testament books and in the various oral stages before these books. The faith and life of the later Church must contain this common core—even though it appears in new forms—if they wish to be an unfolding of what is legitimately Christian, and they must contain it at their centre. The Church, continually taking its norms afresh from the New Testament, must resist wherever this core is no longer present as such, or is reinterpreted and modernized in such a way that its primary aim is lost, or wherever elements foreign to the New Testament are declared to be the core. It must also resist wherever elements present but not central in the New Testament, elements peripheral and merely linked with the centre, are forcibly pushed into the centre with a destruction of the original harmony. Such developments are distortions and must be opposed as such.

Thus, we see how tremendous is the responsibility of this inquiry about the essence of the Christian message common to all New Testament books. The New Testament scholar is very tempted to regard the establishment of the differences in the doctrinal expressions of the various New Testament documents as the goal of his own

particular research. Necessary and important as this work is (particularly with a view to disclosing the common element in all these
books), nevertheless, as was previously said, the question of the common
elements must remain the ultimate aim of New Testament exegesis.
It is a deformation of pseudo-scholarship when this task is lost sight
of, or even branded as unscholarly. Even to refer it to the systematic
theologian is to neglect the task given to the New Testament scholar
as such.[1]

It is primarily a service of the Bultmann school,[2] dominant today
in New Testament scholarship in Germany, that in its own way the
school has raised this question of the essence of the New Testament
proclamation. The school believes that it can see this essence in the
call to decision which gives the basis of a new understanding of
ourselves. Certainly a quite essential feature of the New Testament
is retained in this judgment, and I would like to say at the start that
my difference with the Bultmann school should not be wrongly
understood to mean that I underestimate the address, the claim, the
call to decision, of which Bultmann speaks so impressively. On the
contrary, I, too, feel that this characteristic is essential. My dispute
with him is over his closer definitions of that decision for Christ in
the vague form of 'desecularization'. It is also over the way leading
to this definition. In particular, it is over the *exclusion of salvation
history* in so far as it is regarded as a secondary element, foreign to
decision and self-understanding, or is attributed to a false 'striving
for security' excluding every authentic consciousness of existence.
Are salvation history and Christian existence in the New Testament
really opposites, as the whole Bultmann school asserts? We ought to
attempt in any case to free ourselves from this view which has

[1] The distinction between the work of the exegete and that of the systematic
theologian does not lie here. I have expressed myself on the subject of where it
really does lie in the introduction to the third edition of *Christ and Time*, 1962.

[2] E. Dinkler, who himself belongs to the group, would prefer not to speak of
a 'Bultmann school' in view of the independence of the members of the school;
see his dedicatory letter in *Zeit und Geschichte. Dankesgabe für R. Bultmann*, 1964.
But this volume itself attests to the tremendous dependence of most, though not all,
of the contributors not only upon Bultmann's historical-critical works in the narrower sense (on this level I confess that I agree with him to a considerable extent),
but upon his theological position influenced by existentialism. So the term 'Bultmann school' still seems to me to be adequate and even more suggestive than the
unintelligible expression, 'Old Marburgers'. Furthermore, the unattractive term
'post-Bultmannians' does not seem to be happily chosen, for the concept of a
school covers the temporal and factual aspects included in the prefix 'post', since
a *true pupil* always begins from the standpoint of his teacher and proceeds from there.

almost been raised to the level of a dogma. If we find that not only
call and decision, but also salvation history occupies an essential
place in the books of the New Testament, ought we not then at least
to consider another relation between the two? Is it not more useful
to investigate whether the call to decision is not a call to us to take
our place in a divine sequence of events, overwhelmed by this call,
irrespective of any striving after personal 'security'? The divine
sequence of events we call salvation history, for want of a better
expression. Because of sin and judgment it can also be a history of
disaster (*Unheilsgeschichte*). By virtue of our birth we belong to many
'histories'—the history of our family or the history of our nation, for
instance. By our decision in faith we align ourselves with this very
special history, salvation history.

In a quite proper endeavour to bring the New Testament message
home to the man of today, the Bultmann school, depending upon a
prevailing philosophy, thinks it must divorce the question of existence
in the New Testament from that of salvation history. In premature
abrogation of the separation of subject and object, the school is
thereby misled to see the actual essence of the New Testament
message only at the point where the person realizes that he is addressed today in his understanding of existence. All else is not
included in the *kerygma*, the 'word-event', but is either assigned to a
later stage as an 'objectifying utterance' or is regarded as an irrelevant
form of expression in any case. Because the meaning of a whole series
of events does not seem at first sight to be disclosed in a personal
encounter of faith, but must be ascertained apart from it by an
investigation of successive events and the interpretation of them in
faith by earlier witnesses, even assertions which derive the connection
of these events and interpretations from a definite saving plan of
God are designated objectifying utterances.

The demand to align oneself with a coherent, special, divine history
comprehending past, present, and future is a conception of salvation
far removed from, and alien to, modern thinking. In the words of
Fichte, with which one of the most recent opponents of the salvation-
historical interpretation of the biblical message concludes his work:
'Only the metaphysical, and in no way the historical, gives blessing;
the latter only gives understanding.'[1] It would match the modern
way of thinking to substitute 'existential' for 'metaphysical'. What

[1] *Anweisung zum seligen Leben*, 1806 (Ausgabe Scholz, Dt. Bibel, 1912, p. 98), cited
by K. G. Steck, *Die Idee der Heilsgeschichte, Hofmann—Schlatter—Cullmann*, 1959, p. 61.

the Enlightenment says of the 'accidental truths of history' when it comes to the salvation-historical view of the Bible also dominates modern theological thinking, despite all the differences between the two. What existentialist philosophy and theology mean by 'historicity', in the sense of a 'punctual' event, also stands in opposition to all salvation history.

But is it not immediately suspicious when the very element in the thinking of the Bible which is foreign to modern thought is excluded from the definition of its essence? Should we not instead consider whether perhaps the 'offensive' element, the *skandalon*, does not constitute the essence and centre of the New Testament proclamation, so that it simply cannot be removed from it?[1] This is all the more likely when we find that the assertion that salvation is a history has not become offensive only in modern times, and has nothing to do with a changed world view (as Bultmann thinks), but was felt to be just as offensive in the ancient world. The metaphysics of antiquity and modern existentialist philosophy, which is so different, both share a hostility to salvation history. Consequently, theologies which differ very much from one another in general share this hostility to salvation history and wish to harmonize the Bible with the secular thinking of the times. They also share the attempt to regard the salvation history that is indispensable in the Bible as a mere 'clothing' of a 'true core' of some other kind. In our inquiry into the essence of the biblical message, instead of being led at the start by what is certainly a legitimate endeavour, to make the Bible relevant to modern man, ought we not to start from the extremely dangerous possibility that the very element that we do not think we are able to appreciate, by which *we* do not seem to be addressed or called to decision, could be the heart of their message for the witnesses of the New Testament proclamation, and not just secondary 'objectification'? The standard position legitimatized by existentialism in the Bultmann school fails to catch sight of the possibility that what does not lay claim to us in the testimony of the New Testament could still have been the essential item for those who made this testimony. (Can one not detect here a kind of biblicism from which the school is struggling to be free?)

By its definition of the core of the early Christian *kerygma*, the Bultmann school must exclude *whole* books *as such*—the Gospel of Luke and Acts

---

[1] In that case it is not a 'false' scandal.

in particular, but others as well, because they do not contain the essence but, on the contrary, represent an 'early Catholic' distortion of that core. Certainly there are documents united in the New Testament which are separate chronologically, and one could say that the late origin of some New Testament documents is the objective criterion for a negative criticism of their contents. But the Bultmann school cannot justify its exclusion of some books by the chronology of their compositions, nor does it actually attempt to do this. The very document which is regarded as the chief witness for the true essence of the *kerygma*, the Gospel of John, is dated late, and in any case hardly earlier than Luke's Gospel, even in the Bultmann school. Therefore, quite apart from the recognition of the canon, at least it must be asked whether it is not questionable when the essence of the New Testament message is stated in such a way that whole books from early Christian times in their entirety either are not related to the essence or are related to it at best in a negative way.

All these matters are at present just questions, and the salvation-historical understanding of the common core should not in any way be thought of *a priori* as correct, nor the conclusion reached by way of existential interpretation *a priori* as false. We do not wish to set up the postulate that the core *must* without question be a scandal for modern thought, so that a statement of the essence of the *kerygma* conforming with present-day existentialist philosophy would have to be rejected right at the start. However, the history of dogma teaches us that the *decisive* debate of the ancient Church consisted in its successful *resistance against the Gnostic attempt* to eliminate the salvation history of the Bible by philosophical reinterpretation. Certainly the success of a Christian doctrine is no criterion of its correctness, so long as we do not share the Catholic doctrine of tradition. Let us not therefore regard the salvation-historical understanding of the *kerygma* as justified just because it prevailed in ancient Christianity against Gnosticism. Nevertheless, two recognitions have considerable significance for our problem: first, a victory for Gnosticism in the second century would have struck at the heart of Christianity. The Christian proclamation and the Christian Church would have been absorbed into Hellenistic syncretism and thus led to their ruin. Second, in this struggle the issue was ultimately the *Gnostic exclusion of the basic salvation-historical character* of the Christian message which could not be accommodated into the syncretistic scheme.

2. SALVATION HISTORY AND THE SIGNIFICANCE OF THE ANTI-GNOSTIC DEBATE IN THE SECOND CENTURY

To understand the importance of our problem, vital for Christian faith, and to see that no mere quarrel of theologians was involved, and that to defend salvation history again is not to return to positions long since outdated, let us inquire what was the significance of the second century struggle against Gnosticism. All scholars, Protestant and Catholic alike, are in agreement that it was carried on for nothing less than the very continuance of Christianity. We are bringing Marcion into the debate, although, with Harnack, we do not simply rank him with the other Gnostics. If we ask which side of Christianity was threatened at the time, Marcion and Gnosticism belong together, however great the differences between them may be otherwise.

Common to both is their attack on the Old Testament. But what does the acceptance of the Old Testament by the New Testament witnesses mean? First of all, that early Christianity does not see, as Marcion does, revelation and salvation in a *punctiliar* event, but in a *coherent* salvation happening. For Marcion the gospel is a punctiliar, unbound event, vertical and not horizontal. It comes unprepared; it is the gospel of the 'strange God'. It would be attractive to see Marcion in the light of the present discussion in which *mutatis mutandis* Bultmann wishes to see the saving event only punctually, and not connected with salvation history.

The acceptance of the Old Testament by the New Testament writers further indicates that early Christianity does not, like Gnosticism, preach ever valid truths in mythological garb, for the Old Testament reveals God's action in salvation history.

To be sure, there were already tendencies within Judaism to re-interpret salvation history philosophically by means of allegorical exegesis, not actually denying its having happened, yet placing it on the level of pure myth to such a degree that it was considered no more than the clothing of a completely different core which did not con-sist in an historical event at all. Philo undertook a demythologiza-tion of the Old Testament in this de-historicizing sense. One may ask whether the Jewish religion and religious community would have survived if Philo's system had displaced all other expositions of the Old Testament.

However that may be, Gnosticism, within the province of Christianity, gave an interpretation of the New Testament that eliminated salvation history. It was only natural that the same Gnosticism that rejected the Old Testament no longer took the historical existence of Jesus seriously, and fell victim to Docetism.

Those first Christians who wrote the New Testament books all without exception took over the Old Testament, and this indicates that their faith in Christ is a faith in a salvation history, a story of Christ, not merely a faith in a punctiliar saving event.

Bultmann is operating from much too narrow a basis when he thinks he can explain the whole question of the acceptance of the Old Testament by early Christianity merely from the Pauline discussion of the Law as a custodian (Gal. 3.24), giving proof of an utter 'failure', so that at the same time a *positive* salvation-historical interest is excluded.[1]

The acceptance of the Old Testament in the New is exceedingly important if it means that Christian faith is a faith in a divine salvation happening consisting in a sequence of events especially chosen by God, taking place within an historical framework.

This indicates *that Christian faith, like Jewish faith, was distinguished from all other religions of the time by this salvation-historical orientation*. We must therefore ask whether the surrender of this specific aspect of Christian faith either by its complete exclusion or by demythologization, whether in favour of a metaphysical reinterpretation in antiquity or an existential one in our time, does not amount to the loss of what *distinguishes Christian and Jewish faith from all other religions*. Was not the life and death struggle of the second century Christians against Marcion and Gnosticism primarily over the Old Testament and over the retention or surrender of a salvation-historical approach to the gospel?

Seen historically, the whole debate during the second century amounted to whether Christianity would be enmeshed in general syncretism and thus perish, or whether it would withstand that syncretism and remain an independent faith. The religions of the surrounding world fell victim to that syncretism. *By their unique salvation-historical character*, Judaism and Christianity both resisted it, and thus were saved. The Jewish, and even more the Christian, salvation history simply does not permit union with Graeco-Oriental

---

[1] See R. Bultmann, 'Promise and Fulfilment', in *Essays Philosophical and Theological*, pp. 205ff. Even more one-sidedly, E. Fuchs, 'Christus das Ende der Geschichte', *EvT*, 1948/1949, pp. 447ff., equates the Law with history.

syncretism. The philosophical structure of the latter ultimately represents a Procrustean bed. The other religions could be taken up into it, for the elements in their myths irreconcilable with this structure could be amputated by 'demythologizing'. In Judaism and Christianity, salvation history would have to have been equated with myth to be accommodated thus by reinterpretation to Gnostic syncretism. If this finally proved an impossible undertaking, we can see that salvation history in Judaism[1] and Christianity occupies a totally different place from that of the myths in other religions. It constitutes its inmost essence as a coherent happening.

Judaism and Christianity could only find acceptance in Gnosticism when they were disrobed of this their specific uniqueness, that is, when they were *de-historicized*. This is what Christian Gnosticism attempted and, within its own province, achieved.[2] As soon as the salvation-historical character of Christianity is abandoned, what still remains in some kind of reinterpretation may be adapted to syncretism and its metaphysical framework. But the residue is certainly not the essential core of Christianity. That was what was at stake at the time. No one knew this more fully than Irenaeus. So he carried on his impassioned fight against Gnosticism, for the connection of the Old Testament with the New, for the economy of salvation, for salvation history.[3] Christianity emerged victorious from

[1] This peculiarity of Judaism was demonstrated especially clearly by M. Eliade, *The Myth of Eternal Return*; somewhat differently by H. Gese in 'The Idea of History in the Ancient Near East and the Old Testament', *The Bultmann School of Biblical Interpretation—New Directions* (Journal for Theology and the Church), ed. by R. W. Funk and G. Ebeling (1965), pp. 49ff.

[2] The misunderstanding of 'the historicity of human existence' is there in Gnosticism too, although the essential characteristic of Gnosticism is rather its incapacity to reach a salvation-historical conception of the biblical message.

[3] See *Christ and Time*,[3] 1962, pp. 56f. and the excellent treatment of Irenaeus' theology by A. Bengsch, *Heilsgeschichte und Heilswissen. Eine Untersuchung zur Struktur und Entfaltung des theologischen Denkens im Werk 'Adversus haereses' des Hl. Irenäus von Lyon*, 1957. He shows (pp. 55ff.) that the questions which Irenaeus raises 'point to a disclosure of meaning and an elucidation of the salvation happening. . . . Irenaeus asks, "Why?" He is concerned with the meaning and relationships of what has *happened*.' In the same passage Bengsch rightly refers to the fact that Irenaeus thereby typically dissociates himself from the way Gnosticism formulated its questions which he, along with H. Jonas, *Gnosis* I, 2, 1954, p. 261, defines with the quotation from Clement of Alexandria, *Exc. ex Theodot*. 78.2: 'Who we were, what we have become, where we were, whither we were thrown, whither we hasten, whence we were redeemed, of what is birth, of what is rebirth.' Although modern existentialism's answer to these questions is, 'We do not know', they still form a common point of departure for Gnosticism and existentialism and characteristically distinguish both from Irenaeus' economy-of-salvation thinking.

that decisive crisis because it preserved the only thing that kept it from ruin, namely, the idea of salvation in history.

Far be it from me to charge with heresy other commentators on the New Testament who honestly try to understand it and come to other conclusions than I do. I dare to ask, however, whether that decisive debate in Church history with Marcion and Gnosticism does not contain a lesson for our time. Certainly things are different today. But the situation is still the same as far as the salvation-historical character of Christian faith is concerned. Although in antiquity there was no radio and no one knew of atomic energy, nevertheless this salvation-historical character of Christian faith was even then a scandal for philosophical and religious-philosophical thought just as it is today. The philosophical systems which were to provide the framework for the acceptance of Christianity into syncretism were certainly not the same as the existentialism prevalent today. On the contrary, they were very different from it. But salvation history simply would not be united with those systems, just as it cannot be blended with existentialism and its understanding of the 'temporality of existence'.

Thus it does not mean much when the existential conception of the *kerygma*, as Bultmann presents it, rejects the ancient metaphysics standing behind Gnosticism. The standpoint from which Bultmann reaches this rejection would probably have been thought to be just as dangerous for Christianity as Gnosticism by the earliest opponents of Gnosticism. In his own way Bultmann abandons the salvation-historical basis which is fundamental to the incorporation of the Old Testament into the New, and which justifies such incorporation theologically. In its place he proclaims a 'temporality' and an 'historicity' of man, meaning man's punctual situation of decision which, while not being foreign in any way to early Christian faith, is nevertheless subordinate to, and incorporated into, the salvation-historical perspective. We shall see that the alternative is not either a situation of decision or a salvation-historical conception of the present. The New Testament proclamation does in fact demand a decision, but it does so because it places our existence in a situation belonging inseparably to a divine salvation history which is in the first instance independent of us.

The further history of dogma and theology could be written from the vantage point of the attempts to remove the constant Christian scandal of salvation history from the *kerygma* by reinterpretation. In a very different way, and to some extent in a very questionable way, theological systems were subsequently erected aiming at securing salvation history as *the* distinctive element of Christianity over against every danger from the philosophical side. This was undertaken by Irenaeus, Augustine (in a certain way), Joachim of Floris, and then by Protestant theologians including Cocceius, J. A. Bengel, F. C. Oetinger, Auberlen, G. Menken, J. T. Beck and J. C. K. von Hofmann. Whatever must be said critically about these systems, in the light of the debate already carried on in the second century, it must be regarded as an historical necessity for them to be worked out. They summoned the Christian Church to reflect about what distinguished it and Judaism from all other religions.[1]

From the survey of the most recent theological development that follows, it should become clear that the present theological debate falls into this context.

3. ATTITUDES TO SALVATION HISTORY AND ESCHATOLOGY IN CONTEMPORARY NEW TESTAMENT SCHOLARSHIP

Apart from a few works of the most recent past, the judgment of contemporary scholarship on the role of salvation history within the New Testament is a negative one. To be sure, its presence in the New Testament is not contested. But wherever it is recognized, it is attributed to a later stage of development in early Christian thought, and is placed in contrast to the original eschatology of the Church which was supposedly not at all oriented towards salvation history. The schools of both Albert Schweitzer and Rudolf Bultmann see salvation history merely as a solution which came out of an embarrassment, or else as a faulty development whose origin may be ascribed to the problems arising out of the delay of the Kingdom of God. Elsewhere[2] I have shown how the schools of Schweitzer and Bultmann

---

[1] G. Ebeling asserts in his article, 'Der Grund christlicher Theologie', *ZTK*, 1961, pp. 227ff., directed against E. Käsemann's rehabilitation of apocalypticism, that traditional dogmatics has a salvation-historical outline so that (in accord with the Bultmannian notion) 'it follows the Lucan trans- [and thereby de-] formation of the early Christian *kerygma*' (p. 238).

[2] See O. Cullmann, 'Parusieerwartung und Urchristentum', *TLZ*, 1958, cols. 1ff., and now the introductory chapter to the third edition of *Christ and Time*, 1962.

converge in their negative judgments on salvation history, although both begin with totally different premises. I shall return to this matter later. Although both schools conceive of the essence of Jesus' eschatology in quite different ways, both are of the conviction that any idea of salvation history was completely foreign to Jesus, and that in this respect there is a break between Jesus and the salvation-historical views of the first Christians.

In more recent New Testament research on the problems centring on eschatology and salvation history, we must distinguish three phases: first, the discussion over 'present or futuristic eschatology', which is not directly related to the discussion of the relation between salvation history and eschatology, but nevertheless is highly important for it in an indirect way; second, the discussion in which salvation history and eschatology are seen as contradictions; third, the most recent discussion about 'Revelation as history'. We shall see that the first two phases of the problem cannot be clearly separated from each other in time, and that chronologically at least they are linked together. Categorically the two are quite separate. Since both extend back to Albert Schweitzer, before we speak of each of the three phases in any detail, we must consider in brief Schweitzer's thesis which has determined the course of the development of the problem both positively and negatively up to its climax in the question of the relationship between salvation history and eschatology.

The position of Schweitzer and his pupils is designated 'consistent eschatology'. This expression, which has become a slogan, is, like most of the favourite slogans of theologians, not very happily chosen. Obviously the original meaning of the term was the consistent interpretation of Jesus' eschatology as an expectation of an imminent end. The expression 'consistent eschatology' was, however, extended (especially by Schweitzer's pupils) to the interpretation of the whole development of New Testament theology, and indeed of all Christian theology. The expression is easily misleading because it includes within this later development of theology not consistent eschatology, but, on the contrary, the progressive abandonment of eschatology, that is, a 'consistent de-eschatologizing'.

According to Schweitzer, the whole of New Testament thinking is characterized by a mighty crisis which arose because the *parousia* did not appear at an early date as Jesus had expected and preached it would. All the theological undertakings of the first Christians had as their aim the resolution of this problem in one way or another.

The crisis of the delay of the *parousia* and the accompanying de-eschatologization began in the thought and life of Jesus himself. Originally Jesus expected that the end would come during his lifetime. When he sent out his disciples (Matt. 10.5ff.), he reckoned that it would come during their missionary activity. The first crisis came when the disciples returned (Mark 6.30). The end had not come. Since as a consequence of the evident 'delay' Jesus had to change his prediction, he then announced his own death as the date of the coming of the Kingdom of God. Hence the connection of the Kingdom of God with Jesus' death in his teachings. The extension of the time still remaining before the end, effected in this manner for the first time, contained the theme of all further theological developments up to the salvation-historical conception of the developing Church, in which the emphasis was shifted into the present instead of the future.

This hypothesis could be read out of our sources only while the results of form criticism were not yet being taken seriously. It rests solidly upon the sequence of the sayings of Jesus in the framework of the synoptic writers. Schweitzer's basic work was done before the time of the form-critical research which proved the secondary character of this framework. Thus, Schweitzer's pupils, who took over his idea of the expectation of an imminent end without reservation or criticism, were forced to reject form-critical studies. Schweitzer's thesis is in fact purely hypothetical. (Mark 6.13, 30 says nothing of a disappointment.) His hypothesis, as such, had stimulating effects. But in no case can it be made the basis of a whole structure without any further discussion, as is done by Schweitzer's pupils, who happen to be systematic theologians. Today there is not a single New Testament scholar who advocates the Schweitzer hypothesis in this form.

Schweitzer explains that Jesus' teaching and his ethics (understandable solely as an ethics for the interval before the end, an *Interimsethik*) can only be understood in the light of his eschatological expectation. Schweitzer sharply condemns as inadmissible the attempts made again and again in 'life of Jesus' research (as in the liberal notions of Jesus) to reinterpret the expectation of the imminent end. It must be conceived in a strictly temporal way. He denounces every effort to free the teachings of Jesus from the illusion of the coming of the Kingdom. He departs quite radically from all those New Testament scholars who do not permit the scandal of the illusory expectation to stand in the centre of Jesus' teaching, who push it out into the margin, who minimize it, spiritualize it, who disrobe it of its temporal character, who reinterpret it this way or that.

If the expectation of the imminent end in the life and thought of Jesus really had the primary significance that Schweitzer attributes to it, then in the light of his premises Schweitzer has stigmatized such reinterpretations with a forceful consistency that we must admire even today when we read his *Quest of the Historical Jesus*. The question intrudes whether even the solution of the Bultmann school must not fall under Schweitzer's verdict against exegetical reinterpretation. In the Bultmannian interpretation, the essence of Jesus' expectation is seen as something other than the end of all things soon to come in the temporal sense. For the Bultmann school it is rather an 'always standing in the situation of decision'.

To understand the much wider discussion, especially the later converging of the Schweitzer and Bultmann schools, we must first raise the question whether there was not an inconsistency even in Schweitzer himself. As an exegete and historian he was, of course, thoroughly consistent. Jesus' teaching was without reservation explained by his expectation of an imminent end, temporally understood. This proved, however, to be an illusion. As an *exegete* Schweitzer did not, like Bultmann, find an existential meaning as the actual intention of Jesus behind his futuristic expectation. Thus, from Schweitzer's exegetical premises the conclusion must actually be drawn that Jesus' whole teaching stands or falls with this expectation as its central point, and therefore must fall and be given up. We all know that Schweitzer did not draw this conclusion. We know what Jesus and Paul actually meant for Schweitzer. But he based his own philosophy of life neither on Jesus' expectation that the end was imminent, which was proven an illusion and in no case could be reinterpreted, nor upon some kind of de-eschatologizing 'salvation history' understood as a solution to an embarrassment created by the delay of the *parousia* and therefore valueless because it had its beginning in an illusion. Schweitzer founded his own personal attitude on 'reverence for life'. For Schweitzer, this went hand in hand with a practical Christianity. But theoretically it was neither rooted in the eschatology of Jesus, as Schweitzer understood it exegetically, nor in the eschatological mysticism of Paul, which he rejected because it was worked out in an effort to come to grips with an illusion.[1] Since Schweitzer as an exegete is averse to every reinterpretation of the New Testament, an impassable gap opens between his exegetical and his religious-philosophical attitudes.[2] With his extremely consistent, but purely hypothetical, exegetical account of Jesus' teachings and his flagrant inconsistency in his practical conclusions, Schweitzer's imposing theological work left behind burning and unanswered questions and therefore has determined the debate of the present to an extent which the parties in dialogue today hardly recognize.

We shall see that *three different solutions* of those questions are proposed today: first, it is contested that Jesus expected the coming of the kingdom of God primarily in the near future, as Schweitzer thought. Jesus spoke of a Kingdom that had already come. If that is so, then the delay of the *parousia* does not mean the collapse of Jesus' central expectation (cf. C. H. Dodd). Second, it is contested that the temporal character constitutes the essence of Jesus' eschatology, which is really oriented almost totally towards the situation of decision. Here again the delay of the parousia cannot call in question the substance of Christian faith (cf. Bultmann and his school). Third, the temporal character may not, it is true, be separated from Jesus' expectation; it is not, however, to be thought of as purely future or purely present, but as a tension in time between 'already' and 'not yet', between present and future, which already points the way to the salvation-historical solution of early Christianity in which the delay of the *parousia* represents no fundamental problem (cf. Kümmel and Cullmann).

A. PRESENT AND FUTURISTIC ESCHATOLOGY

We cannot present a complete history of the debate on Schweitzer's thesis here. There are a number of good treatments of the problem prior to the outbreak of World War II.[3] We are concerned for the

[1] In the very course of Paul's de-eschatologizing, his eschatological 'mysticism' (see A. Schweitzer, *The Mysticism of Paul the Apostle*, 1931) implies an evaluation of the present in terms of salvation history.

[2] In his last publication on the question ('Die Idee des Reiches Gottes . . .', *Schweizerische Theologische Umschau*, 1953, pp. 2ff.), Schweitzer tries to retrieve the significance which the Kingdom of God had for Jesus (p. 16) with a Kingdom of God conceived spiritually as an 'ethical entity'. But the hiatus merely becomes even more apparent.

[3] See W. G. Kümmel, 'L'eschatologie conséquente d'Albert Schweitzer jug ée par ses contemporains', *RHPR*, 1957, pp. 58ff.

moment only with the most recent development and shall concentrate on those features which are in the foreground of our problem of 'salvation history and eschatology', especially on the question whether eschatology and salvation history are opposites. First we shall review the works of C. H. Dodd and his pupils and then the discussion in Switzerland carried out between the pupils of Schweitzer (who will be mentioned only in that context) and their opponents during the last war.

The problem we are dealing with here concerns Schweitzer's exegetical thesis of the exclusively futuristic eschatology of Jesus. The direct antithesis to it is advocated most impressively by the English scholar C. H. Dodd. The argument with the pupils of Schweitzer that took place in Switzerland during the Second World War hardly took any account of Dodd's works, and that may be because of the difficulty of international exchange in New Testament studies during the war. This may also explain why it was only after the war that Dodd was recognized as the direct opposite of Schweitzer in his views on the eschatological expectations of Jesus. As a matter of fact, Dodd's thesis is the exact antithesis of Schweitzer's 'consistent eschatology'.

Whereas for Schweitzer the Kingdom of God is exclusively a future entity, and is to be realized in the immediate future, for Dodd it has already dawned in the ultimate sense with Jesus' activity. Dodd develops his thesis of 'realized eschatology' in two books, small, though rich in content, each arising from a series of lectures. One is entitled *The Parables of the Kingdom*. It appeared for the first time in 1935, but since then has been issued in many new impressions. The other is *The Apostolic Preaching and Its Development* and first appeared in 1938.[1] Later[2] Dodd himself found the term 'realized eschatology' not an entirely happy one. He appears at any rate to be in agreement with the expression 'inaugurated eschatology' proposed by Florovsky, and especially with the term advocated by Joachim Jeremias, *'sich realisierende Eschatologie'*,[3] for which he, of course, finds no English equivalent. But in spite of that, the phrase 'realized eschatology' still corresponds best to the thesis Dodd actually represents—at least as

[1] A very good account of this book is given by R. Morgenthaler in his *Kommendes Reich*, 1952.

[2] See C. H. Dodd, *The Interpretation of the Fourth Gospel*, 1953, p. 447 n. 1.

[3] The expression, incidentally, goes back to E. Haenchen. (Translator's note: S. H. Hooke translates this phrase as 'an eschatology that is in process of realization' on p. 230 of Jeremias' *The Parables of Jesus*.)

far as Jesus' eschatological expectations are concerned. He defends the idea that Jesus' eschatology was an eschatology of the present just as consistently as Schweitzer did the futuristic notion. If Jesus took up apocalyptic concepts, only what they portray about the transcendent, as distinct from the futuristic, character of the Kingdom of God is important. In this way Dodd tries to harmonize Platonism and eschatology. All the sayings of Jesus are interpreted by a few of his words in this exclusively present sense. Dodd will allow for Jesus only a prophetic anticipation of events in the impending history of Israel. Jesus never spoke of an actual eschatological event in the future nor of his second coming.[1] The early Church expected the end in the time immediately after Jesus' death and resurrection, but even it did not think of this as a second event distinct from the first act in salvation history. Instead, the Church conceived of it all as part of the same eschatology already fulfilling itself, closely bound to the death and resurrection of Jesus. However, this expectation was disappointed. So even for Dodd the delay of the *parousia* plays an important part. Eschatology in certain circles, whose ideas we meet in II Thess. 2, Mark 13, and in the entire Apocalypse of John, is now referred to the future, which for the first time appears as a separate and second act, signifying a reversion to the pre-Christian level of Jewish eschatology. This reversion is also expressed in the introducing of futuristic features into certain sayings of Jesus contained in the Gospels. Nevertheless, according to Dodd, Paul, I Peter, and the Epistle to the Hebrews follow more closely Jesus' eschatology of the present which is realized in his resurrection. The Gospel of John sets aside completely all 'dark eschatological elements' and so continues the original *kerygma* of Jesus.

As in the case of Albert Schweitzer, a school has also followed C. H. Dodd which takes Dodd's idea of Jesus' eschatology as its starting point. Primarily English scholars belong to it, notably J. A. T. Robinson[2] and T. F. Glasson, but indirectly, and only within the sphere of this question, we have the two German scholars Joachim Jeremias and Ethelbert Stauffer.

In his important work *Jesus and His Coming* (1957), J. A. T. Robinson proceeds from the work of his teacher as well as that of another Dodd

---

[1] Dodd appeals with special stress to R. Otto, *The Kingdom of God and the Son of Man*, 1938.

[2] Not to be confused with J. M. Robinson, influenced by Heidegger and the Bultmann school, about whom we shall speak later.

pupil, T. F. Glasson (*The Second Advent: The Origin of the New Testament Doctrine* (1945)), and thus opposes G. R. Beasley-Murray's *Jesus and the Future* (1954). Robinson portrays an eschatology of the present which he prefers to call 'proleptic eschatology' or 'inaugurated eschatology'. His work, which contains a wealth of suggestive and original observations, goes beyond Dodd to raise the precise question of the origin of the assertion of *Jesus' return*. This came neither from Jesus nor from Judaism. Robinson is unable to find this expectation either with Jesus or in the oldest Gospel tradition. In the light of Daniel 7.13, the saying in Mark 14.62 before the High Priest about the coming of the Son of Man on the clouds, usually cited as evidence for Jesus' prediction of his own second coming, refers not to a return to earth, but to a coming *to God* at the time of Jesus' exaltation. Yet the affirmation of Jesus' return does not go back to Judaism. Robinson believes he is now able to explain its origin from Acts 3.13–26, where an old christology is found. According to this christology it was thought that Jesus' Messiahship was not satisfactorily established by his resurrection. Thus his Messianic act was expected in the future. In the main the view here is the same as that of C. H. Dodd. All the futuristic statements in the sayings of Jesus are referred either to the present or, at any rate, to the coming events of the present and already fulfilled aeon. Whatever cannot be thus explained is regarded as a later addition.

Consequently Robinson agrees with Dodd's exegesis of the parables of Jesus, as well as that of Joachim Jeremias, who in his foundational book[1] partly accepted Dodd's work, but carried it on in his own way.

As we have seen, Dodd's emphasis upon 'realized eschatology' led to a new assessment of the Gospel of John—that it no longer attests to a spiritualization or de-eschatologizing or demythologizing, but that, on the contrary, it presents the authentic ideas of Jesus. In the last chapter of his book, Robinson carries out this thought with even greater boldness than Dodd himself and does not hesitate to make an inference from it as to the date of the composition of the Gospel which deviates completely from the usual estimate.

Not only on this point, but throughout his judgment of Jesus' eschatology, Ethelbert Stauffer belongs in the same class as these English writers, even though a direct connection between them cannot be demonstrated.[2] Stauffer advocates a decidedly present eschatology of Jesus just as Robinson does. In contrast to a certain restraint which he otherwise observes in doubting the authenticity of sayings attributed to Jesus, he declares without hesitation that perhaps the disciples after Easter put the so-called 'highly eschatological' sayings (whose authenticity is least doubted today)

---

[1] J. Jeremias, *The Parables of Jesus*,[2] 1963.

[2] There is a quite astonishing agreement on this point; cf. E. Stauffer, 'Die Eschatologie des 4. Evangeliums' in *The Background of the New Testament and its Eschatology*, 1956, pp. 281ff.

pertaining to the future into Jesus' mouth. Had Jesus' eschatology been characterized by an expectation of an imminent end it would not have been original at all, says Stauffer. This expectation was widespread in Palestinian Judaism at the time. So if Jesus had proclaimed this expectation then he would have been merely one of many apocalyptic preachers of his time who predicted a great transformation of all things in the immediate future. It would then be baffling why Jesus produced such a resounding echo with this message of the future.[1] Stauffer fails to go into the questions raised by the Bultmann school in this regard, and ignores the solution proposed by W. G. Kümmel and myself that Jesus himself combined utterances concerning the present with a futuristic expectation. In this context, Stauffer has this in common with the English scholars just discussed.

Thus, according to Dodd and his followers, there was a break between Jesus' expectation of the end and that held by circles within the early Church. Jesus saw the Kingdom of God realized in the present, whereas its dawning was shifted into the future by certain circles within the primitive Church. According to Albert Schweitzer the break occurred in just the opposite manner. However, both Dodd and Schweitzer are agreed that Jesus' and the Church's expectation of the end were conceived in a temporal way.[2] They suppose there was a break between Jesus and the early Church simply in respect of this temporal conception. So the break between the two, according to Schweitzer and Dodd, was far less radical than is envisioned by Bultmann and his pupils. The latter assert that Jesus' eschatology was not essentially temporal at all. Luke and the ancient Christian writers related to him are made responsible for stressing the temporal character of eschatology with their scheme of making 'periods' in salvation history. However, we shall return to the view held by these scholars in the next paragraph, since it does not properly belong to this discussion of 'present and future', for it ultimately plays off 'temporal' and 'non-temporal' eschatology against each other.

Beside the conflicting theses of Schweitzer and Dodd, a third solution should be noted, represented by W. G. Kümmel and myself. It holds firmly, along with Schweitzer and Dodd, to the temporal

[1] See E. Stauffer, *ibid.*, p. 281, and *Jesus and His Story*, 1960, pp. 156ff.
[2] Only in this respect can one agree with H. Conzelmann, 'Gegenwart und Zukunft in der synoptischen Tradition', *ZTK*, 1957, pp. 277ff., when he speaks of a continuity between Jesus and the early Church in Schweitzer's and Dodd's conceptions.

character of Jesus' expectation of the future as essential to his eschatology. But it rejects the either/or alternatives of 'present and future', insisting instead that the basic feature characterizing Jesus' eschatology was that the Kingdom of God was proclaimed to be at once present and future. This view was advocated in the debate that took place in Switzerland during the last war between Martin Werner and Fritz Buri of the Schweitzer school on the one hand and W. Michaelis, W. G. Kümmel and myself on the other.

Martin Werner pursues the problem of the delay of the *parousia* posed by Schweitzer, with all its consequences, down into the history of dogma in the ancient Church. Albert Schweitzer refers the whole of New Testament doctrine back to the crisis brought on by the delay of the *parousia* in order to account for this doctrine. So too in his voluminous work[1] Werner derives the complete origin of Christian doctrine from that single fact, showing at the same time the dubiousness of this doctrine, since it is finally dependent upon an illusion.

Because of the wartime situation, Werner's work really gained attention only in Switzerland when it was first published. It was later that its effect was felt in the rest of the world. During the war, the thesis of Albert Schweitzer sketched above, which Werner accepted without qualification as the New Testament foundation for his book, was being discussed vehemently by both sides.[2] It was W. Michaelis who especially opposed Werner in that he tried to show that it is possible to speak of Jesus' expectation of an imminent end, but not an end in the very next moment.[3] At a national conference of Swiss pastors at Liestal in 1942, I was asked to give a paper, *The Church's Hope for the Return of Christ*, which Werner answered in an extensive rebuttal.[4] Without advancing the tension between

[1] *Die Entstehung des christlichen Dogmas, problemgeschichtlich dargestellt*, 1941; [2]1953 (ET (abridged): *The Formation of Christian Dogma*, 1957). Cf. O. Cullmann, 'Neutestamentliche Eschatologie und Entstehung des Dogmas', *Kirchenblatt für die reformierte Schweiz*, 1942, pp. 161ff. and 178ff.

[2] Cf. my report, 'Parusieverzögerung und Urchristentum', *TLZ*, 1958, cols. 1ff.

[3] W. Michaelis, *Zur Engelchristologie im Urchristentum. Abbau der Konstruction M. Werners*, 1942. On New Testament exegesis see especially, *Der Herr verzieht nicht die Verheissung*, 1942; *Irreführung der Gemeinden?*, 1942; 'Die grosse Enttäuschung', *Der Kirchenfreund*, 1942, pp. 226ff. More recently: 'Kennen die Synoptiker eine Verzögerung der Parusie?' in *Synoptische Studien A. Wikenhauser dargebracht*, 1954, pp. 107ff. Cf. the replies of M. Werner in *Schweizerisches Reformiertes Volksblatt* and *Schweizerische Theologische Umschau*.

[4] *Verhandlungen des Schweiz. ref. Pfarrervereins*, 1942 in Liestal, pp. 26ff. See further O. Cullmann, 'The Return of Christ' in *The Early Church*, 1956, pp. 141ff., where I have given the substance of my address.

'already' and 'not yet', as I have done in my later works, I took up a position accepting neither the present nor the futuristic interpretation of Jesus' eschatology, finding instead its characteristic and essential feature in the juxtaposition of present and future, thereby assuming that the beginnings of a salvation history could already be found with Jesus.

This thesis was propounded three years later by W. G. Kümmel, who was then at Zürich, in his thorough work, *Promise and Fulfilment*,[1] building on his earlier work[2] in an extensive way. If he deviates from Michaelis and myself on certain details, nevertheless he advocates (as I do) against the schools of 'consistent eschatology' and C. H. Dodd (brought into the debate by Kümmel for the first time) that statements reported of Jesus relating to the present and the future belong together. Furthermore, Kümmel asserts that Jesus calculated that there would be a continuation of this aeon, albeit a short one, after his death. Both conclusions appear to me to be of utmost importance for the whole debate on eschatology and salvation history which is going on at present. I made this juxtaposition of present and future, found already in Jesus himself, and this tension between 'already' and 'not yet', into what is almost a *leitmotiv* of the views developed in my book *Christ and Time*.[3] It is basic also to the reply that I gave in the *Theologische Zeitschrift* to an attack by Fritz Buri of the Schweitzer school.[4] In this article I not only underscore the hypothetical character of Schweitzer's exegesis of the sayings of Jesus in question; I also emphasize especially the fact that, in spite of the delay of the *parousia*, the eschatological expectation in primitive Christianity loses none of its intensity. The only explanation for this is that the root of all New Testament eschatology lies not in the expectation in and of itself that the end is imminent, but in the tension characteristic of the New Testament's salvation history, and that this is already present in Jesus.[5]

---

[1] *Verheissung und Erfüllung*, 1945; 2nd ed. 1953; ET *Promise and Fulfilment*, 1957.

[2] W. G. Kümmel, *Die Eschatologie der Evangelien. Ihre Geschichte und ihr Sinn*, 1936.

[3] I have stressed in the introductory chapter to the third edition (1962) that this, and not the question of the *concept* of time, is the theme of my book.

[4] O. Cullmann, 'Das wahre durch die ausgebliebene Parusie gestellte neutestamentliche Problem', *TZ*, 1947, pp. 177ff. F. Buri's article: 'Das Problem der ausgebliebenen Parusie', *Schweizerische Theologische Umschau*, 1946, pp. 97ff. On this controversy see the reply and rejoinder in *TZ*, 1947, pp. 422ff., 428ff.

[5] 'Consistent eschatology' was contested thereafter in Switzerland by R. Morgenthaler (see especially his *Kommendes Reich*, 1952) and by F. Flückiger, *Der Ursprung des christlichen Dogmas. Auseinandersetzung mit A. Schweitzer und M. Werner*, 1955).

But here we have already arrived at the transition to the second phase to be outlined here, in which not merely the problem of present or futuristic eschatology is involved, but also the question of whether eschatology is to be interpreted existentially or as salvation history. If a *temporal* juxtaposition of present and future was fundamental to Jesus himself, then one cannot speak of a radical break occurring between the eschatology of Jesus and that of the early Church, nor of a radical contrast between eschatology and salvation history.[1] Certainly it is a long way from Jesus to Luke. Nevertheless, not only is the temporal character seen to be essential to Jesus' eschatology in the 'already' and the 'not yet' of his teachings, but also, as we shall try to demonstrate more in detail in our present study, there are already the beginnings of salvation history with Jesus. In this review of the history of the problem, my endeavour was to show that the first phase of the discussion in which the purely exegetical question, 'present and future in the expectation of Jesus', is placed in the fore-ground, is at the same time important for the theological question 'eschatology and salvation history'.

Although Kümmel's service towards the solution of the exegetical question is great indeed, unfortunately he has never carried out the theological implications along the lines that interested me right from the beginning. In a more recent article, 'Futurische und präsentische Eschatologie im ältesten Urchristentum',[1] he advocates anew the idea that the basic New Testament proclamation *right from the beginning* was characterized by the intertwining of present and future. He also stresses along with me that a development unfolded from Jesus to Paul and the early Church, but that this in no way signifies a break.[3] However, Kümmel does not deal with the question as to how this relates to the works of the Bultmann school. In reality, the discussion today is no longer merely about the present-future complex. Instead,

---

[1] It also follows that to throw suspicion on the idea that the later salvation-historical view is anchored in the 'already' and 'not yet' of Jesus' eschatology, dismissing such a notion as due to apologetic tendencies, is out of place. H. Conzelmann insinuates this in the article cited p. 36 n. 2. when he thinks he must comment that this thesis is 'especially agreeable to the church leaders'. Such un-seemly insinuations ought to remain out of a question that is purely a matter of scholarly research.

[2] *NTS*, 1959, pp 113ff.

[3] Quite similarly к. Schnackenburg, *Gottes Herrschaft und Reich*, 1959, pp. 77ff. Likewise W. G. Kümmel gives an excellent survey of scholarship on the most recent continuation of the discussion in 'Die Naherwartung in der Verkündigung Jesu', *Zeit und Geschichte. Dankesgabe für R. Bultmann*, 1964, pp. 31ff.

the question has expanded to whether Jesus' eschatology in essence can be divested of its temporality by an existential interpretation and thus be contrasted radically with salvation history. Or is it the case that there was in what I call a tension between 'already' and 'not yet', if not a salvation history, nevertheless, despite Jesus' expectation of the near end, a beginning from which the way could lead to a salvation-historical approach?

B. THE DISJUNCTION OF ESCHATOLOGY FROM SALVATION HISTORY

We saw that in the case of Albert Schweitzer the results of his exegetical research are out of balance with his philosophy of 'reverence for life'. For him, in contrast to Bultmann, the essence of Jesus' eschatology was its temporal character, that is, the exclusive futurity of Jesus' expectation. This left its stamp on Jesus' whole teaching and ethics and proved to be an illusion. Nevertheless, Schweitzer felt himself to be a Christian. He has not given any foundation to justify this double point of view.

As soon as Schweitzer's exegetical premises are contested, and Jesus' expectation is either, as for Dodd, 'already realized', or seen as a juxtaposition of present and future, as for Kümmel and myself, the difficulty of maintaining Jesus' teaching on the Kingdom of God is lessened even if it does not automatically fall away. But where Jesus' eschatology is regarded in all its depth as an illusion, as by Schweitzer, perplexity must remain.

Martin Werner was somehow sensitive to this problem and as a sort of aside gave an answer to the question left open by Schweitzer. In spite of (and even because of) its being anchored essentially in Jesus' illusion, nevertheless the Christian message can be maintained in saying 'yes' to God. This can be done in spite of a history in which no plan may be discerned. Even so, no actual relationship is established between this and Schweitzer's exegetical conclusions. This information incidentally imparted is, by the way, not at all in the forefront of Werner's interest, which is rather oriented towards the history of dogma. He has, however, reaffirmed it in one of his articles; cf. 'Der Gedanke der Heilsgeschichte und die Sinnfrage der menschlichen Existenz', *Schweizerische Theologische Umschau* 3, 1962, pp. 129ff.

On the other hand, the above-mentioned contradiction and the difficulty inherent in the delay of the *parousia* is actually set aside by Rudolf Bultmann, though he does it in a totally different way. That Jesus expected the end in the near future Bultmann will accept along with Schweitzer, but without going through the questions raised by him. By his whole hermeneutics, however, Bultmann reduces this expectation to its essential core of the 'decision' disclosed by means of existential interpretation without leaving the province of exegesis. Thus Bultmann extracts the pith, so to speak, out of its futuristic shell, which is not at all fundamental since Jesus merely took it over from Judaism.

Although this solution cannot be merged with Schweitzer's exegetical premises, it is nevertheless understandable why it was welcomed by Schweitzer's pupils. On the one hand the point of departure here, as for Schweitzer, is the expectancy of the imminent end. But on the other hand the basic question emerging from the rejection of Jesus' illusory futuristic expectation is solved in such a way that the link with Jesus' eschatology remains visible.

To be sure, the delay of the *parousia* did not stand in the foreground of Bultmann's basic work about demythologizing which appeared in 1941. Nevertheless, the device of 'demythologizing' had been marked, consciously or unconsciously, by a borrowing from 'de-eschatologizing'. From the outset, of course, the main thrust in Bultmann's demythologizing was directed at challenging exegetes to make the New Testament relevant to modern man. Schweitzer and his school came to their conclusions about de-eschatologizing historically, seeing it as a process actually undertaken *by the first Christians*. Bultmann could not speak of de-eschatologizing. As an exegete he was already reinterpreting eschatology existentially in divesting it of its temporality. He does not wish to eliminate the remaining core, the 'punctual eschatology', at all, desiring instead to let it stand as *the* authentic eschatology and *the* quintessence of the New Testament *kerygma*. Whether he is justified in maintaining the term 'eschatology' in this case is, of course, another question, and we shall take it up afresh in one of the following chapters. For our purposes it is enough to show here that, starting with his own premises, Bultmann was unable to plead for de-eschatologizing.

Despite the fundamental distinction between de-eschatologizing and demythologizing, the advocates of 'consistent eschatology' sensed something of common interest in the negation. On both sides, temporal eschatology is given up as an element unacceptable *to us*: Schweitzer did not do this in his exegesis, but only after his exegesis, because of the obvious delay of the *parousia*. By existential interpretation, however, Bultmann already surrendered the temporal eschatology in his exegesis, which eliminated it as something secondary to Jesus himself. For Schweitzer, the expectation of the imminent end signified a heightened temporality, which on that account was subsequently proved an illusion and theologically useless. But for Bultmann, this expectation from the beginning contained a positive core that does away with temporality, for Jesus' eschatological expectation eliminates all linear time.

In their end results, *but only there*, Bultmann and Schweitzer meet. So Fritz Buri, who at that time, with M. Werner, was one of the most resolute pupils of Schweitzer, greeted Bultmann as an ally when his essay on demythologizing appeared. The theological vacuum created by Schweitzer's conclusion that Jesus' error was not something marginal, but basic to his entire teachings, could thus be set aside, for now the 'error' could be banished from its central importance to a marginal one. It must have been for this reason that demythologizing was a welcome development for the advocates of de-eschatologizing. In carrying out his existential interpretation Buri follows Jaspers, whereas Bultmann goes with Heidegger. Buri would also like to de-kergymatize Bultmann. But neither of these points is of chief importance. De-eschatologizing and demythologizing meet in the person of Fritz Buri.

Existential interpretation, as distinct from the idealistic handling of Jesus' teaching in liberalism, starts quite consciously from a *Vorverständnis*, a prior understanding, and on hermeneutical grounds rejects the 'subject-object relationship'. This is tantamount to the kind of reinterpretation that Schweitzer would have condemned because of his principles of exegesis. So perhaps it is not by accident that Buri's theological move was disapproved of in subsequent years by the true Schweitzer follower, Martin Werner.

Independently of the above encounter, and somewhat later, Bultmann and his pupils approached Schweitzer's standpoint on a vitally important question for salvation history, namely, their account of the course of theological development from Jesus to the early Church as far as it is discernible in the New Testament. In exactly the same way as Albert Schweitzer, the Bultmann school declares that the *delay of the parousia* was the impulse to this whole development. According to both, this delay created a 'tormenting' problem that dominated the whole of early Christian thought. There are, of course, differences between Schweitzer and Bultmann that go back to their different points of departure. According to Schweitzer, because of the delayed *parousia*, there had almost inevitably to be an increasing extension of the still continuing time before the end, until finally a salvation-historical conception arose in which this present took its firm place as the time of the Church, and the end was pushed into the distant future. This notion, according to Schweitzer, was rooted in the original illusion, and can only be regarded as a solution inspired by an embarrassment. But it was still the result of a normal development of Christian thought from Jesus' teaching. Bultmann and his school also trace the salvation-historical solution back to the fact of the delay of the *parousia*, rejecting it just as the Schweitzer school did. But the break with Jesus envisaged by the Bultmannians is a more radical one because they are not able to regard salvation history as a further development of the main theme (correcting it) in Jesus' eschatology. They do not understand this main theme to involve a temporal futurity at all, but to present a situation of decision independent of futurity. In the Bultmann school, the salvation-historical solution, in which a lengthy time of the Church, of indefinite duration, is inserted and eschatology is displaced to the margin, thus represents a faulty solution of 'early Catholicism'. This solution, it is said, is not found in all the writings of early Christianity. Instead, the delay of the *parousia* called forth a thoroughly legitimate solution even in New Testament times, one that must also point the way for us to go today. It is the one we find in Paul, but especially in the Gospel of John—that of demythologizing. The illusory expectation that the end was imminent, which was not itself at all central for Jesus, but was adopted simply as a framework, is progressively eliminated. This happens, however, not in order to make way for a salvation history divided into periods, but to maintain the core of that 'always standing in the situation of decision', existentially disclosed in its purity.

Whereas for Schweitzer and his school the delay of the *parousia had to* transform Jesus' eschatology, temporally understood, into a salvation history by one way or another, in a rectilinear lengthening, according to Bultmann and his school the delay induced two totally different developments. One was a legitimate one, freeing the core of Jesus' expectation to be disclosed existentially, and the other was the illegitimate, the salvation-historical one, taking further the temporal element that really should be eliminated. The legitimate development is in Paul and John, for here Christ is the end of all continuous history, and the original core is more and more consciously extracted from the mythological husk of a temporal end. The false solution is the salvation-historical or 'early Catholic' one, as we find it in the Gospel of Luke and the Acts of the Apostles. There, the ultimate root of Jesus' eschatology, to be understood in a punctual fashion, is completely misconstrued; a dividing up of time into periods is undertaken, and the work of the historical Christ is made into the mid-point, already reached, of a whole time line on which the *eschaton* makes up the far distant end and on which the present is extended to an indefinite duration.

The details of this view of the Bultmann school were worked out gradually. My book, *Christ and Time* (first edition in 1946), or rather the rejection of it, contributed to the working out of the notions sketched above, for it caused the pupils of Schweitzer and Bultmann to distinguish their own view of the essence of the New Testament *kerygma* more clearly from the salvation-historical interpretation. I have shown this in the introductory chapter of the third edition, which appeared in 1962. I must emphasize again and again that my aim in the book was not to treat the early Christian concept of time or history in and of itself,[1] but to look at the temporal situation in the New Testament. At that time I depicted it with a particularly relevant illustration: the decisive battle has already been won. But the war continues until a certain, though not as yet definite, Victory Day when the weapons will at last be still. The decisive battle would be Christ's death and resurrection, and Victory Day his *parousia*. Between the two lies a short but *important* span of time already indicating a fulfilment and an anticipation of peace, in which, however, the greatest watchfulness is demanded. Yet it is from the decisive battle now won and the Victory Day yet to be achieved that this span of time gets its meaning and its demands. If this interval of time is given greater and greater extension there will, of course, be consequences that must be described in detail. But the *constant* factor is from the outset the presence of this tension. This means that I see the general foundation for the whole New Testament in a salvation-historical orientation. This is all the more true as the victory achieved in that decisive battle is understood in retrospect

---

[1] See the foreword to the present book as well.

as the obvious consequence and crowning of the preceding events.

The attack on the above view made immediately by the schools of Schweitzer and Bultmann concerns first of all my assertion of the generality of this New Testament foundation. On the basis of Schweitzer's interpretation it must be contested in the case of Jesus' message since, according to his exclusively futuristic conception, everything still awaits fulfilment. Furthermore, if at some later date a salvation-historical significance is attributed to the intermediate period, the solution is inspired by an embarrassment and is valueless because it does not rest upon a positive appreciation of the 'already fulfilled', but upon the illusory expectation of the events which are still 'not yet'. This expectation proves to be something negative, since the 'not yet' becomes more and more a 'still not yet', placing the decisive character of the battle, already supposedly won, in question. This objection was raised against me by Fritz Buri in his polemic already mentioned above.[1]

After that, the attack made by Rudolf Bultmann on *Christ and Time* in his much cited article, 'History of Salvation and History'[2] became much more important. He had to deny that there is a salvation-historical basis throughout the New Testament, for the 'historicity' of Jesus' eschatology could not be 'salvation historicity', since his eschatology conceived of history as a point, just as Heidegger does. This was emphasized even more strongly by Ernst Fuchs in his article, '*Christus, das Ende der Geschichte*',[3] in which, with reference to the Pauline formulation, 'Christ the end of the Law', he completely dissolves time in an existential solution.[4] Nevertheless, Bultmann grants in his article in *Theologische Literaturzeitung* that the salvation history which I (wrongly) found at the basis of all New Testament thought is present in the Acts of the Apostles. In this way he announced the theme that was developed by his pupils and even by

[1] See above, p. 38, n.4.

[2] *TLZ* 1948, cols. 659ff. ET by Schubert M. Ogden, *Existence and Faith. Shorter Writings of Rudolf Bultmann* (1960), pp. 226ff.

[3] *EvT* 1948/1949, pp. 447ff.; E. Fuchs, *Studies of the Historical Jesus*, 1964, pp. 176ff. The true significance of the statements by reason of which the Law is designated merely a happening 'in the meantime' (Rom. 5.20; cf. Gal. 3.17), and which show that the 'cessation of the Law' cannot be equated with the 'cessation of salvation history', does not seem to me to be recognized here.

[4] Cf. the remark by E. Käsemann, 'Zum Thema der urchristlichen Apokalyptik', *ZTK*, 1962, p. 280: 'It is most clearly evident . . . that Paul by no means wants or is able to speak of an end of history that has already come about. Instead, he sees the end time as already having dawned.'

Bultmann himself in his later works on 'history and eschatology'.[1] This was done always in rejection of my book which thus, in a negative way, determined the discussion.

The demythologizing of the New Testament became more and more the statement of the right relationship between (punctual) eschatology and salvation history. In this development the first work to be mentioned is P. Vielhauer's sensational article, 'Zum "Paulinismus" der Apostelgeschichte'.[2] What Bultmann in his book review only casually referred to, Vielhauer carried out, trying to make the author of Acts responsible for the origin of the 'early Catholic' idea of salvation history. Salvation history is essentially a foreign element in Paul, and the apostle was contrasted by Vielhauer with the author of Acts. In the final section of the article the further development within the Bultmann school was anticipated with abundant clarity. Hans Conzelmann has carried out Vielhauer's views consistently and extended them to Luke's Gospel.[3] What I designated in *Christ and Time* to be the essence of New Testament thought pure and simple is for Conzelmann primarily a creation of Luke. Dealing only with the Lucan theology, he even chose as the title of his work the concept that I advanced, *Die Mitte der Zeit*, the mid-point of time. In this way, he wished to make it clear that the whole construction is not the view of the New Testament but that of Luke—or better said, that it is the Lucan distortion. With his salvation history Luke abandoned the essence of Jesus' eschatology, thrusting aside once for all the remaining scandal of the unfulfilled expectation of the imminent end. This he accomplished with his salvation-historical scheme of 'periods', which shifts the emphasis into the past and present and substitutes the activity of the Holy Spirit for the Kingdom of God soon to come.

I have often emphasized that I can regard the conclusion of Conzelmann's work in a certain way as a supplement to *Christ and Time*. Thanks to his analysis it is now established that Luke is really the main participant in completing the salvation history, and to this extent I am in agreement with Conzelmann's work. However, Conzelmann intended this book to be an antithesis to *Christ and Time* which it is only when viewed from the premises that Conzelmann shares with Bultmann and his entire school. According to this school,

[1] First in his article, 'History and Eschatology in the New Testament', *NTS* 1954–55, pp. 5ff., and then in his book *History and Eschatology*, 1957, the Gifford Lectures for 1955.

[2] *EvT* 1950–51, pp. 1ff.

[3] *Die Mitte der Zeit*, 1954. ET *The Theology of St. Luke*, 1961.

by his method Luke abandoned Jesus' eschatology, which must be interpreted punctually and existentially. Luke did this because of the delay of the *parousia*, which was being represented more and more in the Bultmann school, along with Schweitzer, as a 'tormenting' problem which, as Bultmann said in his review, I had minimized. Because of these premises (which are not actually the object of Conzelmann's book) it came to the point where, within the Bultmann school, the justification for leaving the Gospel of Luke and Acts in the canon was put in doubt, and one spoke of the 'error' common to Luke and myself.

In its extremest form, this whole view is represented in E. Grässer's work, *Das Problem der Parusieverzögerung in den synoptischen Evangelien und in der Apostelgeschichte*.[1] The way in which the two very different schools of Schweitzer and Bultmann meet throughout this phase of the problem becomes quite clear. The scheme of 'salvation history as a transformation of the expectation of the imminent end caused by the delay of the *parousia*' is carried through to its final consequences with all the one-sidedness of a beginner's work. A conclusion of this work that went beyond that of Conzelmann was that Luke is less original with his construction than it may appear, for the same process can be shown not only in the Synoptic Gospels, but also in the oral tradition later used by the Synoptic writers. So, in any case, the salvation-historical basis in the New Testament is expanded, although Grässer (who dealt only with the Synoptics) was far from saying that it would be extended to Paul, John, or even Jesus. On the contrary, for Jesus the brief present is nothing more than a 'dark interval' without any theological significance.

The contrast indicated in this paragraph between punctual eschatology and salvation history dominates the interpretation offered by the Bultmann school so much that it has actually become a principle for classifying the books of the New Testament. Thus, Erich Dinkler classifies the Synoptics, Acts, the Epistle to the Hebrews, the Catholic Epistles (excluding the Johannine letters), and Revelation among the writings evidencing a salvation-historical view, making allowance, of course, for their differing stages of development.[2]

---

[1] Supplement to *ZNW*, 1957, [2]1960. See my book review article, 'Parusieverzögerung und Urchristentum', *TLZ*, 1958, cols. 1ff.

[2] E. Dinkler, 'Geschichte und Geschichtsauffassung', *RGG*[3], II, col. 1430, and 'The Idea of History in Early Christianity' in *The Idea of History in the Ancient Near East*, 1955, pp. 171ff.

C. 'REVELATION AS HISTORY'

The latest phase of the discussion concerns the same problem, but the perspective is slightly altered, inasmuch as the point of departure is less the essence and role of eschatology in the New Testament and more salvation history itself. The question comes from another direction. Certainly this discussion may not be too clearly separated from the previous one, for even now, of course, works are coming out which belong topically to the previous one, or even to the first.[1]

Bultmann and his pupils stand by their totally negative judgment on all salvation history—even that of the Old Testament. As the history of Israel, the Old Testament does not address us. This happens only after its history has been subjected to an existentialist interpretation. This history, as such, has been 'done away with' for us, and it is part of our Western history only in the sense that one could say 'that the Spartans fell at Thermopylae for us and that Socrates drank the hemlock for us'.[2] Thus continuity with the Old Testament salvation history is not essential for the New Testament. Ernst Fuchs, for whom, as we have seen, the 'end of the Law' means the 'end of history', in the same way denies that for Paul the continuity with the Old Testament had any significance whatever.[3] For Gerhard Ebeling, too, salvation history, as such, can be of no theological relevance, except in the sense of an existential 'encounter' with history. This is so because the distinction between 'word-event' (*Wortgeschehen*) and 'objectifying' utterance leaves no room for a positive evaluation of a continuous salvation history.[4]

Yet, to be sure, at least at one point a certain interest in history has been awakened among Bultmann's followers, and that is in the debate about the 'historical Jesus' which has again become dominant for a time. They sensed again and again the danger of Docetism that must arise whenever no more than 'the fact that' Jesus has come is retained. This alone was, of course, decisive for Bultmann in understanding Jesus as 'an eschatological phenomenon'.[5] Otherwise, he

[1] Thus E. Jüngel, *Jesus und Paulus*, 1962, in an especially radical way resumes the attempt to deny the temporal character of Jesus' expectation of the future.
[2] R. Bultmann, 'The Significance of the Old Testament for the Christian Faith' in *The Old Testament and Christian Faith*, ed. B. W. Anderson (1963), p. 31.
[3] See E. Fuchs, *Studies of the Historical Jesus*, 1964, pp. 175ff.
[4] See G. Ebeling, 'Wort Gottes und Hermeneutik', *ZTK*, 1959, pp. 230ff., and *The Nature of Faith*, 1962; *Word and Faith*, 1963.
[5] For instance *Kerygma and Myth* I, 1953, p. 117.

refers the little that we know of the historical Jesus to the history of
Judaism and assigns the teachings of Jesus merely to the 'presuppositions of the theology of the New Testament', not viewing them
as 'a part of that theology itself'.

Probably Bultmann thought that he could banish the danger of
Docetism with his emphasis on holding fast to 'the fact that'. But
this tie between the Christ of the Church's faith, who claims us in the
kerygma, and the historical Jesus appeared still too loose to his pupils.[1]
Since the *kerygma* has the historical Jesus as its object, some continuity
must exist between the historical Jesus and the Christ of the *kerygma*.

The distinction between the '*historisch*' (historical) and the '*ges-
chichtlich* (historic) Jesus is traced back to the important and oft-cited
work of Martin Kähler, *The So-called Historical Jesus and the Historic,
Biblical Christ*,[2] and was rediscovered during the' twenties when form
criticism first appeared—not just by the younger followers of Bultmann during the period of demythologizing. With this distinction,
Kähler tried to show that faith in Christ is independent of any
biography of Jesus put together by scholars, and that only the Christ
proclaimed by the early Church is decisive. But the important thing
for Kähler (as distinct from those appealing to him today) was to
find evidence in his research on the 'historic', biblical Christ, as the
Church portrays him in the Gospel tradition, that this Christ-figure is
also accurate 'historically'. The historical Jesus continues his work in
the historic Christ, and hence only in this Christ of faith do we encounter the historical Jesus—not in a 'life of Jesus' of modern scholarship.

The scepticism towards every attempt to distinguish in any
scholarly way an historical Jesus from the Christ of faith was strengthened by Albert Schweitzer's demonstration of the utter collapse of the
whole 'quest of the historical Jesus'. The break-up of the 'quest'
became clear in his work by his proof that the Jesus reconstructed
historically was dependent on contemporary philosophical currents.
So immediately after the First World War, before form criticism was
influenced by Bultmann's personal turn toward Heidegger's existentialism,[3] it renounced the attempt to press back to the historical

---

[1] How easily even this link can be broken is shown by F. Buri's attempt mentioned above to de-kerygmatize Bultmann's theology.

[2] 1892; [2]1896; reprinted 1928, 1953, 1956; ET 1964.

[3] In my article, 'Out of Season Remarks on the Historical Jesus of the Bultmann
School', *Union Seminary Quarterly Review*, Jan., 1961, pp. 131ff., I have tried to
show that form criticism originally had nothing to do with existentialist interpretation, contrary to the usual combining of the two nowadays.

Jesus, maintaining a deliberate neutrality in this regard. It limited itself instead to making the Christ of the early Church's faith its object of research. However, it was not just the distance between the inaccessible historical Jesus and the Christ of the Church's proclamation that was originally to be stressed by limiting the form critical inquiry in this way. Consideration was also given to Kähler's positive intention, namely, to approach the historical Jesus in such a way that he was deliberately not set up as the final goal of study of the Gospels.

Hans Conzelmann is therefore out of line with Kähler's intention and the actual neutrality observed by the first proponents of form criticism when he says that the mark of a contemporary form critic is 'thinking in terms of a break', that is, a break between the historical Jesus and the kerygmatic Christ.[1]

Encounter with the Christ preached by the early Church seemed to be perfectly sufficient once he was interpreted existentially as the one basing our 'self-understanding' in decision. So an historical Jesus, different from him, disappeared theologically from view and was termed not only historically inaccessible, but also theologically irrelevant. If the only matters at stake are decision in faith for Christ and understanding ourselves in a new way, then the first Christians' witness of faith fulfils this purpose without the existential necessity of relationship to the historical Jesus. The stress upon 'the fact that' the historical Jesus had come is thus just a final insurance, more or less theoretical, against Docetism.

Recently the Bultmannians Käsemann, Fuchs, Conzelmann, Ebeling, and Bornkamm have attempted to go beyond 'the mere fact that' (*das blosse Dass*) of their teacher to establish a continuity between Jesus' preaching and that of the early Church.[2] In this way,

[1] H. Conzelmann, 'Gegenwart und Zukunft in der synoptischen Tradition', *ZTK*, 1957, pp. 277f.
[2] Of the almost boundless literature I mention only: E. Käsemann, 'The Problem of the Historical Jesus', *Essays on New Testament Themes*, 1964, pp. 15ff.; E. Fuchs, 'The Quest of the Historical Jesus', *Studies of the Historical Jesus*, 1964, especially pp. 11ff.; H. Conzelmann, G. Ebeling, E. Fuchs, 'Die Frage nach dem historischen Jesus', *ZTK*, 1959, Beiheft 1. Assenting to these efforts without reservation is J. M. Robinson's report, *A New Quest of the Historical Jesus*, 1958. Representatives of the Bultmann school and their opponents have their say in the omnibus volume, *Der historische Jesus und der kerygmatische Christus (Beiträge zum Christusverständnis in Forschung und Verkündigung*, edited by H. Ristow and K. Matthiae, 1960). G. Bornkamm, *Jesus of Nazareth*, 1960 (see especially the foreword), is, of course, under Bultmann's influence, but his view of Jesus is less conditioned by existentialist interpretation than is usually the case among pupils of Bultmann.

it was thought, one could somehow take into account what Kähler actually wanted. This endeavour at first appeared to answer the following questions, which were really urgent because of Bultmann's position described above.

Are we portraying the faith of the first Christians correctly when we fix our attention only upon their act of faith and its meaning for their, and our, self-understanding? Does not a *context of events* stand as the actual basis and *object* of their faith in their statement, 'Jesus is the Christ'? Can we really ignore the events which are intended by the subject of that statement of faith, 'Jesus' (that is, the 'historical' Jesus), as well as the events which in the early Church's faith sanctioned the identification of this 'Jesus' with the 'Christ' (the empty tomb and the resurrection appearances)?[1] If, however, the meaning of the first Christians' faith relates to a series of events, must we not, in principle, keep with the first witnesses in seeing *the events* as the *object of faith* in the Gospel account, even if we can only with difficulty detach the events in the Gospels from their meaning? Must we not ask, even where obviously legendary features are present, whether faith is not making use of them to make clear that connection of events, so that even in this case the historical Jesus stands in the foreground of faith's field of vision?[2] If that is so, then is there not implicitly a distinction between events and the interpretation of faith that creates the connection with those events? Must not the question of the continuity between the historical Jesus and the Christ of faith then be raised for both historical and theological reasons?

For Bultmann, these questions do not arise in the same way, because for him the events as such are not decisive in their objective character, but only our encounter with them, the act of faith itself, decision and self-understanding. Bultmann's disciples, who want to go beyond 'the mere fact that' of their teacher, do not raise the questions mentioned above as we have just formulated them either. Nevertheless, the excessively loose connection with the historical Jesus does not satisfy them, for they are now urgently stressing the need to show the continuity between the historical Jesus and the

---

[1] I say 'sanctioned' intentionally rather than 'called forth'.

[2] I also raise these questions with respect to my own article on form criticism, 'Les récentes études sur la formation de la tradition évangélique', *RHPR*, 1925, pp. 459ff.; 1926, pp. 564ff., in which I was in complete agreement with the view advocated by Bultmann at the time. I was, of course, already aware of the danger of Docetism and made a plea in the concluding chapter that a point of contact be found with the historical Jesus.

kerygmatic Christ. But to realize this aim, would they not have had
to revise the whole Bultmannian notion of the relationship of faith
and objective event? Would they not have had to revise, above all,
their attitude towards salvation history? But, in fact, they deliberately
hold fast to the basic presuppositions of existentialist interpretation,
wishing from the Bultmannian position to raise afresh the problem
of the historical Jesus, handled so completely differently in earlier
times. Thus, they never reach a rehabilitation of salvation history, as
their concern for a 'continuity' might have suggested. For them,
salvation history remains now as before a distortion of the inmost
essence of the New Testament message. They do not finally get
beyond Bultmann, and the consistent and clear position of Bultmann
on the 'historical Jesus' appears instead to be darkened.

Anyone who speaks of a continuity between the historical Jesus
and the Christ of early Christian faith is implying a salvation history,
whether he wants to or not. This is why this most recent discussion
on the historical Jesus is so important for our problem and must be
mentioned in this historical survey of attitudes to salvation history,
even though those who have enlivened the discussion protest expressly
against involvement with salvation history.

The representatives of the so-called 'post-Bultmannian' theology
whom we mentioned still do not ultimately reach a continuity in the
sense intended by Kähler as the conclusion of their research. He had
thought of an actual development of the salvation event as such from
the life of the incarnate Christ to its continuing effect in the early
Church, at the same time manifesting itself as a revelation of that
life. For Bultmann's pupils, the important thing is not a salvation-
historical continuity, meaning by that a continuation of the work of
the historical Jesus in the Christ of the present, but rather the *existential constant* between the historical Jesus and the kerygmatic Christ. In
an article already mentioned,[1] I have tried to show how this constant
is seen in the Bultmann school in an existentialistically cramped
picture of an 'historical' Jesus that emerges in a way that must fall
under the verdict of Albert Schweitzer when seen in the light of the
'quest of the historical Jesus'. Thus, it is of secondary importance that
while in the time prior to World War I only an unconscious influence
of nineteenth century philosophical idealism was exerted upon the
'quest', now we have a deliberate renunciation of thinking in terms

[1] See the article cited p. 49, n.3.

of a subject-object schema. For the New Testament scholars mentioned above, the historical Jesus, like the kerygmatic Christ of the Church, is considered only in the light of his address to our self-understanding. So from the outset one could not expect that the constant would be seen in anything other than 'the call of Jesus to decision' (Bultmann), 'Jesus' faith' (Ebeling), or in 'Jesus' behaviour' (existentially interpreted) (Fuchs). Basically the Bultmann pupils hardly go beyond their teacher at all. For he himself sees an 'indirect' christology already implicit in Jesus' 'call to decision', afterwards made explicit in the early Church.[1] We find, then, that Bultmann, remaining critical towards the questions of his pupils on the historical Jesus, is more consistent with his own presuppositions, which they hold as well.[2]

This school of New Testament scholars, dominant in Germany, is in the main uninfluenced by the rest of the world, as Johannes Munck's work, *Paul and the Salvation of Mankind*, 1959, shows. How fruitful it would be if this school adhered less rigidly to its existentialist presuppositions is shown by the discussion, which is much more fruitful for our problem, at present going on in the field of Old Testament scholarship. Although German Old Testament scholarship has not remained completely untouched by the discussion on hermeneutics in the wake of existentialist philosophy, nevertheless it is much more open, and the positions taken in this field have never gone exclusively along existentialist lines. The problem of salvation history is also discussed much more impartially in this field, and, as is often the case, New Testament scholars could learn much from Old Testament scholars. I am thinking here of the works of G. von Rad, C. Westermann, W. Eichrodt, H. W. Wolff, W. Zimmerli, H. J. Kraus, F. Hesse, R. and T. Rendtorff, and B. S. Childs, who are concerned with our question.[3]

The problem of continuity between the historical Jesus and the

---

[1] See R. Bultmann, *Theology of the New Testament* I, 1951, p. 43, and even his position as early as 1929 in 'Die Bedeutung des geschichtlichen Jesus für die Theologie des Paulus', *Glauben und Verstehen* I, p. 204.

[2] See his article, 'Das Verhältnis des urchristlichen Christuskerygmas zum historischen Jesus' in *Der historische Jesus und der kerygmatische Christus*, pp. 234ff., and 'Das Verhältnis der urchristlichen Christusbotschaft zum historischen Jesus', *Sitzungsbericht der Heidelberger Akademie der Wissenschaften*, 1960.

[3] G. Fohrer, 'Prophetie und Geschichte', *TLZ*, 1964, col. 481, offers a selection from the very rich Old Testament literature. For Fohrer's own rejection of the emphasis on salvation history in the Old Testament, which seems to me to presuppose a narrow conception of its essence, see below p. 86, n. 1

interpretation of him given in the early Church is ultimately no different from the problem raised by von Rad in his *Old Testament Theology*[1]: the progressive reinterpretation of Israel's old traditions is continually awakened by new events in the present. This development of the traditions is itself salvation history, and stands in continuity with the original event basic to the traditions, even if what originally took place concerned individual tribes only. The analogy between von Rad's conception of the Old Testament and the cluster of New Testament problems we are discussing also concerns the fact that in both cases faith, while not depending upon the history worked out by historical criticism, is nevertheless referred by criticism to that history as being an interpretation in faith.

The fact that these problems are handled in Old Testament scholarship apart from the question of existential interpretation makes the discussion much more productive of results. To be sure, F. Hesse[2] accuses G. von Rad of putting the *kerygma* in the place of 'real history', and W. Eichrodt[3] in a similar fashion represents him as being close to Bultmann. But in reality, a greater agreement exists between these three scholars than perhaps they themselves think, and for all their differences they stand on common ground—which is not the case among New Testament scholars of opposing camps. Despite all its emphasis upon a charismatic-kerygmatic interpretation, von Rad's approach goes along the lines of salvation history,[4] and I hope that this will become clearer in the explication of my own concept of the relation between events and their continuing salvation-historical interpretation in the New Testament.[5]

[1] German edition, Bd. I 1957, Bd. II 1960; ET Vol. I 1962, Vol. II 1965.

[2] See especially F. Hesse, 'Die Erforschung der Geschichte Israels als theologische Aufgabe', *KuD*, 1958, pp. 1ff.; *id.*, 'Kerygma oder geschichtliche Wirklichkeit?' *ZTK*, 1960, pp. 17ff.

[3] *Theology of the Old Testament* I, 1961, pp. 512ff.

[4] See von Rad's answer to F. Hesse in the introduction to the second volume of his *Old Testament Theology*. On the whole problem see also J. A. Soggin, 'Geschichte, Historie und Heilsgeschichte im Alten Testament', *TLZ*, 1964, col. 721ff.

[5] In this respect I naturally find von Rad's discussion on the New Testament in the second volume of his *Theology* much less enlightening for New Testament study than the parts in which he deals only with the Old Testament. In the chapters on the New Testament he is occupied for the most part with demonstrating an analogy between the Old and New Testaments rather than showing a further salvation-historical development such as is already characteristic within the Old Testament. Analogy belongs to salvation history too, but salvation history is not exhausted by the category of analogy. Cf. the discussion on typology below pp. 132f.

If the problem in the New Testament is raised *mutatis mutandis* in the same way as in the Old Testament, and if the formation of the canon is governed by the same principle in both cases, we may then ask whether the reason for this is not that the common motif in the development of Old and New Testament notions of salvation and in the origin of the canon encompassing both is salvation history.

In view of this Old Testament discussion, which again takes seriously the salvation history repudiated by the Bultmann school,[1] it is puzzling that K. G. Steck in 1959 wrote a work completely rejecting salvation history.[2] He tried to do justice to my exegetical attempt to understand the essence of biblical thinking as salvation-historical. But he put it in line with past attempts in the history of dogma more or less influenced by conceptions drawn from philosophies of history, such as Hegel's, and thus, despite a noteworthy effort, his way was barred to a proper understanding of my work.

Although in certain details I approach the salvation-historical ideas of Hofmann and Schlatter, nevertheless my basic conception is essentially different from theirs. This fact could have become clear from *Christ and Time*, but to be fair to Steck, it should be said that the point really becomes obvious only in the present work. Steck's criticism does not take into account the fundamental distinction, which I make clear in my earlier book on the basis of the New Testament, between salvation history and history. How would it otherwise be possible for him to include me in a work in which salvation history is declared incompatible with the Bible because in the Bible there is no history as historical coherence in the modern sense—that is, an unbroken, causally connected chain of historical facts that is controllable and provable in such a connection?[3] I have emphasized from the beginning that the salvation-historical faith is definitely *not* faith in an 'unbroken' causal connection, but faith in a connection revealed only by God, resting upon a completely incalculable selection of individual events. Therefore the question may even be raised whether one may properly use the expression 'salvation history' (*Heils-Geschichte*). I shall try to answer this terminological question with reference to Bultmann also.[4] But in no case is it admissible to criticize me for a concept of

---

[1] J. Barr, 'Revelation through History in the Old Testament', *Interpretation*, 1963, pp. 193ff., tries, of course, to explain the emphasis upon revelation as history in the Old Testament as an apologetic answer to the philosophical theories of history during the nineteenth century which endangered the authority of the Bible.

[2] K. G. Steck, *Die Idee der Heilsgeschichte. Hofmann—Schlatter—Cullmann*, 1959.

[3] See K. G. Steck, *op. cit.*, pp. 10f.

[4] See below p. 77.

history which is completely foreign to my concept of salvation history. Since Steck rightly recognized that I make no use of the concept of historical 'organism', it was therefore improper of him to classify me where he did in the history of theology.

It seems to me that my view is also oversimplified in a similar way by R. Marlé, *Bultmann et l'interprétation du Nouveau Testament*, 1956, and by L. Malevez, especially in his article which appeared just recently, 'Les dimensions de l'Histoire du Salut', *Nouvelle Revue Théologique*, 1964, pp. 561ff. I hope that the present work may show that their primary criticisms fail to deal with my actual position.

Steck's main objection against me is that my whole salvation-historical interpretation is weakened with the introduction of the category of the 'prophetic' into the biblical idea of salvation history, that is, the taking up of elements which are not historical. Thus, he bypasses what von Rad and I say about the relation of history and interpretation, for the prophetic interpretation not only *relates* to history, but itself *belongs* to salvation history in its development. Thus it is not surprising that Steck ultimately comes to the completely negative judgment that the concept of salvation history is 'ambivalent, ambiguous, misleading'.[1] The idea of salvation history has 'really stood the test so poorly that it is better not to make any use of it'.[2] I hardly believe that this completely negative conclusion will cause theologians in the coming years to give up thinking of the Bible's content as a salvation history. But it may spur them on to define more closely not what the systematic theologians and philosophers of the last two hundred years have said, but what the men of the Bible have understood by salvation history. Then, in view of the more recent expositions of the Old Testament, some stand will need to be taken toward Steck's surprising assertion which he also extends to biblical history: history, because it is past, is 'first and always a field of graves and dead men'. The present work will be concerned with another opinion of Steck and others, that salvation history lacks a living relationship with the present, that it does not call to a decision, and that one could in this respect contrast the Word of Scripture as a living proclamation with salvation history as a dead past. Steck does this when he distinguishes the letter ('it is written'), which remains binding, from the 'history of ancient and modern Israel', which falls under the verdict 'all flesh is like grass'. Bultmann's question of the existential significance of the biblical message will in

---

[1] *Op. cit.*, p. 56.   [2] *Op. cit.*, p. 61.

fact be taken up, but it will be applied to salvation history. Herein lies Bultmann's positive service, to which a salvation-historical view is indebted, despite its wide difference from the Bultmann school.

K. G. Steck's work may have contributed to bringing the term 'salvation history' even more into discredit than before. Although the writer stands closer to Karl Barth than to Rudolf Bultmann, the work may be thought of as a dogmatic confirmation of the negative estimate of all salvation history by the Bultmann school. Nevertheless, it did not prevent the formation of a group of young theologians at about the same time, including W. Pannenberg, R. Rendtorff, T. Rendtorff, and U. Wilckens. After publishing various small preparatory studies,[1] in 1961 the group came out publicly with a programme that did not emphasize the expression 'salvation history', but in fact came close to my view in *Christ and Time*, despite its divergence on details. The collection of essays put out by the writers just mentioned bears the title *Offenbarung als Geschichte (Revelation as History)*.[2] The problem is actually seen from the vantage point of revelation rather than that of salvation. But as Pannenberg himself recognizes in passing,[3] the two concepts can hardly be separated. The main concept in the New Testament appears to me to be rather that of salvation,[4] but Pannenberg sees salvation as subordinate to revelation. He notes[5] in passing that he did not unfold the relationship of revelation to sin and salvation. I chose the title of my present work, *Salvation in History*, before I knew the Pannenberg group's *Offenbarung als Geschichte*. It should not therefore label my book as an antithesis to this work; however, it may indicate the quite different perspective from which I set about the problem.

Pannenberg's work seeks to rehabilitate history as the source and place of revelation, and its clear statements are a contrast to much of the modern theological literature of Germany, obscure in its sophistication. In distinction to the theology influenced by existentialism, history, and not the single act of God, is designated as a revelation of the one God, indirect, but uniquely complete, over against which the direct self-revelations of God, for instance through

[1] See W. Pannenberg, 'Heilsgeschehen und Geschichte', *KuD*, 1959, pp. 218ff., 259ff.

[2] Edited by W. Pannenberg, 1961. ET in preparation.

[3] *Offenbarung als Geschichte*, p. 101 n. 14.

[4] On the relationship between the history of revelation and salvation history see below pp. 89ff. and 294f.

[5] *Ibid.*, p. 99 n. 12.

his name or his Law, always communicate merely 'something' definite. There is an indication of the connection between history and the revelation of the end of history which alone discloses the actual essence of history. Other important aspects of this set of problems are formulated in a series of theses. Nevertheless, a more exact definition of this history, which is what we are trying to formulate here, is not clearly made in all directions. This has already led to many misunderstandings and given cause for criticism. Above all, Pannenberg does not take sufficient account of the distinction between events and their Spirit-directed interpretations in relation to new events, which will be spelled out below.

A further item is closely related to this. Although Pannenberg rests his position in a commendable way upon the exegetical studies of the Old and New Testament scholars who belong to this group, it is still clear that the premises of his thought are taken mainly from a philosophy of history. In his conclusions the transition from exegesis to dogmatics is not always clear.[1]

The exegetical contribution of U. Wilckens, 'Das Offenbarungsverständnis in der Geschichte des Urchristentums',[2] is, of course, of particular interest to us here. It shows how suited this new approach is for loosening up the rigid fronts of New Testament studies in Germany. This is all the more evident because Wilckens is indebted to the Bultmann school to a large degree and apparently does not wish to remove himself from it. Nevertheless, since he does not share its existentialist basis, he deviates from it at crucial points: in his positive estimate of events, and therefore in the question of the historical Jesus as well, since he lays emphasis upon the 'fate' of Jesus; in the significance attributed to apocalyptic; above all, however, in the recognition of the great service of Luke who, with his salvation-historical theology, has preserved 'the knowledge fundamental for the Christian faith about the historical self-revelation of God that has occurred',[3] and whose thinking is 'in the direction of' Paul[4] (with this one of the fundamental pillars of the Bultmannian approach is destroyed!). Moreover, Wilckens' contribution, of course,

---

[1] Everything said here about Pannenberg was written before the appearance of his great work, *Grundzüge der Christologie*, 1964. Since his latest work came to me just as this book was being printed, unfortunately I could not consider it in this treatment.

[2] *Offenbarung als Geschichte*, pp. 42ff.

[3] *Op. cit.*, p. 90.

[4] *Op. cit.*, p. 74.

contains many judgments which raise the question whether Wilckens ought not really to have come to other conclusions because of the premises of the position laid down in the whole volume. I am thinking here, for instance, of his statements about the title Son of Man, which he claims was first applied to Jesus by the Church; but above all, of his statements about the Gospel of John, in which he, with the Bultmann school, sees Jesus' career divested of its historical character.

The discussion of the volume by the Pannenberg group is still going on. Its programme is completely rejected, of course, by the Bultmann school. One of the school's youngest members, G. Klein, approaching the book from the existentialist position, subjected it to a purely negative criticism in a long article.[1] Klein says there can be no 'decision' made for a 'disclosed' revelation, otherwise it would be superfluous as an answer. Furthermore, he reproaches Wilckens for having a formal time scheme and a 'subject-object schematism'. That he, like others, sees a contrast in the book between history and revelation as the interpretation of history (therefore denying to history a revelatory character) may be partly at least due to a lack of precision on Pannenberg's part.

More fruitful is the sympathetic criticism contained in a supplement of *Evangelische Theologie*[2] devoted to the whole question of salvation history, whose contributors partly reject and partly accept the salvation-historical interpretation of the biblical message and also level a criticism against existentialist exegesis.[3]

The loosening of the theological positions, which has attended the attempt to find a new appreciation of the role of salvation history in the Old and New Testaments (which we have already noted in Wilckens), is now making itself felt in the form of a break-up of the uniformity of the Bultmann school itself over the present discussion on apocalyptic. We have seen that the question of the historical Jesus put the teacher in opposition to his pupils. The problem of apocalyptic, which is closely connected with salvation history, has opened up a new and far-reaching divergence between one of the

[1] G. Klein, 'Offenbarung als Geschichte? Marginalien zu einem theologischen Programm', *Monatsschrift für Pastoraltheologie*, 1962, pp. 65ff.
[2] *EvT*, 1962, Heft 1/2, pp. 1ff., with contributions by G. Bornkamm, W. Zimmerli, J. Moltmann, R. Bohren, and H. G. Geyer.
[3] R. Bohren's lively written article is important in view of the assertion that it is not the salvation-historical, but the existentialist interpretation alone that has kerygmatic value. Here a practical theologian explains that the work of preaching is not furthered by existentialist exegesis at all, but is rather encumbered by it.

most eminent champions of the school, Ernst Käsemann, and its other members. We have already mentioned the significance the Pannenberg circle ascribes to apocalyptic, saying that it is far from being 'excessive fantasy', and that it introduces the historical notion of a consummation. D. Rössler attempts to provide an historical basis for this new assessment and rehabilitation of apocalyptic in a short and oversimplified, but suggestive, work, *Gesetz und Geschichte im Judentum*.[1] He contrasts (too schematically, of course[2]) apocalyptic with rabbinic Judaism which lacks a sense of history, saying that apocalyptic extends God's plan of history to the whole of humanity, thus bringing about the 'historical achievement' of a universal theology of history. Here it becomes evident that in a contrast between rabbinic and apocalyptic Judaism, Jesus belongs on the latter side. Thus, apocalyptic ceases to appear merely as the most extreme, mistaken development and caricature of true eschatology (to be interpreted existentially according to Bultmann), and the calculating of dates is no longer seen as its essential mark.

With very different argumentation, while working out the significance of the experience of Easter for the origin of Christian theology, Ernst Käsemann comes to a high regard for the role of apocalyptic,[3] which he views as the thought structure of the early Church. Thus, indirectly at least, a significant place is allotted to salvation history in the rise of early Christian theology. So it is not surprising that both Ernst Fuchs and Gerhard Ebeling reacted negatively towards his article, warning against such a rehabilitation of apocalyptic.[4] They referred to the fact that the characteristic literary form of earliest Christianity is not the apocalypse but the Gospel. This is certainly a correct observation, but it can be interpreted otherwise than in the terms of existentialist exegesis. Käsemann's rejoinder[5] stresses even more strongly that the earliest Christian theology is not to be under-

[1] *Untersuchungen zur Theologie der jüdischen Apokalyptik und der pharisäischen Orthodoxie*, 1960.

[2] Independently of Rössler's work, W. D. Davies took issue with and rejected this kind of separation of apocalyptic from rabbinic Judaism (without overlooking the differences between the two) in his article, 'Apocalyptic and Pharisaism', *Expository Times*, 1958, pp. 233ff., reprinted in the volume *Christian Origins and Judaism*, 1962, by W. D. Davies. In the discussion of this problem note should be taken of the important work by A. Jaubert, *La notion d'alliance dans le judaïsme aux abords de l'ère chrétienne*, 1963, in which the theology of history in the *Book of Jubilees* and the Qumran writings is treated.

[3] E. Käsemann, 'Die Anfänge christlicher Theologie', *ZTK*, 1960, pp. 162ff.

[4] Both in *ZTK*, 1961, Heft 2, p. 227ff., 245ff.

[5] 'Zum Thema der urchristlichen Apokalyptik', *ZTK*, pp. 257ff.

stood in the light of the '*leitmotif* of human existence', but in the light of apocalyptic.

The new direction that J. M. Robinson has begun with this stress on Heidegger's concept of '*Lichtungsgeschichte*' (history seen as 'clearings') may ultimately be regarded as symptomatic of the same break in the homogeneity of the Bultmann school.[1] Although he proceeds independently of the discussion on apocalyptic sketched above, still this departure from the main stream of the school indicates a turn towards salvation history. Robinson, of course, even with this new orientation, is walking very much in the steps of the philosophical master standing behind the Bultmann school—Heidegger. He faithfully follows the shift which he thinks he discerns in 'the earlier Heidegger'. In Heidegger's 'self-disclosure of Being in history', ('*Lichtungsgeschichte*'), Robinson sees a way leading back even to the salvation history of Hofmann. Salvation history is now, so to speak, fashionable, thanks to the terminology from Heidegger in which it is now clothed. It becomes a 'speech-event, in which the history of Israel is given utterance'.[2] But is the philosophy of Heidegger with its manifold evolutions, or any philosophy at all, really necessary for a proper appreciation of the biblical salvation history?[3]

Although Robinson says in his article in *Interpretation* that because of this new philosophical tendency since 1961, the Bultmannian system has now lost its solidarity, nevertheless it is the attachment to the principles of either the younger or the older Heidegger that still binds the Bultmann school together. Robinson finds support in Heinrich Ott's book, *Denken und Sein* (1959), in which the author evaluates the philosophy of the earlier Heidegger. In this book, as in his earlier work, *Geschichte und Heilsgeschichte in der Theologie R. Bultmanns* (1955),[4] and also in his brief study, *Eschatologie. Versuch eines dogmatischen Grundrisses* (1958), Ott attempts to fulfil Bultmann's demand for an existential interpretation while at the same time trying to go beyond Bultmann by means of the later Heidegger and even to take Karl Barth into account. In point of fact, he leaves Bultmann when he sees, with the New Testament, facts where

[1] Besides the article, 'Basic Shifts in German Theology', *Interpretation*, 1962, pp. 67ff., see 'The Historicality of Biblical Language', *The Old Testament and Christian Faith*, ed. B. W. Anderson, 1963, pp. 124ff.

[2] *EvT*, 1962, p. 137.

[3] Such a dependence does not seem to me justified by the often emphasized fact that Heidegger owes much in his hermeneutics to his theological studies.

[4] See the excellent book review article by F. Lieb in *EvT*, 1955, pp. 507ff.

Bultmann only sees myths. But ultimately Ott, like Bultmann, considers only those eschatological statements in which the individual believing witness understands himself to be claimed in his existential understanding. I cannot see how anyone, despite his efforts to come nearer to the actual state of affairs, can really go beyond Bultmann as long as he basically holds to the demands of existential interpretation.

Quite differently from Ott, W. Kreck, in his book *Die Zukunft des Gekommenen* (1961), rests completely on Karl Barth's concept of eschatology. He holds, as Barth does, in principle to the futurity of eschatology, but does not want to see it actually incorporated into a salvation history. In the introductory chapter of the third edition of *Christ and Time*, I have pointed out that he, like nearly all Barthians, has misunderstood the book in thinking that I wished to present the 'concept' of time as such and to impose on the New Testament a non-Christian scheme of linear time. Actually I wrote the book for the purpose of treating the 'time scheme' that Kreck makes the basis of his own statement on eschatology, the 'already' and the 'not yet'. Whether we like it or not, in the New Testament there really is a tension in *time*, and in my opinion the unbreakable connection between salvation history and eschatology rests on this tension. Eschatology is not thereby 'dethroned', and does not become just a 'doctrine of the last things', as Kreck thinks. He is still influenced by certain biasses of the Bultmann school in his judgment of the New Testament sources. I hope that the present work may show more clearly that Kreck is not as far removed from me as he thinks.[1] On the other hand, it may show where the distinction lies between the Barthian conception he shares and mine regarding the tension between 'already' and 'not yet'. Unfortunately, Barth's eschatology has not yet been written. The statements he has made so far on this point seem to express the demarcation of his view from that of Bultmann less clearly than on all other doctrines. I think the reason for this is that he does not sufficiently explain the relation between eschatology and salvation history. But so long as the doctrine of eschatology (that we hope he will still be able to write) has not yet appeared in Barth's dogmatics, we must reserve a final judgment about it.

This survey of the most recent developments in the main currents of theology may have placed the central importance of the problem

---

[1] I could sign my name to everything he says on pp. 120ff. about the methodological movement from today to tomorrow and back again to today.

of salvation history in its proper light. It seems paradoxical, therefore, that on the one hand salvation history is rejected today by leading Protestant theologians, while on the other hand the problem is still very much with us. Is this not an indication that this salvation history is still the heart of the total Christian message?[1]

Some works appearing in the English-speaking world also indicate that the problem of salvation history has not been disposed of. I mention: E. C. Rust, *Salvation History: A Biblical Interpretation*, 1962; A. Richardson, *History Sacred and Profane*, 1964. The latter seeks a solution to theological problems by confronting them with modern theories on history.[2]

If I have pursued here mainly the development of the problem in most recent *Protestant theology*, that is because this development is closely connected with it in particular. The appraisal of the early Christian concept of history on the part of Catholic theologians and philosophers could also be given. In France a lively discussion on the problem of history has been going on for some years in which the Christian concept of history has been included. If I do not take this debate directly into account in this work, it is only because through a lack of time and space I must limit myself here to the discussion going on within Protestantism. But I hope that in some special publication, if not I, then one of my pupils, will introduce the works being written in France to this discussion.[3]

Among the writings of Catholic theologians one should mention the works of J. Daniélou, who is probably the best-known advocate of salvation-historical theology within Catholicism (above all, *Le Mystère de l'Histoire*, 1953, and *Approche du Christ*, 1957, finally *Jean-Baptiste Témoin de l'agneau*, 1964), A. Mouroux (*Le problème du Temps*), T. G. Chifflot (*Approche d'une Théologie de l'Histoire*, 1960), H. J. Marrou and R. Jolivet, *L'homme et l'Histoire*, 1962 (Actes du 7e Congrès des Sociétés de philosophie française), then J. Feiner, 'Kirche und Heilsgeschichte', in *Gott in Welt, Festgabe für K. Rahner zum 60. Geburtstag am 5. März 1964*, also those of H. U. von Balthasar, *A Theology of History*, 1963, K. Rahner, *Schriften zur Theologie I–V*, 1954ff., ET, *Theological Investigations*, J. Hessen, *Griechische oder biblische Theologie*, and especially H. Fries, *Handbuch theologischer Grundbegriffe*, 1962/63. I have heard through the author and editors, of an ambitious work now in preparation by A. Darlapp, *Theologie der Heilsgeschichte*

---

[1] The problem is well formulated by G. Crespy, 'Une théologie de l'histoire est-elle possible?', *Rev. de Théol. et de Philos.*, 1963, pp. 97ff.

[2] A book dealing with our problem written by Prof. John Knox (New York) has been announced and must certainly be suggestive, but unfortunately I was not able to use it.

[3] This is all the more a matter of concern to me since J. Frisque, writing from a Catholic position, has made my salvation-historical conception the object of a book in his *Oscar Cullmann. Une Théologie de l'Histoire du salut*, 1960; cf. G. Delling, *TLZ*, 1962, cols. 40ff.

(*Mysterium salutis, Grundzüge heilsgeschichtlicher Theologie*, 1. Bd.), being edited by J. Feiner and M. Löhrer, which has not yet appeared. To compare it with the present work would be especially fruitful.

The problem is dealt with in connection with Bultmann's formulation of the question by R. Marlé, *Bultmann et l'interprétation du Nouveau Testament*, 1956, and L. Malevez, who builds on his earlier work in 'Les dimensions de l'Histoire du Salut', *Nouvelle Revue théologique*, 1964, pp. 561ff. (see above p. 56). Both these writers are strongly influenced by Bultmann, although they offer criticism against his 'fideism' (the expression appears in Malevez, *op. cit.*, p. 564), and they try to salvage the salvation-historical thesis from his denunciation of it. G. Hasenhüttl in *Der Glaubensvollzug. Eine Begegnung mit R. Bultmann aus katholischem Glaubensverständnis*, 1963, shows further dependence upon Bultmann.[1] The problem is well treated with regard to my own position, not only by J. Frisque (see p. 63, n. 3), but also by L. Bini, *L'Intervento di O. Cullmann nella discussione bultmanniana*, 1961. A. Luneau, *L'Histoire du salut chez les Pères de l'Eglise*, 1964, studies an important problem.

Among the philosophers, W. Kamlah, *Christentum und Geschichtlichkeit*, 2. Aufl., 1951, sharing the Bultmannian conception, rejected mine completely. However, as is well known, K. Löwith devoted the final chapter of his *Meaning in History*, 1957, to the biblical interpretation of history. Here he takes up my view in *Christ and Time* which he calls 'the most illuminating and consistent treatment of the "salvation event".'

4. PRELIMINARY REMARKS ON THE QUESTION OF HERMENEUTICS

We can deal here only with *preliminary* remarks on the hermeneutical question, for only the work to follow *in toto* can give the basis of a hermeneutics of salvation history. We shall come back to this point in the final part in which we try to draw out the implications for the systematic question.[2] I must therefore ask my readers not to try to derive my 'hermeneutics' from these introductory remarks made by way of summary.

[1] A Catholic position on the ideas emanating from Bultmann which his pupils represent is offered by the American scholar, R. E. Brown, 'After Bultmann, What? An Introduction to the Bultmannians', *Catholic Biblical Quarterly*, 1964, pp. 1ff.

[2] Part V, Chapter 4, 'Salvation History, Faith, and Exegesis'. What is said in the chapter, 'The Beginnings of Salvation History with Jesus', in the methodological section on pp. 187ff. is also relevant.

The aim of interpreting New Testament texts is to understand the faith of the first Christians, its origin, its content, and the manner in which it is fixed in the New Testament. The latter would call us to the same faith. It is not wrong to say that the ultimate goal of exegesis is fully attained only when this faith is subsequently achieved by us. But this is where the difficulty arises: how is such a thing possible without our knowing what the qualities of New Testament faith are, since they are what we are supposed to arrive at by our interpretation? To meet this difficulty, the hermeneutics of today has introduced the concept of the so-called 'Vorverständnis' (pre-understanding) and includes the person of the exegete right at the start. A resigned acknowledgement that our exposition can never be completely free from presuppositions is not felt to be enough. Today, under the influence of the works of W. Dilthey, B. Croce, and R. G. Collingwood, who have dealt with the problems raised in interpreting history, the inclusion of the interpreter's own person in the question brought to the text is raised to an exegetical principle requiring the deliberate abrogation of the distance between subject and object. The striving after 'objectivity', the exclusion of one's own person, heretofore demanded of the exegete as a hermeneutical prerequisite, is retained, to be sure, so far as one's 'personal wishes with regard to the conclusions of interpretation' are concerned,[1] but the effort at objectivity is intentionally dropped in the case of the questions with which one is faced. Because the object is deliberately no longer seen alone, but only in relation with the subject in the 'address', in the 'encounter', it is natural that hermeneutics now gains a significance that it did not have before.

Never before has so much been said and written about hermeneutics by New Testament scholars as today.[2] But is exegetical achievement thereby greater or better than in the time when one impartially concentrated upon the object of exegesis separate from the subject,

[1] See R. Bultmann, 'The Problem of Hermeneutics', *Essays Philosophical and Theological*, 1955, pp. 234ff.; *id.*, 'Is Exegesis without Presuppositions Possible?', *Existence and Faith*, ed. Schubert M. Ogden, 1960, pp. 289ff.

[2] The book of K. Frör, *Biblische Hermeneutik*, 1961, contains an excellent critical survey of the whole discussion which was first opened by K. Barth, but now has been carried on by Bultmann and his students in a quite different way. The work also includes the debate in Old Testament scholarship—primarily being dealt with in connection with G. von Rad's *Old Testament Theology* (see above pp. 53f.). The stimulating dissertation by L. Steiger, *Die Hermeneutik als dogmatisches Problem*, 1961, which takes its premises from H. Diem, belongs more to the debate itself rather than being a survey of scholarship.

and (perhaps in too naive an optimism which was in danger of self-delusion) thereby strove obediently to 'listen to' the text from a conscious distance? Certainly hermeneutical reflection is necessary. But today when, in the name of existentialist considerations, hermeneutics in general is exalted as the main problem both for New Testament scholarship and dogmatics, I cannot help thinking of the well-known scene (Act II, Scene 4) of Molière's *Bourgeois Gentilhomme*. Monsieur Jourdain, eager for learning and wishing to climb higher socially with the help of education, is instructed by the philosophy teacher about the distinction between prose and poetry. The teacher reveals to him that everything he speaks is prose, whereupon the delighted Monsieur Jourdain expresses his joy at finally knowing that for forty years he had spoken prose without realizing it. Knowing about prose has become more important to him than speaking prose. It seems to me that today endless discussion on hermeneutics is succumbing to a similar danger.

By this I do not mean to ridicule the present work on hermeneutics. In the case of witnesses to faith this is in fact a complex problem. But I do wish seriously to raise the question whether the goal of all interpretation would not be better realized if we took to heart, as the first hermeneutical requirement, the concentration upon the object of exegesis in the discussion of the means to attain our end. Of course, this questions the 'overcoming of the subject-object schema' as it is propounded today. Is it really so certain that one's 'being claimed' ought to be included right from the beginning in the study of a biblical text in the interest of understanding it? Should this not be reserved as an exegetical aid for a second phase in interpretation? It is an undisputed fact that what the Bible proclaims demands a decision in faith from us. But is that to be construed in such a way that we ought no longer to distinguish between two phases: a simple listening to the content of the proclamation, and then the encounter of faith, that is, the existential decision?

It is surely correct that an exegesis without presuppositions is an illusion. If I wish to understand a love-song, I must know what love is.[1] If I wish to understand what faith means, I must know what faith is. Furthermore, I must take into account as an exegete that

---

[1] Cf. E. Schweizer's remark in his review of K. Frör's book, *Neue Zürcher Zeitung*, July, 1962: 'A purely grammatical-philological exegesis in the narrower sense of the term would have to conclude that a maiden must be seriously ill if her cheeks are "redder than wine", as the song states.'

no interpreter can exclude his own characteristic experience of love or faith. There was a time when it was necessary to make exegetes mindful of this.[1] Today this has become an obvious point we no longer need to labour. It seems rather that the time has come to warn against an over-emphasis on the impossibility of exegesis without presuppositions. Certainly there is no exegesis without its presuppositions. But to make this conclusion (almost hackneyed today) into a principle appears to me far more dangerous than not to observe it at all. The fact that complete absence of presuppositions is impossible must not excuse us from striving for objectivity altogether, going so far as to regard such striving primarily as an outmoded standpoint, and making a necessary fact into a virtue. To interpret a love-song I must certainly know what love is. But the confrontation with the love I have experienced or expressed happens quite automatically while reading the song. For this a particular effort is seldom necessary. On the contrary, a *special effort* is needed if I am not simply to ascribe my own love experiences of a particular kind to the writer of the love-song, who could have had very different experiences. So it seems to me, now as before, far more important than all the philosophical observations about the object-subject relationship, to take to heart the simple necessity that has become a perennial principle of all sound exegesis. This principle is, not to interpret myself into the text, in the exegesis of a text. This is fortunately carried out in practice to a large extent even where it is unnoticed theoretically. When it comes to interpreting witnesses of faith, this, of course, means that I must know from my own experience what faith is. But even in this it holds true that I must try not to read my own, individually marked, questions of existence and faith into the witness of faith, thereby running the risk of hearing a false address from it. The world of faith, perhaps completely foreign to me, standing behind the text being interpreted, will only become evident to me in its strangeness when I reckon not only with the strangeness of the answer, but also with the strangeness of the *question*. Obviously as a Christian I shall interpret the Koran differently from a Moslem. Yet in my interpreting, I shall try continually not to impose my Christian questions and notions of faith upon it.

This same *requirement, first of all of a simple listening*, without being

---

[1] I personally put special emphasis on this aspect in one of my very first publications. See O. Cullmann, 'Les problèmes posés par la méthode exégétique de K. Barth', *RHPR*, 1928, pp. 70ff.

aware that I am 'addressed' in my existence (*Ek-sistenz*), should also be a valid principle in studying the text of the New Testament, even if I am a believing Christian exegete. In this case my own faith in Christ, if it is ultimately like that of the New Testament witnesses, must surely be a factor added to deepen my understanding. On this I am in agreement with what is being asked for by modern hermeneutics. But this is a second act in the work of exegesis. To start with, I am not at all sure whether the *Vorverständnis* that I bring with me and the question I raise actually correspond with the essence of *New Testament* faith. In the course of church history up to the present, very different expressions of Christian faith, and even degenerations of it, have appeared, which simply rest upon different subjective ways of putting the question.[1]

Certainly the experience of Christ in the Church of today, of which I as an exegete am a member, forms an important presupposition for a legitimate *Vorverständnis* of New Testament faith. But even on this basis, when I approach the text as an exegete, I may not consider it to be certain that my Church's faith in Christ is in its essence really that of the writers of the New Testament. The conviction of the continuity of Christ's work in the present Church ought to be taken very much into account hermeneutically,[2] for the Church is the place analogous to that in which the Scriptures of early Christianity originated. But now we are getting to the question of tradition in relation to Scripture, which is to be dealt with later. Inasmuch as we do not believe in the infallibility of the teaching office of the Church,[3] necessary though it is, we cannot exclude the possibility that some sources of error have been accepted in the Church of the present. In the same way, my personal self-under-

---

[1] An item related to this is the 'selection' within the New Testament of the heart of the gospel, differently defined in each case. H. Küng's suggestive article, 'Der Frühkatholizismus im Neuen Testament als kontroverstheologisches Problem', *Tübinger Theol. Quart. Schrift* 4, 1962, taking issue with E. Käsemann and H. Diem, is very illuminating on this point.

[2] H. Diem rightly stresses this in his reflections in which he carries out K. Barth's hermeneutical ideas. See especially *Grundfragen der biblischen Hermeneutik*, 1950, and *Was heisst schriftgemäss?* 1958. Despite my basic assent, I would still like to say a word against even this *Vorverständnis* on behalf of deliberate effort at impartiality.

[3] It is understandable that my Catholic critic, J. Frisque, *O. Cullmann. Une théologie de l'histoire du salut,* 1960, pp. 206ff., by recourse to the teaching office of the Church, would find a substitute for what he terms my 'positivism'. That may appear in a more proper light in the present work.

standing and my personal experience of faith must not only be seen as exegetical aids, but also as possible sources of error.

When as an exegete of the New Testament I study the faith of its writers, I may not be sure in advance that I am raising my *questions* in a proper way. I may not imagine that the proclamation of faith by the early Christian witness and the call to decision implicit in it necessarily correspond to an answer to the question *I* put. It could be that out of this proclamation I might hear a call to decision unlike the one intended by the writers. An error could arise from my being too sure that the New Testament faith presupposes the question of existence in the way I put it. Surely J. A. Bengel's plea '*rem totam applica ad te*' (apply the whole thing to thyself) ought to be taken to heart, but not in the sense that one reckons only with such an '*applicatio*' that corresponds to the question one raises.

Today it is, of course, asserted that an understanding of New Testament faith is barred completely if the 'false and outmoded philosophy' of separation between subject and object is not given up. One must start instead with a conceptuality that clears away this separation, and this is the conceptuality of the Bible to which Heidegger's corresponds. Because of this, the distinction may not be drawn between 'objective' saving events and their subjective appropriation in faith nor, therefore, between two phases of exegesis. Whether this distinction is a 'false philosophy' or a philosophy at all may be left unanswered. What interests us is knowing whether the New Testament distinguishes between God's acting and the believing subject. Is not faith for Paul of such a quality that this distinction *belongs to its essence* independently of any conceptuality? Does not faith for Paul mean believing that someone else has already accomplished the saving work *for me*, precisely because it has been done completely *independently of me and my believing*? Certainly an appropriation in faith is indispensable. The divine event, together with its interpretation revealed to the prophets and apostles which, as we shall see, belongs in that event, extends a claim to me about which I must make a decision, as Bultmann rightly emphasizes. But in this case decision does not mean a vague decision for the 'wholly other', or 'that which is not at my disposal', but a decision to align my existence with that concrete history revealed to me, with that sequence of events.

If this is the concept of faith found in the New Testament, then it has hermeneutical consequences. On the one hand we need a neutral study of events and the correct rendering of the interpretations of these events communicated to us by others. On the other hand, for a deeper comprehension of that interpretation of faith, we need a personal act of faith by virtue of which we align ourselves with the saving events in our place and time in the same way as the first witnesses did in theirs. This means that in exegesis two things are warranted and required: the exclusion of the exegete's own person and at the same time its inclusion.

With regard to our problem of salvation history, it may be said concretely that the proclamation of the New Testament writers issues the call to decision in the form of an announcement about divine events. The call of the New Testament to us is always founded in the *indicatives* concerning events in which, at the outset, we do not participate at all. It is not a certain matter (as existential interpretation assumes) that those indicatives amount to no more than objectifications which must be demythologized because this is the only way in which they can become a call to decision for us in view of our *Vorverständnis*. If the decision of faith intended *in the New Testament* asks us to align ourselves with that *sequence of events*, then the sequence may not be demythologized, de-historicized, or de-objectified. But this means that the message about these events must be taken seriously as a report about something that has happened objectively.

The 'application of the subject matter to myself' presupposes that in complete subjection to the text (*te totum applica ad textum*), silencing my questioning, I struggle with the *'res'*, the subject matter. But that means that I must be ready to hear something perhaps foreign to me. I must be prepared to hear a faith, an address, running completely contrary to the questions I raise, and in which I do *not* at first feel myself addressed. If my question about my self-understanding is put in such a way that the call to decision cannot come to me in the form of a demand to align myself with a sequence of events brought about by God *extra me* (apart from me), it need not follow that the proclamation of the first witnesses cannot have had this character, in other words that the sequence of events itself cannot be the actual object of their faith, but only its objectification. Such an attitude to the text is not the listening required of us as exegetes. Otherwise, we run the risk of wanting to know what the first witnesses believed better by virtue of our *Vorverständnis* than they themselves.

The demand for an obedient listening to the text and for a listening for a claim independent of my own immediate experience of being claimed, or my own decision in faith, is in harmony with the distinction made by Paul between hearing and believing. In Romans 10.17ff. he states the sequence: first, revelation through the Word of Christ; second, hearing; third, believing. Hearing precedes believing: 'Faith comes by what is heard, and what is heard comes by the Word of Christ.'[1]

The *scholarly* requirement to find out first of all by means of the philological, historical method what the text has to say to us that is new and perhaps completely foreign, thus coincides with the *theological* requirement to listen to the Word of Scripture as to a revelation completely new to us and to let ourselves be given *new questions* by that Word.

But is such simple listening possible at all if we are not at the same time claimed in our own self-understanding? Against the present-day hermeneutical tendency, I dare to answer this question for the present in the affirmative. I can hear the message and its claim even if I 'lack faith' myself, even if the message does not address me at all, inducing neither assent nor rejection. I can in this case describe correctly the essential statements of the message. I can also interpret a text of a pagan religion correctly without belonging to this religion. Otherwise, all scholarship on the history of religion would be impossible.

However, I do not in any way want to dispute that a *believing* pagan can penetrate deeper than I can into the understanding of a text of his religion. Later we shall see that there is a being-claimed by a message, as opposed to its mere explication, and that only after assenting to the faith of the first witnesses is a deepened understanding of what the first witnesses regarded as revelation possible.

My primary concern is to stress that there can be a preliminary hearing, reading, and studying of the New Testament in which the element of personal claim is excluded so far as possible. I refuse to give up what is to me the duty of keeping my own notions of faith away from my interpretation, whether I am able successfully to realize this or not. With the faith of the New Testament, there is a possibility of hearing apart from the encounter of faith, because this faith is communicated to us as a faith in *events*. As we shall see, this

---

[1] As the quotation from Isa. 53.1 in v. 16 shows, here ἀκοή has the sense of 'what is heard', that is, 'what is preached'. In the whole context of the chapter, however, the active sense of 'hearing' certainly stands in the foreground. The following verse (18), 'Have they not heard?', indicates this too.

involves, to be sure, a sequence of events *already interpreted by faith.* But the interpretation, in which even mythical elements can serve to expound the meaning of the events, does not at all prevent this sequence of events from being told as a 'biblical history' that can be unfolded quite irrespective of whether an encounter in faith comes to us or not. Granted that, without faith, from an *historical* standpoint we shall find this interpretation meaningless. But even in what appears to be meaningless from a purely historical standpoint, this interpretation can nevertheless be heard and told as a sequence of events. Furthermore, the significant *connection* of events created by the first Christians can be communicated in a concrete, reflective unfolding within the framework of this special history, even if we ourselves do not share this faith. This preliminary acceptance of biblical history is not the conceptuality presupposed by existential exegesis, but seems to me to be the *Vorverständnis* actually corresponding to the real state of affairs.

It must, however, be granted (and here is where the justification for the question posed by modern hermeneutics lies) that I shall penetrate deeper into the understanding of the New Testament texts, and more fully comprehend the interpretation of the events they relate, if I come to cease to regard the 'biblical history' as meaningless, and not only hear and unfold the interpretation given by the first witnesses, but am claimed by it in my existence, and am thereby called to decision, believing in it *with and in the Church.* Only then will I be in a position by my faith, *which must be purified from everything extraneous to the New Testament witnesses,* to study their faith more deeply. Only then, when I am in some way sure that my faith is the same as that of the first Christians, will the circular procedure[1] between my faith and that of the first Christians, between subject and object, be fully justified. This is why the separation of both phases of exegesis is so important as a matter of principle.

Naturally the effort at objectivity must remain at the *start* of the exegetical road. But on the other hand it should also accompany all the exegete's further work. In a circular procedure analogous to the one mentioned above, what I believe I have gained in understanding the New Testament faith must always be examined anew in the light of the text. I must thus be determined to be instructed by this text ever anew and must eliminate from myself everything alien to it.

[1] I stressed the necessity of this circular procedure myself in 1928 in the article mentioned above p. 67, n. 1.

If we succeed in bringing ourselves to the encounter of faith to which the New Testament would call us, we are confronted with an incomparable source for a deeper understanding of the New Testament message. However, if we impose another faith upon that of the New Testament, then our faith is simply a source of error. In this case an unbelieving historian, operating within his own boundaries, beyond which he cannot press to an ultimate understanding of New Testament faith, will more correctly *describe* the faith than the theologian.[1]

Therefore, now as before, I hold it to be of utmost importance that in the first exegetical inquiry of the text an effort should be made to exclude the danger of a source of error present in the person of the exegete. Naturally this will always be no more than an *effort*, for perhaps we shall never fully succeed in avoiding subjective presuppositions extraneous to the text. But despite my reflections upon the more recent hermeneutical insights, it seems to me desirable and in the interest of collaboration among exegetes that the attempt again be taken up purposively to achieve this goal.

Now this effort is in no way merely theoretical wishful-thinking, for the *philological, historical-critical* method is available to us to help us approximate its realization. We can be thankful that in the various camps of New Testament scholarship there is widespread agreement as to the necessity of applying this method, and in actual practice it plays the same important role almost everywhere. Nevertheless, in the view represented here it takes on a greater importance. It is, in a manner of speaking, the only guarantee for the objectivity sought after in hearing the text's proclamation, independent of faith, to which we attached so much importance in the preceding discussion. Inasmuch as we take New Testament faith seriously as faith in *events*, the importance of historical-critical research is apparent just from the subject matter itself. Furthermore, if salvation history turns out to be basic to New Testament faith, it takes on an added theological significance. Just as *eyewitnessing* is a fundamental accompaniment to a witness of faith for the apostle, and one cannot be thought of without the other (εἶδεν καὶ ἐπίστευσεν John 20.8), in the same way, research on the narrated events with any available means precedes faith in the interpretation of the events for the exegete.

[1] Thus I have found again and again that my non-theological colleagues in certain circumstances come closer to understanding a topic of New Testament faith than some theological exegetes.

Once we have recognized the character of the salvation history of the New Testament, above all its relation to history, and the place taken by the history of its interpretation, we shall be able to show how the role of the historical-critical method is to be more closely determined. Only then can we raise the question whether by means of the historical-critical method we can attempt to search out the naked facts apart from the interpretation of them in faith (as in the problem of the historical Jesus), and whether the interpretation of the events, itself belonging to salvation history, can also be elucidated by this method.

Thus I emphasize again that the actual hermeneutics basic to the salvation-historical understanding of the New Testament will become clear in connection with the discussion to follow in the next chapters. I thought it important, however, at least to indicate the most important lines of the way I am trying to follow, for the essence of New Testament faith is defined in a totally different way by other theologians, and the reason for this lies ultimately in another hermeneutics.

5. TERMINOLOGY

Although terminology belongs within the area of preliminary questions, we are already touching on problems of central importance in speaking of the use of the expressions 'salvation history', 'eschatology', and 'apocalyptic'.

A. 'SALVATION HISTORY' ('ECONOMY OF SALVATION')

Many theologians are unsympathetic towards the expression 'salvation history'. They make no attempt to preserve it by reinterpretation, as they do with the word 'eschatology'. The expression 'salvation history' is simply avoided by a whole group of theologians,[1] and not just by those seeing the thing itself as a distortion for which Luke is primarily to blame. For many, the word has something disreputable about it, for in the history of theology it has acquired a pietistic, or

[1] An article by H. J. Kraus, 'Schöpfung und Weltvollendung', *EvT*, 1964, pp. 462ff., seems to me to be characteristic of this. On p. 484 at the conclusion of this notable work, he writes, 'the salvation-historical perspective is eliminated', whereas in reality he develops one.

even 'conservative' (in *malam partem*) apologetic significance. There is a fear that to take a positive stand on salvation history is to fall into bad theological company. In the last century there was a theological school whose adherents, so to speak, wrote the expression *Heilsgeschichte* on their banners, or were given the label *Heilsgeschichtler* by others to designate their theological position.[1]

It is certainly a welcome thing when people do not wish to approach New Testament exegesis informed by a certain dogmatics, especially since the school just mentioned was greatly dependent upon the Hegelian philosophy of the time. Since theologians, at least in the German-speaking part of the world, almost automatically connect the expression 'salvation history' with the earlier systematic theologians, it easily gives rise to misunderstandings. There is a temptation to impute ideas held by the earlier theologians to anyone using the term to describe the essence of New Testament faith, even though that person does not represent such views at all.[2]

So it must be granted that the term *Heilsgeschichte*, hard to translate into other languages, is not a very good one. It has become a slogan, and the cherished usage of slogans, among theologians in particular, tends to be detrimental to the matter in question. But the term 'salvation history' is not entirely a happy choice for two other reasons. As a term, it is not biblical, and thus *a priori* it arouses suspicion that anyone using it is trying to bring into the New Testament a category foreign to it. Furthermore, the word 'history' can be misunderstood, inasmuch as the characteristics constituting the concept of 'history' are, of course, absent here.

In point of fact, the expression 'salvation history' is to be found nowhere in the New Testament. The Greek word οἰκονομία, found in the New Testament, is, however, very close to what, for lack of a better expression, we call 'salvation history'. Even in its secular usage it includes the thought of a plan, of an administration, of a 'household', sometimes in the passive sense, and sometimes in the active sense of 'keeping house'. In this sense it occurs particularly in Colossians and Ephesians, tending to be connected with the concept of the divine mystery that Paul uses in Romans and Corinthians

---

[1] On this see G. Weth, *Die Heilsgeschichte, ihr universeller und ihr individueller Sinn in der offenbarungsgeschichtlichen Theologie des 19. Jahrhunderts,* 1931.

[2] Even I was not spared this fate entirely. I experienced it not only in the work mentioned above, written by K. G. Steck, who regards me as an extension of this line of theologians, but also at the hands of many critics of my book *Christ and Time.*

wherever he speaks of a supernatural revelation he has had of the divine *plan of salvation* (Rom. 11.25; I Cor. 4.1; 15.51). Eph. 3.9 speaks of the οἰκονομία of the mystery, hidden up till now, which is now revealed. Of special interest is the phrase in Eph. 1.10, 'οἰκονομία of the fulfilment of the times'.[1] In an analogous sense, Ignatius of Antioch uses it to refer particularly to the divine plan which finds its fulfilment in Christ: Jesus was born of Mary as the fruit of the body κατ' οἰκονομίαν θεοῦ (Eph. 19.2). He wishes to enlighten his readers about εἰς τὸν καινὸν ἄνθρωπον Ἰησοῦν Χριστόν (Eph. 20.1). In I Tim. 1.4 the οἰκονομία θεοῦ ἡ ἐν πίστει is contrasted with the speculations of false teachers. Here the radical opposition between salvation history and Gnosticism is grasped well.

How the apostle himself and his office belong to this οἰκονομία is shown in passages such as I Cor. 9.17, 'I am entrusted with the οἰκονομία', and Col. 1.25 and Eph. 3.2. The revelation of the divine plan of salvation to the apostle and the commission issued to him belong in that plan, and thus in salvation history itself. The apostle is steward of the mysteries of God (I Cor. 4.1).

For Irenaeus' theology the concept of the οἰκονομία is of basic importance. He uses it, like later writers, in the sense of a salvation history, and this is in fact what is intended in the New Testament passages mentioned.

Since the New Testament term οἰκονομία actually relates to what we call salvation history, one could ask whether it would not be better to say 'salvation economy' instead of 'salvation history'. But then an even less intelligible word would be introduced into theological terminology, and a foreign word at that. Furthermore, the idea that God carries out his plan in connection with specific, temporal events, included in the New Testament use of οἰκονομία, is not sufficiently expressed in the Greek word. This thought, however, is basic for the thing intended in the whole New Testament, even in the passages just cited. To speak of the carrying out of the divine plan always refers to a *series* of divine events linked together. Although the term 'salvation history' is not a biblical one, nevertheless we prefer it. The objection that it introduces a category foreign to the New Testament should be invalidated by the present work. It ought

---

[1] The question, much discussed at one time, whether the genitive τοῦ πληρώματος τῶν καιρῶν means that the 'fulfilment of the times' is itself the object of the οἰκονομία (so v. Hofmann), or whether the οἰκονομία in view here takes place in the fulfilment of the times, does not change the significance of the concept οἰκονομία very much.

also to be obviated by the fact that there is the other word, οἰκονομία, in the New Testament for the *matter* intended.

It is, of course, asserted by the opponents of salvation history that the essential features constituting history are absent in this salvation history. This is the second difficulty. Actually, it will be one of my prime concerns in the following chapters to bring out what radically distinguishes New Testament salvation history from all other history, and to stress the connection, meaningless from a purely historical standpoint, of a few specific events. We shall see that no philosophy of history is involved here, for if this were the case it would connect a philosophical idea with immanent historical vantage points, selecting a particular grouping of events, whereas the selection of events encountered in salvation history cannot be found in the historical regularity of a principle, being ascribed instead to a *revelation* about history. Moreover, the 'by-passing' not only of many events, but of whole periods of history, such as we shall find particularly in the salvation-historical view of the New Testament, contradicts the law of continuity,[1] important for all history.

This stressing of the distinction between salvation history and history, which is so important to me, has already indicated how wrong it is to associate my exegetical treatment of New Testament salvation history with the salvation-historical dogmatics of the last century. As a result of its philosophical premises this dogmatics was often, though not always, more interested in how salvation history and history go together than in how they part company.[2]

Thus the terminological objection which says that the expression 'salvation history' is in any case unsuitable because no history at all is involved here seems all the more justified. But the connection of salvation and history ought to be indicated by tacitly setting the second word of the phrase in quotation marks. 'Salvation' and 'history' in the usual senses of the terms do not, of course, fit together. This produces a deliberate contradiction, which is characteristic of the subject matter. If this happens, then its use is particularly meaningful.

---

[1] Cf. the discussion below pp. 153ff.

[2] K. G. Steck's objections against me (see above pp. 55f.) have their partial basis in the way he argues as though I were equating salvation history and history, even though he recognizes that I make no use of the concept of organism (*op. cit.*, p. 44). He then accuses me of inconsistency because I still operate with concepts like 'prophetic', which do not pertain to history.

Certainly this opposition to history in the usual sense is not enough to justify retaining the expression. The *analogy* between salvation history and history must also be seen.[1] The two are not identical, but there is an analogy between them. We can elaborate on this only in the chapters that follow. But even here reference should be made to three essential points in which this analogy comes to light: First is the fact that we are concerned with a *connected series of events*, even if the principle of the connection is not arrived at historically. Second is the fact that within the divine plan a place is left for historical contingency, for human resistance, sin, and the mysterious 'detours' taken because of this resistance and sin—in other words, salvation history also includes a history of disaster (*Unheilsgeschichte*). Third is the fact that the essential *individual events* constituting this series of events belong to history.[2] Hence, in the New Testament the event which is above all the centre and norm of all that happens is Christ's death on the cross. This double analogy to history is, as already mentioned, a very important aspect of what we call New Testament salvation history. A sequence of real events represents an analogy to history that is worthy of note, even though their selection cannot be explained historically. Despite the undeniable disadvantages noted in the reservations above, the use of the term 'salvation history' seems to me not only justified, but even required in the absence of a better expression. Only when a term which is really a better description is proposed can the disputed word be given up.

B. 'ESCHATOLOGY'

'Eschatology' is derived from τὰ ἔσχατα. It is conjectured that the expression comes from Ecclus. 7.36: 'In all you do, remember the end', in Hebrew, *aharith*. In the section in the older dogmatics dealing with the future, for instance that of Johannes Gerhard, ἔσχατα is translated '*novissima*' (*locus de novissimis*). Just when the word 'eschatology', derived from the Greek, was used for the first time is yet to be determined. Today, it has passed into general theological parlance and has become a technical term, like the adjective derived from it, 'eschatological'.

[1] Cf. below the whole chapter, 'New Testament Salvation History and History', pp. 150ff.
[2] The fact that mythical elements are adduced to *interpret* the individual events does not change this fact.

For some time now the word, and particularly the adjective, has gone through a noteworthy transformation in meaning, which ties in with a general development of the understanding of eschatology. Today, it is often used in a way hardly justified by the literal sense. Any situation of decision is often described as 'eschatological'. The writings of Kierkegaard, the existentialism connected with them, and especially the application by Bultmann of the term to New Testament eschatology, all play an important part in this transformation. Because for Bultmann's approach, with his question concerning self-understanding, the ultimate meaning of Jesus' eschatology is the 'always standing in the situation of decision', this extension of the concept undertaken by him and his school appears perhaps justified. Still, because this interpretation cannot be taken exegetically as a general and valid interpretation of the *essence* of Jesus' expectation of the end, nor taken as a point of departure, this wider and misleading usage ought to be avoided. It is also misleading in its use by Bultmann and his pupils because etymologically the word has only a temporal significance. If, as happens in the Bultmann school, the temporal element in the sense intended by the expression ἔσχατα is given up, one should also give up the term itself. This is even more so since there are adequate expressions at hand from the language of existentialist philosophy corresponding to the idea retained as essential. The words 'eschatology' and 'eschatological' relate to the end time, not the time of decision. Certainly the end time is a time of decision, but every time of decision is not an end time; therefore, we shall use the expression 'eschatology' and 'eschatological' in their etymological sense of 'end time'.[1] That, of course, does not mean that in the New Testament they are not related to the present. On the contrary, as we shall see later, it is characteristic of the New Testament situation that the end time is *at once* a future and a present. However, the concept of the 'end time' is not to be understood in an existential way, but in the temporal sense of 'final time'. That means that it remains closely bound up with the concept of salvation history. To speak of 'final time' only has meaning when it stands in connection with a preceding time.

[1] It is encouraging that N. A. Dahl, 'Eschatologie und Geschichte im Lichte der Qumrantexte' in *Zeit und Geschichte. Dankesgabe für R. Bultmann*, 1964, pp. 3ff., also proposes a return to the 'old-fashioned use of the word'. Incidentally, he thinks he already sees a preparation for the transformation into the present usage in Albert Schweitzer (p. 4).

C. 'APOCALYPTIC'

It is customary to distinguish apocalyptic from eschatology by taking the content of late Jewish books designated as apocalypses as a starting point. All items associated with these books, so far as time and subject matter are concerned, are called 'apocalyptic'. In this sense the word, as substantive and adjective, relates to a type of literature belonging chronologically to late Judaism. On the other hand, the expression has a topical significance, distinct from that of eschatology, and which tends more and more to assume a derogatory character. In this sense, it is customary to term 'apocalyptic' those descriptions of the future which serve as pure speculations merely to satisfy human curiosity, without any actual interest in salvation.

This depreciatory qualification is not justified by the etymology of the word. As distinct from the word 'eschatology', apocalyptic relates not to the object, but to the means of knowledge: a 'revelation' directly issuing from God. The object of eschatology, of course, is recognized only by way of divine revelation. Therefore, if information about the end designated etymologically as 'revealed' is referred to as 'apocalyptic', this amounts to merely a difference in degree. Apocalyptic relates to *final*, divine secrets, lying beyond the usual revelations entrusted to the prophets. These secrets look to events no longer having a direct point of contact with the events to which we are witnesses. They are primarily, if not exclusively, of cosmic nature.

Thus the revelations to the apocalyptic 'seers' do not usually come in the same way as the future predictions made through the prophets and apostles, who usually learn of God's message about the future in an event during the present. Here is a real distinction.[1] Often the 'apocalypses' do not have the connection with salvation history which is so characteristic of biblical eschatology in the Old and New Testaments. Where no sort of connection with salvation history exists any more, where the future no longer enlightens the whole divine history of salvation, nor at the same time is enlightened by it, where only a plan of God for the future without a firm connection with his whole plan is involved, there the noun and adjective 'apocalyptic' may be applied in the derogatory sense. Certainly there are writings

---

[1] G. von Rad, *Old Testament Theology* II, pp. 306ff., rightly says that apocalyptic obscures its historical context and stands under the influence of the theology of the Wisdom movement. But see the next footnote.

among the late Jewish and Christian apocalypses that can be characterized in this way.

Nevertheless, caution is required here, for this characteristic by no means always remains true. There are both late Jewish and Christian apocalypses completely anchored in the events experienced by the seer in his own present. The connection with the remaining salvation history is usually very much stressed, although less from the vantage point of events in the present than from the doctrine of the two aeons. The recent debate on the positive or negative value of apocalyptic suffers from a serious lack of distinction between the different apocalypses in this respect. Therefore both the defenders and the opponents of apocalyptic are sometimes right and sometimes wrong.[1] By and large it is true, however, that injustice is done to apocalyptic by the derogatory use of the word, and the rehabilitation of apocalyptic undertaken by Rössler, Wilckens, and, in another way, by Käsemann, should be regarded as a fitting reaction.

For this reason it is perhaps advisable to drop the derogatory use of the word 'apocalyptic'. There are Jewish and Christian apocalypses containing detailed descriptions merely satisfying human curiosity, and as speculations floating about in the air they have no connection with salvation history. This is true, for example, of the calculating of dates. It is fitting to view them as degenerations, indeed, as caricatures of true eschatology. But it is wrong to use the expression 'apocalyptic' in such a way that everything deriving from this literary and theological bent belongs in the category of distortion. I urge instead that the word 'apocalyptic' only be used in a neutral sense to designate a special literary type and the items belonging to it within the province of its theology.

Whether we are encountering a legitimate continuation of prophetic eschatology or distortions of the kind just mentioned must be decided in each case. If we avoid the label 'apocalyptic' in the derogatory sense, our judgment will be more unbiassed. But where, then, is the distinctive criterion? For existential interpretation, 'apocalyptic' in the derogatory sense is everything that cannot be directly interpreted existentially. On that basis practically *everything* in the apocalypses must fall under this category. It may be a related fact

[1] Even von Rad's judgment in the previous footnote is nevertheless given too summarily and would have to be compared with the results of D. Rössler's work, *Gesetz und Geschichte*, 1960. Rössler for his own part neglects the other side too much when he places the universal relationship of apocalyptic to history too exclusively in the foreground.

that the extension of the derogatory usage has been helped along by this circle of theologians.[1]

We must in reality be on our guard that we do not judge all descriptions of the future by this too narrow category. Otherwise, we would not be able to judge properly, for instance, the powerful witness of the Apocalypse of John. Here, in a genuinely prophetic way, the future is seen from the standpoint of present experience, that is, persecution, mission,[2] and above all the experience in worship anticipating the future. The future is seen, as in all salvation history, in connection with the tradition of the history of salvation that has been handed down. The whole book, but particularly chapter twelve, shows how the salvation history of the past is seen in the closest relationship with the events of the present and future.[3] We ought not, therefore, to toss out as 'apocalyptic' and as eschatologically irrelevant every statement about the end time whose relation to our self-understanding is not directly evident.

Of sole critical importance for our judgment should be whether the vision of the future is anchored in the total history of salvation, and in the light of the New Testament, above all, whether this vision is anchored in the central Christ event. Only where this connection is lacking, and where pure speculations floating in the air are present, is there a departure from the legitimate, biblical-eschatological tradition.

We shall find as the essential characteristic of all biblical eschatology that cosmic events are bound up with historical events; that cosmology is, in a manner of speaking, demythologized and historicized. Furthermore, we shall note that the whole cosmic process is linked with what happens to humanity, and in this way the cosmos is tied in with sin and redemption. Therefore, the habit often observed of discrediting every mention of cosmic events in an apocalyptic-eschatological description, saying 'there is a distortion', meaning 'apocalyptic' in the bad sense, is unjustified. Statements concerning cosmic events of the future are not completely absent

---

[1] Hence the sharp reaction in *ZTK*, 1961, Heft 2, pp. 227ff., 245ff. by E. Fuchs and G. Ebeling against E. Käsemann's article, 'Die Anfänge christlicher Theologie', *ZTK*, 1960, pp. 162ff. Cf. the clear movement away from the 'leitmotif of existence' in Käsemann's reply, 'Zum Thema der urchristlichen Apokalyptik', *ZTK*, 1962, pp. 257ff.

[2] On this whole subject see M. Rissi, *Zeit und Geschichte in der Offenbarung des Johannes*, 1952, pp. 109ff.

[3] For a survey of exegesis of Rev. 12, see P. Prigent, *Histoire de l'exégèse d'Apokalypse* 12, 1959, and M. Rissi, *op. cit.*, pp. 122ff.

from the total salvation-historical view of the Bible. For this reason, the step so eagerly taken in the exegesis, for instance, of the Synoptic apocalypse of Mark 13, which *a priori* views every saying of Jesus about cosmic upheavals as unauthentic, is a dubious one. There can be good literary grounds for regarding them as secondary. But in no case should this be done on the false premise that every futuristic statement about the cosmos is a degeneration of true eschatology.

The exclusively derogatory use of the word 'apocalyptic' is, to a great extent, to blame for this premature conclusion. We shall therefore use it in the neutral sense of 'revelation of the final secrets'. These secrets can be loosed from the total salvation-historical perspective of the Bible and become theologically irrelevant speculation; but this need not necessarily happen.

II

THE GENESIS OF THE SALVATION-HISTORICAL APPROACH

H OW DID THE message preached to us in the New Testament as a witness of faith arise? The answer to this question cannot be gained from any direct information relating to it. Instead, it must be disclosed indirectly from the study of the main characteristics of this message itself. We must therefore anticipate some of the conclusions of the next part of this book,[1] selecting individual points of importance. The basis of the New Testament message is the narration of interpreted events. The Gospel as an account of the life of Jesus is the specifically Christian type of literature.[2] Even if the majority of the New Testament Epistles were composed earlier than the written Gospels, the Gospel *material* is still older than the Epistles and is presupposed by them. Quite in accord with the fundamental meaning of the Gospels, from the beginning of the second century the word εὐαγγέλιον was used exclusively as a designation for an account of the events of Jesus' life, even though the Epistles could have been called εὐαγγέλια just as well.[3] To be sure, the Book of Acts does not have the title of εὐαγγέλιον. But everything points to the fact that the writer of the two works placed them both on the same level, with Acts as a sequel to the

---

[1] In view of the necessary anticipation of such conclusions, it might seem more suitable for the phenomenological treatment of the essence of New Testament salvation history to precede the genetic treatment. Upon careful consideration, however, the sequence here seems to me to be better.

[2] G. Ebeling, 'Der Grund christlicher Theologie', *ZTK*, 1961, p. 232, rightly emphasizes this, and so does E. Fuchs, 'Das Neue Testament und das hermeneutisches Problem', *ZTK*, 1961, p. 201. But neither has drawn the real conclusions from this fact.

[3] As a matter of fact we find this term applied to a Pauline letter in an exceptional case; cf. I Clem. 47.1f.

πρῶτος λόγος, that is, our Gospel of Luke, thus attributing the same importance to it as to the Gospel itself.[1]

This fact ought not to lessen the importance of the New Testament letters or the didactic parts of the Gospels. It does make clear, however, that everything in the Epistles, indeed all the doctrine of the New Testament, is spoken from, and must be understood against, the background of events. Thus, even the Sermon on the Mount is to be understood only in relation with everything we know about the life of Jesus. 'But I say to you' is more than merely an introductory rhetorical formula.

In stating the essence of the New Testament message, the earliest confessions of faith indicate that a series of events is not just an exterior framework, but the basis of that essence. The confessions are, of course, especially important for establishing the core of the New Testament message, for in them the first Christians sought to portray only what they regarded as the primary matter. In the oldest creed cited, I Cor. 15.3ff., *events* are spoken of, albeit interpreted ones.

A further observation of fundamental importance must be added: the account of events is connected with the Old Testament by the first Christians. This is particularly evident in Matthew's Gospel,[2] but in the others as well, and probably extends back to an earlier stage of the Synoptic tradition that was set down in writing in the so-called '*testimonia*' which can perhaps still be reconstructed from early Christian literature. The aim of the *testimonia* is to show the new events as the fulfilment of the earlier ones witnessed to in the Old Testament.[3] The very early creed, mentioned above, that Paul cites in I Cor. 15.3ff. also connects the central events of the crucifixion and resurrection with the Old Testament (κατὰ τὰς γραφάς). The New Testament writers seem to have thought mainly of the prophetic predictions of the Old Testament. But in the Old Testament, prediction by the prophets belongs to the divine events. Although there is often a parallelizing typology (we shall have to discuss the differences between typology, allegory, and salvation history[4]) in the

---

[1] There is much to be said for the hypothesis that the two parts were separated only when the Gospel of John came between them in the canon, bringing about the present form of the prologue. Cf. P. Menoud, 'Remarques sur les textes de l'ascension dans Luc-Actes', *Neutestamentliche Studien für R. Bultmann*, 1954, pp. 148–156, and E. Trocmé, *Le 'Livre des Actes' et l'Histoire*, 1957, pp. 31f., 41ff.

[2] K. Stendahl, *The School of St Matthew*, 1954.

[3] P. Prigent, *L'Epître de Barnabé I–XVI et ses Sources*, 1961.

[4] See below pp. 132ff.

New Testament citation of Old Testament accounts, behind this juxtaposition there is still the attempt to connect the present events not just with the Scriptures in a rabbinic sort of way, but with earlier events. It must never be forgotten that whatever 'is written' has first of all 'happened'. In I Cor. 10.11 Paul makes a clear distinction, 'Now these things happened to them τυπικῶς, but they were written down for our instruction, upon whom the end of the ages has come'. This means that Scripture as such wishes to invite us to perceive a divine plan in the way events correspond with one another and develop further. Because a divine plan is perceived in the relationship of present and past, the past can be 'presented' in the present.

Finally, we note that in the genesis of New Testament salvation history, all events, the past, the present, and the ones expected in the future, are summed up in *one* event as their high-point and mid-point: the crucifixion of Christ and the subsequent resurrection.

In view of these characteristics of New Testament salvation history, the New Testament acceptance of the Old Testament is especially important for our problem. Whether the concentration is seen to be on historically verifiable events or on the historical development of traditions, the great majority of scholars are agreed that the Old Testament is oriented toward a salvation history.[1] At any rate, the acceptance of the Old Testament by the New indicates that the phrase 'Christ as the end of the Law' cannot in any case be understood to mean that only a punctual, unbound event is envisaged by Jesus and early Christianity.[2] In view of such an understanding, we

[1] G. Fohrer, 'Prophetie und Geschichte', *TLZ*, 1964, cols. 481ff., reacts against the notion of 'salvation history' by showing that salvation and disaster (*Unheil*) balance each other out. This indicates a narrow concept of salvation history, for obviously disaster also belongs in salvation history; see below pp. 123f. The 'history of decision' which Fohrer contrasts with salvation history (col. 498) involves the decision to *return* (cf. the text from Jer. 25.3ff. which he cites, '. . . dwell upon the land which the Lord has given to you and your fathers from of old and forever'). The fact that a decision is always made in the *present* is an element integrating all salvation history and therefore is not a point which can be used to support Fohrer's thesis. Fohrer goes on to say (col. 499) that the aim of God's action is the rule of God over world and nature which strives for a relationship of fellowship between Yahweh and Israel. But this aim is characteristic of salvation history, as we shall show in the present work.

[2] E. Fuchs, 'Christus, das Ende der Geschichte', *EvT*, 1948/1949, pp. 447ff., and R. Bultmann, though somewhat differently, make the equation: 'end of the Law' = 'end of the history of salvation'. But the Pauline problem of the Law is only a partial problem in salvation history and offers too narrow a basis for this far-reaching judgment on the question of salvation history in the New Testament. See above p. 25.

must again refer to the danger of Marcionism for which indeed the Christ event is only punctual. The concept of fulfilment, so important for salvation history, indicates that the new covenant does not bring an end to a chaotic situation of the past, but that the past remains very real in the present and determines the Church's 'self-understanding' so that it views itself as the 'new Israel'.[1]

Everything vital for the genesis of the Old Testament salvation-historical perspective must be considered in the question of the origin of the New Testament salvation-historical perspective because of the Church's consciousness of the continuity of the two covenants. The New Testament's progressive completion of the salvation-historical *kerygma* continues the process begun in the Old Testament. We can say that the process continues in the New Testament according to the same 'laws'. At the same time, we must note that this regularity does not show the same constancy as that by which ordinary traditions develop, for the development of the salvation historical *kerygma* is ascribed to divine revelation and to its comprehension through the Holy Spirit by the people assisting in elaborating the *kerygma* in relation to new events. Thus, any regular rhythm is excluded. On the one hand, this distinguishes biblical form criticism from general form-critical laws, despite far-reaching analogies between them. On the other hand, it allows the continuity between the development of the Old Testament and New Testament *kerygmata* to stand out all the more clearly in relief.

We should, therefore, always start from what must be said about the salvation-historical message in the Old Testament. Whatever is ascertained there must be applied afresh to the New Testament. Nevertheless, if everything in the New Testament *kerygma* appears in an entirely new light, both as to origin and to phenomenological characteristics, the reason for this is not that for the first time a change in the development of salvation history appears on New Testament premises, and that before this change salvation history remained more or less stationary. We shall see that, on the contrary, in the Old Testament the *complete understanding* of the divine plan *evolves* in relation to new events in the present and sometimes passes through far-reaching changes. The New Testament does not bring

[1] F. Nietzsche in his *The Dawn* terms the whole effort of early Christianity to show this as 'that unheard-of philological farce about the Old Testament' (Walter Kaufmann's translation in *Nietzsche: Philosopher, Psychologist, Antichrist*, Meridian Books, 1950, p. 301; the phrase is cited by H. J. Schoeps, *Paulus*, 1959, p. 248).

something new in principle in this formal respect, but rather in the conviction of faith that the present event, which has *now* brought about a new understanding, is the decisive and normative event for all times, past, present, and future.

1. EVENT AND INTERPRETATION: THEIR MUTUAL RELATIONSHIP THROUGHOUT THE BIBLE

How does the salvation-historical perspective in the Old Testament arise? We shall speak for the moment only of the origin of the salvation-historical perspective, and not of that of the concrete descriptions of salvation history. We cannot go into all the details of the debate stirred up primarily by von Rad's *Old Testament Theology*. According to von Rad, the historical traditions of Israel, the theologies of history of the Yahwist, Elohist, Deuteronomist, and the prophets, continued to develop, usually in relation to *new events* occurring in the writer's own times. This fact is important for the genetic problem to be discussed here of the progressive origin common to the Old and New Testament *kerygmata*.

An objection made against this view is that it detracts from the role of history in favour of a *kerygma* lying beyond history; but this objection is unjustified when the stress is placed (perhaps more so than with von Rad) upon the continually *new events* which bring about, and *are incorporated in*, the new interpretations. Each new event recognized in faith as belonging to salvation history[1] is linked in its verticality with earlier interpretations of earlier events by the Old Testament writers. In this way light is thrown from the earlier events upon the new, but likewise a totally new light is also thrown from the new upon the old.

Salvation history does not arise by a simple adding up of events recognized in faith as saving events. Instead, each time *corrections* of the interpretation of past saving events *are undertaken in the light of new events*. This, of course, never happens in such a way that an earlier account is disputed. Rather, aspects formerly unnoticed are by virtue of the new revelation now placed in the foreground, creating a correspondingly wider horizon.

---

[1] Obviously it can mean disaster and judgment in the total plan of God, which includes human resistance and sin.

Here a particularly important item enters that we must keep in mind for the whole discussion to follow: The act of interpretation, which the prophets ascribe to revelation, *is regarded as belonging to salvation history itself.* The mediator of revelation, in the Old Testament the prophet, and in the New Testament the apostle, aligns himself, his function, and the revelation he has received, with the salvation history which he is interpreting anew. The fact of revelation, which has come to him together with the commission to communicate it, is therefore conceived of as belonging to salvation history itself. We shall see that this inclusion of the saving message in the saving events is quite essential for the New Testament. However, it is also present in the Old Testament, sometimes implicitly and sometimes explicitly. Revelation history and interpretation history are very closely connected with salvation history, but salvation history is still the over-arching concept.[1] On the other hand, however, this means, too, that the *predictions* of the prophets, the fulfilment of which is confirmed in the New Testament, cannot in principle be separated from Old Testament *events* which the first Christians saw to be paralleled and fulfilled in the present events of their own time.

The process by which the salvation-historical perspective originated is no longer completely comprehensible everywhere in the Old Testament. In the first place, the historical occasions for the origins and further development of the oldest traditions cannot always be told with certainty, especially when oral traditions or oral *kerygmata* are often involved, which were then set down in liturgical confessional formulas. To establish that these traditions were often first *fixed* in the *Sitz im Leben* of worship is to say nothing about the origin of the older *kerygma*, for instance, of the Exodus from Egypt. It is only in the great historical conceptions, and particularly in the prophets, that we are able to become better acquainted with the origin of the salvation-historical interpretations and reinterpretations.

This process is portrayed in the Old Testament (and this holds true for the New Testament as well) schematically as follows:[2] In a single event, either in political history or in his own life, the prophet experiences a revelation of a divine plan concerning this event. In order that the divine plan can be perceived as such,[3] he places this

---

[1] See what was said above, p. 57, about the title of this book.

[2] I am fully aware that this is too schematic a treatment. Otherwise a whole theology of the Old Testament would be needed.

[3] See J. Fichtner, 'Jahves Plan in der Botschaft des Jesaja', *ZAW*, 1951, pp. 16ff.

event in a series with past events and past revelations concerning these events. This association is given him by the tradition, whether in a prophetic historical work or in a confessional formula of a liturgy. Not every prophet offers a whole salvation history in each case. He can be content to show merely those links in history which are at the moment crucial for him, although in the background there is usually a total view of history.[1] In our treatment, this must be said in passing: in the light of the new event and this association with the salvation-historical tradition, the time-line can be extended forward to eschatology and backward to creation and primeval history. This perspective is also influenced by the new perspective which is linked with the events of salvation history. In describing the characteristics of the salvation-historical perspective, we shall come back to the importance of this widening in both directions.

We therefore distinguish: first, the naked event to which the prophet must be an eyewitness and which is seen by non-believers as well, who are unable to see any revelation in it; second, the revelation of a divine plan being disclosed in this event to the prophet, with which he aligns himself in faith; third, the creation of an association with earlier salvation-historical revelations imparted to other prophets and the reinterpretations of these revelations.

As a rule, the first and second acts take place simultaneously, although this does not always happen. The third may often be brought about in a longer process of theological reflection. Still, a present event recognized in faith as a saving event is fundamental to the third development. Only in certain apocalyptic predictions is this salvation-historical element lacking.[2]

Because the event is usually communicated only in connection with the revelation about it, there is a temptation to underestimate the role of the event in the origin of the salvation-historical conception. However, the *eyewitness quality* represents a *quite essential element* in the process described above. Granted, apart from revelation and faith in this revelation, the event may signify nothing. Since, however, the revelation and faith in this revelation are related *to the event*, it is of central importance that the bearer of revelation be himself an eyewitness to the event. This will be important, too, for the New Testament concept of apostleship. It is, however, already true for

---

[1] See pp. 127ff. below, where I intend to show that this is even more frequently the case in the New Testament—indeed, almost a rule.
[2] See above pp. 8off.

the Old Testament prophet. It is not by accident that Docetism is the primal heresy of ancient Christianity, the only one which we can distinctly see to be attacked by the New Testament. Up to the present day it emerges again and again wherever the event is underestimated in favour of the *kerygma*.

For this reason, whatever can and must be said critically in certain details about the Pannenberg group, I still regard its reaction as a healthy one over against the theses of the Bultmann school. The fact that the need to do justice again to the historical Jesus was felt by the Bultmann pupils themselves shows better than anything else that the exclusive emphasis upon the *kerygma* is always in danger of succumbing to Docetism.

When one of the younger Bultmann pupils, G. Klein, in his article cited above, 'Offenbarung als Geschichte? Marginalien zu einem theologischen Programm', argues against W. Pannenberg that the event in itself does not reveal anything at all, since unbelievers experience the same event without anything being revealed to them, not only is he in the closest proximity to Docetism with this objection, but he misses the actual question being posed. The question is not, does the event or the *kerygma* mean revelation for everybody? For the outsider, neither the event *nor the kerygma* (which he can also hear) signifies revelation. Rather, the question is, what role does the event play *for the recipient of revelation*?

In the origin of biblical salvation history, we are therefore dealing with a kind of *chain* of salvation-historical insights and representations in which each time a new event and a new revelation about it are aligned with the previous revelation, so that the previous revelation is at the same time placed in a new perspective. The new perspective will become for its own part an object of a new interpretation to come still later, and usually this new interpretation is caused by a new event and a new revelation about it. Often several existing traditions are assimilated into a new perspective. The analogy of a chain must not mislead us into a schematic conception in which a first event would be related to a first interpretation, to which a second interpretation would attach itself, and then a third, and so on. The works of Martin Noth and Gerhard von Rad have shown how individual events and interpretations only coalesce in a later kerygmatic view.

In this continual association of different traditions, a divine plan of salvation becomes more and more clear as a constant in the province of the Old Testament, in the middle of which stands *Israel's election* for the salvation of mankind. This election may be traced through all its further developments. Even where the topic shifts to condemnation, this background is presupposed. Still, no philosophy of history motif, theoretically imposed on the history of Israel, is involved here. Instead, the idea of election *took form* out of different revelations about precise events. Thus the whole *kerygma* of the Bible and its main theme of election are the results of a developing recognition which has been disclosed as a revelation through the Holy Spirit. In this process it is presupposed that the prophet recognizes the salvation history handed down to him to be what it is, a divine salvation happening. This was actually the case with the Old Testament prophets. The history of salvation was accessible to them in a written tradition, in the confession, and in the liturgy representing a 'presentation' of salvation history. The prophet is not just a solitary man;[1] he still stands in the salvation-historical tradition. When because of new events and revelations he places this tradition in a new perspective, for instance in prophesying judgment, nevertheless the *constant* of the tradition, the *election of Israel* for the salvation of mankind, is not done away with, but is more closely defined on the basis of new events, and thus the idea of election is corrected.

The prophet is an eyewitness only of the event he himself has experienced, in which a revelation has been imparted to him. So far as the past events are concerned, he is in the same situation as we are in relation to the whole biblical salvation history. He is referred to the believing witness and the mediatorship of those who went before, but the events of the past become actual for him by association with the event he himself has experienced. He can place the new event on the same level in the same association, and at the same time the 'presentation' of past events is strengthened by this association.

Because the prophet already has at his disposal a kerygmatic account of history that has been handed down to him, the notion could be entertained that in the *kerygma* contained in that presentation, the 'Word', and not the new event, is uppermost for him in the new revelation. It could also be proposed that this *kerygma* caused the prophet subsequently to regard the events of his time as events of salvation or divine judgment (*Unheil*). Certainly the *kerygma* con-

---

[1] K. Frör in *Biblische Hermeneutik*, following G. von Rad, *Old Testament Theology* II, p. 129, and H. J. Kraus, *Prophetie und Politik*, 1952, pp. 19ff., writes thus: '[The prophets] are not the solitary geniuses they were reckoned to be during the time of the cult of the personality.'

tained in the traditional salvation history has its own impetus, and as a rule there is a *reciprocal relationship* between present event and traditional *kerygma*. Indeed, it may even have happened that at one time only the given *kerygma* was the point of departure for subsequent reflection about a new event. How much must be attributed to the *kerygma* and how much to the new event can hardly be determined in any single case. But the fact that the new event is not simply placed in the traditional kerygmatic account, but rather that this account is *interpreted afresh*, indicates the considerable significance of the event. If the traditional *kerygma* were the actual point of departure, then the new event would simply be inserted into it and subordinated to it. However, the *kerygma* itself is, on the contrary, *interpreted anew in each case on the basis of the present event!*

With this idea a further thought must be considered which, to be sure, does not lead to a depreciation of the role of the *kerygma*, but should expose the basic significance of the event and remove the character of an abrupt alternative from the problem 'event or *kerygma*' which is so acute today: the traditional *kerygma* has events as its object. It has as its aim the leading of the person to whom it is delivered to this object, that is, to the (interpreted) events.

The salvation-historical *interpretation*, as we shall see, uses non-historical elements alongside the historical reports or by investing the accounts of historical events with legendary, mythological, and bold relief. It does this in two ways: either by placing the non-historical elements alongside the historical reports or by investing the accounts of historical events with legendary, mythological, and fabulous elements. This material has in common with an historical report of events the fact that it, too, is communicated in the form of narratives. The men who interpreted a given *kerygma* anew did not make any distinction between historical report and mythical interpretation in the account passed on to them, a distinction we carry out with our methods of scholarship. Thus, it is often hard today to distinguish between the two in biblical narrations.

One may not, however, conclude that myth and historical event played the same secondary role in the original process, and that the event, so far as its function is concerned, is no more important than the myth.[1] It may not be said that both merely served the purpose of depicting in an objective way a *kerygma* lying beyond myth and history, to be understood, for instance, existentially. We shall see[2] that in reality

[1] In a sense this is actually the case for R. Bultmann.   [2] See below pp. 136ff.

these mythical materials have been historicized in the Old and New Testaments, that is, subordinated to the historical report. Thus, the impetus to their being introduced came from the event, or more specifically, from a sequence of events. The mythical elements are intended to make a kerygmatic meaning clear, but this is a kerygmatic meaning of *events*.

This historicizing, of course, increases the difficulty for the modern exegete of distinguishing between myth and history in the original process. Besides, the longer the chain of connecting links is, the more obscure the historical motives for the oldest narrations naturally become, especially if *kerygmata* passed down by word of mouth alone are involved.

This difficulty has led many modern exegetes to renounce entirely any effort to carry through a distinction between myth and history. Some are satisfied simply to ignore the history and to describe the *kerygma*, its origin and characteristics. In so doing they overlook the fact that it is not possible to ignore history in seeking the origin of the *kerygma*, since the *kerygma* is not a finished entity in the Bible, but develops further with *the coming of new events* which are themselves usually absorbed into the *kerygma*. Every inquiry concerning the *Sitz im Leben* of a kerygmatic tradition is a question concerning history, which in turn becomes a part of the *kerygma* in a subsequent stage of the biblical development.

Let us select an example from the province of the New Testament, where the chain of connecting links extends through a shorter space of time and is therefore easier to survey. If I say that the development of the oral gospel tradition towards the written Gospels owes its origin to the events and situation in the Church of which the Gospel writer was a member, then I must be acquainted with this historical situation. If I project my inquiry concerning the origin of the oral Gospel tradition behind the time of the Gospel writer, I come up against the events of Easter. However these events are to be evaluated, I must make an effort to explore them historically if I am ultimately to trace the origin of the oral tradition back to them. *Otherwise I am explaining the unknown with the unknown.* We shall see that the question about the historical Jesus is posed in a similar way. If we do not want to fall into Docetism, we must inquire further: What kind of events motivated Jesus himself to the *kerygma* he proclaimed?

It is an illusion to think we could escape the difficulty of exposing the history in its various connecting links by saying that we are dealing only with the origin of the *kerygma* without raising the question of historical events. Because the *kerygma* arose by a development in connection with events, it cannot be investigated at all without an attempt to distinguish history and interpretation, history and myth at its very origin. There is also a need to go beyond interpretation to history in the question about the process by which the individual traditions in the Old Testament arose—for example, in the particularly difficult question of the Red Sea episode. Even if research comes to the conclusion that in this case the historical core was nothing more than the destruction of a band of chariots, this event is not irrelevant as one of the causes of the *kerygma* which has effects that extend right into the New Testament. Through all the further developments, there still remains one constant which was already at work in that first event, however insignificant it may appear. The difficulty inherent in such a scholarly undertaking may no more excuse us from the task than the uncertainty of our conclusion.

A remarkable argument, which incidentally goes beyond the limits of the exegetical discussion, again and again takes the field in the present debate to justify a refusal to raise the historical question on grounds of principle. It is said that our faith must not be dependent upon the uncertain conclusions of scholarship. This is actually a truism that hardly anyone will seriously dispute. It is obvious that there can and must be a believing encounter with the Bible independent of all scholarly exegesis. Furthermore, an analysis of the *kerygma* which deliberately ignores the question of the historical event can lead only to conclusions whose 'certainty' is just as little a settled matter. Despite all that, we must work at scientific exegesis just as we do at scientific theology in the interest of faith because it can be a means of furthering faith. We know that despite all the erroneous ways exegesis has gone and goes, it is not only an impediment, but also a help.

The attempt to distinguish history and interpretation is also an example of such an aid in faith. In our study of the origin of the salvation-historical perspective, we are specifying precisely the roles played by both history and interpretation. In this way we learn what history meant for the faith of the biblical witnesses, and at the same time what it can mean for our own faith.

Here, of course, there is a hermeneutical difficulty which must be taken into account. As exegetes, we are not in the same situation today as the biblical witnesses were. We have seen that on the one hand they possessed a traditional kerygmatic interpretation of events, but on the other hand, as eyewitnesses, they came up against events which in turn became for them objects of a new kerygmatic interpretation. In the Bible we have, of course, *only* kerygmatic interpretations before us, and not a simple report of facts that could influence us as the events of the present influenced them. It would seem that we approach their understanding in faith if we at least *dare to make the attempt*, however uncertain its success may be, to place the events alongside the interpretation in such a way that in the naked events disclosed to us the interpretation of those events is forced upon us as it was upon the biblical witnesses. Do we not comprehend the interpretation even better if we also *allow it to come to us out of the naked events* which for us, of course, lie in the past? When we become acquainted with the naked event as well, does not the *reliving of the event in the present* become more real for us? Since we, in contrast to the biblical witnesses, possess scholarly methods allowing us to make the past present, we should and must make use of those methods, however unsure they are, and however great the danger may be of creating a source of error if we make a false separation between history and myth, as happened so often in the 'quest of the historical Jesus'.

To be sure, this involves us in a *circle*. Only through the interpretation can we come to the historical event; but by the same token the historical event should then bring us nearer to the kerygmatic interpretation which the biblical witnesses have communicated to us, since this event was the cause for the interpretation in the first place. Therefore, the attempt to distinguish between history and myth is required both dogmatically and exegetically.

So we should not look at form criticism so one-sidedly, as if its only aim were to impress us with the impossibility of bridging the distance between *kerygma* and history. It ought to permit us to pass from the *kerygma* to the event which gave rise to the new interpretation, and thence to other kerygmatic interpretations handed down orally and to the events they rest upon. Then we shall be in a position, together with the men of the Bible, to pass in the opposite way from events to their interpretations, so that we are clear not only about the distance, but also about the positive connection between event and interpretation, in which the biblical witnesses saw the saving revelation. That there were distorting influences involved in the interpretation of the historical character and the kerygmatic meaning of the event should certainly not be disputed. That would amount to disputing that the revelation in salvation history belongs to the incarnation within the human situation. It is wrong, however, from a scholarly point of view to reckon only with misrepresentation and to designate form criticism as a 'thinking in terms of a break'.[1]

To sum up: the question whether the event or the *kerygma* is decisive for the faith of the witnesses who have given us the biblical salvation history may not be answered in the form of an alternative. The process through which kerygmatic accounts originated must also be reckoned with. It follows that, on the one hand, the events of their own present gave the biblical writers the impulse to faith and reinterpretation, and, on the other hand, a *kerygma* was already given them about other events to which they were not eyewitnesses and which were available to them only in kerygmatic form, that is, in association with myths and legends. If we keep this development in mind, we must say that a reciprocation takes place between present event and traditional *kerygma*. Word and event are not separable in the mind of God himself, and, accordingly in the biblical view, the Word is an event, and conversely the event is a Word.[2] Nevertheless, from the human point of view, we must acknowledge that the event has priority. On the one hand, the first impulse to the specific bearers of revelation, the prophets in the Old Testament and the apostles in the New, was from the present event of their own time. On the other hand, we dare not forget that past events stood behind their *kerygma*. These events were made present as they were interpreted kerygmatically, as they were recited in worship, and as they were confessed in the creed. In this way their effect as events was further extended. This continuing effect of the event through all the further *kerygmata*, however, concerns particularly the Christ event proclaimed as the central occurrence in the New Testament.

2. EVENT AND INTERPRETATION IN THE NEW TESTAMENT

Up to this point we have followed the process of how the salvation history common to the Old and New Testaments arose. We must not be misled by the literary separation of both Testaments into

---

[1] See H. Conzelmann, 'Gegenwart und Zukunft in der synoptischen Tradition', *ZTK*, 1957, pp. 277ff.
[2] See below p. 137.

accentuating a distance between them that does not exist. The continuous advance of the same salvation-historical development, and the continuity between the bearers of revelation, prophets and apostles, constitutes the unity of both Testaments and gives the canon its inner justification. Therefore, the following remarks are understandable only against the background of the previous chapter.

When we duly take account of the common basis of both Testaments, we shall understand where, in the framework of this continuous development, the radical *'novum'* in the New Testament lies.

Constitutive of all salvation history is the fact that the disclosure of it is attributed by its own authors both in Old and New Testaments to a spiritually comprehended *revelation* about particular events *and* their relationship with other events. Salvation history does not come by way of reflection about history, as if it were a case of philosophizing on history, something Bultmann wrongly imputes to me. Rather, it comes primarily because of a consciousness of having received a special prophetic revelation through the Holy Spirit. Therefore, salvation history is not concerned with a philosophy of history, but a *prophecy of history*.

As in the Old Testament, this revelation in the New Testament relates to an interrelationship of historical fact and interpretation. Here again, the revelation consists in both—in the event as such and in its interpretation. The fact that not only the interpretation, but also the event itself is regarded as a revelation of a divine saving drama, rests in the importance attributed to *eyewitness*. It is particularly emphasized at the end of the crucifixion narrative (Mark 15.40 and parallels) in the reference to the women (Luke 23.49 adds 'acquaintances', and John 19.25ff. adds the mother of Jesus and the beloved disciple). The oldest detailed creed of the Church, cited by Paul in I Cor. 15.3ff., stresses the eyewitness of those who saw Jesus' resurrection appearances and relates them to the saving process. The Gospels stress the women's eyewitness to the empty tomb (John 20.2ff. emphasizes that of the two disciples as well).

In the Gospel account of the empty tomb and the resurrection appearances, it is not said how the resurrection itself happened. This is stated for the first time in the apocryphal reports. Instead, events are narrated which alone could be the object of eyewitnessing. Both the empty tomb and the appearances do not in themselves prove to an outsider that Jesus arose bodily, just as the events of Israel's history without the revelation shared by the Old Testament witnesses could hardly signify salvation for others. We know that the empty tomb has been explained in various ways —a theft of the body, for instance.[1] Visions of dead persons were not absolutely unique at the time. Only on the basis of the interpretation communicated by the witnesses—'he has arisen bodily', 'he has appeared' —did these events become a revelation of the new aeon that had dawned. However, it is significant that a greater testimonial importance was attributed to those historical facts as such from the start; and eyewitnessing played an important role, *being reckoned with the saving events* (I Cor. 15.3ff.). This ought not to be forgotten in the present discussion on history and *kerygma*. The historical facts ought to show that the resurrection has to do with a setting in history.[2]

In the New Testament as in the Old Testament we are dealing with a continual *development* of the *kerygma* onward in relation to new events. There is also a *continuing connection* of present events experienced by the witnesses with a *kerygma* already present, and a reinterpretation given with the *kerygma*.[3] Again, in the New Testament the adaptation of this *kerygma* as a rule proceeds in a threefold manner. First, the event, with the new revelation relating to it, is assimilated into the old *kerygma*. Second, on this basis the old *kerygma* is interpreted anew. Third, the recipient or recipients of the revelation with their functions are themselves assimilated into the *kerygma*, as we see in the case of the witnesses to the resurrection.

Nevertheless, there are significant differences. First of all we have seen that the present event, the starting point of the new interpretation, was regarded as the *decisive* event and norm of the whole salvation history. Everything that happened heretofore tends toward this one event, and everything still to come is an unfolding of this event. The taking of a norm from *one* event in this way was never found in the previous reinterpretations. A present event formerly determined the *perspectives* into which all the earlier events were placed. But all these events were still located on the same level. In the New Testament, however, we have an event which belongs within the structures of history, but which according to its own

[1] See especially H. von Campenhausen, *Der Ablauf der Osterereignisse und das leere Grab*, ²1958.
[2] On this point see below p. 143.
[3] In his chapters devoted to the New Testament (*Old Testament Theology* II, pp. 319ff.), G. von Rad's aim is in principle to pursue this Old Testament reinterpretation in the New. But he does not carry this through as we are attempting to do here. He actually reckons with only *one* reinterpretation of the Old Testament in the New. But as in the Old, so also in the New Testament, the process continues in *self-developing kerygmata*, albeit compressed into a short space of time.

revealed interpretation, so surpasses in importance all other interpreted events that it is the decisive point of orientation for them and
assumes cosmic dimensions in its consequences. It contains within
itself the whole salvation history of the past, present, and future. Just
as the whole plan of salvation encompassing every period of time is
present *in God himself*, so this plan appears in its entire fullness, as it
were, compressed in that one event, only now in such a way that
neither the past history, which is fulfilled in this event, nor the
future, in which it unfolds, becomes superfluous.[1]

So an event is involved whose *verticality* emerges more clearly than
that of other events in the history of salvation. The vertical contains
the horizontal within it. God's speaking by his Son 'in these last
days' (Heb. 1.2) is, in fact, of another kind than his manifold speaking
by the prophets. But in its verticality, his speaking belongs in the
horizontal saving process. The writer of the Epistle to the Hebrews
expressed this very clearly in his prologue. Not only does God's
speaking by the Son belong on the same temporal-historical line,
but in supplying both norm and meaning it is also related to everything occurring on the horizontal level. *The event in the Word-made-
flesh contains within itself the entire salvation history that came before and
that comes afterwards; but it also aligns itself with this history.* It is no good
giving up the horizontal while appealing to the normative significance of the Christ event, as happens today.[2] But neither will it do to
fail to single out the unique character of the Christ event from all
other events in the history of salvation.

Accordingly, much more than just a new perspective is at issue
here. The Old Testament interpretative constant, 'the election of the
people Israel', remains, of course, the constant for the New Testament as well. But now it becomes the election of one person. Towards
this election the whole election of the people of Israel tends, and from
it the whole election of the new Israel proceeds.

The Old Testament constant, 'the election of the people of Israel',
is surely not a motif from the philosophy of history. Starting from the
principle of the election of the people of Israel, no philosopher of
history would arrive at the idea that the hanging of a Jew condemned
as a Zealot on a cross is the central event of history with representa-

---

[1] We shall see that the writer of the Gospel of John understands the life of Jesus
precisely in this way. See below pp. 268f.
[2] H. U. v. Balthasar, *op. cit.*, concerned to work out a theology of history, has
not escaped this danger in his most recent publications.

tive significance. But this unheard-of new revelation, declaring that here the decisive event has taken place, is related to the old *kerygma* of election. The movement of New Testament salvation history which I have designated in *Christ and Time* as a line has its origin here, in the idea of substitution; the way leads in a progressive narrowing from mankind to the elected people of Israel, from Israel to the remnant, from the remnant to the one man, Christ. From this mid-point it then proceeds, ever-widening, to the circle of the apostles, to the first community, and from there to the Church made up of Jews and Gentiles. Thus, the idea of election is retrogressively retained as a constant, and yet in the light of the revelation in Christ it is given a completely new orientation. The vertical aspect of the Christ event does not set aside the horizontal aspect of the salvation happening, but interprets it afresh.

Linked to this radically new orientation towards the event, recognized as decisive by faith, is the consciousness of revelation, tremendously heightened in the New Testament. Hence there is a strong emphasis upon the *eyewitness* to this event *which we do not find in the case of any Old Testament saving event*. Consequently, in the New Testament, the incorporation of the apostles, the new mediators of revelation in salvation history into the new covenant, has more significance than the incorporation of the Old Testament prophets into the old. Not only salvation, but also the saving revelation, has reached a high-point with Christ. From now on all revealers are organs of the one revealer in a direct way. This accounts for the heightened consciousness of revelation.

Furthermore, the compression of the new saving events, and con-sequently of the new interpretations, into a very short space of time is new in comparison with the Old Testament development. Whereas the Old Testament salvation history, even the part belonging to history rather than primeval history, encompasses centuries, its ex-tension in the New Testament is a matter of a few decades, although in keeping with their crucial character mentioned above they are extraordinarily full. Here the saving events are, as it were, forced together. We have already spoken of the various new interpretations appearing in this short space of time. Disregarding later writings such as some Catholic Epistles and the Apocalypse, approximately at the end of this space of time are the written Gospels—not the oral Gospel tradition itself, which, on the contrary, belongs at the beginning. Recent research on the redactional stages of the individual

Gospels has been concerned with the kerygmatic theology contained in them. The Gospel writers merely offer a kerygmatic description of the life of Jesus, as form criticism for a long time has taught us. Their *kerygma*, too, is influenced by events occurring in the second half of the first century. The consciousness of being a revealer is especially clear in the writer of the Fourth Gospel, but it is also present in the Synoptics. The oral tradition, which for its own part had interpreted afresh the *kerygma* going back to Jesus in the light of recent events, above all, the Easter event,[1] was already available to the Gospel writers.

It is, however, significant that a double link of new events in salvation history takes place each time. On the one hand, it occurs with the event regarded as central, together with Jesus' own *kerygma* about it; on the other hand, it occurs with the *kerygma* found in the Old Testament. The first happens immediately; the second happens more during the course of reflection, especially since the Old Testament salvation history is already codified as 'Holy Scripture', and is in part, though not entirely, accessible only through the medium of the biblical interpretation of the time.

We shall speak later about this second link.[2] The new interpretation through the Church's oral tradition, applied to the message preached by the incarnate Jesus himself, interests us particularly. Here the first witnesses of the new events surrounding the resurrection, as eyewitnesses of the incarnate Jesus, were at the same time guarantors of the *kerygma* going back to him. They did not need to link the new events they experienced after Jesus' death with events some time in the distant past, experienced by earlier witnesses, as the men of the Old Testament did. Instead, they linked the present events with ones to which they were themselves witnesses—the events of the life of Jesus. Therein lies the unique position of those apostles who were at the same time disciples of the incarnate Jesus over against all other apostles.[3] All apostles were eyewitnesses of the resurrection; but beyond that, the twelve had to guarantee the continuity between

[1] It is not just a matter of the empty tomb and the resurrection appearances (see above pp. 98f.), but also of the various manifestations of the Spirit in the Church.

[2] See below pp. 112ff.

[3] The question of the historical origin of the *office* of apostle, as it is raised by W. Schmithals, *Das kirchliche Apostelamt. Eine historische Untersuchung*, 1961, cannot be discussed here. The question dealt with by M. Barth, *Der Augenzeuge*, 1946, is important for our problem.

the new events and the *kerygma* given them concerning events to which they were also witnesses. This means that they had to witness that the incarnate Jesus and the exalted Christ are identical, or, that the incarnate Lord continues to work on as the exalted Lord. The principle of continuity, characteristic of all salvation history, is personified here at the high-point of the whole process *in the person of Jesus Christ*. The new events which sum up those preceding are fulfilled by one and the same person.

Those apostles who were at the same time eyewitnesses of Jesus' life are not related in the same way to the past events they experienced a short time ago as they are to the new events which occurred after Jesus' death. The interpretation of the events transpiring after Jesus' death is disclosed to them simultaneously with the events. They see Jesus appearing, and at the same time the fact is revealed to them that he has arisen bodily, that death is vanquished. In the case of the incarnate Lord, they were, of course, witnesses at the time of the event, and they heard Jesus' own interpretation of this event. But this interpretation was at best sporadic for them, and had been at most a dim revelation. Now and again an understanding of the reality contained in what was seen and heard showed through,[1] only to be lost sight of once more, and often a faint glimpse was bound up with a fatal error that Jesus himself had to thrust aside as 'devilish'.[2] For this reason the Gospels, and particularly the Gospel of John, make a point again and again of the disciples' failure to understand Jesus. We shall see that it is the leading thought of John's Gospel that the salvation-historical meaning of the life of Jesus made its impact upon the disciples only after his death (the Johannine 'remembering'), because of the Paraclete who leads them 'into the truth'.

Before the *full* revelation, the disciples did not understand the whole significance of what had happened in the life of Jesus. This revelation was made manifest to the early Church for the first time in retrospect, in the light of the Easter events. Despite this lack of

---

[1] See my article, 'L'apôtre Pierre instrument du diable et instrument de Dieu: le place de Mt. 16.16–19 dans la tradition primitive', *New Testament Essays. Studies in Memory of T. W. Manson*, 1959, pp. 94–106. Unfortunately E. Dinkler in dealing with this problem does not appear to know this article in his essay, 'Petrusbekenntnis und Satanswort', *Zeit und Geschichte. Dankesgabe für R. Bultmann*, 1964, pp. 127ff., although he comes very close to my thesis.

[2] Cf. the political misunderstanding of Jesus' consciousness of his mission; see O. Cullmann, *The State in the New Testament*, 1956, and *The Christology of the New Testament*, 1959, pp. 111ff.

understanding, it was still of greatest importance that at least some of the members of the Church saw the events and heard Jesus' own interpretation of his revelation. In connection with the new events, the 'remembering' gained the highest revelatory significance for its reinterpretation of the *kerygma* from the fact that its originator was Jesus himself.

It became subsequently clear to the disciples that everything they had previously seen and heard in Jesus' life and preaching had been the decisive saving revelation of God. It became clear to them that the life Jesus lived and the doctrine he preached together represented the central *kerygma* in which the whole history of salvation came to a climax. They had to *transmit* the *kerygma* they received from Jesus and *at the same time* interpret it anew. In the case of Jesus' life, they did not need to create afresh the interpretation of the events they had witnessed. The recent debate about the 'historical Jesus' often suffers from failing to take into account that not only the events but also their salvation-historical interpretation—in the proclamation of Jesus—were given with the historical Jesus, and that the disciples were not announcing this interpretation for the first time after his death. Instead, after Jesus' death his interpretation was newly discovered by the disciples simultaneously with the new interpretation which they then shared in for the first time. For this reason the Johannine concept of the recollection effected through the Spirit is a particularly apt expression for this state of affairs.

In this *kerygma* given to the disciples and then rediscovered, Jesus himself was the originator of the saving event and its revelation. *At this high-point, the blending of the saving event with the revelation about this event is complete.* Jesus creates salvation by his works, and does so by proclaiming the meaning of his works and their consequences throughout all his teachings. Here the close relationship between salvation and revelation is seen in special clarity.[1] Even the instructions of the Sermon on the Mount disclose the revealer who is at the same time the bringer of salvation. Jesus reveals himself as the high-point of the whole saving process. Because quite specific things are brought to pass through him, the Kingdom of God has come in his person (Matt. 12.28 and parallels). The prophets placed themselves in the saving events revealed to them, and the apostles will do the same. But Jesus incorporates himself here in such a way that it becomes clear that all salvation history has unfolded with him in view, and that in him,

[1] See above p. 89.

and in his death, the decisive event occurs which fulfils the idea of election and representation, so that the whole history of salvation is summed up in him.[1]

In the light of the Easter events it becomes clear to the disciples that not only the events, but also the revelation *that* these were really saving events, could already have been available to them at the time. It becomes evident that there was *already an interpretation, a kerygma,* reaching back to Jesus himself.

To be sure, this *kerygma* did not exist in written form. Jesus left no personal writings whatever. The disciples could not take any text for granted in their new interpretation. They had to write one for the first time and then hand it on. Thus we know Jesus' *kerygma* only through the disciples. Because they were custodians of that *kerygma* and were also those who interpreted it anew in the light of the Easter events, the *kerygma* and the new interpretation in the light of the events of the disciples' lifetime appear very closely related. This is why the *kerygma* of Jesus, the one the disciples were given, may not be separated from the new interpretation of it in the way possible for many Old Testament traditions, where the old often remains alongside the new and therefore may be more easily picked out.

In the light of the revelation of the resurrection, the first Christians took the *kerygma* (of which some of them were eyewitness guarantors) that they received from Jesus and associated it so closely with its new interpretation that any separation between the two is extremely difficult. Thus, it is understandable that Bultmann even regards it as impossible. Therein lies the whole problem of the relation between the 'kerygmatic Christ' and the 'historical Jesus'.

This close connection of *kerygma* and reinterpretation is related to the revelation imparted to the disciples which tells that the risen Lord, present in the resurrection appearances and celebration of the Lord's Supper,[2] is identical with the Jesus who accomplished his decisive work on earth and whose entire present activity has its basis in the events of the life of this incarnate Lord. The conviction of this continuity even draws the process of reinterpretation into the relationship between the incarnate and exalted Christ. Behind the apostles' tradition of the deeds and words of the incarnate Christ

[1] We shall later speak in detail of what is taken for granted here, that Jesus did not preach the Kingdom of God by itself, as an entity independent of his person, but that he himself interpreted the events that happened *through him* with reference to it.

[2] See O. Cullmann, *Early Christian Worship*, 1953, part I.

stands the exalted Lord himself, according to decisive affirmations in the New Testament. The consciousness of being an organ of Jesus Christ, who as the exalted Lord creates the post-Easter tradition about his own earthly work, is once more particularly apparent in the Gospel of John (14.26; 16.12), but the *whole* Gospel tradition is inspired by it.[1] The stronger this consciousness is, the firmer the faith that there can be no difference between the *kerygma* of the incarnate Jesus and that of the exalted Christ. Hence the difficulty of distinguishing the two *kerygmata*—on the one hand, that which Jesus in his incarnation proclaimed about himself, and which the disciples had to transmit from their own memories; and, on the other hand, that which the same disciples interpreted anew, simultaneously with that memory, as Christ stood behind them as the exalted Lord.

Now it is essential to the biblical tradition to develop itself further. So if we wish to uncover the process of development which the New Testament itself traces back to a revelation moving from the incarnate to the exalted Lord, we must still consciously distinguish between the two *kerygmata*.

This is the problem of the 'historical Jesus', properly seen by the Bultmannians who, unfortunately, try to solve it from their too narrow basis of existentialism.

In principle, we must first of all concede that because of the general characteristics of the continuing *development* of the salvation-historical *kerygma* in relation to new events, it must therefore be our task right from the start to demonstrate that there is a development from Jesus' interpretation to that of the disciples made on the basis of the Easter event. On this point there is widespread agreement among most commentators today. There is also general agreement that some continuity between the *kerygma* of the 'historical Jesus' and that of the disciples must exist. To a certain measure it is agreed that the continuity between the two is seen in the conviction that the turning-point of the aeons is in the immediate future. However, this already introduces the contrast we spoke of in our survey of this history of the problem of present and future in Jesus' expectation of the end. It raises the question whether this turning point is already introduced in Jesus' message, not simply in his preaching of the proximity of the Kingdom of God, but in the happenings of his life itself.

---

[1] See the exegetical evidence in Paul's case: I Cor. 11.23, I Cor. 15.3, as well as the sayings of Jesus that he cites; O. Cullmann, 'The Tradition', in *The Early Church*, pp. 59ff.

This leads us to a disputed point on which opinions diverge completely: What is the relationship existing between the function Jesus attaches to his own person in his *kerygma* and that which the early Church ascribes to it? It is true that Bultmann's pupils (and Bultmann himself, with a less emphatic interest, of course) try to construct a continuity along these lines. But they define it by starting with their existentialist premises.[1] According to Bultmann, the continuity is assured by Jesus' call to decision which already implies 'an indirect christology'. For G. Ebeling it is by 'Jesus' faith', and for E. Fuchs by 'Jesus' behaviour'.

The idea that the continuity rests on what earlier was called the 'Messianic consciousness' is expressly rejected by the whole Bultmann school. In no way did Jesus conceive of his task as defined by one of the honorific titles which the Old Testament and Judaism used to designate the role of the redeemer. He regarded himself neither as the Son of Man[2] nor as the Suffering Servant of God.

Jesus' message, therefore, is not an interpretation of what he accomplished in relation to the salvation history of the Old Testament. A *kerygma* about this event at whose centre stands Jesus himself was the product of the early Church and not of Jesus. He was not the actual originator of the radically new interpretation of the *kerygma* related to his own person of which we have spoken. Thus, when Bultmann in his *Theology of the New Testament* assigns Jesus' teachings to the presuppositions of New Testament theology rather than to that theology itself, *from his own vantage point* he is right. Any salvation-historical self-revelation of Jesus, in terms of his incorporating himself into the previous salvation history given in the Old Testament, is out of the question. The faith making the proclaimer an object of the *kerygma* in this way, allowing the proclaimer to become the one proclaimed, arose for the first time in the early Church.

But is it not an illusion to think that in spite of all this the continuity between Jesus and the first community is assured? It is still undisputed that the unique centre of the first community's *kerygma* is the proclamation that Jesus by his work brought about the new aeon.

[1] Cf. my article, 'Out of Season Remarks on the Historical Jesus of the Bultmann School', *Union Seminary Quarterly Review*, Jan., 1961, pp. 131ff.

[2] P. Vielhauer in 'Gottesreich und Menschensohn in der Verkündigung Jesu', *Festschrift für G. Dehn*, 1957, pp. 57ff., tries to deny that Jesus conceived of himself as the Son of Man because of the fact that the two concepts 'Kingdom of God' and 'Son of Man' are never connected.

Can one really go on speaking of a continuity if the incarnate Jesus did not preach himself, but the Kingdom of God apart from his person, and only in this way called the disciples to decision? Does not the assumption of an actual continuity require that it be related to that main, unprecedented, bold theme of the first community's message declaring that Jesus regarded himself not just as a proclaimer, but as a fulfiller of Israel's whole salvation history, and that he thought of his death in particular as an atoning death fulfilling the meaning of this entire salvation history?

Certainly the salvation-historical christology, like all salvation-historical revelation, *developed* in relation to events. In their going behind Jesus' *kerygma*, referring in their reinterpretation to the *kerygma* of the Old Testament, the first Christians certainly elaborated the christology further. Certainly they went beyond Jesus' self-declarations and constructed further links with the Old Testament. But could they really do this without any kind of self-declaration by Jesus? If the interpretation given in my *Christology of the New Testament* is correct, it was the earliest Christians who explicitly gave Jesus the title of Messiah (Christ) for the first time Jesus could have applied this title to himself in a new sense, but because of the danger of its being misunderstood politically he always avoided it.[1] After Jesus' death, when this danger no longer existed, Christians could bestow this title upon him along with others which Jesus also gave himself, and give it special emphasis. This thesis actually concerns a further development with which I am reckoning fully. But can we really speak of such a further development if, as is asserted nowadays, Jesus in no way assumed one of Israel's titles of honour from its salvation history and in no way incorporated himself into the history of salvation? Are we not instead dealing with a μετάβασις εἰς ἄλλο γένος?

Thus, the Bultmann school contests what I believed I could prove, namely, that Jesus regarded himself as the 'Suffering Servant of God' and the 'Son of Man'. Since according to the Bultmannian theses any idea of salvation history was far removed from Jesus' mind, the school must of necessity reject the idea of such a self-designation, implying as it does an incorporation into salvation history.

The title Son of Man is denied Jesus as a self-designation with particular vehemence. So in a way hardly in harmony with the findings of form

[1] See my *Christology*, pp. 111ff.

event and criticism, the literary sources are played against one another (*Logia* versus Mark). Even U. Wilckens follows the works of the Bultmann school, whose conclusions are summed up in Tödt's dissertation, *The Son of Man in the Synoptic Tradition* (ET 1965), F. Hahn's *Christologische Hoheitstitel*, 1963, and A. J. B. Higgins' *Jesus and the Son of Man*, 1964 (see below p. 192 n. 1). The form-critical consideration that Jesus' designation as the Son of Man does not accord with the Church's christology, I regard now as before to be weightier than the arguments introduced against the use of the title as a self-designation of Jesus.[1]

The historical fact that Jesus was condemned by the Romans (of course in complete misunderstanding of his 'self-consciousness') as a Zealot, as a pretender to the throne (cf. the '*titulus*' on top of the cross),[2] seems to me to be almost irrefutable proof that Jesus in some way made himself the subject of his preaching on the Kingdom of God soon to come.

If the primitive community was the first to make the proclaimer into the one proclaimed, the leap from the *kerygma* of Jesus to the *kerygma* of the community would be a tremendous one indeed, and *on this assumption* I would rather side with the old liberalism and speak of a break rather than a continuity, saying with Harnack that only the Father, and not the Son, belongs in Jesus' gospel. However, Bultmann's pupils now seek a continuity between the kerygmatic Christ and the historical Jesus. But the accomplishment of this task is encumbered by the fact that they all hold fast with an almost dogmatic faithfulness to Bultmann's assertion that Jesus could not have applied any of the Old Testament titles of honour to himself. Actually, despite the thesis of the 'Messianic secret' (taken over from Wrede, likewise without qualification, as a theory about Mark's Gospel—it can be explained in a much more appropriate way[3]), no more than an hypothesis is involved in this question. If this hypothesis is taken as fundamental, then along with classical liberalism the admission ought rather to be made that there is a mighty leap from the 'gospel of Christ' to the Church's 'gospel *de Christo*'. In this case, are not talk of 'indirect Christology' and the somewhat tortuous explanations of a continuity which we have described a minimizing of that leap?

Certainly the Easter event was experienced by the first disciples

---

[1] On this question see E. Schweizer, 'Der Menschensohn', *ZNW*, 1959, pp. 185ff.

[2] See O. Cullmann, *The State in the New Testament*, 1956, chapters 1 and 2.

[3] See O. Cullmann, *The State in the New Testament*, 1956, on Jesus' wish to avoid the political misunderstanding suggested by the title of Messiah.

as an earth shaking occurrence and one which had to lead to a new interpretation of Jesus' *kerygma*. But the fact remains that this re-interpretation does not directly relate in the first instance to the Old Testament salvation-historical *kerygma*, but to the *kerygma* of the historical Jesus himself, and that it reaches back to that of the Old Testament only through this *kerygma*. In this case, the new interpretation ought to be more than the usual reinterpretations. It indicates the *remembering* (in the Johannine sense) by the eyewitnesses of Jesus' *kerygma*. It is a *remembering of revelation, darkened by misunderstanding*, but made alive by the Holy Spirit.

Hence, within the framework of our study of the origin of salvation-historical conceptions in the New Testament, the question is posed as follows: Is the boldness by which Jesus was proclaimed as the centre of history in relation to the Old Testament salvation history only to be attributed to the Church's reinterpretation of the *kerygma* brought about by Easter? Or, was it accomplished by Jesus himself, not just 'indirectly' through his preaching of the Kingdom of God, but consciously in his teachings and life? We could put the question this way: in Jesus' message, is there a salvation-historical *kerygma*, belonging in the series of salvation-historical interpretations and reinterpretations found in the Old Testament, albeit as a decisive fulfilment of them?

On the above question of the intertwining of Jesus' and the Church's *kerygmata* there is endless debate, especially since the principle of a development from Jesus to the Church is accepted by both sides, though in very different ways. Actually, it is my view that the salvation history of the Bible in essence develops not just by aligning new events one after another, but by interpreting them as well.

I accept that with the following considerations I shall not be able to demonstrate to the defenders of the opposing thesis[1] that Jesus regarded himself not merely as a decisive herald, but as the decisive mediator, *creating* salvation by his death, thereby being the one who completes the divine saving plan. In the final analysis we are dealing with a question of greater or lesser evidence for which no absolutely objective criterion exists.

Operating within this reservation I start from two facts: First, at the centre of the early Church's new interpretation is this tremendous statement that Jesus of Nazareth, whose earthly life is known to the

[1] The historical fact of the condemnation of Jesus as a Zealot mentioned above on p. 109 ought to be convincing proof for *everybody*.

first witnesses, is the one who fulfils the whole history of Israel in carrying out the divine plan and is the one who brings salvation to the world. Second, the early Church does not refer directly back to the Old Testament *kerygma* for this new interpretation, but goes to the *kerygma* of the historical Jesus, his life and his preaching.[1] Hence its primary interest in the 'life of Jesus'.

Although the disciples did not understand Jesus' life and teaching during his earthly ministry, they were still witnesses to his life and teaching. Therefore, could the early Church's immediate reference back to the life and teaching of Jesus be hazarded in the interest of reinterpretation if the revolutionary and radically new thing in the reinterpretation were present only indirectly in Jesus' life and teaching, as would have to be assumed when speaking of his 'call to decision', 'Jesus' faith', or his 'behaviour'? Certainly many features of Jesus' life and teaching are presented in the light of the resurrection, so that interpretation is involved with the facts. Here is the reinterpretation. The central assertion, however, that the coming of God's Kingdom is dependent not only upon Jesus' preaching but also upon his work, above all upon his death, I cannot completely attribute to this reinterpretation. For I am keeping in mind that the first disciples structured their *kerygma* so that it was oriented completely toward this assertion. They sought at the same time to build it upon the foundation of Jesus' *kerygma* by their recollection as witnesses who saw and heard. These same disciples had the awareness of being the *guarantors* of the life and words of Jesus.[2] The process of linking the new *kerygma* with the *kerygma* of Jesus starts immediately after Easter. If this took place for the first time a generation later, when there were no more eyewitnesses, then I could understand that the later generation attempted to unite two *kerygmata*, in reality not having the same centre at all, in the illusory belief that they were both the same.

The first witnesses of the resurrection did, however, see and hear the incarnate Christ. That, of course, did not prevent them from attributing to Jesus sayings and deeds coming not from their memory, but from their interpretation in the light of the resurrection—some-

---

[1] See above p. 102.
[2] At the same time note must be made of H. Riesenfeld's thesis, *The Gospel Tradition and its Beginnings. A Study in the Limits of Formgeschichte*, 1957, and its confirmation and extension by B. Gerhardsson, *Memory and Manuscript. Oral Tradition and Written Transmission in Rabbinic Judaism and Early Christianity*, 1961.

thing occurring much more frequently in subsequent generations. But could they really link the *central* new revelation, 'Jesus is the fulfiller of the divine salvation history', with Jesus' own *kerygma*, if the latter did not contain this revelation at all? Were that so, it would be not so much the subsequent process of completing the *kerygma* as the origin of a deliberate reference back to the incarnate Christ that would seem to me to be very hard, if not impossible, to explain.

Does this not become much more evident when we assume that the new revelation imparted to the disciples in the resurrection event consists in the fact that what they previously saw *and heard*, and at best understood sporadically, now became a certainty? The faith they obtained in the Easter revelation was a faith in Jesus' *self-revelation*, that is, the faith that Jesus himself was completely conscious of his position in salvation history not merely as a herald, but at the same time as the one who carries out the plan of God decisively through his work. In a special chapter I shall return to the point that the early Church's faith was faith in Jesus' self-revelation, just as in the province of the Old Testament every reinterpretation in the history of salvation always implied a faith that the mediators of earlier *kerygmata* were really bearers of divine revelation. However, the early Church's faith in Christ's revelation was infinitely bolder, but also more momentous, because it was self-revelation. Here was a faith that the revelation this time related to the revealer as the *centre* of all history.

I emphasize this point in view of Bultmann's thinking that *our* faith is identical with the early Church's if we regard Christ as the Messiah even though we deny that he believed in his own Messiahship. This seems to me to be an illusion. The early Church believed in Christ's Messiahship only because it was convinced that Jesus himself believed it, and that it belonged to the essential content of his message. The Messianic faith as faith in Jesus' revelation about the Kingdom of God is not the same as the Messianic faith in Jesus' revelation about himself.

In this case the historical Jesus himself gave the impulse to his own incorporation into salvation history. Like all the earlier revealers, he who proclaimed the crisis of history also believed that he belonged to this history in a decisive way as the revealer of the crisis (*Entscheidung*). This means, however, that he belonged to it in a manner different from the mere 'heralds' of earlier times. There is no 'interruption' between the Old Testament *kerygma* and the early Church's.

Between the two stands Jesus himself. He aligned himself and the *kerygma* he lived and *preached* with the Old Testament *kerygma* in such a way that he now stands in the decisive position.

In evaluating this beginning of the early Christian perspective, specifically its link with the preaching of Jesus, the opinions of New Testament scholars diverge and probably will always diverge. But as was already mentioned in passing, agreement exists about the fact that the Christian *kerygma developed* within the New Testament in a way analogous to the development of the Old Testament salvation history. The early Christian *kerygma*, interwoven most closely with the *kerygma* of Jesus, is bound up even further with the Old Testament *kerygma* in relation to new experiences and events in the Church. This *kerygma* passes through new interpretations more radical than all those undertaken within the sphere of the Old Testament because they are all subsequently oriented toward the Christ event. But because the *kerygma* of Jesus, its self-revelation in his words and work, is regarded once for all as the decisive turning-point, the early Church refers back again and again to the incarnate, or as we say today, the historical Jesus. For this reason, the evangelists still offer their reinterpretation in the form of a life of Jesus at a relatively late stage in the formation of the primitive Christian *kerygma*.[1] This holds true not just for the Gospel of John, but, as the more recent works on the redactional history in Mark, Matthew, and Luke's theological witness have shown, for the Synoptics as well.

Like the Old Testament reinterpretations, these reinterpretations are called forth mainly by new events and experiences associated with them and are often brought about within the structure of lengthy reflection on the Old Testament witness to Christ. At any rate, this re-working is accepted as being inspired by Christ himself, especially since he is seen as the exalted Lord at work in the new revelatory events, experiences of worship, and manifestations of the Spirit. What we read in the Gospel of John may certainly have been the conviction of the writers of other New Testament documents: the link of the events of Jesus' life with the Old Testament became apparent to the disciples only in the light of later events: 'When therefore he was raised from the dead, his disciples remembered that he had said this; and they believed the scripture and the word which Jesus had spoken' (John 2.22). It is the Paraclete who in the same

---

[1] We have seen that interest was focussed on the *oral* Gospel tradition in the earliest stage.

way will instruct the disciples about everything the incarnate Lord said to them (John 14.26; 16.12ff.). Although there is already a new *kerygma* closely bound up with the *kerygma* of the historical Jesus, it is again and again referred back to the incarnate Christ over a lengthy period in the subsequent development. We shall see that the Gospel of John has as its main goal the reference of the present experiences and events of the Church closer and closer to the life of the incarnate Christ in accordance with salvation history.[1]

There is agreement among New Testament scholars only over the fact of the development, and not over the character of the events in the early Church leading to the reinterpretation. For the Bultmann school, as well as the Albert Schweitzer school, the delay of the *parousia* is the great impetus, the key, explaining all further growth, while the *positive* causes discovered by form criticism and established as the '*Sitz im Leben*' for the Gospel tradition fade into the background.[2] For our part we are not going to underestimate the 'extension of time' for an understanding of the development of the New Testament *kerygma*. Instead we shall attempt to assign to it a proper place among the controlling causes for this development. On this point at least it ought to be possible to come to a greater agreement if it is already acknowledged in principle by both sides that the message about Christ undergoes a development within the New Testament. It still remains for us to discuss the primitive Christian belief that this whole process of development of revelation belongs to salvation history itself. Within the Bible, an essential item of all salvation history is the fact that the revelation of saving events and how they are linked together in the divine plan was disclosed to definite witnesses. Another essential item is that these witnesses believe that the saving events belong together. And the witnesses proclaim this faith that all may share it.

In view of the importance of this fact for dogmatics, we shall have to devote a special chapter to the question to what extent salvation history can be an object of our faith even today.

---

[1] See below pp. 268ff.

[2] A related fact is that the conception of form criticism now held by its younger exponents is different from the original one. See my article, 'Out of Season Remarks on the Historical Jesus of the Bultmann School', *Union Seminary Quarterly Review*, Jan., 1961, pp. 131ff. Because the *positive* motives have receded today, the possibility is no longer entertained that they are of positive relevance in disclosing the historical Jesus, inasmuch as the first disciples discovered a profound harmony with the historical Jesus in their present experiences.

3. THE FAITH OF THE WITNESSES IN SALVATION HISTORY

Does faith relate to salvation history in the New Testament?

Is it at all possible for a *sequence* of events to be the object of a faith which is more than mere intellectual assent? The negative answer to this question, and the thought that it is not the insight into the relationship of different events with each other, but only the 'punctual' encounter with the message about a definite event confronting our existence that can become an address to us, are often at the bottom of the rejection of, and contempt for, all salvation-historical theology. Although it is often customary to dispense with salvation history as a pietistic product, the disagreement with it often comes ultimately from an outspoken pietistic understanding of faith on behalf of which an appeal is made to Luther, but hardly with good reason.[1] According to this notion, being overwhelmed intellectually by a revelation about events leading to an insight like Paul's in Rom. 9–11 does not belong to the act of faith nor to the saving event. The act of faith in such a conception appears remarkably narrow—even pietistically narrow. Being overwhelmed by a revelation about divine events whose saving character almost essentially depends upon one's non-participation in them is, according to this understanding, no element of the act of faith. It should not be said that Christ is Christ 'for me' because he is the Christ. Instead it must be said that he is Christ because he is Christ 'for me'. In reality, however, the act of faith is much more complicated. Both sides are implied: Christ is Christ 'for me' because he is the Christ; and he is the Christ because he is Christ for me. If it is correct that faith for Paul (cf. Romans) means believing that one's salvation has been effected apart from and before one's faith, this implies that address and decision do not relate primarily to a revelation about one's existence, but in the first place to a revelation about a divine series of events, and that *only thus* do they relate to this revelation about one's existence. It is fruitless to try to understand Paul better than he understood himself. And is it right to appeal to Luther when only the positive statements about one aspect of the act of faith agree

[1] Writing from the Lutheran standpoint, G. Gloege has subjected the programme of Bultmann to a critique that is very penetrating on this point in his *Mythologie und Luthertum. Recht und Grenze der Entmythologisierung*, [3]1963.

completely with his conceptions, while negative remarks about the saving event being independent of faith would have been rejected by him quite decisively and with his own peculiar severity?

The question can be phrased in the general form in which we posed it at the beginning of this chapter: can a series of events be an object of our faith today? It is a question belonging more to dogmatics, and must await treatment in the final part of this book. Here, as always, we are primarily occupied with the exegetical problem: for the biblical witnesses, can the sequence of events in the history of salvation be the object of an act of faith? Again, what we have repeatedly stressed is important: It is constitutive of salvation history that the revelatory process is incorporated in it. For this reason, the first witnesses' faith is at the same time a decision in faith for their own alignment with a *series* of connected events. They see a divine extension of a saving work begun long before them in the fact that a new revelation has been imparted to them. They have the self-consciousness of being instruments of the divine plan of salvation, in so far as they must proclaim it. This divine plan overwhelms them. It is for this reason, and not because they are looking for 'security', that they subject themselves to it. The saving plan (*Heilsplan*) also includes disaster (*Unheil*) which appears in a very immediate fashion. A series of events becomes an address for the biblical witnesses and leads them to a new 'existential understanding', to a 'decision'. Faith in the account of salvation history is given in and with their faith in the divine salvation history itself. This must be understood in a twofold way: the witnesses believe in the account of the divine plan of salvation given to *earlier witnesses*, and they also believe in the account of it which has come to them. All faith in salvation history is, therefore, at the same time faith in the witnesses' revelatory function. There, too, lies faith in Scripture. It is simply an extension of the faith existing *before the formation of the canon* in the divine appointment of the previous witnesses of the history of salvation.[1]

This inclusion of the revelatory process in salvation history is characteristic of the whole biblical notion, and it finds its decisive culmination in the New Testament. Thus, it is here that faith in the divine history is at once faith in the bearer of revelation, in

---

[1] For this reason G. Steck's playing off of Scripture against salvation history (*Die Idee der Heilsgeschichte. Hofmann-Schlatter-Cullmann*, 1959, pp. 10f.) does not seem to me to do justice in any way to the relationship of salvation history to Scripture.

Christ, who is also the perfecter of salvation. Here the identity of the revealer with the revealed is precisely the *object* of the *kerygma*.

If the above interpretation is correct, then it can rightly be said of the incarnate Christ that in preaching the Kingdom of God he preaches himself. Like all the revealers of the divine salvation history, he includes himself in the event happening at the place in which he stands. But the new revelation now consists in his proclaiming this as the *decisive locus* of all salvation history. He aligns himself in such a way that in his case actually one can no longer speak of alignment, since he is now manifest as the basis of the whole process, past and future. Here not only does the proclaimer *also* belong to the proclamation; the one proclaimed is himself the revelation, in his own person, and because of this the salvation history reaches its highpoint.

In a secondary way the inclusion of the revealers in the history of salvation continues in the apostles through whom Christ works on. It is not as if their consciousness could be equated with that of Jesus. Rather, their apostolic consciousness is comparable with prophetic consciousness. On the other hand, it surpasses prophetic consciousness because they have the certainty of belonging to the incarnate Christ as eyewitnesses, that is, of being members of the saving drama become flesh in Christ. They know that they are called to align themselves and their preaching with the high-point of all history, and the answer of their faith consists in obedience to this call.

This apostolic consciousness is heightened even more because it rests upon the conviction that it is Jesus himself who now as the exalted Lord continues to reveal himself through the apostles.[1] For this reason it is not possible to present the christology of the New Testament without treating the process of how it arose as an integral part.[2] One must show how the incarnate Christ first reveals himself, how here and there, in a still faint suspicion, an understanding emerges among the disciples that is temporary and often dimmed by error. It needs to be shown how Christ manifested himself to them

---

[1] See O. Cullmann, 'The Tradition', *The Early Church*, 1956, pp. 55ff.

[2] This is something several critics of my *Christology of the New Testament* have not noted. M. Barth in his reviews of the book, *Journal of Religion*, 1958, pp. 268ff., and *The Christian Century*, 1959, pp. 1503f., even reproached me for having represented the continuing christological revelation within the New Testament as belonging to the christology itself. As the author of a book on the 'eyewitnesses' (*Die Augenzeugen*, 1946), he of all people should have known the place of the witnesses of revelation within the salvation history of the Bible; see above p. 102, n. 3.

at Easter as the resurrected Lord, how his presence as the exalted Lord is experienced in the celebration of the Lord's Supper, and how the reflection ascribed to inspiration by the Spirit produces the relation to the Old Testament salvation history, and thus to creation as well. In all this, according to New Testament faith, there is no human struggling with theoretical problems here, but the self-revelation of Christ, that is, not a revelation about salvation history, but salvation history itself.

Paul shows particularly clearly how the apostle aligns himself with the history of salvation in the decisive place where he stands, in the obedience of faith. His whole theology is a presentation of the divine plan of salvation as it was revealed to him by Christ on the basis of an ἀποκάλυψις (Gal. 1.12ff.). At the same time, however, a particular commission was imparted to him in and with this revelation: to preach the gospel of Christ to the Gentiles. Whether Colossians and Ephesians originate from Paul or not, certainly what we read in Col. 1.20 (Eph. 3.1ff.) about the economy of God entrusted to Paul is in accord with Paul's self-consciousness. The whole salvation-historical proclamation of Rom. 9–11 about Israel and the Gentiles is bound up in the closest way with Paul's own calling as the apostle to the Gentiles. Hence the firm tie between life and theology in Paul. Everything he reports about himself does not derive from an autobiographical interest; it has a highly theological character. Because the history of salvation has been newly revealed to him, he is himself called to carry it out. Although the whole perspective of Rom. 9–11 immediately presupposes a theological reflection extending over a lengthy period in Paul's lifetime, at the root of it there ultimately lies the call on the road to Damascus. So it is not without reason that at the end of this typical salvation-historical section of Romans, in view of the revelation imparted to him, the apostle cries out: 'O the depth of the riches and wisdom and knowledge of God!' (11.33). What he says in I Corinthians about the 'Wisdom of God' (chapters 1–3) which he contrasts with human wisdom relates to the revelation of the cross granted to him in the same way.

In the letter to the Corinthians, Paul ascribes this σοφία to the Spirit. Thinking of the work of the Paraclete leading him into all truth, the author of the Fourth Gospel in similar fashion views his theological undertaking as telling the life of Jesus in a particular perspective which, contrary to the dominant notion today, we characterize as salvation-historical.[1] There is also the consciousness of being an evangelist. The evangelist who proclaims the life of Jesus belongs in and with salvation history. He represents one of the final members in the salvation history of the Bible. This history then flows into the canon, which is a work of the revelation of salvation history and of faith in it, and represents, in a manner of speaking, the furthermost boundary in its development. We shall discuss this subject later.[2]

We must draw no false conclusions for the problem 'faith and history' from the way in which the reception of the revelation is included in salvation history, as if salvation were effected only in the witnesses' act of faith, as is taught by the Bultmann school. For salvation history to be disseminated, the faith of the prophets and the apostles must follow the revelation to the prophets in the Old Testament and the apostles in the New. This faith must be related to what was revealed to them. To be sure, this revelation also concerns the prophets and the apostles themselves, in a twofold way: they have their place in the revealed history of salvation; and, on the other hand, all salvation occurs for *them*, as for all men. But they are aware that this revelation concerns them in so far as they belong in a series of saving events in which they were not *at first* involved. They provide the link between the event occurring in their own present and the *kerygma* handed down to them. Because they have been overwhelmed by the revelation of events which happened apart from their faith, they therefore understand their own existence and enter into this process of events.

The faith of the apostles in the revelation is thus in the first instance faith in the new divine event and its saving significance. Second, it is faith in what has been handed down by others before them concerning a divine event. Third, it is faith in the association of the two, and in the role that they themselves must play in this association. It is *essential to faith* as it is found in the New Testament, and as it is asked of its readers, that it be related to events not instigated by the readers, *nor by the readers' faith*; events having taken place apart from their faith—*pro nobis*, but *extra nos*. Even on the circuitous route of faith, redemption dare not become self-redemption.

The biblical witnesses do indeed enter into this process with their faith and their decision in faith. They do this not by regarding the

[1] See below p. 268.   [2] See below pp. 293ff.

question about their 'self-understanding' as the object of the saving process, but by concentrating completely on the event coming to pass outside themselves.[1] The paradox of their faith consists in the fact that they reach a new 'self-understanding' *not by seeking it*, but by knowing they are constrained to align themselves with an historical process extraneous to themselves, which began long before them and now continues on and will continue on afterward: 'Woe to me if I do not preach the Gospel' (I Cor. 9.16). The preaching of the Gospel which they are commissioned to perform brings the fulfilment of the divine plan of salvation, which they did not set in motion, to its end.[2]

The faith of the biblical witnesses as an answer consists in their aligning themselves with that sequence of events. Although their hearers and readers, aligning themselves with the saving process, do not participate in it in the same way as do the prophets and apostles, nevertheless this decision in faith is also required of them.

According to Bultmann, a saving encounter can take place only in a punctual event. The depreciation of salvation history, so much in favour these days, goes along with a disdain for the idea that a *sequence of events* can lead to an encounter of faith. It is also said that no room is left for a decision if the revelation of the divine plan is so obvious.[3] In reality, however, the revealed sequence of events with which one must align himself is not at all self-evident. This particular selection and this particular connection of events are, of course, historically speaking meaningless even in the ancient world. They are a scandal evoking opposition and therefore require the decision of faith. This scandal is only taken seriously in its strangeness when it is not made innocuous existentially—as if it went against the pre-understanding of the biblical witnesses in an existential sense.

---

[1] The points made about faith in Christ by K. Barth in his study, 'R. Bultmann, An Attempt to Understand Him', *Kerygma and Myth* II, 1962, pp. 83ff., and by H. Gollwitzer, *The Existence of God as Confessed by Faith*, 1965, on the question of faith in God's existence (both with Bultmann in view), are true for the history of salvation too. Faith is not faith in faith. H. Braun tries to defend the Bultmannian point of view against Gollwitzer in 'Gottes Existenz in meiner Geschichtlichkeit im Neuen Testament', *Zeit und Geschichte. Dankesgabe für R. Bultmann*, 1964, pp. 399ff.

[2] See my article in *RHPR*, 1936, pp. 210ff. on κατέχων.

[3] G. Klein's objection ('Offenbarung als Geschichte? Marginalien zu einem theologischen Programm', *Monatsschrift für Pastoraltheologie*, 1962, pp. 65ff.) against W. Pannenberg amounts to this. Cf. below pp. 122ff. for the relationship between the divine plan (the constant) and historical contingency.

It was not revealed to the men of the Bible how they must 'understand themselves', but first of all how God made the particular events take place in history which, when linked together, mean salvation for the world. *Only in their function in this historical process do the witnesses belong together in salvation history.* Their faith can have no other object than the revelation that has come to them.

If the saving event for us is limited to what Bultmann and his pupils regard it to be, in other words the act of faith, and if faith consists primarily in self-understanding, must it not then be said that the faith of the New Testament witnesses has another object than the faith of the man of today? The revelation of the divine plan having come to the apostle 'now', νῦν, belongs in the saving process, not as a punctual act always repeated, but on the contrary ἐφάπαξ, as a part in the whole process. The 'now' of the New Testament witness's decision does not mean for him an 'always standing in the situation of decision', it means a decision at a particular point of time in a coherent salvation history, namely, after the death and resurrection of Jesus and before his return. It means a decision to accept the meaning of the present supplied by salvation history and to assume the obligation that follows. The meaning of this present is disclosed, however, only within the framework of the total salvation history. Otherwise, the decision becomes a decision for anything at all.

Bultmann is right in laying stress upon decision in a very impressive way. Certainly the New Testament speaks from beginning to end of the decision of faith. At this point the reproach of introducing a subject alien to it cannot be raised against Bultmann's understanding of the New Testament. This decision, however, is not defined in accordance with New Testament exegesis when Bultmann conceives of it as a decision with respect to an existential understanding that is supposed to ignore events and the salvation-historical link between them as objectifications. The decision of the New Testament witnesses is not the vague decision for existentialist philosophy's 'what is not at my disposal', but for an alignment in a definite divine plan. Certainly this plan is not at human disposal. Neither does it unfold in a straight line, but rather in a fluctuating line, and during the present its details are obscure to our minds.[1] Still, in its total movement it tends toward a definite goal known to the prophets and

---

[1] See below pp. 124f., 299, 311.

apostles, and through them, and finally through Christ himself, it is revealed and comprehended with the aid of the Holy Spirit.

This faith and these decisions do not arise from a 'need for security', as is again and again asserted. They come instead from being overwhelmed by events and insight into their relationship with each other. Anyone who sees here only a need for security may with L. Feuerbach refer *all* faith back to this need.

4. THE SALVATION-HISTORICAL REVELATION AS A PROGRESSING DEVELOPMENT WITHIN THE CONTEXT OF THE BIBLICAL PERIOD

(*Constant and Contingency*)

We have seen that all biblical salvation history progresses. This conclusion would be a truism if we had in mind only the *events* which constitute salvation history. In reality, we must also remember the continual forward development of the salvation-historical *kerygma*, in other words, the *interpretation* of those events. Each time a new event is added, the whole perspective is simultaneously changed in the light of it, and so also is the relationship to the eschatological events yet to come. It must not, of course, be forgotten that the new events give the cause for the reinterpretations, and that the *kerygma* therefore develops further because it is bound to a sequence of events.

We shall wait until the last part of this book, devoted to a dogmatic standpoint, to deal with the question whether and how salvation history develops further beyond the time of the apostles. On the other hand, we shall attempt to show that the limitation of salvation history implicit in the thought of a canon grows directly out of the reinterpretation of the New Testament described in the previous chapter, on the basis of the thought that in Christ the highpoint of the whole saving process is reached.[1]

Here our task is to analyse the salvation history found in the biblical framework. The notion of development is in fact quite basic to the Bible. For this reason an historical treatment of the Bible is a theological necessity. The paradigm for the manner in which this

[1] See below pp. 293ff.

development proceeds is offered by the canon encompassing the Old and New Testaments. When I speak of the 'canon', as always I mean not its final fixing, but the appearance of the notion of the canon in the second century. What is indicated by this idea is, as it were, typified in the whole development proceeding step by step as we have pursued it through the Old and New Testaments in our inquiry into the origins of salvation history undertaken up to this point. Two items must be taken up both for the idea of the canon and the whole preceding development in the history of salvation: *continuity and change*. We could also say, change in continuity.

Each time the perspective is changed. In placing the books of the New Testament together with those of the Old, as is done in the canon, all reinterpretation reaches its final expression. Whereas individual biblical passages afford only partial insights into salvation history, based, of course, on a total view, the canon offers a total survey including the whole salvation history from the creation, 'In the beginning was the Word', to the promise at the end, 'Surely I am coming soon.' The position of the New Testament after the Old shows it as the high-point and hence the key to interpreting the whole process. For this reason much of what was previously central is displaced to the periphery and appears to be dispensed with in the light of the Christ event. Still, what was dispensed with remains significant and is not simply suppressed in a Marcionitic misunderstanding.

This is the way in which the whole salvation-historical development has already been taking place. The perspective is expanded step by step with each new event, encountering at the same time corrections and even a certain break with previous statements. We may recall, for example, the prophetic message of judgment which superseded the prophecy of salvation alone. To a great extent the history of salvation is the history of disaster (*Unheil*). Yet even here the continuity is preserved, and later the proclamation of salvation is in turn taken up without the preaching of judgment disappearing. So it is certainly not in harmony with Paul's intention to speak of the miscarriage of the Old Testament, appealing to what he indicated as the impossibility of the way of the Law.[1]

The progress of salvation history and salvation-historical revelation means change and correction, but the faithfulness of God is nevertheless guaranteed. That means that historical contingency is also

[1] See above p. 25.

a part of salvation history, and we may and must, therefore, take this very much into account in our theology. Nevertheless, salvation history may not be dismissed as falling under the verdict of Lessing regarding the 'accidental' truths of history. The failure to determine exactly the relation between salvation history and history leads again and again to the much too simple justification for dismissing salvation history along with the 'accidental truths of history'.

It will not do, however, to oversimplify the whole development so that it is forced into the favourite scheme of 'promise and fulfilment'. This scheme does not do justice to the contingency of the saving process which occupies a large place. The scheme is not apt because any particular fulfilment is very often a promise of something greater to come.[1] A typical example is John 14.12, where the Johannine Christ predicts that through the disciples he will perform even greater works than he did in his incarnation because he goes to the Father. Fulfilment within the biblical framework is never complete. Salvation history continues to develop. Although God remains true to his promise, it is fulfilled in a way hard to survey in detail and in a manner not at the disposal of human knowledge once for all. For one thing, man's *sin* as resistance to the plan of God must be noted. In Rom. 3.2ff. and Rom. 9–11, Paul shows how in mysterious ways God can turn the unbelief and sin of men to good use to carry out his plan. The inference that man is therefore not responsible for his sin Paul repudiates with indignation. The divine plan and human responsibility belong side by side for Paul, and both are retained as indispensable ingredients of salvation history. Thus the very disbelief of Israel opens the way for the full number of Gentiles to come in—without abandoning God's plan that had its start in the election of Israel.[2]

From the human point of view, quite apart from man's sin, contingency belongs to the manner in which God's plan develops. In the Bible the movement and purpose of the plan are revealed at the start, but not the particular stages in it. They are disclosed for the first time in the events as they occur. The continuing execution of the divine plan, and its association with contingency, lapses, and

---

[1] This was already recognized by J. C. K. v. Hofmann, *Weissagung und Erfüllung im alten und neuen Testament*, 1841/44; see now G. v. Rad, *Old Testament Theology* II, p. vii.

[2] K. E. Skydsgaard, 'Vom Geheimnis der Kirche', *KuD*, 1964, pp. 137ff., refers to the significance of guilt within the history of salvation.

detours, is expressed in a Portuguese proverb cited by Paul Claudel as the motto for his *Soulier de satin*: 'God writes straight, but with crooked lines.'[1]

Saving events unforeseen by men enter in, and new revelations come to new witnesses. The corrections of the traditional *kerygma* brought about by events would not otherwise be possible. The corrections, however, never mean giving up the movement of the divine plan expressed in the preceding salvation-historical perspective. At particular places there is a disavowal of earlier statements inasmuch as they were linked with perspectives not yet sufficiently wide, but in the perspective created by new events they can always find their places in the corresponding new interpretation.

This consideration is relevant not only for the relationship of salvation and judgment in prophecy, but also for the question of the delay of the *parousia*, forcefully advanced today by both the Schweitzer and Bultmann schools. This matter is regarded as the one great concern that is supposed to have occupied early Christianity unremittingly as a 'tormenting' problem. For our study of the relationship between salvation history and eschatology, we shall have to inquire whether there really was such a disappointment that the Kingdom of God did not come as quickly as Jesus predicted, which caused the reinterpretation of the *kerygma* by extending the interval between his resurrection and return. Are there not instead, as in all previous reinterpretations, new saving events, positively experienced, such as the workings of the Spirit in the Church? Without signifying an actual break with the expectation of an imminent end preached before, and without calling forth a crisis, did not these experiences cause the inclusion of the extension of time within the biblical framework as an almost organic development of the *kerygma*?

If it is really essential for all salvation history in the Bible to undergo development (and not just in relation to human sin that counteracts God's plan, though still being used by God for good in harmony with his purpose, but also in relation to new events experienced as revelation), then the much discussed extension of time, as found, for instance, in the writings of Luke, can no longer be regarded as a break with Jesus' message, nor as the result of a faulty theological development, as is done today. The Gospel tradition

---

[1] *Dieu écrit droit, mais avec des lignes courbes.* I am grateful to Père Y. Congar, O.P., who in a conversation referred me to this proverb corresponding precisely to what I would like to show in this book.

handed down sayings of Jesus about an imminent end without re-flecting on them at a time when it was already established that 'the bridegroom delays'. This is confirmation for the fact that without an actual crisis, and without creating a tormenting theological problem, as was the case among the rabbis, the early Church linked Jesus' *kerygma* with the *kerygma* interpreted anew in the light of the workings of the Spirit, in which the intermediate period, the time of the Spirit, mission and the Church, underwent a natural lengthening in the Church's *kerygma*. Jesus' sayings about the imminent end were not suppressed in the light of the new *kerygma*, and were probably even retained in their original wording, but were now read in the context of the whole reinterpretation.

Jesus probably preached that the Kingdom of God would come within the time of his own generation. He did not speak of centuries. In a later chapter[1] I shall have occasion to reject all interpretations of his sayings speaking of the Kingdom's imminent coming that try to explain away this fact forcibly. I shall emphasize all the more strongly that the Bible's salvation history itself developed further at this point, and that this further development, like *all* biblical re-interpretation of the salvation-historical *kerygma*, at once means correction and continuity. We shall see that the continuity consists in the fact that the beginnings of a salvation history are already present with Jesus since the salvation-historical tension between 'already' and 'not yet' is basic to his eschatology. We shall also see that his preaching already knows an intermediate period, albeit a very short one, lying between his death and the end, and this interval is important in terms of salvation history, in spite of its short duration.

When we deal with this question in connection with everything that we have established about the origin and progressive develop-ment of salvation history, aspects will unfold that will put it in a new light.

[1] See below pp. 236ff.

5. THE WRITTEN CONSOLIDATION OF SALVATION-HISTORICAL EXCERPTS* IN THE NEW TESTAMENT

(*Salvation History, Typology, Allegory*)

Up to now we have spoken of the salvation-historical perspective, basic to the whole of New Testament thinking, and of the origin of this perspective, neither of which is summed up anywhere in the Scriptures in a neat and concise way. Only in a certain sense is it visible in the Gospels and Acts, where the central saving event is presented and is taken as the standpoint from which the past is seen in retrospect and the future is anticipated. The Gospel of John connects the life of Jesus, as the centre of the whole process, especially closely with the total salvation history.[1] However, we shall discuss this presentation of the life of Jesus in later chapters. We now turn to the salvation-historical excerpts given to us by the other books of the New Testament. They, too, presuppose the same total view of salvation history. But in contrast to the Old Testament, the New Testament never offers us the *whole* chronological connection of events in salvation history in a written, fixed form, but only excerpts from it. This is why the presence of a total view of salvation history in the New Testament has been disputed. As a matter of fact, in the excerpts found in the New Testament there is very often only *one* connection between a concrete problem of the present and one or several events of the Old Testament salvation history. Hence, the conclusion is often prematurely drawn that the relation to the past in the New Testament is only 'punctual-momentary'.[2]

A second argument advanced against the presence of a general salvation-historical view in the background of the New Testament finds support in the expectation of an imminent end in early Christianity. So long as this expectation was alive, it excluded an actual interest in salvation history. To this it must first be said that the

---

* Translator's note: An 'excerpt' in the context of this chapter carries an unusual and perhaps unique connotation. An 'excerpt of salvation history' (*heilsgeschichtlicher Ausschnitt*) is a specialized and technical term. It means a line drawn from one or more persons or episodes found earlier in salvation history to some concern in the present. The line can also be extended to something in the future. In this way things separate chronologically are drawn together to show their relevance to each other.

[1] See below pp. 268ff.

[2] H. Conzelmann, 'Gegenwart und Zukunft in der synoptischen Tradition', *ZTK*, 1957, p. 290, favours this view.

impetus for the New Testament efforts to solve a concrete problem on the basis of Old Testament events is in fact 'punctual-momentary'. The *manner*, however, *in which the problem is dealt with* is not punctual, but salvation-historical, that is, it inserts the theological or ethical problem emerging in the time of the writer into salvation history.

Even where attention is directed to the future coming of the Kingdom of God expected in the most immediate future, for the first Christians the necessity of binding the proclamation of this coming with the past saving process of the Old Testament arises. It is a forcible modernization of New Testament thought to say that from the expectation of the imminent end one must come to an existential stance irreconcilable with any endeavour to produce a connection with the Old Testament saving activity of God. By such argumentation one merely shows that one is not taking into account the importance of the anchoring of even the early Christian perspectives in the Old Testament. Anyone who is as steeped in the history of Israel as were the first Christians, and lives in it as they did, must bring his most ardent eschatological expectations for the immediate future into relationship with the Old Testament. He must understand them as the fulfilment of a promise, but also as a completion of a *process* already in effect. This is already true in the case of Jesus himself.

We shall see that the intensity of this hope is involved in the fact that it grounds the expectation of what is yet to come in faith in what has already become a reality in the past. Along with the acceptance of the Old Testament, this is the decisive indication that the various links with the Old Testament found in the New are not detached from a total view of salvation history which is implicitly present. However near the expected future may be, the place of the present in salvation history must be determined in relation to the near future, and this is only possible if its relationship to the salvation-historical is also indicated. The present is self-fulfilling future only when it is the fulfilment of the past. The early Church was forced to survey the *whole* history of salvation, for only in this way could it be sure of its special position as the *elect people of God*, as the new Israel. This should be heeded more in the present discussion. It is hardly disputable that the Church regarded itself as the *true* Israel. This, however, implies a total salvation-historical perspective towards the past, present and future.

The treatments of salvation history in the New Testament must be read and understood against this background. If, therefore, Paul, for instance, displays just *one* particular relationship to the Old Testament in a concrete question of faith or life in the Church, this is still done in the light of salvation history, even though only one aspect is singled out. Thus, we no longer have relationships immediately experienced as revelation, but subsequent theological reflection taking that revelation as its point of departure. We could also say that problems emerging in connection with the life and instruction of the Church are answered in the light of salvation history.

The passage Gal. 3.6–4.7 is particularly instructive in this regard. Its theme is faith in Christ as the basis for appropriating salvation. The apostle treats it by presenting a 'salvation history of faith'. Although the point of departure is the faith of those living in Paul's own present, the Pauline discussion proceeds chronologically. It begins with Abraham, to show how the descent of the people of God, as bearers of the promise, is founded upon Abraham's faith in the divine promise, and how by his faith in Isaac's birth the way leads beyond the parenthesis of the Law to the One, to Christ, as the object of faith, and thence to those baptized in Christ and believing in him who become 'sons'. History serves here as an 'example'. Abraham is more than an 'example from Scripture', more than just any example of an Old Testament witness who believed. Rather, his story is recalled as an event historically understood, the starting point for a *development* leading to the baptism of those believing in Christ.

In Rom. 4, the same line is drawn from Abraham up to the present, but now in a somewhat different direction, that is, in regard to the problem of 'faith and circumcision', as it is seen in the Epistle. Here the argument is influenced by a rabbinic exegetical principle.

In Rom. 5.12ff., Paul draws a line, not from Abraham to Christ, but from Adam to Christ. Here a typological parallelism is produced between Adam and Christ. We shall speak below of the distinction between salvation history and typology. Nevertheless, even here the salvation-historical perspective is not lost sight of, nor are the intermediate stages bypassed. Typology is imbedded in a total salvation-historical understanding: 'from Adam to Moses' (v. 14). Less explicitly, but nevertheless clearly enough, the statements about the Law in Rom. 7 rest upon a salvation-historical view of the paradise story.[1] It is quite obvious that the whole section in Rom. 9–11 is

---

[1] See S. Lyonnet, ' "Tu ne convoiteras pas" (Rom. VII.7)', *Neotestamentica et Patristica. Freundesgabe für O. Cullmann*, 1962, pp. 157ff., and *id.*, 'L'Histoire du salut selon le chapitre VII de L'Epître aux Romains', *Biblica*, 1962, pp. 117ff.

oriented towards salvation history. The view begins with Abraham, but again the same story is seen in another perspective, namely, from the vantage point of the theological problem of 'Jews and Gentiles'. Accordingly, another development is indicated, but still within the same salvation history. The stress is on the genuinely prophetic vision into the future, resting upon a prophetic understanding of the story of the Christian mission in Paul's own present, and this vision includes the past as well. There is a Pauline theological reflection here, but this reflection stands in immediate relationship to the personal revelation of the divine saving plan imparted to Paul, as the outcry at the end of this section shows: 'O the depth of the riches and wisdom and knowledge of God!' (Rom. 11.33ff.).

We have already established with regard to Rom. 5.12ff. and Rom. 7 that in these salvation-historical excerpts answering theological questions, primeval history is regarded as a part of the same process. Discussions like Rom. 8.18ff. show this too. Here the solidarity of the whole creation with man is spoken of. It is treated as the participation of creation in the *whole* development of salvation history. The origin of this is seen in the way in which Adam's curse draws the whole creation into the consequences of his sin.[1] After that, the creation shares in the whole Christ event in the present and future, even in the 'groaning' of the Spirit during the present. This is a sign that the Spirit as a first fruit in the present directs us towards the future in anticipation of it. The relationship between primeval and present events is established more indirectly in Phil. 2.6ff. There, in order to derive the exaltation from the humiliation, and to establish Christ's present lordship over all, the hymn to Christ begins with a clear reference to Adam's fall, resting upon the disobedience of one who was supposed to have been the image of God, but who was not satisfied with that and wanted to usurp equality with God 'as robbery'.[2] In the next part of this book we shall speak about the connection between primeval history and history.

Salvation history is spoken of only in relationship to a theological problem dealt with at a particular moment, and this explains why time and again just *one* aspect of it is thrown into relief. The salvation-historical orientation is not simply an external form, as a concession

---

[1] It should not be doubted any longer that Adam (Gen. 3.17ff.), not God, is meant by διὰ τοῦ ὑποτάξαντος (Rom. 8.20). On the question of creation and salvation history, see below pp. 145ff., 255ff.

[2] See O. Cullmann, *The Christology of the New Testament*, 1959, pp. 174ff.

to the thought structure taken over from Judaism, but the core of the answer to the theological problem.

In the Acts of the Apostles, Peter sees the pouring out of the Spirit upon the Church as the fulfilment of Joel's prophecy, according to which at the *end* time the Spirit ceases to be a privilege of individual men of God and instead comes upon all. Here again we do not *just* have a rabbinic citation of a passage of Scripture, but a salvation-historical insight into a development in the work of the Holy Spirit. Thus the fulfilment of the passage in Joel implies, so to speak, a history of the Holy Spirit in the background. Furthermore, Peter's Pentecost sermon unfolds the salvation-historical perspective of present history from the Jews' rejection of Jesus, his predicted death, his resurrection and the apostles' attestation of it, to the miracles of the exalted Christ. Although the 'proof from Scripture' is important to the writer, so is the way in which the events follow one another. Certainly Luke's involvement in this as well as in other speeches in Acts is great.[1] But it can surely be assumed that he makes an effort to distinguish between the speeches of Peter, Stephen, and Paul on the basis of the traditions at his disposal, especially since they often contain trains of thought which are not specifically Lucan.[2] Hence the proof of the necessity of Jesus' suffering will in fact have been important for Peter.[3] Stephen's speech contains a salvation-historical survey carried out in detail to demonstrate a quite concrete fact, namely, that Israel consistently resisted the Spirit's working in that it bound God's revelation and presence *locally*, whereas the history of salvation proves that this was definitely not God's will. Thus the line from Abraham to Christ is again drawn with respect to a quite specific current problem, namely that of the temple.[4] Surely Luke is not developing his own theology here.

In the Epistle to the Hebrews there are likewise excerpts of salvation history which are always seen from a particular theological perspective, although the history of their development is not so

---

[1] Cf. especially U. Wilckens, *Die Missionsreden der Apostelgeschichte*, 1961, ²1963.

[2] See B. Reicke, *Glaube und Leben der Urgemeinde* (*ATANT* 32), 1957, p. 40: 'If one does not demand the impossible of this historical writer and the tradition behind him, then it must be granted that there is always a perceptible effort at individual characterization in the speeches.'

[3] I have tried to show this in my *Peter: Disciple—Apostle—Martyr*, rev. ed. 1962, pp. 67ff.

[4] See my article, 'L'opposition contre le Temple de Jérusalem motif commun de la Théologie johannique et du monde ambiant', *NTS*, 1959, pp. 157ff., and B. Reicke, *op. cit.*, pp. 136ff.

involved as in Acts. This is true from the first verses about God's previous 'speaking by the prophets to the fathers', and about his 'speaking at the end of these days by a Son' (1.1ff.),[1] up to the cloud of witnesses in Chapter 11.

In the Epistle to the Hebrews a problem is forced upon us which we have already raised in connection with Pauline passages: to what degree is there a typology here rather than a salvation-historical exposition? What is the relationship between the two? We cannot, of course, deal with the complex problem of typological and allegorical exegesis here.[2] Instead, we shall call attention merely to the aspects of the problem relevant to the view of salvation history developed here.

Typology merely establishes a parallelism between two figures or phenomena. Now we have seen that every presentation of the history of salvation in the narrower sense in the New Testament offers just one excerpt of the whole and draws out just certain lines of salvation history. Thus far, hardly any distinction exists between salvation-historical exposition and typology. Conversely, typology presupposes a wider salvation-historical framework and connects two points on this background. In typology, however, the connection is limited to the two points being dealt with. Those parts and members of the salvation history which fall in between the two points are either passed over or are not considered in this manner of confrontation.

It is rightly emphasized that typology at the same time stresses analogy and heightening, repetition and consummation, with respect to the two points in contrast.[3] In this measure analogy or, specifically, repetition, plays a role in typology. Analogy and repetition contain an element which threatens to destroy the salvation-historical

---

[1] The juxtaposition of the 'speaking by the prophets' and 'speaking by the Son', with the stress upon the latter, confirms what was said above pp. 99f. about the relationship between the vertical and the horizontal. The vertical does not abolish the horizontal, but interprets it.

[2] Cf. L. Goppelt, *Typos* (*Beiträge zur Förderung christlicher Theologie*), 1939; H. de Lubac, 'Typologie et allégorie', *Rech. Sc. Rel.*, 1947, pp. 180ff.; J. Daniélou, *Sacramentum futuri, Études sur les origines de la Typologie biblique*, 1950; R. Bultmann, 'Ursprung und Sinn der Typologie als hermeneutische Methode', *TLZ* 75, 1950, pp. 205–212; F. Michaeli, 'La "Typologie" Biblique,' *Foi et Vie* 50, 1952, pp. 11–18; W. Eichrodt, 'Ist typologische Exegese sachgemässe Exegese?' *TLZ* 81, 1956, pp. 641–654; G. v. Rad, *Old Testament Theology* II, 1960, pp. 116, 273, 323ff., 364; S. Amsler, *L'Ancien Testament dans l'Église, Essai d'herméneutique chrétienne*, 1960.

[3] R. Bultmann, *op. cit.*, points this out especially.

THE WRITTEN CONSOLIDATION

character of development, but need not necessarily destroy it. The salvation-historical interest actually recedes to the degree that the stress is placed more strongly on repetition than upon consummation. On the other hand, the salvation-historical interest always accompanies the principle of heightening and the notion of consummation, and the more preponderant this interest is, the more the typology is oriented toward the history of salvation. All typology, at any rate, presupposes a salvation-historical background, namely, the relationship between the Old and New Testaments understood from a salvation-historical point of view. This is true for the typological juxtaposition of baptism and the events in the wilderness in I Cor. 10.1ff. where it is finally said in v. 11 that the events in the wilderness *happened* τυπικῶς, but were written as an admonition for us on whom the end of the aeons has dawned.

This background is only given up in *allegory*. In allegory the salvation-historical meaning of Scripture is eliminated, making it merely a form for expressing some truth divorced from salvation history.[1] In allegorical interpretation the historical development between the Old Testament text and the New Testament situation has no significance whatever. Only in a very few Pauline passages is such an allegorical interpretation offered in the New Testament, where the fact as such is merely a clothing for something else.

There is, of course, the danger of slipping off into allegory even in certain typological parallelizing as soon as the parallelism, loosened from the events, is regarded as the essential thing—as soon as merely a parallelism of texts and not a parallelism of events is involved. The boundaries between salvation-historical exposition and typology on the one hand, and typology and allegory on the other, are not hard and fast, and there are bridges between them. There is actually no contradiction between typology and salvation-historical exposition in principle. However, in principle allegory must be separated from typology and still more from salvation-historical exposition. Within the total framework of the New Testament, typology is legitimate, but allegory is not, for pure allegory certainly does not accord with the essence of the New Testament, and in the very few passages where it is present we really have no more than the acceptance of an exegetical method stemming from rabbinic Judaism. But in view

---

[1] Despite the great differences between the Bultmannian method of demythologizing and allegory, both concur in trying to make biblical texts credible to modern man by the aid of an interpretation that eliminates all salvation history.

of the ultimate intentions of the whole New Testament witness, even here it serves a conception of the Old Testament that is not basic to allegorical method, but presupposes an inner relationship to the saving process of the Old Testament.

In the New Testament problem 'salvation history, typology, allegory', the question is ultimately one of the first Christians' understanding of Scripture: is this understanding, on the one hand, oriented toward the biblicist-rabbinic, formal principle in which the only important thing is to show that the letter of the Old Testament is fulfilled this way or that; or, on the other hand, is it to show that in the plan of God revealed in Scripture the Old Testament process is fulfilled in a further *event*? Starting from the formal rabbinic understanding of Scripture and the corresponding conception of promise and fulfilment, allegory is inevitable. But the question is not properly put in the form of an alternative. It must be granted that the rabbinic principle of interpreting Scripture is present in the whole New Testament and especially in Matthew's Gospel, and plays a considerable role.[1]

There is a grain of truth in Conzelmann's exaggerated assertion ('Gegenwart 'und Zukunft in der synoptischen Tradition', *ZTK*, 1957, p. 290) that whatever belongs farther back in the past than John the Baptist no longer interests Mark as history, but as prediction, and that the relationship to the past does not extend to the events narrated in the Bible.

However, if we study the proofs from Scripture, we come to the conclusion that where the New Testament uses arguments stemming from the rabbinic understanding of Scripture, there is usually at bottom a deep insight into the plan of God accomplished in *events*. This emerges in the 'typological' passage at I Cor. 10.11 where the distinction is expressly made between the event and the written fixing of this event. This insight into the plan of God is exactly what differentiates the New Testament writers' understanding of Scripture from that of the rabbis, despite everything they have borrowed from the latter. The evangelists' strong salvation-historical interest in John the Baptist[2] can be rooted only in a total understanding of the old covenant which extends far beyond that of the rabbis and grasps the concept of fulfilment much more deeply—in much the same way the prophets understood it.

---

[1] For the Gospel of Matthew, see K. Stendahl, *The School of St. Matthew*, 1954.
[2] This fact is acknowledged even in Conzelmann's work mentioned above.

The first Christians' theological reflection on and exposition of Scripture borrows, to be sure, from rabbinic exegesis, but never so that the total salvation-historical perspective is lost.[1] The early Christians ascribed the origin of this perspective, which we have studied in the foregoing chapters, to a revelation. There is certainly a difference between the immediate salvation-historical knowledge of the divine plan in relation to the newly experienced event and, on the other hand, the written fixations of salvation-historical perspectives. But in the New Testament the ground of that knowledge is never abandoned.

---

[1] Although in the exegesis from the Qumran sect the sect's own community is very much in the foreground (as the 'remnant'), the exegesis is oriented much more towards the formal principle of interpreting Scripture than towards an actual salvation-historical conception. See O. Betz, *Offenbarung und Schriftforschung in der Qumransekte*, 1960.

III

PHENOMENOLOGICAL
CHARACTERISTICS

1. THE RELATIONSHIP BETWEEN HISTORICALLY
CONTROLLABLE AND HISTORICALLY
UNCONTROLLABLE ELEMENTS: HISTORY
AND MYTH

WE HAVE SHOWN the mutual influence of event and interpretation to be the main motive of the *origin* of the biblical
salvation history. Up to now, however, we have only looked
at the *genetic* question—to what degree did the event, and to what
degree did the preaching of the Word lead to the biblical view of
salvation history? Is the 'Word' or the event the starting point of
revelation and salvation? We have seen that the question cannot be
answered in the form of a clear alternative. Inasmuch as earlier
biblical interpretations have affected later interpretations, a greater
significance is attached to the *kerygma*, the 'Word'. It is utterly impossible to make a chronological distinction between Word and
event *in God himself*. But from the human standpoint we stressed
some degree of primacy of the event, in two respects. On the one
hand, the event primarily affects the interpretation as *kerygma*, and
the interpretation is not imposed upon the event. This is confirmed
by the fact that within biblical time the reinterpretations correcting
and refining earlier interpretations are on each occasion called forth
by new events. In other words, the primacy of the event is clear in the
development of all biblical salvation history. On the other hand, all
interpretations and reinterpretations have as their objects events in
which God's activity is recognized. They are interpretation in so far
as they produce an *association* between the individual events which
results from the confrontation of new events with earlier interpretations given to earlier events.

Moving from the genetic question, we turn in what follows to the study of the *phenomenological* characteristics of the salvation-historical perspective and ask how event and *kerygma* relate to one another in the fully developed history of salvation.

First of all, it must be remembered here that *the biblical notion of the Word as an event, or vice versa, of the event as Word,* corresponds with the actual interrelationship of history and interpretation and their co-existence in God himself which we previously mentioned. The Old Testament uses the same designation for 'event' as for 'word' (*debarim*). In the Gospel of John, the divine Logos, the 'Word', already appears as an event 'in the beginning', as the same Logos that is revealed at the centre of all history in the life of the one who has appeared in the flesh. The word goes out 'Let there be light!'— and there was light. The Word occurs (*geschieht*) and the event (*Geschehen*) becomes the Word. The Holy Spirit speaks by acting; he acts by speaking. The same revelation by the Holy Spirit is at work in the event as such, *and* in the kerygmatic interpretation of the event.

Despite this close connection, and even because of it, we need to distinguish how the proclamation of events and the interpreting preaching of the Word are related against this background in the Bible, and especially in the New Testament, with which we are concerned. The first question here is, to what degree is it possible to verify certain events communicated in the Bible as such? Do not many of them actually belong, as myths, not to history itself, but to the preaching of the Word, to interpretation? If that is true, then is there any justification at all for speaking of the *history* of salvation, if events of creation which are not history, but myth, stand at the beginning of this history and if at its end events are predicted which are to take place for the most part in the cosmic sphere and cannot be termed historical because they belong to the future?

Actually, historical reports and mythical materials are involved very closely together—so closely that it is extraordinarily difficult to distinguish between them. This is even more difficult because the myths have a narrative character. The histories of the beginning and the end time can be separated from the historical central portion (history of Israel, the life of Jesus, the history of the early Church and mission) relatively easily. But even in the telling of the central portion itself there is an amalgamation of historically controllable and historically uncontrollable elements. The latter we can term mythical.

The Bultmann school finds support in the continual appearance of myth for its assumption that myth has primarily characterized the salvation-historical perspective of the Bible. Accordingly, the sequence of events purporting to be a divine-ontic process is merely external clothing that can be stripped off. Common to myth *and* event is the existential meaning, my understanding of Being, that is fundamental to both. The *connection* of events made between the historical elements themselves, as well as between them and mythical elements, would in this case need to be eliminated as mythology (or 'objectifying utterance') in order to disclose the existential understanding of Being which binds myth and history. The hermeneutical course of 'demythologizing' *all* salvation history, advocated by the Bultmann school, accords with this understanding of the co-existence of myth and history.

Bultmann's view has the advantage that it takes note of the unity made by the biblical writers between the specifically mythical materials and the historical elements of the Bible by viewing and treating them together as mythology. The Bultmann school employs the same principle of interpretation for both: the connection of events in terms of a divine-ontic process is eliminated. The existential meaning affecting my self-understanding, which results from hearing and being claimed by the biblical message, is retained.

We too are trying to stress the unity that is produced in the biblical salvation history between myth and history in the manner which has been described above. But whereas for Bultmann the form of expression of the whole salvation-historical approach is characterized by mythology, on the contrary we see the basic principle creating the connection between history and myth in what for Bultmann is merely an objectifying mythological utterance that is to be eliminated. The connecting link here, therefore, is not the existential meaning of both history and myth, but an element which Bultmann derives from the history (*Historie*)[1] he depreciates, an element which in the main belongs to salvation history and admits of historical research. This is the conception of an event revealed to me as a divine event, having happened independently of me and my faith, an event with which faith requires me to align myself inasmuch as I am claimed by it. We, too, want to make the myths embedded in this process understandable to modern thinking, but not by claiming that their existential meaning is the key to the understanding of the whole

---

[1] Preferring what he calls '*Geschichtlichkeit*', namely as encounter.

biblical message. Instead, we take account of the true *meaning* they are given *within the biblical message*, which reveals the divine process to us.

When we study the myths utilized for the beginning and end of biblical history *independently* of their tie with the historically controllable central portion of biblical salvation history, they must not be interpreted as they are when we judge them as parts of this salvation history. For the Bible, even the Old Testament, has already *demythologized* the myths by placing them on one and the same level with the historically controllable middle portion of biblical history, thereby *historicizing* them.[1]

Thus within the Bible they are already disrobed of what constitutes the deeper meaning of myth. It is, therefore, incorrect to explain biblical myths as if they were independent of their present context. That would mean overlooking their function and their transformation resulting from this function.

Demythologizing may, therefore, be recognized and required as one of the aims of exegesis, only it must be undertaken in the biblical sense, that is, in terms of historicizing the myths, i.e., interpreting history, and not adapting them to an extraneous philosophy, whether it be a metaphysics, as in Philo, or existentialism, as in the Bultmann school.

The Old Testament historicized myths by firmly attaching them to Israel's history. In this, the New Testament went still further by subjecting all myths more rigidly to *one* event in history—the death of Jesus and the events connected with it which immediately followed. The myths are placed at the service of the salvation-historical perspective at whose mid-point stands an historically controllable event.

Myths serve to *interpret* the connection of the various saving events. Demythologizing rightly understood is the correct recognition and definition of this *interpretative character* of the myths, in other words, of their relationship to history. We shall see how demythologizing can and must be carried further in the intention of the Bible.

The central portion of salvation history, open to historical investigation, is made up of individual events belonging to secular history which are placed in a definite connection not disclosed by history

[1] On the following see my article, 'The Connection of Primal Events and End Events with the New Testament Redemptive History', *The Old Testament and Christian Faith*, ed. B. W. Anderson, 1963, pp. 115–123, and in the volume of my collected articles to appear shortly. The same problem is dealt with in a somewhat different view, yet close to the way we are treating the question here, by J. Hempel, 'Glaube, Mythos und Geschichte im Alten Testament', *ZAW*, 1953, pp. 109ff., and B. S. Childs, *Myth and Reality in the Old Testament*, 1960.

itself. This is a feature of the salvation-historical development of revelation indicated above. The knowledge of the divine origin of this connection is attributed to a direct communication to those who bear the biblical revelation, the prophets and apostles. In the New Testament, this connection is defined by the central place of the historical event of the death of Jesus. The purpose of myth in the service of interpretation is to bring this central place into relief, showing, on the one hand, that the whole historical process is summed up in this event, and, on the other hand, that all past history tends toward this centre, and that all present and future events proceed from it. This is true for the events belonging to history like the past history of Israel and the prophetically predicted future events taking place within the framework of history, such as the destruction of the Jerusalem temple.

Furthermore, myth expresses the fact that beyond the solid block of historically controllable events all the events in the historical process, including those which are not accessible to historical research, are bound *as divine events* to this historical central portion. Thus, in the whole salvation-historical conception of the Bible, primeval and end events must be attached to this central portion in the closest kind of relationship. These events are seen entirely in the light of the event at the mid-point and are not meaningful in themselves. Nevertheless, they are not mere appendages, but are constitutive of the total process.

The interpretative function of myth is therefore a double one. On the one hand it determines the position of the historical process constituting the central portion of salvation history, which in its absolute breadth encompasses the whole divine process. For myth *extends* the process both backwards and forwards beyond the time of the historically verifiable. On the other hand, *within* the framework of the historical central portion itself, myth makes visible the connection created by God between the various historical events by being inserted into the narration of these events. Thus the principle of *election*, which proves to be the motive of the whole salvation history, especially in its historical part, is made particularly clear by the coupling of historical[1] elements with non-historical, mythical ones. Hence the intertwining of history and myth is especially close.

---

[1] In this chapter we do not use 'historical' in the sense of a secular historical coherence but to refer to individual events that take place in the historical framework. Cf. the argumentation in the following chapter.

So it is most difficult to distinguish between the two, particularly since myth makes use of the same literary form of narration as historical reporting does.

To fulfil this double function, myth is robbed of its mythical character, but not its narrative form. Outside the Bible it is characteristic of myth that human *situations* are told about as events in a naive way. Outside the Bible these myths can therefore be interpreted according to the general rules of the study of mythology, so that the naive narrative character of the myths is recognized as a form of expression for something more profound, and hence is eliminated. But the character of event is completely *indispensable* to the myths now historicized in the Bible as a consequence of their close connection with the historical central portion of the biblical narration. Certainly the use of myth in the Bible is naive to the extent that the writers do not distinguish between historically controllable and uncontrollable events. Only in this regard is demythologizing a hermeneutical necessity, as we shall show later. But the character of event must be retained as essential. By its connection with the historical central portion, myth contains an importance and seriousness that it did not possess when it was not yet historicized, for myth is not just *linked* with the historical portion. It is first of all transformed by it. It is not as if an idea basic to pre-biblical myth, and dealing in its essence with some human situation, were imposed upon the historical central portion in order to interpret it. On the contrary, the *occurrence* of which pre-biblical myth speaks is moved into the foreground by virtue of its connection with the events of biblical history and is given a significance formerly foreign to it. In this way, by a kind of reciprocation, myth for its own part fulfils its function as a myth which is now historicized, making the all-inclusive central place of that historical event visible in a twofold way. On the one hand, within the historical framework, it intensifies significantly the line running through the historical central portion. On the other hand, it prolongs this line backward into primeval time and forward into the end time.

In both cases the important thing is that an *occurrence* outside the historical framework and outside historical time is assumed, analogous to the one taking place on the historical level.[1] As was already mentioned, the exegete must, of course, distinguish on the basis of

[1] K. Barth, *Church Dogmatics* III/2, 1960, p. 446, thinks that events can be historical occurrences (*Geschehen*) without being historical facts. R. Bultmann in

modern thinking between an historical and a non-historical level and may not simply suppose the mythical to be historical. But he must allow the essential factor in the biblical association of history and historicized myth to stand, that is, the belief that a divine, if not also an historical, *event* is revealed in both the historical event and the interpretative myth reaching into the non-historical level. The distinction between the historical level and the non-historical one thus concerns only a formal aspect in the light of the biblical revelation and not the core of the revelation. In this extension into primeval time, clarified with the help of creation myths now historicized, events without human witnesses and without the possibility of historical control are involved.[1] Thus, all historical 'proofs' about this period in the fashion of the slogan, 'The Bible is still right',* are a highly questionable undertaking from the start. But the important thing about these historically uncontrollable narratives is that events are at issue here, and not Being, and that these events are in closest connection with the ones which take place on the historical level. In like manner, the events of the Eschaton, inasmuch as it speaks of historical upheavals and events before the divine throne, are beyond historical control. But here again an *event*, not a human situation, is involved, an event in which the same divine motives operate as in the saving event on the historical level.

It is very significant indeed that in Jesus' preaching about the end in the Synoptics there are only descriptions of events of the end time, and not the human situations in it. Exceptions are the statement about not marrying (Mark 12.25 and parallels) and possibly those about the Messianic banquet (Matt. 8.11f.; Luke 13.28f.), which are meant to express the constant close association with Jesus.

The mythical features included in the central portion of biblical history also serve to clarify the saving character of historical events. To be sure, they have to do with historically uncontrollable events; still, these matters are occurrences that must be understood as *events*,

---

'The Problem of Hermeneutics', *Essays Philosophical and Theological*, 1955, p. 260, asks, 'What does Barth understand by [*Geschehen*] and [*Geschichte*]?' Much in fact would be gained in mutual understanding if Bultmann could accept *such* an historical occurrence (*Geschehen*).

[1] R. Prenter, 'Die Einheit von Schöpfung und Erlösung', *TZ*, p. 166, is in favour of this view.

* (Translator's note: '*Die Bibel hat doch recht*', the title of a book by the German newsman, Werner Keller.)

even though on another level. All the statements about the conquered 'angelic powers' belong in this context. It is an unrelinquishable New Testament conviction that things inaccessible to empirical investigation really *happen* in that province which correspond with historically verifiable events.[1] It would be wrong to conclude from our heavy emphasis upon temporality that we may deny the New Testament assumption of a world *beyond*. But this world must not be conceived as metaphysical and non-temporal; it must be included in the *temporal* process.

Similarly, in the resurrection accounts of the canonical Gospels, the *occurrence* of Jesus' resurrection, which is not itself accessible to historical control, and not described in the Gospels, is linked with facts at least theoretically provable within the historical framework —the resurrection appearances and the empty tomb. The preaching of the resurrection itself is merely one possible interpretation of these facts. Only the apocryphal Gospels tell about the occurrence itself with the use of mythological elements. The canonical Gospels are satisfied with the simple statement interpreting those facts: Christ is risen. But even here the essential thing again is that this statement concerns a divine event, incapable of historical demonstration. Furthermore, it is an integral feature of the New Testament resurrection accounts that they bind the level of the historically uncontrollable so closely with that of the historically verifiable that certain historical events which can be interpreted quite differently on the historical level become a confirmation of the divine event of the resurrection. Thus the resurrection accounts indicate that the divine occurrence is revealed in empirical events. The linking of the historically controllable and the historically uncontrollable levels belongs to the matrix of the New Testament message, proclaiming that at this high-point in salvation history, in the life of the incarnate Jesus, heaven and earth make contact in a special way.

The same union of historically controllable and historically uncontrollable elements is present in the New Testament birth stories of Matthew and Luke. These stories do not show the reticence of the resurrection accounts about what is historically uncontrollable. At least by way of allusion they tell 'how' the Son of God is born.[2] But

[1] The Apocalypse presupposes historical occurrences taking place on two different levels (cf. especially the 'angels' of the churches, Rev. 1–3).
[2] How reserved the childhood stories of the canonical Gospels are in this respect is shown by comparison with the *Protevangelium of James*, chs. 17ff.

here again it is important that a divine event is communicated to reveal the divine origin of a historically verifiable event in the activity of Jesus' life.

If we note that it was important to the biblical writers to emphasize the character even of the historically unverifiable saving occurrence as an event, and if we glance back at the origin of the salvation-historical perspective, we understand why they used myths for interpretation. By virtue of their narrative form, myths may be historicized in the way mentioned earlier. Even though in *pre*-biblical myth this narrative form often has only the objectifying role of representing human situations, the biblical writers surely chose it for another reason, because they felt that this narrative character was particularly suited to speak of the happening referred to by the events which were historically accessible to them. For this happening they could find support neither in their own eyewitnessing nor in that of others.

Of course, they did not take this association of the historically verifiable with the historically non-verifiable, which we call mythical, so far by their lack of a developed historical sense that they did not distinguish at all between the two levels. In this regard they retained a naive way of thought, and we shall see that for the modern exegete this presents a problem in separating the two levels, from which he cannot extricate himself with the excuse of the difficulty implicit in the complex way in which the two are intertwined.[1]

Thus, the creation narratives also to a large extent belong to a complex of myths traceable in the broad stream of non-biblical religions. These myths originally offered a cosmogony free from all history, partly to satisfy a purely speculative interest, partly to depict human situations in narrative form. But despite the formal incapacity of the biblical writers to distinguish between the two levels, on the premises of the Bible, the creation story still assumes a quite different character. As a result of its association with the historical central portion, which is at the same time significant for the whole saving process, the interweaving of the two levels ceases to be merely naive and acquires essentially a deeper meaning. The account of creation now fulfils the function of indicating the solidarity of creation with man and its tie to salvation history which comes to pass because of human sin.

---

[1] See below pp. 148f., 192. See also above pp. 95f.

The final, still less the most important word is not said by showing that the Bible, even the Old Testament, did not distinguish between the two levels of history and myth. Even though we stress the non-historical character of the account of the first man's sin we still maintain all the more firmly that this story offers a revelation just as the historical events of the Bible do. It is not revelation about the sinful *situation* of man,[1] but revelation about an *original event* in which man resisted his divinely appointed destiny. So we cannot abandon the Pauline remarks in Rom. 5.12ff., that our sinning is dependent upon a primeval event. That is a fundamental theological element which cannot be given up in the historicizing of myth. The historicized myth incorporated into salvation history in this way ceases to be an actual myth.

Thus in the Old Testament, for instance in Deutero-Isaiah[2] and the Psalms,[3] creation is connected with Israel's election. In early Christianity this historicizing, even of the creation narrative, is carried much further than in the Old Testament. Since the entire saving process has its high-point in the fulfilment of Israel's election in the one man Jesus Christ, the entire saving process is a Christ event. The association of myth and history is now so close that the historicized creation myths are no longer placed merely alongside or prior to history. The creation story is told anew in the Gospel of John as creation through the Logos who is identical with the incarnate Christ. This Gospel, beginning with the same words as Genesis, ἐν ἀρχῇ (*b^ereshith*), presents a new account of creation in the light of the Lord whose decisive saving acts are recounted in the twenty chapters that follow. Furthermore, in the remainder of the New Testament the creation is spoken of in this way. The important matter now is the role of the mediator of creation, 'the Son', to whom the creation of heaven and earth is ascribed as the work of his hands (Heb. 1.10). The story of Adam's fall appears in Paul in the light of the one who as second Adam fulfils in obedience the task which

---

[1] At any rate this is not its primary purpose as in myth apart from the Bible, even though this original intention of myth shines through in a secondary fashion. The aspect depicted here was not noted by P. Ricoeur, who in various works attempts to come to a new understanding of biblical myths from the philosophical side. See for instance his 'Herméneutique des symboles et réflexion philosophique', *Il problema della demitizzazione*, edited by E. Castelli, 1961, also appearing in *Kerygma und Mythos*, Bd. VI, 1.

[2] For instance, Isa. 51.9ff.

[3] For example, Pss. 65.8; 89.10ff.

God assigned to man when he created him in his image, a task to which man became unfaithful in disobedience through the primal sin (I Cor. 15.46; Rom. 5.12ff., and especially Phil. 2.6ff.[1]). The myth is, as it were, disrobed of its substance as myth by historicization.

In Rom. 8.19ff. the solidarity of creation with the whole saving process is carried up to the period of salvation history in which Paul lived. The creation already shares in the consequences of Christ's work, which are made known as an expression of the Holy Spirit. The Spirit moves creation to groaning that simply bears witness to the hopeful expectation of the deliverance of every creature from the deathly power of the σάρξ. In the same way, the Synoptics speak of cosmic signs (darkness and earthquakes)[2] at the place where the historical saving process reaches its high-point. All these mythical features in the Bible serve to manifest the awesome importance of the saving process, which has cosmic dimensions.

For this reason I do not believe it is exegetically proper to seek an understanding of Being as the essential core in the primeval myths *as they have been worked over in the Bible*. At bottom, the procedure of the Bultmann school is not demythologizing, but dehistoricizing, and thus a *remythologizing*, so far as those primeval myths are concerned. Here again the myths are dealt with as if they were separate myths, in which one may indeed find an expression of an understanding of Being.

The myths of the *eschaton* are also consistently historicized in the New Testament. This is the significance of Paul's associating the resurrection of the dead completely with the resurrection of Jesus of Nazareth, 'the first fruits of those who have fallen asleep'.[3] Therefore, everything said about our future resurrection body in the same chapter of the letter to the Corinthians must be understood against the background of faith in the bodily resurrection of Christ, that is, in an event. Furthermore, the historicizing of all the eschatological myths is accomplished by equating the appearance of the Son of Man expected by Daniel on the clouds of heaven (Dan. 7.13) with

---

[1] See O. Cullmann, *The Christology of the New Testament*, 1959, pp. 174ff.

[2] Apart from the Bible, see the hymn inserted into ch. 18 of the *Protevangelium of James*. The hymn tells how nature stood still at the moment of Jesus' birth. The Bible attests to a link between salvation history and creation which does not seem to me to be heeded by Teilhard de Chardin.

[3] I Cor. 15.12ff.; see also the description, 'first-born from the dead', Col. 1.18; cf. Col. 1.15; Rom. 8.29.

the returning Jesus of Nazareth.[1] Now all eschatological events are dependent upon the one who was on earth. They are connected with the work accomplished by the incarnate Lord. The cosmic events, related for instance in the Synoptic apocalypse (Mark 13 and parallels), coincide with the Lord's penetration of the spheres of the astral world on his return. When at his return he passes through the cosmic sphere, the tremendous upheavals mentioned in the Synoptic apocalypse will occur, to usher in a new creation. He is its mediator as he is mediator of the first creation. If the historical life of Jesus is really the centre of all history, the same Jesus must also be the mediator of the events of the end time.

The future expectation is, of course, important for all early Christian thinking, and consequently in interpreting the New Testament message it is necessary to take eschatology into account in the form of an expectation of an imminent end, as Albert Schweitzer does. Still, it must not be forgotten (not only in the question of the origin of the salvation-historical perspective in the New Testament, but also in that of understanding it) that eschatology is determined primarily by its connection with historical events and not *vice versa*.[2] If salvation at the significant climax of the decisive mid-point of history is an event, it must also hasten towards its consummation, and the *essential* factor for the mid-point of history must come to its consummation at the end.[3] This finds its clearest expression in the Apocalypse, where it is the *slaughtered* lamb that appears (Rev. 5.6 and elsewhere). On the other hand, the expectation of the eschatological consummation yet to come expresses the meaning of all history in such a perfect way that an interaction appears here, and now light from eschatology falls back upon the central portion of history.

Nothing shows more clearly how fundamental the thought of a *process unfolding* within as well as beyond historical time is for all salvation history in the Bible than the very close connection between

[1] Following Glasson, J. A. T. Robinson, *Jesus and His Coming*, 1957, p. 22, rightly noted that in Daniel the Son of Man on the clouds does not descend to earth, but ascends to God. But as soon as the Son of Man is identified with Jesus of Nazareth (or if Jesus identified himself with him, as I think he did), his eschatological coming *must* become a coming to earth. See below pp. 225f.

[2] See p. 14 of N. A. Dahl's article, 'Eschatologie und Geschichte im Lichte der Qumrantexte', which I cited above p. 79 n. 1.

[3] Again and again I must call attention to the fact that I do not understand the 'mid-point of time' in terms of a chronological mid-point, as though it divided the whole saving process into two chronological sections of equal length.

futuristic myths and historically controllable events. A saving process so conceived must continue on to the end,[1] and cannot be concluded where its high-point is attained, so long as its unfolding has not touched every creature. How the present, lying between the historical central period and the eschatological future, finds its place in this continuing movement, we shall see later.

The question could arise whether the expected event of the *eschaton* will take place partly in the framework of political events of the future, such as the destruction of the temple, or in a cosmic event, which myth alone could describe. However, this question is without primary significance for the total salvation-historical perspective of early Christianity because the cosmic myths are historicized and placed in a relation to Jesus' resurrection and the coming of the Holy Spirit who transforms the whole creation into the new creation (Rom. 8.19ff.; I Cor. 15.35ff.; Rev. 21.5).

For this reason, the manner in which political predictions and cosmic prophecy about the future lie side by side may not be used as a pointer for literary source criticism within the Synoptic apocalypse.

As has often been indicated in this chapter already, this demythologizing, already undertaken by the biblical writers in their work of historicization, does not excuse the exegete from distinguishing *between the historical and non-historical levels* in his interpretation for the modern reader. Obviously this distinction was not only impossible for a biblical writer, but also unimportant. The important thing for him was to show that the historical saving process is the centre of *all* history, including primeval and eschatological history. However, for our modern thinking, the distinction between the two levels is unavoidable. We must show here how the historicized myth serves to interpret the historical events, which must be distinguished from the myth itself, by extending the historical process to the non-historical level as well. This is necessary, not only because our modern knowledge requires us to separate historically controllable and historically uncontrollable events from each other, but also in order to set ourselves back, so to speak, into the situation in which the first witnesses found themselves. Only when we have learned what interpretation (extended to the non-historical level) and historical event are, shall we be in a position to see revelation both *in interpretation and in the*

---

[1] Cf. J. Moltmann, 'Exegese und Eschatologie der Geschichte', *EvT*, 1962, pp. 31–66. Unfortunately, I could not use his most recent book, *Theology of Hope*, ET 1967.

historical event. Then we shall recognize that the historical event as such is revelation for the prophets and the apostles and caused them to form their interpretations. Revelation takes place in both event and interpretation.[1] The task of advancing by means of modern methods of research to find out what really happened historically may not be renounced because of a theological interest. The problem of making this historical judgment is difficult because of the close dovetailing of history and interpretation, history and myth; but this difficulty may in no case justify its renunciation. It is probably impossible to arrive at completely certain results by historical-critical exegesis. This is true, as we have seen, in the question of the 'historical Jesus'. The effort to separate history and interpretation in the use of historical-critical criteria is unavoidable, even though these may still be problematic. Indeed this effort is imperative if one is to see how revelation and salvation are given not only in the interpretation employing myths, but *in history itself* (and not simply in the encounter directed at my self-understanding). If we attempt first of all to separate the two levels, we shall understand the theological importance of their being intertwined in the Bible, as we have already attempted to do at certain points.

For example, to understand what is meant in the New Testament when Christ is contrasted with Adam, we shall start from the fact that for us Adam does not belong on the same level as Jesus of Nazareth, and we shall distinguish the two levels at the point where the New Testament traces Jesus' genealogy back to Adam. In this way we shall be open to the connection existing between the two levels from a salvation-historical, divine vantage point, which is the important thing to the biblical writers.

In this *legitimate* sense, demythologizing has always been undertaken by all sound exegesis long before the slogan fascinated a whole generation of theologians. It was not previously practised according to a standard derived from an extra-biblical myth aided by existentialist philosophy, rather than one derived from biblical salvation history. Demythologization of the Bible is legitimate only so long as it continues in the same way as the historicizing demythologization in the Bible itself. That is, it must indicate more clearly *the relationship*

[1] Important and interesting for this relationship is the controversy between G. v. Rad, F. Hesse, and W. Eichrodt. Cf. the preface to the second volume of G. v. Rad's *Old Testament Theology*, and also A. Soggin, 'Geschichte, Historie, und Heilsgeschehen im Alten Testament', *TLZ*, 1964, cols. 721ff.

of the biblical myths to history in the framework of the Bible's salvation history by distinguishing the *levels* of myth and history, in order to work out more clearly what is *positively* common to both. The important thing theologically is not the inability of the biblical writers to separate the two levels from each other, but rather their deep understanding in faith that the biblical event which has come to pass in history is the centre of all history and therefore also includes a revelation about world history at its beginning and end. It is theologically important that these writers placed an *event*, and not a state of Being, at the beginning and at the end. The interpretation of the life of Jesus concerns the history of human sin; and the effect of this life of Jesus is extended to the creation. For this reason there must be a divine process at the beginning and end of history which speaks of sin as an original event and in connection with that tells of a cosmic event at the beginning and of a new creation at the end.

We shall rightly understand the Bible's *intention* in the use of myths when, departing from the Bible, we separate the two levels, but afterwards, *with* the Bible, rightly understand their common functions, placing the whole saving process in the light of the saving revelation in Jesus of Nazareth.

Demythologizing in the biblical sense does not mean eliminating salvation history, but, on the contrary, deepening it.

2. NEW TESTAMENT SALVATION HISTORY AND HISTORY

Many misunderstandings in the debate about New Testament salvation history are due to a failure to take account of the relation between salvation history and history. This is true both for those who regard salvation history as representing the essence of the New Testament message and for those who see in it simply a secondary construction that must be eliminated. It cannot be disputed that at least some advocates of the classical school of salvation history of the last century failed to pose this question sharply enough, sometimes directly imposing Hegel's view of history on salvation history. Despite all his services, perhaps even Schlatter contributed to the discredit of salvation history by not carrying through quite clearly the distinction between history and salvation history. Recently W. Pannenberg has worked on the problem,[1] but seems to me to fail to take note of some essential items.

However, the failure of the theologians on this point in no case justifies running to the opposite extreme, condemning wholesale every attempt to understand the Bible in terms of salvation history. Nor does it justify the current adversaries of salvation history in their neglect to ask what separates biblical salvation history from history and what the two have in common,[2] rebuking without hesitation anyone who speaks of the history of salvation for confusing the two entities.

That a radical distinction exists between history and salvation history follows from the connection of history and myth which we indicated in the previous chapter. Such an amalgamation of historically verifiable and non-verifiable events is excluded from the province of secular history. For secular history, historical events are not interpreted by their relationship to a wholly different event, occurring on a non-historical level, which is nevertheless thought to be just as real as the events it interprets. A fundamental distinction exists here *a priori*. For this reason, we began our exposition of the characteristics of New Testament salvation history by throwing that characteristic association into relief.

In what follows, we shall now compare the historically verifiable elements of the Bible's salvation history, that is, what we have called the historical central portion, with history. It could appear that biblical history was history *per se*, apart from its primeval history and its eschatology. In this chapter caution is urged against this error, at the same time, however, still paying heed to what is common to the two.

We shall not at this point return to what was said earlier about the *origin* of the Bible's description and view of history. We recall that a secular view of history does not originate in the same way as the biblical perspective. To be sure, both have a double origin—accounts found in sources and one's own experiences of events. Both go back to facts and their interpretation. With respect to their *origins*, however, the thing that distinguishes history from salvation history is the role played by revelation in salvation history, both in the

[1] 'Heilsgeschehen und Geschichte', *KuD*, 1959, pp. 218ff., 259ff. Partial ET in *Essays in Old Testament Interpretation*, edited by C. Westermann, 1963, pp. 314ff.

[2] K. Löwith, in *Meaning in History*, gives an exciting presentation of the older theological treatment of the problem in a philosophical perspective.

experiencing of events and facts, and in the appropriation of the accounts and their interpretation ('*kerygma*') through faith. Here events are experienced as divine revelation,[1] and likewise the accounts and interpretations are ascribed to divine revelation.

Thus we are no longer occupied with the question of origins in the progressive development of the salvation-historical perspective in the Bible. We turn instead to study the characteristics which both unite and distinguish what we call history (*Historie*) and the central portion of salvation history presented as a finished entity in the Bible. We shall come back later[2] to the important question touched on earlier[3] of whether the divine plan presupposed by salvation history is reconcilable with general historical contingency. Before doing this, we shall call attention to other points which become relevant in a comparison of historical contingency and salvation history. The finished portrayal (interpretation) of an excerpt of salvation history is far more closely linked to the causes (event and interpretation) of its origin than is the case in secular history. This is because the *act of revelation* as a saving event is always included in salvation history and therefore is included in the narration of salvation history.[4] The developmental character constitutive of *all* history appears even more prominently in salvation history, to the extent that here the development of the *view* of history itself belongs to the development of the *events* of history.

Thus, we find that first of all salvation history has in common with history a *sequence* of events somehow connected. At least there is a noticeable *analogy* here, which despite all the differences justifies our speaking of salvation *history*.

Furthermore, the individual events constituting the historical central portion *take place completely within the historical framework*. This is particularly evident in the Old Testament, where primarily the history of a people is involved, a history which is, of course, closely linked with the history of neighbouring peoples and world empires in particular.

In the New Testament, whose concern is the life of a man and then

---

[1] Here again the point must be stressed against G. Klein (see above p. 91) and others as well that obviously the events are not revelation for non-believers of and by themselves, just as the *kerygma* is not revelation for non-believers. But *for the believer*, not only the *kerygma*, but also the *event as such* is revelation.

[2] See below pp. 158f. and p. 161.

[3] See above pp. 123ff.

[4] See above pp. 89.

of a small community, the saving process is not coupled with the history of the times in the same measure. Still, even here this process unfolds quite within the framework of general history whose course we perceive from afar. We hear of Herod the Great and his sons and successors, but also of the Roman Empire, of Caesar Augustus, of the census, of Tiberius, of Roman governors and proconsuls—Pontius Pilate, Felix, Festus, and Gallio. They are mentioned only on the periphery, but that is enough to remind us that events in which a divine plan is revealed to the Christians have history as a background, even if these events may have been quite insignificant for those who 'made history' at the time.

Also indicative of this is the question of Zealotism, a purely political consideration with which Jesus had to deal daily.[1] It has a very close relationship to the centre of salvation history, since Jesus was crucified as a Zealot. The conquest of Jerusalem appears in Jesus' message for the future only as a prediction like the prophetic predictions of the Old Testament. Although many books of the New Testament were written after the fact was historically accomplished,[2] remarkably, it is nowhere reported as such. Still, it must have claimed the attention of Christian thought, and we find at least traces of it in many New Testament passages.

A positive relationship to history in general is established by the fact that salvation history involves a sequence of events taking place within history. Salvation history is therefore not a history *alongside* history (a notion that has wrongly been attributed to me[3]); it unfolds in history, and in this sense belongs to it.

As soon as we examine this sequence more closely, fundamental distinctions arise, proving that despite this contact, salvation history and history can in no case be equated. The events constituting salvation history indeed run in a *chronological* sequence as do those of history. But whereas events of history unfold as a general chrono-logical, historical sequence without interruption, and the record of them is accordingly set down without any gaps, it is essential to

---

[1] Cf. O. Cullmann, *The State in the New Testament*, 1956, and M. Hengel, *Die Zeloten, Untersuchung zur jüdischen Freiheitsbewegung in der Zeit von Herodes I. bis 70 n. Chr.*, 1961.

[2] Apart from S. G. F. Brandon, *The Fall of Jerusalem and the Christian Church*, 1951, New Testament scholars have not paid sufficient heed to this question up to now.

[3] E. Grässer, *op. cit.*, p. 15 n. 4, does this through a misunderstanding of my book, *Christ and Time*.

biblical salvation history that it shows *gaps* which are quite remarkable from an historical standpoint, and which unfold entirely by leaps. *Isolated events appear differentiated and sorted out of the total historical process, historically speaking, in an arbitrary way.* Nevertheless, a *connection* exists between them. However, this connection cannot be defined according to immanent historical perspectives nor according to views taken from a philosophy of history. We have seen that the understanding of this selection and connection is traced back to the progressing divine revelation in events and the interpretation of them. The result of this revelation interests us here. All biblical salvation history rests upon the tacit presupposition that the selection of events is reached by the decision of God, and that the principle of this selection, that is, their being placed in connection with each other, is determined in the *plan of God.* The selection and association of events in which God brings about salvation both rest upon the completely irrational theological idea of the divine *election*, which cannot be proved. God elects a people for the salvation of mankind, and in this people he chooses the remnant, and finally the one man; then the Church of those believing in the one man enters into this election for the salvation of all. Therefore *this* history must run its course in a completely different fashion from history in general, even though it unfolds in world history and is constantly in a real relationship to it, as we have seen. Hence there are great chronological gaps within this process, completely inexplicable for history and philosophies of history. These gaps do not exist merely within one and the same period. Whole periods as such are 'bypassed'.

Within the Old Testament these gaps are less apparent, because here the history of the elected people of Israel is involved. The bearer of salvation history is a people in its entire course of history. The divine election consists primarily in the fact that all history, even that of other peoples, is placed in the light of this people elected for the salvation of mankind. The whole course of the history of Israel represents *grosso modo* the history of salvation. The same events would not be represented by the secular historian as the history of the *elect* people, but would be connected with the histories of other peoples. Thus, the accents are at any rate differently distributed, and therefore neither the salvation history of Israel nor the description of it simply coincides with the history of Israel. Even in the case of Israel's own history, according to biblical faith, a selection of specific events takes place, some of which are verified by the secular historian, but are thought to be hardly worth mentioning. On the other hand, other events of supreme importance for the historian are hardly worth noting so far as salvation history is concerned.

The divine selection of a few events out of the total historical process by virtue of the reduction of election to the central event of the mid-point makes itself felt even more forcefully in the New Testament. The history of the whole people of Israel is no longer at issue here. The progressive reduction,[1] already present in the prophets, particularly in their stress upon the 'remnant', attains its decisive point in the New Testament. The story of the life of one man, Jesus Christ, appears in place of the history of one people as the fulfiller of Israel's history. After that come the events of the life of the little community that takes Israel's place as the people of God. So now, the divine selection of a few events out of the whole of history appears more clearly for two reasons: first, much of what occurs even *within* the life of Jesus and the Church does not belong directly to the divine saving and is bypassed. Second, the shift in accent contrary to historical principles becomes apparent particularly in the New Testament.

This 'bypassing' is illustrated in the description of the life of Jesus. The four evangelists of the New Testament have in common with one another the telling of only a small excerpt from the life of Jesus, because they are convinced that only in the quite specific events of this life which they now report did God bring about salvation. For Mark, the Gospel (and thus the actual salvation history) begins with the baptism of Jesus. Matthew and Luke include his birth because, by virtue of revelation, they, like the writer of the Fourth Gospel in another way, see the divine saving event in operation in Jesus' incarnation in an especially striking way. However, a large gap opens up between the birth and the baptism of Jesus. The story of the twelve year old Jesus in the temple (Luke 2.41–52), as well as the short note at the end of the Lucan birth story, 'The child grew and became strong, filled with wisdom' (2.40), are not able to fill this gap.[2] Only the apocryphal Gospels were interested in these 'gaps', trying by means of various legends to fill them in. This is evident in

---

[1] Cf. O. Cullmann, *Christ and Time*, 3rd ed., 1962, pp. 115ff.

[2] Thus W. Schmithals, 'Paulus und der historische Jesus', *ZNW*, 1962, pp. 145–60, has exaggerated the difference between Paul and the Gospels, inasmuch as the Gospels are also interested in just the narrow time line during the life of the 'historical Jesus'.

all the apocryphal Gospels and is perhaps especially clear in the Gospels dealing with Christ's childhood.[1] Thus the Gospel of Thomas[2] gives an account of Jesus' boyhood years. With their interest in filling in the 'gaps', the apocryphal writings merely prove that they have not understood anything about the essence of the divine salvation history, and that they do not know that the εὐαγγέλιον, like all salvation history, rests upon the *divine selection* of events within the whole of history.

The writer of the Fourth Gospel, unlike the apocryphal writers, strongly emphasized this. At the end of his book (20.30f.) he expressly notes that Jesus accomplished many other 'signs' not written in this book. He adds in the next verse, 'these are written that you may believe that Jesus is the Christ, the Son of God . . .', thereby showing that he reports only those things in which he sees the divine saving work intended to become the object of faith. We shall see[3] that the Gospel of John, contrary to the generally accepted notion, depicts the life of Jesus as *salvation history* in a quite obvious manner. So it should not surprise us that this book understood so completely the main characteristic of all salvation history, the divine selection of a few events, and that in this respect it is distinguished from the apocryphal Gospels in a quite definite way.

What is true in the case of the Gospels is also true of the various Acts of the Apostles. As opposed to Luke's work, the apocryphal Acts of the Apostles show their complete lack of understanding of God's selection in salvation history. They are not satisfied with the facts that Luke reports. The latter limits himself to the points at which he sees the working of the Holy Spirit. The omissions in the canonical Book of Acts which impede so much our understanding of the historical picture of the early Church are due to the fact that not all the events of the early Church were revealed to Luke as saving ones. This may be the reason why events so important from the historical standpoint as the deaths of Peter and Paul are not narrated. Thereby Luke shows that he understood the main distinction between salvation history and history: salvation history belongs, to be sure, to history, but still is not to be identified with it, since it forms only a narrow line within history.

[1] See O. Cullmann, 'Infancy Gospels', in Schneemelcher—Hennecke—Wilson, *New Testament Apocrypha* I, 1963, pp. 363ff.

[2] Not to be confused with the newly found Coptic Gnostic Gospel of Thomas.

[3] See below pp. 268ff.

We could extend the same observations to the apocalypses, in which similarly the limitation to real *saving events* of the future is to be regarded as the criterion of the legitimacy of these 'revelations'. Anything that simply satisfies curiosity, apart from any interest in salvation, deserves the derogatory estimate often wrongly extended to *all* apocalyptic.[1]

The 'gaps' relative to the rest of history that are found in the New Testament, which no longer tells merely the history of a people, are much more extensive than in the Old Testament. Not only this, but the distance of salvation history from history is greater to the extent that the different *shifting of accent* referred to above is made far more noticeable here. All the events of the New Testament were, in fact, quite uninteresting for those who 'made history' in those days, although they took place within the historical framework. Even the event that is the centre of all revealed saving events, the execution of Jesus of Nazareth condemned to death as a Zealot, was no more than a sundry news item. In the news reports of the time it would have probably been put under a heading on the equivalent of the crime page of one of our newspapers. Even less attention was given to occurrences attributed by the Christians to the Holy Spirit: healings, the sharing of property, the missionary message, its acceptance and rejection.[2] Still, in all of this, historically verifiable events are involved. In certain events like those narrated in I Cor. 15.3ff. it is essential to their saving character that their historical verification be attested. Hence the witness is handed on with great chronological precision ($K\eta\phi\tilde{q}$ . . . $\epsilon\tilde{\iota}\tau a$ . . . $\tilde{\epsilon}\pi\epsilon\iota\tau a$ . . .). Related to this is the fact that the very concept of the office of apostle is linked with the verification of historical facts.[3]

The salvation history of the Old Testament, more closely coupled with secular history, is appropriated by the first Christians into the New Testament and is taken over as a whole. At the same time, from an historical standpoint, a very great *chronological gap* becomes visible, *extending from the last Old Testament prophet to John the Baptist*. Here it is no longer just a matter of bypassing a series of events within a period. Rather, in the New Testament salvation-historical perspective, which

[1] See above pp. 8off.
[2] For the conception of the Pauline mission as a saving occurrence see O. Cullmann, 'Le caractère eschatologique du devoir missionaire et de la conscience apostolique de saint Paul. Étude sur le $\kappa a\tau\epsilon\chi\omega\nu$ (−$o\nu$) de II Thess. 2.6–7', *RHPR* 16, 1936, pp. 210–45, and J. Munck, *Paul and the Salvation of Mankind*, 1959.
[3] See what is said above pp. 91 and 102f. on the eye witness of the apostle.

also begins with the creation of the world and ends with the new creation, a *whole period*, so to speak, drops out. In this period things happened which were important to secular history and the history of the Jewish people, but not a single one of them is salvation history for the New Testament. Thus, we hear nothing in the New Testament of the Qumran sect, important for history as it is.

We shall later discuss the question of whether the gap between the last of the Old Testament prophets and John the Baptist provides an analogy to our own time, lying as it does between the end of the apostolic age and what is revealed in the New Testament about the end time yet to come.

Up to now we have spoken of a divine selection of events. We have seen that the *connection* between these events, selected arbitrarily from an historical standpoint, is revealed progressively to the prophets and apostles, and in the New Testament is attributed to a divine plan. If it were the case that this divine plan determined in advance the course of events in all their details in a fixed way, then one could hardly speak of a salvation *history*. In fact, it has been said that the concept of salvation *history* is completely unsuited to describe what is intended, because contingency, the feature which constitutes all history, is lacking in it. But here we must remember what we have said about the developmental character of all salvation history, and it now becomes clear why we have placed so much stress on it. In salvation history we are in fact dealing with the amalgamation of a constant, namely, the divine plan, with a contingency, that is, the development of divine, individual events, unforeseen by this plan itself (above all, the opposition to God's plan). This seems to me to be of fundamental importance to the whole discussion of salvation history.

Within salvation history we find clarifying corrections called forth by new saving events. If everything were really prescribed in the plan previously given, then the *events* themselves would no longer really mean revelation and salvation. Then the divine plan, the Word, would be everything. *In the course of* salvation history, however, the divine plan, as it was revealed through earlier events and interpretations, is clarified by later unforeseen ones, is set into a new perspective, and transformed in its presentation. Thus we see the way in which constant and contingency go together in the prediction of salvation and judgment in the Old Testament. More particularly, on the New Testament level, we gain a true perspective on the complex described by theologians as the delay of the *parousia*.

It is quite essential to the biblical salvation history that constant and contingency are not mutually exclusive. This is the way in which the problem of 'predestination and freedom' is posed in the area of salvation history. Although salvation history is quite different from history, because of what has been said above we may and must still speak of history in relation to it. This does away with the objection that the salvation-historical understanding of the Bible leaves no place for any kind of 'decision'.[1]

This is also the reason why the movement of the Bible's salvation history is not exactly described by the expression 'promise and fulfilment'. In reality, the progressing development again and again surpasses the promise.

In John 14.12, a promise itself refers to this fact: 'He who believes in me will also do the works that I do; and greater works than these will he do . . .' The question must be raised here whether the new creation will surpass the first creation. This purely speculative problem is, of course, never dealt with as such in the New Testament. But the christological hymn in Phil. 2.6ff. implicitly contains an answer to it when it uses the term ὑπερύψωσεν in v. 9, which is more than merely a rhetorical formula. Christ receives more by virtue of his obedience than Adam lost with his disobedience: more than being in the image of God (μορφή = εἰκών = d^emuth), namely, being equal with God, a status given with the position as Lord.[2] Apart from this passage, the whole Pauline eschatology assumes that the believer, when he partakes of the divine δόξα and receives imperishability, will at the end have more than the first man. The first man possessed life along with his being in the image of God, and he was not subject to death. But he could lose this life, and he could become mortal.

Up to now we have dealt with the *formal* side of the relationship between salvation history and history, and we have come to the conclusion that the divine selection of the one people and of the individual events following from this selection is not at all historically conditioned, and yet is revealed completely in history and becomes effective in it. The study of the *theological* relationship to the subject will confirm this complex connection between both and will indicate their deeper anchorage. In view of the fact that God's election proceeds in a completely free way, it cannot be grasped from an historical

---

[1] Thus G. Klein, 'Offenbarung als Geschichte? Marginalien zu einem theologischen Programm', *Monatsschrift für Pastoraltheologie*, 1962, pp. 65ff. On the question of decision, see below pp. 196f. and above pp. 102f.

[2] J. Héring, *Le Royaume de Dieu et sa venue*, 1937, p. 163, and O. Cullmann, *The Christology of the New Testament*, 1959, pp. 176f.

standpoint why Israel in particular was elected and why Christ did not appear among some other people. But the election of God is toward a goal—the salvation *of all mankind*. Hence, from the beginning an intrinsic link exists between salvation history and history. Because of this relationship, we can speak of salvation history in the wider sense along with the actual salvation history which is the object of our study.[1] The progressive divine reduction is completely non-historical, and yet is the principle of all biblical salvation history.[2] Its direction is: creation, mankind, Israel, the remnant, the one man. Then it returns again towards multiplicity: apostles, first community, Church made up of Jews and Gentiles, world. This movement from the beginning had *all mankind* in view. Israel is elected for the salvation of humanity. Because mankind is envisaged from the outset through the concept of the election of Israel, humanity remains in a salvation-historical perspective throughout its entire extent. This is why the Old Testament never loses sight of the history of the Gentiles, despite its limitation to the history of one people. This is not merely because it makes up the framework for what takes place among the elected people, but because, historically speaking, in an utter reversal of perspectives, they now are seen and understood in the light of this little people. The more or less tacit presupposition of all salvation history becomes clear in the Old Testament eschatological hope. The Gentiles at the end come to Jerusalem, of course, in subjection. In the transformation of this eschatological expectation from its first beginnings in the Old Testament to the expectation of the Kingdom of God in the New, what we said about the developments, clarifications, and corrections of biblical salvation history is again confirmed. Above all, the way in which constant and historical contingency lie side by side is confirmed as well.

Humanity and its history are never lost sight of in the New Testament sphere. It might appear at first sight that a concentration on the history of the life of one man and then on a tiny community might discourage theological interest in the world at large, and that it might be considered merely as a framework for the events of the new covenant. In reality, it is the case that the narrower the framework of salvation history becomes, the *wider the salvation-historical influence radiates*. In the universal extension of salvation history, the

---

[1] Cf. K. Rahner's remarks, *op. cit.*, and those of J. Feiner, *op. cit.*, on the relationship of 'special salvation history' to 'general salvation history'.

[2] See O. Cullmann, *Christ and Time*, pp. 115ff.

principle of *election* remains the foundation without which every universalism loses all relationship with the Bible. Anyone who does not grasp the principle of election can understand nothing of salvation history.

This is why during the second session of the Second Vatican Council a number of bishops could not understand why in one of the texts formulated at the Council the Jewish people were not discussed in the same way as those adhering to other non-Christian religions. There is in fact no reason to make a distinction between Jews and other non-Christians apart from their relationship to salvation history.

God's election is the consequence of the *sin* of men. Apart from human sin, the whole history of salvation would be unintelligible. The sin of all leads to the election of some, with the salvation of all as its purpose. But sin does not stand simply at the beginning of the divine plan of salvation. It continually resists the history of salvation. Consequently the whole salvation history is at the same time conditioned by the constant of this plan and the contingency of history. In the New Testament, God makes use of both sin and unbelief to carry out his plan of salvation and to realize his universal purpose—to bring the whole of history into salvation history (cf. the Law for the sake of transgressions in Gal. 3.19; Rom. 5.20).

We must always see both aspects of salvation history—it aims at all humanity, and the means to realize this aim is the selection of a minority. Anyone who ignores the first aspect falls into a sectarianism foreign to the Bible. Anyone who ignores the second aspect falls into a syncretism equally foreign to the Bible.

The teaching that all humanity remains within the vision of the New Testament salvation history, now even more than it was at the beginning, may be traced through the whole New Testament. Although Jesus limits the missionary preaching to the lost sheep of Israel and commands the disciples, 'Go nowhere among the Gentiles, and enter no town of the Samaritans' (Matt. 10.5f.; cf. Mark 7.27), his whole attitude towards the Samaritans (Luke 9.51ff.; 10.50ff.; 17.11ff.) as well as towards the Gentiles (Matt. 8.5ff.; Mark 7.29) nevertheless shows that he is merely following the path to a saving plan that is ultimately universal. Consequently the first Christians who founded the mission among the Samaritans (John 4.35ff.;[1]

[1] See O. Cullmann, 'La Samarie et les origines de la mission chrétienne', *Annuaire 1953–1954 de l'École pratique des Hautes Études, Section des Sciences religieuses,* Paris, pp. 3–12; ET in *The Early Church,* pp. 185ff.

Acts 8.4ff.) and Gentiles correctly interpreted Jesus' own meaning in his sayings limiting the mission. The latter sayings were surely known to them from the tradition and were probably played off against them by the Jewish Christian opponents of the Gentile mission. It becomes especially clear in Paul's view of salvation history (Rom. 9–11) how in the plan of God the concentration of salvation history given in election ultimately has universalism as its goal. The one man Jesus is the *saviour of the world* (John 4.42).

Of course, early Christianity's missionary thinking, which consciously sees the Gentiles included in the saving process, does not have an actual interest in world history. But it shows not only how all history is always kept within the province of the saving process, but also how the strong New Testament concentration on a very narrow line running within history aims at funnelling all history into this line, merging all history into salvation history. Political history then becomes mission history. In the Old Testament, where the history of the Gentiles is seen only in the light of the salvation history of the one people Israel, there begins a development that is completed in the New. There the meaning and goal of all history is its eschatological entry into salvation history so that finally there will only be the saved πᾶς Ἰσραήλ (Rom. 11.26) comprising the converted Gentiles and the converted Israel. The development that as a consequence of the preaching of the Gospel the conversion of the whole Gentile world to faith in Christ displaces the eschatological streaming of the vanquished nations to Jerusalem, is in accord with what we have said about the clarifying and correcting reinterpretations which are given as salvation-historical events progress. Whereas in the Old Testament's political vision of the future the Gentile nations will at the end be joined to Israel, according to Paul the procedure is reversed. The Jews who still disbelieve will at the end be incorporated into the people composed of believing Jews and the full number of believing Gentiles. The earlier view of salvation is not thereby given up, since now all the nations enter into the salvation history given in the election of Israel. The saving way back from the one to the many is here complete. The narrow saving line has been expanded to the universe.[1]

This objective of the whole salvation history means that past and present political history, without being an actual salvation history,

[1] Cf. the exceptionally rich treatment in *Die apostolische und nachapostolische Zeit*, by L. Goppelt, 1955ff., in the series *Die Kirche in ihrer Geschichte*.

still enter into a factual relationship with salvation history. Thus pagan rulers indirectly become instruments of the divine plan of salvation, either as unconscious scourges of Yahweh, as in the early prophets, or as unconscious mediators of salvation, as Cyrus in Deutero-Isaiah.[1] In early Christianity, an indirect role of the same kind is allotted to Herod and Pilate who, as unconscious instruments of the divine saving plan, crucify Christ, and against their own wills thereby contribute to the overthrow of the demonic 'powers' (I Cor. 2.6). The allusions to current history in the Apocalypse[2] refer to the persecution of the Church by the Roman rulers, who also have a place in the divine plan of salvation.

Apart from these indirect points of contact, the New Testament does not, of course, draw any direct lines leading from the history of the peoples of antiquity to salvation history. Still, Acts 14.16 mentions the Gentiles whom God allowed to go their own way, and in Paul's speech on Mars Hill (17.26) it is said that God determined for the Gentiles 'allotted periods and the boundaries of their habitation'. But here there is no relationship to salvation history in the narrower sense.

It would be exciting to attempt to show the *hidden* ways in which, *in the light of the biblical revelation*, the preparation for salvation history was made in the history of the Gentiles and their religions. At the same time it would have to be remembered that we are not on the same sure grounds as we are with our knowledge of the salvation history revealed in the Bible. But such an undertaking would be possible if we were constantly to orient ourselves in the strictest way by this norm given to us. We would thereby find ourselves in the same situation as when we determine the way in which salvation history unfolds in post-biblical time.[3] There, too, it is a question of a hidden saving process which we can attempt to disclose only with the help of the normative saving process in the Bible.

Thus, theoretically, one could visualize a history of religion which could actually be written in the light of the centre of the total revelation of the Bible. Such an attempt has not been undertaken since the apologists of the second century—I am thinking particularly of Justin Martyr.

Behind the post-Easter salvation-historical interest in the Gentiles stands the early Christian faith in the present *lordship* of Christ over the world. The world does not yet know that it is already ruled by

[1] Cf. E. Jenni, 'Die Rolle des Kyros bei Deuterojesaja', *TZ*, 1954, pp. 241ff.
[2] See S. Giet, *L'Apocalypse et l'Histoire*, 1957.
[3] This will be discussed in the last part of this book. See below p. 299.

Christ, for this lordship will be apparent only at the end and is still invisible. It is only visible to faith. The believing members of the Church already know about it, and as knowers they have a special position within the present lordship of Christ.[1] They understand how what they expect at the end already becomes a reality in the present. For they are convinced that they stand in the end time which has already begun. So they see how world history is already being merged into salvation history (not how salvation history is being merged into world history!) In political events, in the manifestation of the imperium, they see those invisible 'powers and authorities' at work which play such an important part in the salvation-historical drama that they are spoken of in all the ancient Christian credal formulations.[2] The earthly rulers are merely the executive organs of these powers and authorities. Not only Herod and Pilate, but all the earthly lords of this world are unconsciously placed in the service of the Christ event.

In the message of Jesus, a political event predicted for the future forms the immediate bridge to the prediction of the eschatological events yet to come, to wit, the destruction of the temple. This act is more than merely the framework for the introduction of the future saving events. It stands in an immediate theological relationship to them. The Old Testament predicted the building of a new Temple in the Messianic end time. But even though Jesus may have shared this expectation, still his prediction is associated with the question of Zealotism which in his day did, in fact, dominate the scene. So here at the same time is an instance of a prophetic, political prediction of the Jewish war belonging with those of the prophets.[3]

The words spoken by Jesus on the way to Golgotha (Luke 23.28–31) point in this direction as well.[4] As in the case of the Old Testament prophets, the political future is here predicted and interpreted by the events of the present. In the light of saving events still to come, a political event is recognized here as a crucial saving event. Therefore a special significance is attached to it in Jesus' preaching because it brings about the turning-point. Jesus' saying about the temple, according to which 'no

---

[1] See O. Cullmann, 'The Kingship of Christ and the Church in the New Testament', *The Early Church*, 1956, pp. 105ff.

[2] See O. Cullmann, *The Earliest Christian Confessions*, 1949.

[3] Against W. G. Kümmel, *Promise and Fulfilment*, 1957, p. 101. C. H. Dodd, *The Parables of the Kingdom*, 1936, pp. 60ff., also interprets this prediction by Jesus as a political one. Cf. below pp. 223f.

[4] For a commentary on v. 31 see O. Cullmann, *The State in the New Testament*, 1956, p. 48.

stone will be left upon another' (Mark 13.2; see also Matt. 23.38; Luke 13.35), comes to the foreground in the so-called trial of Jesus.[1]

The early Church took up this prediction, and, in an expectation of the future which left its stamp on the Synoptic apocalypse (Mark 13 and parallels) in its final form, the event appears (in a manner characteristic of all salvation history) on the same level as the cosmic events of the end.[2] The reinterpretation of the Old Testament hope of a new temple follows the manner of all biblical reinterpretations and is related to the political events of the Zealot uprising[3] which led to the destruction of Jerusalem and the temple. This became a reality in the year AD 70, that is, in a time to which a large part of the New Testament writings belong. At that time a new interpretation of this event became necessary without the abandonment of the old. Likewise, in a vision of the history of salvation, Paul includes it in the μυστήριον (Rom. 9–11) before the event happened, again without giving up his earlier hope from the standpoint of present events of his time, namely, *the work of the Christian mission*. This showed that Israel as a whole rejected the gospel while the Gentiles accepted it. The temporary separation of the new Israel κατὰ πνεῦμα from Israel κατὰ σάρκα is necessary in the history of salvation in order that the 'full number of Gentiles' may come in. When the destruction of Jerusalem and the Temple in AD 70 actually came about, this separation of salvation history from its close connection with the history of Israel found its confirmation without, of course, any forgetfulness of the function of Israel in salvation history.

It is not actually said in the New Testament writings that the destruction of Jerusalem leaves the way more free than ever for the triumphant march of the gospel through the world and for the preaching of the gospel to all the nations, for whose sake the time before the end is still lengthened. But indirect traces of such an assessment of that event, judged so completely differently by the historian, may be found in some passages of the New Testament.

We come to the conclusion that, according to early Christian faith, the main element of salvation history is actually a history developing

---

[1] J. Schniewind, *Das Evangelium nach Markus* (*Neues Testament Deutsch*, 1937, p. 158) rightly stresses that this is no secondary construction like a *vaticinium ex eventu*; so also E. Lohmeyer, *Das Evangelium des Markus*, 1937, p. 268, and W. G. Kümmel, *op. cit.*, p. 100. The prediction was not at all fulfilled in its precise form since the temple was destroyed *by fire* in AD 70.

[2] The 'strictly eschatological significance' that W. G. Kümmel, *op. cit.*, p. 101, rightly sees is therefore not at all excluded by our assumption of a political prediction, as Kümmel apparently thinks it is.

[3] M. Hengel, *Die Zeloten. Untersuchung zur jüdischen Freiheitsbewegung in der Zeit von Herodes I. bis 70 n. Chr.*, 1961, and O. Cullmann, *The State in the New Testament*, 1956.

in time to the extent that it is composed of events following one another in the framework of history, preserving the character of contingency belonging to all history. But we also note that a radical distinction exists between salvation history and history, since salvation history does not have an uninterrupted sequence of events. According to New Testament faith, God selects only specific events bound together by a developing connection. This saving connection God reveals to the prophets and apostles in an act which itself belongs to salvation history. The material relationship between salvation history and history, theologically speaking, is that salvation history in essence rests upon election, on reduction to a very narrow line, and that this line continues on for the salvation of all mankind, leading ultimately to a funnelling of all history into this line, in other words, a merging of secular history with salvation history.

3. PRESENT AND FUTURE

*The Salvation-Historical Tension between 'Already' and 'Not Yet'
as the Key to the Understanding of New Testament
Salvation History*

According to the New Testament view, all the epochs which make up salvation history are oriented towards the happening of the decisive period, the cross and resurrection of Jesus Christ. The *whole* salvation history present in God's plan is latently contained in this one event. All the preceding history of salvation tends towards the occurrence of this period. The present period in the history of salvation issues from it, and the whole future of salvation history portrays it in its universal and permanent consummation. To change Ranke's dictum that every historical epoch is 'immediate to God',[1] in this case it must be said that every epoch in the history of salvation 'is immediate to this mid-point in salvation history'. Salvation history is not oriented to the 'beyond' of history, but *to a saving event*. Yet each individual epoch has its special significance, its special task, in relation to this period. The past indicates, with special clarity, the movement of the whole development of salvation history in terms of election and reduction. The present, in contrast to the past, proceeds

---

[1] L. V. Ranke, *Über die Epochen der neueren Geschichte*, 1917, p. 217.

from the decisions now realized and still presses towards the consummation for this very reason. The future portrays what is realized and revealed as salvation, as the goal of the whole development of salvation history, universally and permanently extended, but compressed into the temporal, dateable point in the period towards which it is oriented (the cross and the resurrection). From this perspective the future, too, supplies an orientation for all the epochs of saving history, but not in the same way as the occurrence of the decisive period, since the future itself is also oriented from a salvation-historical, not a speculative, point of view towards what has occurred in Jesus of Nazareth.

The mutual connection of all the epochs continually operates within the whole saving process. Because these epochs are all held together by the event of the decisive period, which provides an orientation, they are co-ordinated one with another. Although they are all placed in a continual forward movement towards a temporal end, and although one presupposes the other in a temporal sequence, there is nevertheless at the same time an influence of future events still to come upon preceding events, in the opposite direction.[1] This is because of the co-ordination of the vertical and the horizontal. Because of this mutual effect, eschatology refers back to the past salvation history in that it contains the promise of a *new* Exodus, a *new* covenant, and a *new* David.[2]

We shall now speak of the *present period* in salvation history, that is, the epoch lying between Christ's ascension and return. It must be stressed that we shall speak only of that part of this time span that belongs in the biblical framework of the New Testament, not of its post-biblical extension in which we stand today, the possibility of which most of the New Testament writers did not even take into account. New Testament salvation history has to do only with the interval of time concluded by the end of the apostolic age, or at any rate by the end of the first phase of Christian history. It may be asked whether the post-biblical present belongs to salvation history at all,

---

[1] In this respect I am supplementing the argumentation of *Christ and Time* (1st ed. 1948, 3rd ed. 1962). The play on words with the German term for 'future', *Zukunft*, which presupposes something that 'comes to me' (*auf mich zukommen*), therefore contains a kernel of truth in the sense intended above. But it must not be employed in the service of non-futuristic eschatology.

[2] Cf. H. W. Wolff, 'The Understanding of History in the O.T. Prophets', *Essays in Old Testament Interpretation*, edited by C. Westermann, 1963, p. 342. The Qumran sect undertook a reinterpretation of eschatology on the basis of current events; see N. A. Dahl, 'Eschatologie und Geschichte im Lichte der Qumrantexte', *Zeit und Geschichte. Dankesgabe für R. Bultmann*, p. 14.

or whether it represents one of the 'historical gaps' we spoke of in the previous chapter, so that only the time during the apostolic age would then be regarded as the salvation-historical, intermediate present. But that question belongs in the dogmatic part of this book. Here we are merely expounding the New Testament concept.

The Bultmann school thinks that no uniform view of the biblical present can be found in the New Testament. The present is understood as an *intermediate period* of salvation history, linked with the past and the future only in the later, 'early Catholic' writings of the New Testament—primarily in the Gospel of Luke and Acts. But by Jesus, Paul, and John the present is not considered as an intermediate period in salvation history. The reason why it is not so understood by Jesus is because there was no place at all for such a period in his expectation of the imminent end. For Jesus, Paul, and John the saving event in the momentary present is only the punctual 'encounter' with the 'wholly other' that addresses me in an unbound event in history. That is the authentic notion of the saving event. Christ is the end of all history. Salvation history, on the other hand, is a secondary distortion of this original '*kerygma*'.

In the above view this much is correct: in the salvation-historical interpretation of the time separating the decisive Christ events from the end, we can discern a development in the books of the New Testament. This was associated with new events and concerned the *length* of that time. Accordingly, in this respect a correction was progressively undertaken of the account given by Jesus. Jesus preached that the end was coming within the generation living in his time. Later on, the New Testament writers reckon with a longer interval of time, of uncertain duration. We have seen that such 'developments' and corrections in salvation history, associated with new facts perceived as saving events, and accompanied by a retention of the constant *kerygma*, not only occur in the Old Testament, but are a constitutive part of all biblical salvation history.[1] The question is simply whether in assessing the significance of the intermediate period of salvation history the *duration* of this period may be separated as an element capable of development and correction from a *constant*, *temporal* defining of its essence. In that case, one would need to follow the progressive clarification of the interval from Jesus' message to the late Second Epistle of Peter. Then the differences to be noted

---

[1] See above pp. 123ff.

between Jesus and the later New Testament writers would not amount to a break, but only a development. Such is the thesis of the present book. It stands in opposition to the above-mentioned approach of Bultmann and his school.

In Bultmann's thought a break is *necessary*, for he interprets Jesus' original message in the above mentioned existential sense. The answer to the question whether a salvation-historical view is characteristic of the whole New Testament (even if it is only incipient in Jesus' message and reaches completion in Luke) is, therefore, particularly dependent upon one's understanding of the relation of present and future in Jesus' teachings. If Jesus' teachings must really be interpreted existentially, then every saving event is a *punctual* present as an encounter with the 'wholly other', and only that. It is no longer a present *bound* to salvation history. In that case there is not actually any *fundamental* distinction between epochs in salvation history such as we see to be the presupposition for all biblical salvation history.[1] Thus for Bultmann and his school, the situation of the Christian 'addressed' by the New Testament *kerygma* is a 'continual standing in decision for Christ'. Certainly on New Testament premises we can and must formulate the situation thus. But we place the 'now' beside the 'continually' with greater emphasis—a 'now' bound up with salvation history. Only in this way is the decision bound to a precise content, even though each time it occurs it receives a new and individual stamp.

The distinction at first appears insignificant, but is really fundamental. The New Testament 'now' is accurately fixed by the boundary between Christ's ascension and his return and presupposes the whole salvation-historical past of the Old Testament as well. That fact distinguishes *this* 'now' from all other 'nows'. It is not an 'eternal now' (*nunc aeternum*), but a 'now' linked forward and backward. As we shall see, its content is defined by the concrete command that within this time span the gospel of Christ's cross and resurrection must be proclaimed to all the world in the Holy Spirit, who is already at work, and by the Church, which is looking towards the end. Every moment of this 'now' is bound up in such a way with the past and future. The 'now' of the present is bound up with the history of

---

[1] To be sure, for Bultmann a special significance is attached to the Christ event as such quite apart from the 'encounter'. But this significance is only punctiliar in effect and not salvation-historical. For the inconsistency attributed to Bultmann by theologians closely associated with him, see below pp. 180f.

salvation because the decisive Christ event is itself bound in this way. It is not, as Marcion taught, unprepared-for, nor has it appeared merely in a vertical fashion. The whole struggle of the ancient Church, particularly of Irenaeus, against Marcion was meant to defend the New Testament link of the Christ event with the history of salvation against the Marcionitic doctrine of the unknown God. In other words, the struggle was over the horizontal foundation of verticality.

It is indeed true, according to the New Testament, that one must decide; but not for a vague 'desecularization', but for one's incorporation into a saving process which has already begun beforehand, and which will go on afterwards, and which has now reached the point in time at which one stands. Obviously within the present period of salvation history there is room for individual, 'punctual' decisions, to take up an expression of the Bultmann school. But these individual decisions need not be within the structure of a vague desecularization, nor be made for an even vaguer 'Wholly Other'. They may remain within the structure of the present period of salvation history, the significance of which is that during this time the gospel is proclaimed before the end by the Church of Christ, to which the Holy Spirit is already granted.

Far be it from me to accuse Bultmann and his pupils of the kind of 'decision' that their philosophical master, Heidegger, came to in 1933 when he, among others, said in his famous appeal in the *Freiburger Studentenzeitung*, November 3, 1933: '. . . The *Führer* himself, and he alone, is the present and future German reality and its law. Learn to know ever more deeply: From now on each thing demands *decision* and every action responsibility. Heil Hitler!'

Nevertheless, this attitude shows where the 'conceptuality' which, according to the Bultmann school, must be applied to the New Testament, *can* lead if the decision to be arrived at is freed from every association. In that case it can indeed be a decision for anything or for anyone, and the joke of Heidegger's students, 'I have decided—but for what, I do not know',[1] is not at all beside the point. To be sure, Bultmann only wants to use Heidegger's *conceptuality*, and for Bultmann, in contrast to Heidegger, a decision *for Christ* is at issue. Nevertheless, this decision is so vaguely defined in relation to the programme of demythologizing that the 'continually standing in decision' even dispenses with the norm that is implied in early Christianity, with the salvation-historical significance which it accords to its present time.

[1] Cited by G. Gloege in his article, 'Karl Löwiths Kritik der geschichtlichen Existenz', *TLZ*, 1962, col. 84.

In the New Testament view, the significance of the present in salvation history creates a structure for all the decisions of the Christian, and this structure has its specific character. It is conditioned by the past as by the future and is oriented towards the decisive Christ event. It is natural that the prime interest of early Christianity is turned towards the present period of salvation history. This is shown in its christology, which stresses in the first instance faith in the exaltation of Christ, his present sitting at the right hand of God, his present lordship not only over his Church, but over the whole world—even over the invisible 'powers and authorities'.[1]

The oldest confessional formulas found in the New Testament give us the proof for this dominance of the present period in the thinking of the first Christians about salvation history. These short summaries of the early Church's faith retained only the essential elements, and are therefore especially important for our problem. What they retain has to do primarily with the present, but that is the present conceived of in its place in salvation history. Ps. 110, from which comes the statement about Christ's present sitting at the right hand of God and his victory over the powers, is the most frequent Old Testament citation to occur in the New Testament, and therefore the statement is to be found in almost all the old confessional formulas. It can take the form of a short *Kyrios* confession. Thus the hymn used by Paul in Phil. 2.6ff. finds a climax in the mention of all the 'powers' who bow before him on whom the name of *Kyrios-Adonai* is bestowed, who 'is above every name', because he himself is the name of God and the sign of his own lordship.

However, that does not mean that this present lordship of Christ was isolated in the thinking of early Christianity. Rather, it is firmly anchored in the whole history of salvation. The *decisive* events are Christ's death and resurrection, and although the early Christian attitude towards the present naturally stands in the foreground, it is still oriented toward those events. The events of the rest of the saving epochs, chiefly those of the future, are mentioned for the first time in later creeds. This is an indication that they do not stand in the

---

[1] I have stressed this in all my publications, but above all in 'The Kingship of Christ and the Church in the New Testament', *The Early Church*, 1956, pp. 105ff., and in *Earliest Christian Confessions*, 1949. The objection has been raised against me by Bultmannians that because of my stress upon the present, I ought to take a positive stand towards existential exegesis. However, from the above discussion it ought to become clear that in the New Testament the present should be conceived not existentially, but salvation-historically.

foreground of interest. They are, nevertheless, not forgotten in all the statements about the present period of salvation history.

Indeed, because the New Testament present is already understood as an *end time*, expectation of the future naturally plays an especially prominent role for the present in the thinking of the first Christians. Nevertheless, it is not accurate when the present is one-sidedly designated as 'eschatological'. Important though eschatology is for the understanding of the New Testament present, it is *not* the really characteristic feature of the new covenant. The Old Testament and, above all, the theology of late Judaism are to a large extent characterized by eschatology. It would be far better to designate the Qumran sect as 'eschatological' than to apply the adjective to the early Church.[1] Even the expectation in the New Testament that the end is imminent is not entirely new.[2] This idea existed before Jesus— one has only to think of John the Baptist.

The *new element* in the New Testament is not eschatology, but what I call the *tension* between the decisive 'already fulfilled' and the 'not yet completed', between present and future.[3] The whole theology of the New Testament, including Jesus' preaching, is qualified by this tension. Hence, what is termed the enthusiasm of the early Church is not called forth by the expectation of the end as such, but by the 'already' that gives a foundation to it. The expectation is only a symptom. Certainly the first Christians did expect a near end. But if this were *all* that characterized them, then it would not be understandable why this group stirred up such a sensation, and why it prevailed over the others.[4] Certainly the whole New Testa-

---

[1] In the article cited above, p. 79 n. 1, N. A. Dahl thinks he finds a 'realized eschatology' in the Qumran sect. But there an actual 'tension' is lacking.

[2] On the question of the expectation of an imminent end in late Judaism, see the book by A. Strobel, *Untersuchungen zum eschatologischen Verzögerungsproblem auf Grund der spätjüdischen-urchristlichen Geschichte von Habakuk* 2.2ff., 1961, which discusses much very valuable material. Unfortunately, the author feels compelled to pay his tribute in the final pages to the theology in fashion these days. But that does not affect the important conclusions of his study.

[3] Unfortunately, in our modern languages no adjective can be found that expresses this idea. One of my students suggested 'taseological' to me because the word 'eschatological', strictly speaking, simply refers to the end time in a general way. It does not express the *tension* between present and future which makes up salvation-historical eschatology. The word 'taseology' (from the Greek τάσις, 'tension') would come closer to what is intended by eschatology in the New Testament sense. But our theological jargon is already so heavily loaded that it is better not to increase it with further unintelligible foreign words.

[4] Unfortunately, such fundamental questions as this one are usually not even raised.

ment takes up the message of the Baptist (Matt. 4.17): the Kingdom of God is at hand. But alongside that, and bound up with it, is another series of statements which are new: 'I saw Satan fall like lightning from heaven' (Luke 10.18); 'If it is by the finger of God that I cast out demons, then the Kingdom of God has come upon you' (Luke 11.20; Matt. 12.28); 'Death is vanquished', 'Christ is risen'. Here I have deliberately combined statements of Jesus with affirmations of the early Church to indicate that, with all their differences, all the books of the New Testament are in agreement in this juxtaposition of 'already' and 'not yet'.

At this point there is no break whatever between Jesus and the early Church, despite all the differences between them that must not be overlooked. This notion at the same time separates Jesus and the early Church from Judaism.[1] But this can have no other meaning than that *salvation history is the common basis of the whole New Testament.* We hold that there is in the New Testament a temporal tension between faith in a decision already made and hope resting upon it for what is not yet fulfilled. If this is what is *new* in the New Testament, and if it is basic to *all* New Testament thought, then the above inference cannot be escaped, even though Jesus, in contrast to Luke and other New Testament writers, only reckoned on a very short intermediate period of time. For if this 'already' and 'not yet' of salvation history relate to the present, then the present is linked to salvation history in both directions. In that case, we stand in an ever progressing movement. This is why a clear exposition of the tension between faith in the fulfilment already achieved and hope in its consummation is so important to me. Anyone who admits the existence of this tension ought not to assent to the popular polemic of today in which the idea that salvation history is the common basis of the New Testament is rejected *a priori.*

On the other hand, salvation history must be contested by all those who allow this tension for the later, so-called 'early Catholic' writings of the New Testament, but ascribe to Jesus either a purely futuristic or a purely present expectation of the Kingdom of God. For them, the salvation-historical tension does not in fact belong to the original New Testament message. This is why the whole discussion of Albert Schweitzer's 'consistent eschatology', applied to Jesus' message, and of the 'realized eschatology' of C. H. Dodd is so

---

[1] For this reason, in a theology of the New Testament I would not put the chapter on Jesus' message among the Jewish presuppositions, as Bultmann does.

important for the question of salvation history.[1] Both Schweitzer's thesis (only futuristic eschatology) and that of Dodd (only already realized eschatology) exclude the salvation-historical tension of the present in their one-sidedness.

When Dodd diametrically opposes Schweitzer, at first glance it might seem that his thesis, in which according to Jesus the Kingdom of God is already realized, retains the specifically new element in Jesus' message over against the futuristic eschatology of late Judaism. It is true that C. H. Dodd actually comes much closer to the truth with his stress upon Jesus' sayings concerning the present than Schweitzer does, in so far as the revolutionary newness in Jesus' message is actually to be seen in the conviction that the Kingdom of God is already here, rather than in the expectation shared with wider circles of late Judaism that it is coming soon. But in fact even Dodd's interpretation does not take account of the specific newness of New Testament thinking. It is characteristic of New Testament thought that the future statements about the coming kingdom retain their futuristic character and are associated most closely with the present statements about the dawning of the Kingdom which has already taken place. The solution of scientific exegesis cannot be to strike out one of the two series of statements, those concerning the present, or those concerning the future, which are both present in the entire Synoptic tradition. It must instead rest in the acknowledgement that their juxtaposition is itself the essential item in Jesus' message.

At the same time it must be noted that within this tension the futuristic sayings are the same as those of late Judaism and really relate to the temporal future, and that they still acquire a new significance precisely by their connection with the sayings about the present. The immediate nearness of the coming Kingdom is now based on the present which has already been realized. What is yet to come *will* come *because* the crucial event *has* occurred. Dodd does not take this tension into account. He renders innocuous what in Jesus' preaching is still to come,[2] and makes it at most an appendage of no fundamental importance. Hence it is understandable why for him eschatology could finally come to a Platonic reinterpretation.

The whole problem of salvation history is ultimately concentrated in the question whether what I call the salvation-historical tension

[1] See above pp. 32ff.
[2] Even he allows for coming events. In oversimplified treatments of his work, Dodd is unfairly accused of permitting no more future events at all to stand.

is really a secondary distortion, or whether it belongs to the decisive New Testament witness at its high-points (Jesus, Paul, and John). The next part of this book will enter into this question in detail.[1] However, at this point it should be emphasized that Jesus' teachings can be freed from this tension only by a highly arbitrary and scientifically questionable method, in which either the present sayings (Schweitzer's school) or the future sayings (Dodd's school) are termed 'community formations'. The essence of what is called Jesus' eschatology consists in the juxtaposition of both of these series of statements.

It might seem a concession to the salvation-historical conception presented here that E. Käsemann, following the lead of E. Haenchen, G. Florowski, and J. Jeremias, instead of using the term 'realized eschatology', speaks of 'an eschatology that is in process of realization' (*sich realisierende Eschatologie*), an expression which Dodd, too, can accept.[2] In fact, a *salvation-historical* appraisal of the present in one's interpretation of Jesus' eschatology should follow from this. But Käsemann does not follow this route to its end, even though the historical sense again and again seems to triumph over the philosophical presuppositions of the Bultmann school from which he starts, although it does not ultimately prevail. Käsemann does not draw the conclusion that for Jesus the present (even though it is short) must have its specific, salvation-historical significance, even if, on the one hand, the present is not yet eschatology, but, on the other hand, it stands in a special, *temporal* relationship to eschatology, as the participle in the term *sich realisierend* indicates. But in order not to fall into conflict with modern philosophical tendencies, there is a refusal to acknowledge linear temporality (as distinct from Heidegger's *Zeitlichkeit*) as an essential feature of the New Testament or to admit that the present lies in a definite, *theologically meaningful* movement between past and future.

How much the whole of present-day Protestant theology is dominated by prevailing currents of thought in its exposition of the Bible is shown by the book of the Barthian W. Kreck, *Die Zukunft des Gekommenen* (1961), which in general attests to a deep insight into the essence of New Testament eschatology. The title expresses quite correctly the tension between present and future, and in the study

[1] To show the tension between 'already' and 'not yet', basic to the whole New Testament, is the actual nerve centre of the present work.
[2] See above p. 33.

itself 'already' and 'not yet' are spoken of again and again. But in accord with one of the tendencies found in many Barthians, which is probably traceable to a position on New Testament eschatology not quite clear in Barth himself, the linear temporality, the horizontal movement of time that unquestionably forms the background for the 'already' and 'not yet', is nevertheless not taken seriously. The 'already' is a vertical break-through since it contains the whole salvation history in latent form, and yet *this 'already' is aligned with a horizontal process*. The very fact that it is 'only' an anticipation proves that the New Testament revelation has as its object continuous time hastening toward the end. In no way may this tension be reinterpreted statically. Its character of temporal movement must be retained.

So it is understandable that Kreck (pp. 35f.) appears influenced by E. Fuchs' critique which dissolves the temporal side of the tension with the thought that Jesus is the 'end' and not the 'mid-point'. Here he misunderstands my term 'mid-point', used in *Christ and Time*, to mean a turning-point between two periods of equal length instead of a decisive, temporal high-point. The notion that Jesus did not reckon on an *extended* interval of time is not disputed by any serious exegete. It does not follow, however, that for Jesus salvation history is done away with: even if Paul writes that Jesus is the end of the Law, this does not mean he is the end of salvation history. Kreck misunderstands the essence of the New Testament tension, its anchorage in a special salvation history, and the intertwining of vertical and horizontal. Here I can only refer to my illustration of the crucial battle and the cease-fire yet to come. Although this tension is to be taken seriously, it is still relaxed to the extent that the futuristic expectation of the realization of the 'not yet' is *established* in faith in the 'already'. When Kreck asserts that eschatology is dethroned by the linear-temporal conception and degraded into an appendage like the 'last things' (see below), New Testament eschatology, despite his every intention to the contrary, is in danger of being dissolved into a philosophical *'nunc aeternum'* in which the tension between 'already' and 'not yet' is no longer a real tension. Of course, the end is anticipated in the decisive period of the Christ event, compressed into a brief time of revelation, and in this respect the tension is already relaxed (see below). But the characteristic of the New Testament tension, presupposed by the concept of salvation history unfolded here, is precisely that the tension remains, and yet is relaxed because of the mid-point already reached in Christ.[1] It continues to exist because the anticipation of the end in Christ is indeed only an *anticipation in him*, and

[1] See below pp. 184, 259 and 269.

because the Christ event is unfolded in its universality and permanence only at the end.

All reinterpretations of New Testament eschatology rest upon the misunderstanding that because the end, like all salvation history, is contained in Christ, it will bring *nothing new*. Behind that, however, lies the assumption that what is still to come is simply the fact that at the end the 'cover' will be removed from the table that so far has always been covered (cf. K. Barth). Philosophically and dogmatically it may be right that *in* God himself the whole history of salvation is already present, and the systematician may be permitted to extend his line of reasoning in this way. But it cannot be stressed enough that the Bible is not occupied with the 'Being' of God, but with his saving activity.[1] On this level what is still to come is actually a *new* act of God, and the future is really future. The speculative question, permitted only for the systematician, whether the future is future in the eyes of God, the Lord of time, does not exist at all within the province of the New Testament, for its object is only the activity of God in time. Certainly the future already exists in the plan of God according to the New Testament. God reveals it to the prophets and apostles. But what pertains to the future has yet *to happen*.

We should remember that the whole history of salvation past and future is summed up in Christ. So to say that decisive future events are anticipated in the life, death, and resurrection of Christ, and that therefore nothing is now left that is still to be realized, is like arguing that because events in the Old Testament recur in the Christ event, it is not necessary for them to have happened at all prior to the coming of Christ. Again, it must be remembered that in the New Testament the vertical and the horizontal do not exclude each other. A new event is coming which is more than an uncovering of what is already present. Only because in the New Testament the fact is taken seriously that more things of importance will happen at the end yet to come, is the whole saving process in the time of Jesus and the Church taken seriously without reservation. Everything associated with the resurrection of our bodies and their transformation by the Spirit (I Cor. 15) and with the super-human new creation (Rom. 8) *is yet to come*, even though there is already a resurrection body, the body of the 'first-born of the dead' (Rev. 1.5), and even though in the

[1] See my answer to Catholic critics of my *Christology of the New Testament* in *Choisir* 9–10, 1960, pp. 20–23, and now in the volume of my collected essays, appearing shortly.

present time belonging to Christ, anticipations of the time when the Spirit will finally take hold of the body occur in all the New Testament miracles of healing. But they are only anticipations. Only in the future resurrection will *we* have a body finally transformed by God (σῶμα πνευματικόν), when the same Spirit remakes the whole creation.[1] The victory over the 'flesh' (σάρξ) and sin which has already been achieved, the overcoming of death by which our inner man is already being renewed (by the Spirit) from day to day (II Cor. 4.16), will then take effect bodily. It is an unjustified modernization of the substance of Pauline thinking to interpret this event otherwise than as *something still to come in time*. The dependence of our resurrection upon that of Christ is not only in point of fact, but also in the order of time. Christ is the 'first born' of those who have fallen asleep, and only at the end will *our* resurrection occur (I Cor. 15.23: ἔπειτα . . . ἐν τῇ παρουσίᾳ αὐτοῦ).

In this sense we may confidently speak of 'last things', for the New Testament writers themselves spoke in this way, and not just those accused of 'early Catholicism'. It is almost a fashion these days to shun every interest in an end event yet to come. It is regarded as an expression of a lower form of religion. The 'last things' in the New Testament which relate to the resurrection of the spiritual body and the new creation do not in any way belong to a final chapter designed to satisfy human curiosity. We have seen that purely speculative apocalyptic with no relationship to salvation history has, in fact, no legitimate place in the New Testament proclamation. However, the futuristic statements in the New Testament are involved in the typical salvation-historical interaction with the whole saving process and the event of the mid-point, Christ. Apocalyptic can only be called Christian with full justification if it rests upon the 'already', preserving its relationship with a human redemption which requires faith, and if it does not regress to become speculation floating in the air. The future is no longer conceivable in the New Testament without the victory over death already won by Christ. But the

[1] It is the opinion neither of the writers of the Synoptic Gospels nor of the Gospel of John that those raised from the dead by Jesus will not die again. The resurrection of 'many bodies' at the moment of Jesus' death (Matt. 27.53) was probably understood by the evangelist only as an anticipation of their final resurrection. Only of Jesus himself does Paul (Rom. 6.9) say that 'being raised from the dead' he 'will never die again'. The implication for us, of course, is that 'he who raised Christ Jesus from the dead will give life to [our] [as yet] mortal bodies also through his spirit which dwells in [us]' (Rom. 8.11; see Phil. 3.21). Cf. O. Cullmann, *The Immortality of the Soul or the Resurrection of the Body?*, 1958.

futuristic statements, so rooted in the victory of Christ, point towards a final point in the whole saving process which is nowhere finally realized before the end.

Wherever eschatology is merely 'desecularization', as in existential theology, we are no longer dealing with eschatology at all, and the expression has become meaningless. In that case, we have an 'eschatology without hope'[1] and there is no more room for the tension between present and future which seems to us to be the key to understanding the whole New Testament.

Both Albert Schweitzer and Rudolf Bultmann, following his lead, think that they should explain this tension as a secondary, makeshift solution because the imminent expectation of the end is contradicted by the actual continuation of history. But in fact the temporal tension between 'already' and 'not yet' is present even before this expectation has been disturbed by the actual course of events. Hence *in the New Testament* this future expectation has from the start a character unlike all late Jewish eschatological hopes. That is because it rests upon the 'already', expressed not just in signs of the *end*, but in an *effective anticipation in Christ*. The actual relationship between expectation and tension is just the opposite of what the Schweitzer and Bultmann schools presume it to be. The tension between 'already' and 'not yet' is not a consequence of a (disappointed) expectation of a near end. On the contrary, the expectation in the New Testament is a consequence of the certainty that the coming Kingdom is *already* existent in Christ. Thus in the New Testament, the expectation that the end is near, which is not new in itself, is heightened tremendously.

With Jesus himself, it is anchored in his own self-consciousness. The 'already' is now manifest for Jesus in his certainty that he himself is already here as the fulfiller of the coming salvation. For this reason, the Bultmann school, which in contrast to Schweitzer denies that Jesus had such a self-consciousness, cannot see an actual tension between 'already' and 'not yet', between present and future, in Jesus' eschatology.

We shall see in the chapter on Jesus[2] that futuristic temporality and the question of the time of the end must be distinguished in his eschatology. The problem of dating (the limiting of the time still to

[1] H. Grass, 'Das eschatologische Problem in der Gegenwart', *Dank an P. Althaus*, 1958, p. 64.
[2] See below pp. 203ff.

elapse to the generation then living) actually belongs among those elements of salvation history which undergo a correction in connection with new events without the *constant* being affected. In this case the constant is the futuristic temporality of eschatology in its relationship of tension to the present, and this is not contradicted in the slightest by the failure of the *parousia* to come.

In his article 'New Testament and Mythology', *Kerygma and Myth I*, 1953, edited by H. W. Bartsch, tr. R. H. Fuller, p. 5, Bultmann says, 'The mythical eschatology is untenable for the simple reason that the *parousia* of Christ never took place as the New Testament expected. History did not come to an end, *and, as every schoolboy knows, it will continue to run its course*' (italics mine). Here Bultmann does not distinguish between the question of the time of the end (limiting the interval to Jesus' generation) and that of temporality in general. According to him, when the imminent expectation of the end ceases to be a factor, the whole notion of the futurity of the end collapses and is therefore non-essential.[1]

It is common knowledge that Bultmann is accused of inconsistency by groups (chiefly Fritz Buri) standing close to his position which want to 'dekerygmatize' his theology because he allows the cross to stand as an objective, divine saving event. The inconsistency seems to me to become apparent particularly when we compare his attitude towards Jesus' cross with his attitude towards futuristic eschatology patent in the above citation. Is the scandal of the temporality of eschatology greater than that of the temporality of the decisive revelation in Jesus' cross? If we allow ourselves a dogmatic perspective at this point, departing from the exegetical character of this part of the book, it must be said against Bultmann (as Morgenthaler remarks against Dodd[2]) that the assumption that the end could suddenly come at any single point in time is no more nonsensical than the assumption of Bultmann and the first Christians that during the third decade of the first century God brought about his *decisive* revelation. In both instances we have a 'foolishness' in the Pauline sense. The foolishness of the temporal future issues from the foolishness of the temporal tension characterizing the present and belongs within the province of this same 'foolishness'. Thus, because it is as an indispensable part of the New Testament message, the temporal future cannot be included in the process of demythologizing, however proper the latter may be when it is carried out in accord with the essence of this message where mythological elements are really involved.

---

[1] Here we are not touching on the question, treated earlier, whether it is legitimate to view something as non-essential in Jesus' message because it can no longer be essential for us.

[2] R. Morgenthaler, *Kommendes Reich*, 1952.

If, as we shall show in the next chapter, Jesus' eschatology rests upon the tension between 'already' and 'not yet', this same tension cannot be a makeshift solution to the problem of the delayed end where we find it related to prolonged time, as in Luke. Rather, this tension is itself the *common factor* in both the expectation of the near end and in the assumption of an extended interval of time. To be sure, for Jesus the interval has only a very short duration, and its extension to a long 'Church history' is not foreseen in his message. Certainly there is a distinction here between Jesus and Luke that we do not wish to minimize. But the distinction is not fundamental to the question of the continuity of salvation history. If the expectation of the imminent end is accompanied by the idea of a *brief* present indicating precisely *the same essential characteristics* as the *prolonged* interval of the later salvation-historical conception, then we have a *starting point* for incorporating the present into salvation history. *That is where the continuity between Jesus and Luke lies.*

The *abiding factor* in eschatology is not the detemporalized situation of decision, but the retention of the tension, temporally understood. The expectation of the imminent end rests upon a particularly intensive, 'enthusiastic' experience of the tension between 'already' and 'not yet'. Because the 'already' is really present, and hence offers the firm guarantee for the early cessation of the 'not yet', the tension first of all assumes the form of an anticipation of an imminent end. That this expectation is really only an expression of the conviction that the 'already' must make an end to the 'not yet' is shown in the fact that it does not cease with those in II Peter 3.3ff. who scoff because the hope has failed to materialize, saying the end will not come at all, and everything will remain the same as before. Only the assumption of the imminent end is then dropped; the temporal expectation of the end is preserved within the tension even when a lengthy period is envisaged.

Thus, with Bultmann, we look for the abiding factor expressed in the expectation of a near end. But in contrast to him, we do not surrender futuristic temporality to an existential interpretation, but see the constant factor in what is specifically new in Jesus' message and in the whole New Testament revelation; in other words, in the conviction that the decisive event for the end has already happened, and *therefore* the coming of the end *cannot* fail to materialize. The abiding core of the eschatological hope, which is not in any way altered by the failure of the *parousia* to come, is the faith that with

Christ saving time has made a *great leap forward* unforeseen in the natural course of time. Saving time has entered into its *final phase*. That is the significance of the 'already'.

That this final phase was limited by Jesus and the first Christians to the duration of the generation living at the time is merely a way of expressing a special intensity of that faith, conditioned by the thinking of their time. The salvation-historical interpretation of the present developed further in the manifestations of the Spirit in the life of the Church and in its mission, just as all interpretations found in salvation history have developed onward within the Bible while retaining the *constant* factor.[1]

The constant in the appraisal of the present situation in the New Testament is the faith that we stand in the final phase. Hence the *indefinite* duration of this phase is more strongly emphasized. But we find the beginnings of this emphasis in Jesus' words about not knowing the day nor hour,[2] even though they are linked with the limitation of the duration to the generation living at his time. This also shows that this limitation is a secondary feature in Jesus' expectation and in the hope of the first disciples. This judgment does not represent a makeshift solution. Rather it had to be reached, even if the error made in fixing the date had not become apparent.

So long as the fundamental conviction of the 'already' is dominant (and this is the case in the whole New Testament period), the belief in the coming end loses nothing of its intensity, even though an indefinite and longer duration is assigned to the present interval. Even in II Peter, where the extension of the interval has for a long time been a known fact, it remains vibrant. 'Children, it is the last hour' (I John 2.18). This 'last hour' is meant in a temporal sense, even though its length is now indefinite. Only when the faith that we are really in the situation of tension between 'already' and 'not yet' disappears, only when the 'not yet' is taken more seriously at the expense of the 'already', does the eschatological expectation weaken in the course of Church history beginning after the apostolic age. This confirms once more that the constant *basis* of the eschatological hope is faith in the 'already' and the tension of the intermediate period which goes with it, and that the biblical present is properly

---

[1] See above pp. 125, 150f.
[2] See the next chapter for the authenticity of these sayings, which today are readily ascribed as 'secondary constructions' resulting from a tendency to justify the extension of time.

defined neither by a one-sided emphasis on the 'already', nor by a one-sided emphasis on the 'not yet', nor again by the dissolution of temporality in a '*Zeitlichkeit*' to be understood existentially.

The temporal characteristic of the present as the time of a tension stemming from the 'already' belongs to the definition of the theological content of this tension. I find no better comparison than the one used in *Christ and Time*: the decisive battle has been fought, but the war continues on for a still uncertain time. The *concrete* effect of this intermediate period is expressed according to the New Testament by the fact that now is the time of the eschatological *Holy Spirit* who renews everything 'already' (ἀρραβών, ἀπαρχή), the time of *the Church*, the time of the *preaching* of the gospel to the world before the end comes.[1] That is the scope of present time within which the disciple in the New Testament must make his individual 'decisions'.

We are not treating the tension in salvation history between the emphatic 'already' and the resultant 'not yet' as the common link of all the New Testament books for the purpose of forcibly harmonizing diverse expressions of the early Christian faith and hope in the books of the New Testament. We do it instead because exegesis shows, as we shall see in detail, that an intermediate period is an indispensable element of salvation history, even though it was reckoned as being brief at the beginning. Even where the end is expected within the generation living during New Testament times, the salvation-historical movement does not cease. What is being said here in the context of the phenomenological characteristics of the New Testament perspeetive will be borne out in exegetical detail in the next part.

Finally, we must stress one aspect of this New Testament tension to which we have not perhaps paid sufficient heed up to now, although we have referred to it.[2] It is essential to this tension that, on the one hand, it still exists, but on the other hand it is abolished by implication. It is not as if the 'already' and the 'not yet' balanced the scales exactly. Nor does the decisive mid-point divide the time of salvation into two equal parts. The fact that the *decisive turn of events* has already occurred in Christ, the mid-point, and that now the future expectation is founded in faith in the 'already', shows that the 'already' *outweighs* the 'not yet'. The tension is even now 'relaxed'

---

[1] See my article, 'Eschatologie und Mission im Neuen Testament', *Evangelisches Missionsmagazin*, 1941, pp. 98–108.

[2] See above p. 176.

because the decisive turning-point has already been attained during the time of the New Testament, and is now past. A tension in which future and present balance the scales could actually exist only before the decisive point had already come, when the 'already' of the turning-point was not yet attained.

The present period in salvation history is, according to the New Testament, in a preferential position over against the past. Even though in a certain sense there is already a tension between present and future in the past, it is not *the* tension called forth by the decisive turning-point, the 'already', now attained and lying in the past.

The 'already' which was realized during New Testament time does not, of course, merely mean a fulfilment of what had been expected in the future, but a fulfilment of the *whole* past of salvation history lying behind us. Therefore, to understand the New Testament present, we need continually to be oriented towards the past lying before Christ. This is what is meant by the early Church's consciousness of accepting the obligation of Israel and its efforts to demonstrate the 'fulfilment of Scripture'. The 'already' of the present points both ways at the same time.

The solidarity of the whole of the present salvation-historical period with the past already exists, of course, in the Old Testament, which shows how the great salvation-historical events, already lying in the past, were made present time and again in worship. In the New Testament context of the period following Easter this connection of the present with events of the decisive period now past gains a special significance in worship because here the central Christ event, the death and resurrection of Jesus, is made present in the Lord's Supper. In addition, in the same situation of worship, the connection with the future is indicated since the 'breaking of the bread' is an anticipation of the Messianic meal and therefore of a final union with Christ. Thus in early Christian worship the whole fulness of the 'already' is made manifest.[1] But even here the end is only anticipated.

Despite the qualifications made here, the fact remains that important events are still to come which are only implicitly contained in the decisive event already reached. The reality of the 'already' causes the Christian to hope in the overcoming of the 'not yet'. Thus, despite the relaxation of the tension, Christian existence is characterized by standing in faith and hope. The fulfilment of past salvation

---

[1] Cf. the meals following the resurrection.

history does not mean the end of salvation history, even where the end is expected in the impending future. As soon as an interval of time before the end is assumed, however short it may be, a beginning is made towards incorporating an intermediate period into salvation history. This will be shown in the chapters to follow.

IV

THE MAIN NEW TESTAMENT TYPES

T HE VIEW PROPOUNDED in the preceding chapters stands or
falls on the interpretation of the *development* of the New Testament message from Jesus to the end of the Apostolic age as this
development may be traced in the various books of the New Testament. The fourth part of this book is devoted to a study of this
development. The Bultmann school sees a great break primarily
between Jesus, Paul, and John on the one hand, and Luke and the
'early Catholic' writings related to him on the other. The message
of the former group is said to consist in a proclamation calling me
in my self-understanding to a decision. In Jesus' message the temporal eschatology amounts to merely an external garb that can be
stripped off, one necessitated by the times. This garb is, for the most
part, eliminated in Paul, and abolished completely in John. Luke
and the other 'early Catholic' writers have thrust the expectation of
a near end aside, and in substituting an extended interval, a temporal
salvation history for it, they are said to have substituted an alien
element for the existential *core* of the original '*kerygma*'.

According to the view I propose, there is a distinction that must
not be overlooked between Jesus' expectation of an imminent end
and the assumption, which soon prevailed, of a prolonged interval of
indefinite length. However, the *connecting factor* between the two is
the fundamental, *linear* salvation history already existing incipiently
with Jesus. The temporality of this salvation history must not be given
up to make way for an existential *kerygma*.

The approach represented here must now be examined in detail
in four chapters, of unequal length, at the crucial points: Jesus, Paul,
Luke, and John. Because there is widespread agreement as to the
presence of a salvation-historical perspective in Luke and the New
Testament writings related to him, the main stress of this study will

rest upon the chapters on Jesus, Paul, and John, especially on Jesus and John, the points at which opinions diverge the most. Is their message characterized by a salvation-historical perspective?

Much importance is attached to the chapter on the extension of the period in the later New Testament writings, primarily in Luke, for the total argument of this book, as I have a different assessment of the alleged transformation of the original salvation history into a prolonged interval and, indeed, of its origin from that of the Bultmann school.

1. BEGINNINGS OF SALVATION HISTORY WITH JESUS

I speak of the 'beginnings' of salvation history deliberately, for obviously Jesus' message does not offer a fully developed salvation history. We have seen that only portions of salvation history are discernible almost everywhere in the New Testament. These, however, presuppose an overall salvation-historical view. We now seek to determine whether such a view is in the background of Jesus' message and whether his message leads, so to speak, organically to a further developed salvation history. For this reason we must answer the following questions: 1. Is the salvation-historical tension between fulfilment in the present and consummation in the temporal future present with Jesus? 2. Does his eschatology really include an indifference towards the present as a meaningful period of salvation? Does this period of salvation have its necessary place both in Jesus' call to decision and in his ethical instructions? 3. Does the intermediate period, brief as it is, have a very short extension beyond Jesus' death? Does Jesus think in terms of salvation history to the extent that he regards the present as a fulfilment not only of the future, but also of the past which is realized in the present?

A. METHODOLOGICAL REMARKS

When we speak of Jesus we come up against a difficulty already felt before.[1] Which sayings within the Gospels are to be attributed to Jesus? In principle, this difficulty exists for all of us who are schooled in form criticism and do not think in a fundamentalist way. In both

[1] See above pp. 107ff.

the narrative and speech materials we must reckon with the possibility that some 'community formations' have been projected back into the life of Jesus with the intention of illuminating it. But there is a great danger, especially where utterances of Jesus are concerned, that we shall be led by more or less subjective judgments in determining what actually comes from Jesus, and what is from the Church. Certainly this danger cannot be entirely avoided.

At the time of the beginnings of form-critical work, this difficulty for the exegete was felt. Every demarcation of 'authentic' from 'inauthentic' sayings of Jesus was renounced. The Gospel tradition was consistently treated as a whole, and the inquiry was simply to ascertain the principles and motives by which the Church at first preserved orally the tradition containing sayings of Jesus, whether genuine or not. This neutrality was hailed at the time as a great liberation from the arbitrariness with which liberalism often unconsciously used its one-sided theological standpoint, characterized by philosophical idealism, to decree what was 'genuine' and what was not.

I am not going to pursue here in detail the radical transformation that form criticism has undergone in the period that followed.[1] But I would mention that Bultmann's younger pupils, in contrast to their teacher, are again making the historical Jesus an object of research; at the same time, however, they are not being guided by the original endeavour of form criticism (to which they nevertheless appeal). They are controlled by an arbitrariness influenced by a definite, theological, dogmatic standpoint. Far more important to them is their relationship with so-called existential exegesis. This exegesis, however, has nothing more to do with form criticism than the fact that Bultmann is at the same time the founder of both and later brought about the synthesis of the two for his own purposes. In his basic works on form criticism proper, there is no trace of existential exegesis at all.

Certainly the goal of form criticism is to find Jesus in the *Church's witness*, and this aim ought to lead us to regard the *present-day* Church as the place where we can come to a better understanding of the Jesus of the New Testament,[2] taking due account of the temporal

[1] See above pp. 49f., and also my article, 'Out of Season Remarks on the Historical Jesus of the Bultmann School', *Union Seminary Quarterly Review*, January, 1961, pp. 131ff.
[2] See below pp. 325ff. and above pp. 68ff.

distance between the Church of today and that of the first century. The encounter with the Christ present in the Church of today permits us to understand the work of the incarnate Christ, but this work is of a kind that *for* me, but independently of me, leads to Christ's exaltation, making possible my encounter with him in the Church. But that is not what existential exegesis means by 'being addressed' and by 'self-understanding', in which the key to the historical Jesus is supposed to be found. In reality the danger of falling back into the arbitrariness against which form criticism tried to fight has merely become greater by associating form criticism with existential exegesis.

Here I am simply bringing out the points in the present debate on the historical Jesus which seem especially important to me in view of the discussion to follow. If we start with form criticism, it is proper to ask of each saying of Jesus in the tradition: does this correspond with or contradict the tendencies of the early Church which handed it down? If it *contradicts* these tendencies, then we may conclude with a good deal of certainty that we really do have a saying spoken by Jesus, since the early Church preserved it, as it were, against itself. On this point there is agreement.

But in the assessment of those sayings of Jesus which *correspond* precisely to a theological tendency of the early Church, there is an arbitrariness in pronouncing verdicts of authenticity or inauthenticity which is gaining ground at an alarming rate. In such instances the Bultmann school concludes almost as a rule that the saying is a 'community formation'. This premature judgment is unjustified from a scholarly point of view and is particularly irreconcilable with the sound principles of the original form criticism. The Church probably did put some words into Jesus' mouth to make clear its idea of Jesus, but it also used genuine sayings of Jesus for this purpose. It *selected such genuine* sayings of Jesus *as accorded with its own tendencies*, ones that specially emphasized what seemed to it of central importance in Jesus' message.

Thus, the discussion of the question, so important to our problem of salvation history, whether Jesus regarded his death as an atoning one, and whether the sayings of Jesus relative to his death came from him or were secondary compositions, seems to me to suffer from the fact that scholars are led by that wrong principle, either consciously or unconsciously. Once it has been established that the Church in its debate with Judaism had to justify the fact of Jesus' death, and

that it had an interest in placing the dying redeemer in the foreground when confronted with Hellenism, the conclusion is too
quickly made that Jesus himself could not have had the consciousness
of fulfilling the task of the Suffering Servant of God.

To cite another example that will occupy our attention in the
following discussion: it is said that the Synoptic sayings and parables
in which Jesus admonishes wakefulness, confesses his ignorance of
the 'hour' and points to the suddenness of the return of the Lord were
assigned to him for the first time by the Church. These sayings and
parables sought to help the members of the Church to solve the problem of the delay of the *parousia* by this appeal. Now it is, of course,
correct that it was *also* an endeavour of the early Church to admonish
Christians to wakefulness. But why could this not have been the
result of a 'tendency' of Jesus himself, before a 'delay' had actually
occurred? Why could not Jesus have spoken these sayings and
parables to counteract the general feeling of security men wrongly
held?[1] Scholars do not want to appear uncritical toward the early
Church's temptation to make constructions of its own and attribute
them to Jesus—a sound observation established by form criticism.
But do we not risk bringing this legitimate principle into discredit
by over-using it?[2]

It is a requirement of form criticism that account should also be
taken of the manner in which the rabbinic schools passed on the
doctrinal traditions of their masters. On this point, despite the
difference between a rabbinic school and Jesus' circle of disciples,
we should consider seriously what H. Riesenfeld and B. Gerhards-

---

[1] Matters are not improved when H. Conzelmann and E. Grässer from time
to time make the remark that 'Jesus himself could have spoken in this way
too'. They still decide with regularity that 'everything is much better understood
as a secondary construction'. Conzelmann still occasionally makes a statement
such as: the Parable of the Thief in the Night could, though not necessarily, owe
its origin to the fact of the delay of the *parousia* which was established later on
(*ZTK*, 1957, p. 286). However, in explaining the words of the unfaithful servant
in the parable in Matt. 24.48, 'My master will not come for a long time yet',
Conzelmann raises the completely useless question, 'How does [the unfaithful
servant] arrive at this attitude?' (*The Theology of St Luke*, 1961, p. 108, n. 2). He
answers: 'Because the Lord has been long delayed', and assumes as a matter of
fact that the Lord's long delay could have been known only by the early Church.
In the same way, E. Grässer (*Beiheft zur ZNW*, [2]1960, p. 92 n. 4) asks concerning
the Parable of the Doorkeeper in Mark 13.33ff. and parallels: 'But what made
this admonition [to wakefulness] necessary if it was not the assumed fact of the
delay of the *parousia*?'

[2] This should be taken to heart by those who too quickly charge others with
being 'uncritical' (see below p. 192 n. 1).

son,[1] following his lead, have worked out about the memorizing of the words of the master by his pupils. If one speaks of 'community formations' indiscriminately, wherever a saying of Jesus accords with tendencies of the Church, allowing only what contradicts these tendencies to stand as the certain core of Jesus' teachings, and taking this 'core' as the criterion for all decisions in the remaining doubtful cases, an extraordinarily cramped idea of Jesus' teachings arises because the criterion itself is already cramped in perspective. Jesus' eschatological hope is reduced approximately to the statement: the Kingdom of God is at hand.[2] This forced reduction is not mitigated when one seeks to establish the link between the kerygmatic Christ of the Church and the historical core by means of 'existential exegesis'.[3] The basis of my 'being claimed' and of my 'self-understanding' is too narrow, and the historical Jesus approached in this way will ultimately be an existentialist one, just as the Jesus of the nineteenth century was an idealistic one.

Form criticism sought to free us from an arbitrariness in distinguishing the 'authentic' from the 'inauthentic' sayings of Jesus, but today an arbitrariness prevails at least as great as that in the days of the old liberalism. While influence from philosophical idealism remains undetected, it is no help today that the favoured expression is 'community formations' rather than 'inauthentic'; even when a dissolution of the subject-object relationship leads to a deliberate inclusion of the person who is being addressed.

Nowhere does the arbitrariness in the separation of genuine sayings of Jesus from community formations appear more blatant than in the discussion of the fact that in the Synoptics we have some sayings of Jesus proclaiming an eschatology realized in the *present*, and others proclaiming a *futuristic* eschatology. On this point, completely contradictory judgments are given as to which of the two series of statements is to be regarded as secondary. The decision as to which of the contrasting sayings are to be attributed to the Church depends upon one's opinion—whether one thinks that Jesus spoke only of the impending Kingdom, or whether he simply regarded this Kingdom as already 'realized'.

[1] B. Gerhardsson, *Memory and Manuscript*, 1961.
[2] See, for instance, E. Grässer, *Das Problem der Parusieverzögerung* (*Beiheft zur ZNW*, [2]1960).
[3] See the survey of scholarship made by J. M. Robinson, *A New Quest of the Historical Jesus*, 1959.

As Protestant scholars we certainly do not strive towards any 'official' exegesis and are proud of the diversity of our interpretations. But in order to keep our freedom in the interpretation of the Bible from falling into discredit, we ought at least to be uneasy about the distressing fact that often today, by the same methods, and by 'careful analysis', one school regards the statements of Jesus related to the present as community formations, while another puts the decidedly futuristic sayings into this category.

I know, of course, that all of us schooled in form criticism find ourselves in a precarious situation in this respect, since we reckon *in principle* with the possibility of 'community formations'. I make no claim whatever to a monopoly of truth in my view of things. But I think that much would be gained if at least an effort to avoid the influence of subjective judgments were made again seriously in theory. This seems much better than mocking such an effort with remarks about abandoning the subject-object relationship, making a virtue out of the difficulty inherent in the fact that we cannot step out from behind our skins. In view of the self-confidence with which many answer the question of authenticity or inauthenticity, as if the original concern of form criticism to make an end to such judgments had never existed, we all ought to apply the soberest judgment in this respect and impose great caution upon ourselves. Above all, we ought to rid ourselves of the practice of measuring the critical sense of a New Testament exegete by the number of verdicts against genuine authenticity which he pronounces.[1] Even Harnack warned against this naive attitude. In this chapter, wherever a saying of Jesus accords with a tendency in the Church, I shall reckon with the probability of a 'community formation' and therefore shall not attempt to use it to reconstruct Jesus' teachings only in the following cases: first, when a saying contradicts another saying of Jesus found in the tradition so that they are mutually exclusive; second, when a saying presupposes a situation that was really unthinkable at the time of Jesus, and in his surroundings; third, when a literary comparison of the Synoptics suggests or urges the conclusion that a saying was created late. I lay down these principles not for apologetic, but for scientific reasons, not because of conservatism, but because of a concern for a true critical sense that must be alert when

---

[1] See above p. 190 n. 1. Up till now at least English scholars have not as a rule made use of this cheap argument. Unfortunately, A. J. B. Higgins (see above p. 109) has succumbed to this 'method'.

confronted with particular favourite ideas. Following the above line of thinking, the parables must not be given a one-sided preference, nor may the sayings of the *logia* source of Mark be preferred over all the rest of the *logia*, nor may both of the latter be favoured over the special material found only in Matthew and Luke, as is done in the Son of Man question.

Again I cautiously repeat that even with the above rules no absolute guarantee for a certain judgment is offered. But the endeavour to exclude judgments that are too subjective seems to me more important than the continually emphasized awareness that we obviously can never completely suspend our own ideas.[1]

B. PRESENT AND FUTURE IN THE PROCLAMATION OF JESUS

It would go beyond the aim and limits of this book to try to offer here a whole eschatology of Jesus. We are limiting ourselves to those aspects that must be particularly considered in our problem, and in view of the importance of this chapter, we shall need to go into some detail after having discussed some general features mentioned above.[2] The question to be answered first of all, whether the characteristic salvation-historical tension between fulfilment in the present and consummation in the temporal future is present in Jesus, would not exist as a problem if the series of statements concerning the present were not doubted by some, and the series concerning the future were not doubted by others. We must therefore study the *logia* of both series one after another. In order to show that they indeed belong to Jesus' teachings simply because they stand in a *relationship of tension*, the evidence that the present statements also refer to the future, and the future statements rest upon the present, will be important. If, however, the presence of this tension is demonstrated, it must further be shown whether it really includes the beginnings of a salvation history, or whether it is a mere absorption of an ultimately nontemporal future into a punctual present.

[1] There is the danger not only of treating an authentic saying of Jesus as a secondary composition, but also of regarding a secondary composition as an original saying of Jesus. Nevertheless, the second possibility seems to me less able to distort our image of Jesus than the first, for if one observes the three rules laid down above (and this is, of course, a presupposition), then it is possible for a secondary construction which ascribes 'too much' to Jesus by one of the principles of form criticism to serve to illuminate the image of Jesus.

[2] See pp. 166ff.

We begin with those statements in which Jesus said clearly that the Kingdom of God is already present in his own person. These sayings, of course, presuppose Jewish eschatology, but are nevertheless new in their boldness. They are very closely related to what is called the self-consciousness of Jesus. We start with the question of John the Baptist, especially as the answer of Jesus is seldom thought of as a community formation.[1] 'Are you he who is to come, or shall we look for another?' (Matt. 11.3). Jesus' answer utilizes various passages from Isaiah (Isa. 35.5f.; 61.1): 'The blind see again, the lame walk, the dead are raised up, and the good news is preached to the poor' (Matt. 11.5). It has been noted that this is in fact not a direct answer to the Baptist's question. It merely indicates, in essence, that things have happened which characterize the reality of the Kingdom of God. This connection of question and answer (which is not at first apparent) expresses *how* the statements of Jesus about the presence of the Kingdom of God are to be conceived. The question concerns him, and the answer concerns the Kingdom of God. Jesus speaks here of the Kingdom having come only in relation to his own work. The signs of the Kingdom of God show indirectly that he, Jesus, is the one to come, for he is the one who carries out the works of the Kingdom. Hence, the statement may also be reversed: because he that is to come, Jesus, is now on earth, the Kingdom of God is here.

Here we find confirmation of the close association of Jesus' faith with the 'already' and above all see how the link of his faith with the 'already' relates in his self-consciousness to his hope in the consummation of the 'not yet'. The Kingdom of God *is* here because he who *is to* bring it is here. Wherever he is at work, there are more than mere signs; if death recedes before his message to the 'poor', as the healing of the sick and raising of the dead show, then fulfilment is already at hand.[2]

Jesus' answer is only possible because, quite apart from the signs enumerated, he understands himself as the one who is to come. A

---

[1] The situation (John the Baptist's question which still expresses a doubt), the manner in which the question is expressed (the 'one who is to come'), and the discretion of the answer all rule out a late origin of the episode.

[2] So it is not by accident that those who deny Jesus had any Messianic consciousness, while not doubting the authenticity of Jesus' answer, nevertheless play down its reference to the present by shifting the accent so that the point is stressed that only a 'dawning' of the Kingdom is involved (cf. E. Grässer, *Das Problem der Parusieverzögerung, Beiheft zur ZNW*, ²1960).

man other than Jesus could hardly point to the miracles *per se* as proof that he was the one to come. The Pharisees also drive out demons, as Jesus says in Matt. 12.27. Certainly the victory over demons, sin, sickness, and death is an external sign of the Kingdom of God. But only because Jesus is at the same time the one who will accomplish these works in a final way, do the facts enumerated amount to proof.

This interpretation is confirmed particularly by the saying about binding 'the strong man' (Mark 3.27 and parallels). Jesus answers the accusation that he is driving out demons by the prince of demons by saying parabolically that no one is able to break into the house of a strong man and rob his goods without first having bound the strong man himself. This confirms our observation that Jesus adduces the miracles enumerated in Matt. 11.5 as an answer to the question whether he is the one to come only *in connection with his self-consciousness*. The miracles of healing belong in a *total plan* for the vanquishing of Satan, and it is Jesus himself who will carry this plan *to completion*.

H. Grundmann (see ἰσχυρός, *TWNT* III, p. 403) thinks that the passage Isa. 53.12 about the Servant of God who 'shall divide the spoil with the strong; because he poured out his soul to death' lies behind the saying about 'binding the strong man'. If this is true, Jesus' consciousness of his task of bringing in the Kingdom of God through the vanquishing of Satan is related to his conviction that he must fulfil the work of the *Ebed Yahweh*.[1] Jesus' consciousness of fulfilling this work only in death does not alter anything so far as the present victory is concerned. Even what happens in Jesus' death is already anticipated in his earthly work.

Wherever he appears as the final victor over Satan, the power of the demons is already at an end. But on the other hand the figure of the 'strong man bound' (Mark 3.27; Matt. 12.29) calls to mind that his apparent power continues and is still to disappear, even though the stress is not yet placed on the fact that he is *only* bound. The figure of the strong man bound that returns later in another form in the Apocalypse (Rev. 20.2) refers to the salvation-historical tension of 'already' and 'not yet'. In the later view, the typical salvation

---

[1] There is a similar association in the close connection between the stories of the baptism and the temptation in Matt. 3–4 and Luke 3–4. The significance of the story of the baptism lies, of course, in the voice of God citing a passage in Isa. 42.1. This text appears at the beginning of the *ebed Yahweh* songs and addresses the Suffering Servant of God. See O. Cullmann, *Baptism in the New Testament*, p. 16.

historical idea of the 'thousand year reign' finds its basis in this figure.

It is important here that Jesus' statements about the present at the same time imply the 'not yet'.

Bultmann's explanation (*Theology of the New Testament I*, 1952, p. 7) that the Kingdom of God is not yet present, but is dawning, indeed expresses this one aspect of the truth. But when only this is said, the tension is taken away. The other aspect must be added: wherever he who will bring in the Kingdom of God is at work, there and only there is it present. The dialectic here seems to me to be understandable only by virtue of Jesus' special self-consciousness which Bultmann denies that he possessed in this form.

For Jesus himself, the juxtaposition of present and future statements raises no problem because he sees the Kingdom being realized in his own person. Furthermore, *for this reason a problem of the delay of the parousia cannot properly exist for him.*

In most of Jesus' sayings about the present, the victory over Satan stands in the foreground. He takes over the general conviction in Judaism that at the end Satan will be bound (*Test. Levi* 18.12 and *Zeb.* 9.8; *Jub.* 10.8; *Ass. Mos.* 10.1), and that the Messiah will vanquish him (e.g. *Pes.r.* 36). He sees this being realized in his miracles.

If the coming of the Kingdom of God is dependent upon the victory over Satan and death, this presupposes the connection of sin and death which is the point of departure for the whole salvation history of the Bible. Death and Satan prevail because man has fallen in sin. The task of the one who is to come consequently consists in the fact that he frees man from sin, and thereby vanquishes Satan and death. The 'already' and the 'not yet' results from this fact. Jesus forgives sins already, he already heals the sick (all sickness, as an instance of death, is associated with the power of the demons), he already raises the dead; but there are still sick, and the dead who are raised will die again. Satan is already vanquished where Jesus appears, forgives sin, and forces death back.

The forceful saying of Jesus in Luke 10.18 should leave no doubt that for Jesus not only is the future announced in his person, but it is already anticipated: 'I saw Satan fall like lightning from heaven.' That Jesus saw the fall of Satan so concretely indicates that he had the certainty that he was the one who had to conquer Satan both through the miracles of healing and in Satan's own province.

The close connection of the expectation of the Kingdom of God with the victory over Satan is shown by the saying from the *logia* source, cited rightly again and again as proof of the presence of the Kingdom, which is probably in its original form in Luke (11.20): 'If it is by the finger of God that I cast out demons, then the kingdom of God has already come upon you.'

Along with many translators I deliberately add the word 'already', for it is implied in the Greek verb φθάνειν, as R. Morgenthaler rightly emphasizes (*Kommendes Reich*, 1952, pp. 36ff.), comparing its use in Paul (I Thess. 2.16; 4.15; Phil. 3.16; II Cor. 10.14; Rom. 9.31). This is also the case where it is not constructed with the accusative in its classic sense. I would not describe it as a synonym of ἐγγίζειν nor in any way as equivalent to 'to come near' (so Bultmann, *TLZ* 1947, col. 272, and in a modified way even W. Michaelis, *Das Evangelium des Matthäus*, ²1949, pp. 153ff.). Here, as well as in other passages, it is actually said that the Kingdom of God has already broken in with the vanquishing of Satan and his host.

All these sayings refer to the victory over Satan already won and presuppose a self-consciousness in Jesus of being the one who must obtain this victory in its final form, both through his own death and through the eschatological struggle. The question whether or not Jesus thought in terms of salvation history may, of course, be answered in the affirmative independently of assuming Jesus to have been conscious of being the *ebed Yahweh* and the coming Son of Man. However, without this assumption, the juxtaposition of present and future in his eschatology is hardly understandable. It is hardest of all to understand on the basis of the 'indirect christology' that follows from Jesus being a mere 'herald'.[1] So a decision about the authenticity of the sayings relating to Jesus' self-consciousness is especially important.

Along with all these arguments, the fact that Jesus *forgave sins*, seldom disputed and hardly disputable, seems to me to prove that all the present statements about the victory over Satan have their roots in this self-consciousness. How monstrous Jesus' action must have been in Jewish eyes is something which we do not ordinarily realize. It is not as if Jesus merely *proclaimed* that the sins of those addressed by him were forgiven; he actually forgave their sins by his own authority. We ought to consider what kind of blasphemy the Jews would see in the usurpation implicit in that act. We ought

[1] See above pp. 52f., 107, 111f.

to take seriously the reaction of the scribes in Mark 2.7 to Jesus' declaration, 'My son, your sins are forgiven', and ask with them, 'Why does this man speak thus? It is blasphemy! Who can forgive sins but God alone?'[1] The authority to forgive sins which Jesus takes upon himself represents a claim at least as shocking as the boldest statements about himself which many have found much more offensive than this claim to authority. The latter implies a unique consciousness of 'being sent' which is more than that of a 'herald,' and is expressed particularly in Jesus' other statements about himself relating to the *ebed Yahweh* and the Son of Man.

There are New Testament scholars who would grant only that Jesus believed he was the *coming* Son of Man. But if he had this self-consciousness, he could not have ignored so easily as is assumed the urgent question about the salvation-historical relationship between his coming mission and his mission in the present. It is therefore more consistent when Bultmann and his pupils (see for example Conzelmann, $\mathcal{Z}TK$, 1957, pp. 281f.) reject even this belief in any form.

We shall see that Jesus' conviction that the present is not only an anticipation of the end, but at the same time a fulfilment of past salvation history, only becomes understandable if we assume that with his consciousness of fulfilling the mission expressed in the above Jewish titles of honour he aligned himself with salvation history.

Alongside the clear sayings about the victory already won over Satan and death, we must consider a whole series of other *logia* about the realization of the Kingdom of God in the present, all of which we cannot go into here—for instance Matt. 12.41f., Luke 11.31f., 'Something greater than Solomon is here . . . something greater than Jonah is here'; or Matt. 13.17, "Many prophets and righteous men longed to see what you see and did not see it, and to hear what you hear, and did not hear it.' C. H. Dodd adduces a whole series of parables as evidence for 'realized eschatology'[2] all of which do not, of course, relate to the problem of present and future. Moreover, decidedly futuristic statements, such as those about the nearness of the Kingdom of God (Mark 1.15 ἤγγικεν ἡ βασιλεία)[3] or Matt. 10.23, stating that the disciples will not have passed through all the cities

---

[1] Ex. 34.6; Isa. 43.25.
[2] C. H. Dodd, *The Parables of the Kingdom*, [3]1936, since then appearing in numerous reprints.
[3] See below p. 199.

of Israel before the Son of Man comes,[1] may not be taken in support of Dodd's thesis.

The passages that speak of an anticipation of the Kingdom already linked with the time of Jesus' own life are so well and clearly attested that it is not necessary to reinterpret other texts more or less forcibly to get this meaning.

On the other hand, it holds true for the other series of statements relating to the *future* Kingdom yet to come that the *logia* belonging in this series are equally clearly witnessed, and it is enough just to cite them. I shall not go any further into the sayings that allude to Jesus' death as the decisive event for the coming of the Kingdom of God.[2] They, too, refer to a time later than when the *logia* were spoken, and by this we shall see that Jesus' death is in its own way also an anticipation of the consummation. It is not necessary to cite all the passages in which Jesus clearly speaks of his expectation of a future Kingdom. I have already referred to Mark 1.15 where the translation should not be, 'the Kingdom of God has come', but 'has come near'.

Starting from the fact that in the LXX ἐγγίζειν, like φθάνειν, is a translation of the Hebrew verb *naga'* and the Aramaic *meta*, which both mean 'to come', Dodd translates Mark 1.15 as 'the Kingdom of God *has come*'. However, this meaning occurs only as an exception. J. Y. Campbell (*Expository Times* 1936/7, p. 9) and K. Clark (*JBL* 1940, pp. 367ff.) have established that in by far the most cases the verb ἐγγίζειν in the LXX means 'to come near'. Morgenthaler (*Kommendes Reich*, 1952, p. 45) has shown that in thirty-six passages where the verb ἐγγίζειν occurs in the New Testament unconnected with the expression 'Kingdom of God' (twenty-two are found in the Synoptics), the meaning is obviously 'to come near' and never 'to arrive'. W. G. Kümmel (*Verheissung und Erfüllung*, 3. Aufl., 1956, pp. 13ff., ET, pp. 19ff.) extended the study of the use of the adjective ἐγγύς in the New Testament and arrived at the same conclusion—that it describes the imminent future.

The so-called Synoptic apocalypse (Mark 13 and parallels) would be relevant to the problem under discussion; but the majority of

---

[1] See below pp. 216f.

[2] Many New Testament scholars contest the idea that Jesus regarded himself as the *ebed Yahweh* (see my *Christology of the New Testament*, 1959) and not just those belonging to the Bultmann school. W. G. Kümmel and E. Schweizer are among those who doubt this. But actually I find them merely making the assertion, and never showing any proof that all the *logia* making this identification are 'secondary compositions'.

scholars raise objections to assigning it to Jesus, although their arguments actually relate to the composition as a whole more than the individual *logia* contained in it. But even if we ignore this material in the tradition for the time being, the total witness of the Synoptic tradition is so clear in this respect that it can be pushed aside only by violent means. In this case it is necessary to proceed without any literary basis to regard a whole series of sayings of Jesus as community formations, while forcibly reinterpreting the futuristic sayings which remain after this operation.

It is enough to mention the sayings that are of prime importance: First of all, those concerning the coming judgment (Mark 8.38 and parallels; Matt. 10.15 and parallel; Matt. 11.22 and parallel; Matt. 12.41 and parallel; Matt. 19.28 and parallel; Matt. 24.40 and parallel; Matt. 7.1f; Matt. 23.33, and also the description in Matt. 25.31ff.); to deny that all these sayings go back to Jesus would be hard indeed. The same is true of the *logia* about the Messianic meal (Matt. 8.11f. and parallel; Mark 14.25); on there being no marrying in the Kingdom of God (Mark 12.25 and parallel); about the days of the Son of Man (Luke 17.26). The parables mentioned above which command alertness in view of the sudden coming of the Lord refer quite clearly to the future. We shall come back to these again. Decidedly futuristic sayings are the three predictions about the imminent nearness of the Kingdom, to come in the days of the generation alive at the time (Mark 9.1; Mark 13.30, Matt. 10.23). Because they limit the intermediate period so much that they seem to leave no room at all for any kind of positive interest in salvation history during the present time, we shall deal with them separately. The petition of the Lord's Prayer, 'thy Kingdom come' (Matt. 6.10), can be disrobed of its futuristic character only by means of an illicit spiritualization.[1]

I am limiting myself to these sayings, although others could be cited at this point. Now it is significant that we can make precisely the same observation as we made in the case of the sayings about the present. Just as the former contain at the same time an indirect reference to future events still to come, so the above mentioned passages refer tacitly to the 'already' of the present. This seems to

---

[1] It is even further from the truth to think of this petition as a secondary composition. But that is done in the argument that praying for the coming of the Kingdom would make no sense in Jesus' mouth, since he predicted this coming with such a firm conviction. Cf. E. Grässer, *Das Problem der Parusieverzögerung*, [2]1960, pp. 95ff. Such reasoning presupposes a strange conception of prayer.

me particularly important as a basis for the thesis advocated by W. G. Kümmel and myself, according to which the two series of statements, the ones relating to the present and to the future, must be allowed to stand.

This concerns primarily the sayings about judgment, and first of all the *logion* already mentioned in Mark 8.38 and parallels: 'For whoever is ashamed of me and of my words in this adulterous and sinful generation, of him will the Son of Man also be ashamed, when he comes in the glory of his Father with the holy angels.' The future judgment presupposes one already being carried out. Even if the doublet of the Q source in Matt. 10.33 and parallel does not expressly mention the coming of the Son of Man, the future judgment is nevertheless presupposed when the denial by Christ takes place before the Father in heaven (Matt. 10.33) or before the angels (Luke 12.9). On the other hand, this future denial *by* Christ is already implicit in Christ's present denial.

The reference to the present does not, of course, actually indicate that the Kingdom is already in the present, but that the Son of Man is already here. Consequently the attitude of men toward their judge already determines the coming judgment which the Son of Man will speak. This at least brings us near to the Johannine passages (3.18; 5.24) about the judgment. Matt. 25.31ff. belongs in the same frame of reference. In the description of the Last Judgment, so completely new in comparison with all late Jewish descriptions of the Judgment, the present relationship of men towards Jesus is declared as the standard for judgment, 'as you did it to one of the least of these my brethren, you did it to me'. Even if the collective meaning of the Son of Man as the 'people of the Holy One', going back to Dan. 7.13, proposed by T. W. Manson (*The Teaching of Jesus*, ²1935, pp. 227ff.), is not generally acceptable, the double meaning of 'men' and 'the Son of Man' must be reckoned within Jesus' teachings, as T. Preiss points out ('The Mystery of the Son of Man' in *Life in Christ*, 1954, pp. 43ff.; see his book *Le Fils de l'homme*, 1951 and 1953. But see F. Hahn, *Christologische Hoheitstitel*, 1963, pp. 17f.).

If this double meaning really goes back to Jesus, then a further relationship between future and present would be implied: the thought of a correspondence between Jesus and the little band of disciples would be at least already referred to; Jesus, the future Son of Man, is already present in his community. According to the later conception of early Christianity, the coming Kingdom of God is anticipated not only in Jesus' person, but in the fellowship of disciples. The connection lies in the identity of the Son of Man and the People of the Holy One in the Book of Daniel. The election of the twelve described in the saying about the twelve thrones (Matt. 19.28), and the *logion* about the little flock (Luke 12.32), to which the future Kingdom of God is to be given, and not the least the saying about the coming building of the ἐκκλησία (Matt. 16.18), would then be related to this identification,[1] and the statements about the future would be connected with the present. The void that W. G. Kümmel[2] thinks he finds in this regard between Jesus' 'historical consciousness', seeing an anticipation only in his person, and the historical consciousness of the first Christians, seeing an anticipation only in the Church, would not then exist. On the contrary, we would then be dealing with a typical, onward development of salvation history that takes its starting point in the message of Jesus.

According to Jesus' message, the Kingdom of God will come only in the future, but it is already realized and anticipated in his person during his earthly existence. If we take this conclusion seriously, we must regard what I call the tension between 'already fulfilled' and 'not yet completed' as the thing that is *really new* in Jesus' eschatology. This is the beginning of a salvation history. It is *characteristic of all New Testament salvation history that between Christ's resurrection and his return there is an interval the essence of which is determined by this tension.* The 'already' in Jesus' preaching is related to his person, and in the early Church it is related to the ἐκκλησία. This interval was, of course, assumed to be very brief by Jesus and the earliest Church, whereas the later Church reckoned with a long duration of *indefinite* extension. However, we shall raise the question later whether this further development actually justifies our overlooking the *common* judgment made by Jesus and the early Church that the present belongs to salvation history, and whether it is legitimate to construct a radical contrast between Jesus and the salvation-historical perspective.

Jesus did not, of course, *reflect* on this tension. He had no completed salvation-historical system like Luke. But the tension typical of the whole present of salvation history in the later New Testament notion is, nevertheless, the presupposition of all Jesus' activity and sayings and, above all, of what is referred to as his 'ethics'. We may accept the expression 'interim ethics', used by Albert Schweitzer, but not in the same way as Schweitzer, who read out of the intermediate period only the negative side, the 'not yet'. Instead, it must be used to refer to a true interim where the positive side in the 'already', bestowing *lasting* validity on this ethics so long as the authentic

---

[1] See F. Kattenbusch, 'Der Quellort der Kirchenidee' (Harnack *Festschrift*, 1921, pp. 142ff.).

[2] *Kirchenbegriff und Geschichtsbewusstsein in der Urgemeinde und bei Jesus* (*Symbolae Uppsal.* 1943); also *Promise and Fulfilment*, 1957, pp. 138ff.

eschatological tension remains, is just as important as the 'not yet', or even more so. This ethics becomes untenable whenever the 'already' or the 'not yet' becomes debilitated.

In regarding this 'already' and 'not yet' in their juxtaposition and intertwining as the essence of Jesus' eschatology,[1] Kümmel[2] and I are making no attempt to harmonize. I have never advocated forced harmonization. The situation as I see it and describe it in this whole chapter is that there is no scholarly justification for eliminating one or the other series of statements from Jesus' teachings. Such a procedure is indeed merely dictated by predetermined constructions. I believe that I have refuted the objection that Kümmel's and my concept of the 'tension' present in Jesus' teachings is not contained in the *logia* of both sets of statements, and that both are dissociated from one another, by demonstrating that *each of the two sets presupposes the other*: the statements about the present also refer to the consummation, and those about the future rest upon the present ones.

It is important that the *temporality* of this tension should be taken seriously and not be tacitly reinterpreted to refer to a different tension between 'desecularization' and being 'in the world'. There are certainly sayings of Jesus that expressly reject everything speculative, detached from salvation history, repudiating the reckoning of dates and places as refractory and irreconcilable with the sovereignty of God, which is nowhere more impressively shown than in the events of the end time. The temptation is great to refer to these sayings and then state that the temporal character of eschatology is something secondary in Jesus' eschatological expectation and must be reckoned among the elements to be 'demythologized'.

It is true that eschatology uses and must use many symbols to describe the indescribable. Hence, for example, in Jesus' eschatological sayings the 'Messianic meal' is a symbol of a particularly inward relationship with him. But futuristic temporality may not be assigned to these features to be demythologized, for in Jesus' teachings eschatology stands or falls with this temporality.

I have already referred to the play with etymology whereby the German word for future, '*Zukunft*', is itself demythologized, so to speak, by saying

---

[1] Although Kümmel does not directly draw the implications for a salvation-historical conception.

[2] See especially his article, 'Futurische und präsentische Eschatologie im ältesten Urchristentum', *NTS*, 1959, pp. 113ff., and his book, *Promise and Fulfilment*, 1957.

that the essential idea in it is 'what is to come to us' (*das 'auf uns zu Kommen'*), so that something that 'is to come to us' is thought of as being in the call in every decision. In this sense every event calling us to a decision becomes an eschatological event.

C. H. Dodd brings about a reinterpretation of eschatology in another way, particularly in an appendix to his book, *The Apostolic Preaching and its Development*, entitled 'Eschatology and History'. He can see no essential feature in a temporal event of the future because, as he understands it, the expectation of the Kingdom of God is already fulfilled for Jesus. Whatever remains to take place in a future event (even Dodd thinks Jesus expected to be exalted following his death) he reinterprets philosophically. His philosophy is, however, not Heidegger's, as in Bultmann, but Platonism. Hence he speaks of eternity, for which the temporal images of the future are only symbols, and of the Absolute, of timeless reality, of the 'Wholly Other' that has broken into history (Rudolph Otto influenced Dodd in this respect).

Jesus' words about not knowing the 'hour' and about the suddenness with which the kingdom of God comes seem at first to give some justification for eliminating the future and temporal character of Jesus' eschatology. In fact, they cannot be separated from the temporal expectation of salvation history. These *logia* are contained primarily in the parables admonishing alertness, mentioned above.[1] That Jesus varied the same thought in so many different parables shows how important it was to him. Usually they contain the picture of a master of a household away on a journey, which is modified in various ways. In Mark 13.35 he admonishes the gatekeeper in particular to be wakeful, 'Watch therefore—for you do not know when the master of the house will come, in the evening, or at midnight, or at cock-crow.' In Matt. 24.45ff. (Luke 12.42ff.) we read of the unfaithful servant who says to himself, ' "My lord will not come for a long time yet,"[2] and begins to beat his fellow servants, and eats and drinks with the drunken.' In Luke 12.36ff. the master comes back from the marriage, knocks for someone to let him in, and lets the servants he finds awake sit at the table. The same thought is clothed in quite a different image in the Parable on the Thief (Matt. 24.43; Luke 12.39f.): 'If the householder had known in what part of the night the thief was coming, he would have watched and would not have

---

[1] See above pp. 190, 199f.

[2] Properly translated in this way by W. Michaelis, *Der Herr verzieht nicht die Verheissung*, 1942, pp. 6ff.

let his home be broken into.' The admonition 'Watch, for you know not' reappears as a leitmotif in individual sayings as well. In Luke 12.35 it appears in the new image of the 'girded loins'.

The famous *logion* in Mark 13.32, which was placed in context with others for the first time in the composition of Mark 13, must be judged as an individual saying: 'But of that day or that hour no one knows, not even the angels in heaven, nor the Son, but only the Father.' There is no reason for doubting that this saying comes from Jesus. Of course the resurrected Lord makes a very similar statement in Acts 1.7, and the early Church had indeed an interest in handing down such sayings at a time when its members especially needed this admonition. But the kind of tendency mentioned above,[1] in this case the tendency towards a feeling of false security, was just as present among the disciples during Jesus' lifetime as it was later in the early Church after his death, and therefore Jesus himself had the same reason to combat it as did the apostles and teachers of the early Church.

The saying in Mark 13.32 can be explained only with difficulty as a secondary composition of the Church. Even if the early Church wanted to explain the delay of the *parousia* in this way, would it have invented so bold a saying about the limitations of Jesus' knowledge, contradicting all assumed christological tendencies of the early Church? The same argument by which the *logion* in Mark 10.18 ('Why do you call me good?') is found not to be a later invention ought also to be valid for Mark 13.32. Kümmel (*Promise and Fulfilment*, 1957) also regards the saying as genuine, but thinks Jesus' reference to himself as the 'Son' must have been added by the early Church.[2]

The meaning of the Parable of the Ten Virgins (Matt. 25.1ff.) is very similar. It is, of course, true that a 'being ready' is involved here rather than a 'being awake', but this does not make a great deal of difference. What is more important, as is rightly pointed out by G. Bornkamm,[3] is that the parable is different from those discussed before because here the point emphasized is not that the master comes earlier than expected, but, on the contrary, that he comes later. The foolish virgins are rebuked for not having reckoned with

[1] See above pp. 189ff.
[2] But on this point see O. Cullmann, *The Christology of the New Testament*, pp. 287ff.
[3] 'Die Verzögerung der Parusie', in *In Memoriam E. Lohmeyer*, 1951, pp. 120ff.

this possibility. This correct observation, however, makes Bornkamm think that the whole parable is a secondary composition, and he attributes its origin to an advanced stage of the delay of the *parousia* when the fact of this delay was deliberately taken into account, unlike the earlier stage when it was not. But this inference is not necessary. It must not be overlooked that the foolish virgins take along too little oil to begin with even before the delay is an established fact, because they believe the bridegroom is coming too soon, so when he delays they are naturally unprepared. Such situations certainly existed in the primitive Church; real preparedness was jeopardized because the end was expected too soon. Paul struggles against such a mood in Thessalonica where people no longer worked because they expected the imminent end. But did not such a mood exist even during Jesus' lifetime from what we see in his preaching of the nearness of the Kingdom? Reckoning on too early a date could be the reason for Jesus' censure of those who say, 'Lo, the Kingdom of God [according to Matt. 24.23 and Mark 13.21 'the Messiah'] is here or there' (Luke 17.20f.).

In reality the problem is still the same as in the other parables we have mentioned: the bridegroom is coming suddenly, but we do not know when. This *not knowing* includes both aspects: he can come within a certain short space of time, or he can come later. At any rate, the message is: be alert, be prepared, whether he comes early or late. The warning against the feeling of a *false security* is common to both the Parable of the Ten Virgins and the parables on wakefulness. The disciples ought not to be lulled into a mistaken ease either by the thought that the master will not come for a long time yet, nor by the other thought that he will be back immediately (as if they needed to assume no duties extending over a long period of time). In *both* cases, not knowing the date ought to make that feeling of false security impossible.

The suddenness of the coming of the end is described in Luke 17.22ff. in an especially graphic way: 'For as the lightning flashes and lights up the sky from one side to the other, so will the Son of Man be in his day', and the days of Noah and Lot are given as examples of the time when men lived in ease and took comfort in the thought that things would always go on as they were. Just as the upheaval then came quite unexpectedly and suddenly, in the same way, only to a totally different degree, the end will suddenly be here: 'I tell you, in that night there will be two men in one bed; one will be taken and the other left. There will be two women grinding together, one will be taken and the other left' (Luke 17.34f.).[1]

The *logion* at Luke 17.20f. cannot be interpreted with complete certainty: 'The Kingdom of God is not coming μετὰ παρατηρήσεως, nor will they say, "Lo, here it is!" or "There!" for behold the kingdom of God is ἐντὸς ὑμῶν.' Very probably the words ἐντὸς ὑμῶν, whether they are to be translated by 'within you' (Dodd), or 'in the midst of you' (the majority of exegetes), may not be claimed as support for either a present or a future conception of the Kingdom.[2] However, any reckoning on the date[3] of the coming of the Kingdom of God, and probably any special localizing of it as well (this is how the saying is understood in the version in the Coptic Gnostic Gospel of Thomas[4]) is meant to be excluded here. Man's incapability of calculating the coming of the Kingdom is at any rate the important point.

The fact that the suddenness of the coming of the Kingdom and the Son's ignorance of the date belong to Jesus' preaching, does not, however, invalidate his statement about its nearness in time, nor does it contradict that statement. Everything said in Jesus' message about the coming of the Kingdom within the generation living at the time still stands. So there is no contradiction with Jesus' words about the 'signs'. Only when the 'already' and the 'not yet' are conceived as contraries is one inclined to see a contradiction between the words dealing with signs in the present and those about not knowing the date. In reality the latter juxtaposition rests upon the juxtaposition of sets of statements about both the 'already' and the 'not yet'.

At one time it is said, 'Take heed, for you know not when the hour is coming; it will come suddenly.' At another it is said, 'Take

[1] Jewish texts also speak of the suddenness with which the Kingdom of God will come (cf. Strack-Billerbeck IV, 30. Exkurs, 'Vorzeichen und Berechnung der Tage des Messias', pp. 277ff.). So the reason escapes me why sayings expressing this sudden coming would have to have been put in Jesus' mouth by the early Church after it had experienced the delay of the *parousia*.

[2] See H. Conzelmann, *The Theology of St Luke*, 1961, pp. 120ff., 123ff. (see his footnote on p. 120 for literature on the history of the interpretation of this passage).

[3] If A. Strobel's thesis ('Die Parusieerwartung als urchristliches Problem in Lk. 17.20ff.', *ZNW*, 1958, pp. 157ff.) is correct, the term παρατήρησις contains a reference to the night of the Passover. In Jewish circles there was a tendency to set the date of the coming of the Kingdom of God on the night of a Passover. See the recent exposition of A. Rüstow (*ZNW*, 1960), who proposes the translation 'at the disposal of' for ἐντος.

[4] See A. Guillaumont, H. C. Puech, G. Quispel, W. Till, and Yassah 'Abd Al Masih, *The Gospel According to Thomas*, 1959, log. 3, p. 3.

heed, for you know the meaning of the present in which the Kingdom is already so clearly anticipated; know that the Kingdom is coming soon.' The purpose in both instances is the same.

In Luke 12.54, Jesus says to the crowd: 'When you see a cloud rising in the west, you say at once, "A shower is coming"; and so it happens. And when you see the south wind blowing, you say, "There will be scorching heat"; and it happens. You hypocrites! You know how to interpret the appearance of earth and sky; but why do you not know how to interpret the present time?' It is the responsibility of his listeners to recognize the *kairos*, not the *kairos* in which we know ourselves to be addressed in our self-understanding, but the specific *kairos* of Jesus' own present in which the disciples recognize the connection between salvation history and the eschatological future. Here again we have a demand to remain awake. The basis for this is given in the reference to the temporal anticipation of the Kingdom of God in the present, the anticipation of which we have heard in statements about the present like those in Matt. 12.28; Luke 10.18; and Matt. 11.3ff.

The parable of the Fig Tree, which all three Synoptics put at the end of the apocalypse, is to be understood in this way as well. It is right to think that originally this was an individual parable that has been appended to the remainder of the apocalypse as it was finally composed.[1] 'From the fig tree learn a parable. When its branch becomes tender and puts forth its leaves, you know that the harvest is near. So also, when you see this happening, you should know that he is near, at the very gates' (Mark 13.28ff. and parallels). If we regard the parable as an isolated one, it can only refer to signs taking place in Jesus' own present.

The juxtaposing of statements about the signs of the times with others about not knowing the hour confirms that the latter statements must not be misunderstood in such a way that futuristic temporality is entirely irrelevant. In Christ, God gave the disciples a decisive salvation-historical revelation about time, about the past, the present, and the future; they are to know exactly where they stand in the present. But every revelation in salvation history ought to admonish them to usurp God's sovereign lordship over time by human reckoning of dates. Therefore, while being wakeful and ready, they may and should pray for the coming of God's Kingdom.

All Jesus' statements about the suddenness of the coming of the

[1] See W. G. Kümmel, *Promise and Fulfilment*, pp. 20ff.

Kingdom and not knowing when it will come still presuppose that his return at a sudden and unknown hour is to be expected soon. Therefore, we maintain that a salvation-historical conception of time corresponds with the juxtaposition of a Kingdom already anticipated in Jesus' person and a Kingdom still to come. God is the Lord of time. On the one hand, in Jesus he anticipates the Kingdom in the present and reveals to the disciples the nearness of the coming Kingdom in this way. On the other hand, he reserves for himself the setting of a point in time for its consummation. We shall need to remember both these factors when we inquire about the meaning of Jesus' preaching in the context of the three sayings in which he promises the coming of the Kingdom within the generation living at his time. Both the limited temporality and the ignorance of the hour are elements that cannot be given up in Jesus' eschatology.

The *beginnings* of a developed salvation history, as this history is presupposed in the later writings of the New Testament, above all in Luke, are given in both these aspects. It is characteristic of Luke that the date of the end is no longer a problem since, on the one hand, the present is regarded already as a fulfilment, and, on the other hand, ignorance of the point in time which God sets in his authority is emphasized. Both points are made in Jesus' message, although in incipient form. For him as well, because of his self-consciousness, there can be no delay of the *parousia*. The distinction between the later concept and that of Jesus consists in the fact that Jesus proclaims that the end will come *suddenly* in a *short space of time*, whereas the later Church proclaims that it will come *suddenly* in a space of time of *indefinite duration* which can be extended *longer*. The salvation-historical conception of fulfilment of the past in Christ, anticipation of the end in Christ during the present, and the consummation yet to come, is quite untouched by this distinction. But now we shall raise the question whether this intermediate period, thought by Jesus to be so short, is really the object of an interest in salvation history, or whether it merely represents a 'dark interval', as is said by the Bultmann school.

C. IS THE TIME BEFORE THE END GIVEN SALVATION-HISTORICAL SIGNIFICANCE IN THE PROCLAMATION OF JESUS?

It would not be necessary to ask this question if the Synoptic tradition did not contain sayings in which Jesus predicts that the end will be here before all the members of the generation alive at his time have died. If these sayings are genuine and have this meaning, is there any room at all for an intermediate period in the divine plan of salvation? In this case, should not what happens during the brief time of this one generation be understood merely as a 'punctual' eschatological event that puts an end to all saving events occurring in a linear history? Or to express it another way: *for Jesus, is there any salvation-historical significance in the fact that there is still this short span of time?* Concentrated in this question is the whole problem with which we started, whether there is a continuity between Jesus' message and that of the early Church which has the significance of salvation history. The fact that Jesus reckoned only with a very brief interval, while the early Church reckoned with one of indefinite duration does not at all indicate in and of itself that the divinely determined succession of periods in salvation history is different in the two cases. The important thing is the significance of the fact that Jesus reckoned with such a brief period of time.

Without being able to go into all the details, we must discuss, at least in broad outline, the three sayings involved: Mark 9.1 and parallels, Matt. 10.23, and Mark 13.30 and parallels. Within the scope of this book it is primarily of importance to show (1) that these sayings are 'genuine', and (2) that we cannot avoid accepting the 'scandal' that Jesus set a date for the end, if not to the day and hour, at any rate within a limited space of time.

As soon as one considers that Jesus' eschatology need not be futuristic, as Bultmann does, this stumbling block disappears. The limitation of the interval in these three sayings to the time of the generation then living is then included in the general process of demythologizing, together with the futuristic character of all other eschatological statements. From this Bultmannian standpoint, there is no greater offence here in principle than in the temporal-linear conception of the future and in the assumption of a sudden halt in the course of world history in general. In contrast to such a conception, we have stressed the impossibility of abandoning the temporal-linear character of the future, but on the other hand we have referred to the setting of a date as irreconcilable with the respect for God's omnipotence so strongly emphasized by Jesus. We have not made our task easy.

We especially do not want to make it easy by succumbing to the temptation of taking our refuge in the exegetical panacea of explaining that these sayings must be eliminated from Jesus' message as 'community formations'.[1] Such a solution would be especially welcome here. If as an exegete I could really advocate this with a clear conscience, my own over-all interpretation would be facilitated. But I cannot do this, and perhaps what I meant when I spoke of the necessity of an effort at objectivity at the beginning of this chapter, meaning an elimination of our own favourite views, becomes clear in this instance.

In *Mark 9.1* we read, 'Truly, I say to you, there are some standing here who will not taste death before they see the kingdom of God come with power.' This *logion* must be compared with the one cited by Paul in I Thess. 4.15ff., about the fate of the dead at the moment of the *parousia*, who have no advantage over the living. Mark 9.1 is termed a 'community formation' (a 'comforting word') by some, and is interpreted by countless others in such a way that the scandal of a chronological limitation of the end disappears.

Those who dispute its authenticity (in a certain way even Loisy,[2] but particularly Wellhausen,[3] and subsequently Bultmann[4] and his school, including G. Bornkamm[5] and E. Grässer[6]) rightly point out that according to the saying only some, τίνες, will be alive, presupposing that the majority of people will have died. From this it is inferred that Jesus could not have made this statement. The argument goes that it is a 'comforting word' that the Church placed in Jesus' mouth: some at least will yet experience the end. Actually, it is by no means clear that Jesus was of the opinion that *all* the members of his generation would still be alive when the end would come. On the contrary, we shall see how all the indications are that he expected that many would have already died.

Moreover, it is difficult to explain how anyone could have put

---

[1] A. Vögtle, 'Exegetische Erwägungen über das Wissen und Selbstbewusstsein Jesu', in *Gott in Welt, Festgabe K. Rahner*, 1964, pp. 608ff.) regards Mark 13.30 as genuine and relates it to the destruction of the temple (see below p. 214 n. 4). So far as the other two passages, Mark 9.1 and Matt. 10.23, are concerned, he attributes their present form to the early Church, but tries to show how they were derived from authentic sayings of Jesus. Accordingly Jesus' original words do not contain the offensive limitation of time to his own generation, and the scandal is circumvented.

[2] A. Loisy, *L'évangile selon Marc*, 1911, *ad loc*. He thinks that Jesus said πάντες, and the Church altered it to τίνες.

[3] *Das Evangelium Marci*, 1909, p. 68.

[4] *The History of the Synoptic Tradition*, 1963, p. 121.

[5] 'Die Verzögerung der Parusie', *In Memoriam E. Lohmeyer*, 1951, pp. 116ff.

[6] E. Grässer, *op. cit.*, pp. 131ff.

such a *logion* into Jesus' mouth since it speaks of people who must
have been alive at the time the saying originated. It is said of them
that they 'stood by' at the time when Jesus said these words. How
could such a precise statement of Jesus be invented when it would
easily have been disputed at the time of its appearance?

G. Bornkamm, *op. cit.*, p. 117, apparently sensed this difficulty. Thus he
thinks the saying is a 'prophetic oracle'. But even so, the later transference
of the oracle to Jesus and his contemporaries presupposes a long and complicated process of development that does not explain the above-mentioned difficulty satisfactorily.

For those holding this saying to be a 'comforting word' to the
Church which was later disappointed because of the delayed *parousia*,
there is an added difficulty in the fact that the word 'some', τίνες,
does not stand in contrast to πάντες. To be sure it tacitly presupposes
that most will have died, but it is *nowhere emphasized* that 'some' will
still be alive. It is not constructed like I Cor. 15.51 where Paul expressly says, 'we shall not all sleep'. The τίνες without stress seems
to me to prove that the saying cannot be understood as a reaction
to the delay of the *parousia*, but must be seen as proof that Jesus
expected the end to be very near, but not immediately near (most
will have died!).

The saying of Jesus cited by Paul in I Thess. 4.15ff. accords with
this. The problem there, of course, is not the date of the *parousia*,
but the fate of those who have died before it arrives. It assumes as
self-evident that at the moment of the *parousia* some of those who
were members of the Church from its beginnings will have died while
others will still be alive. The situation thus seems to be that those
still living will be more numerous than the dead, while in Mark 9.1
the opposite seems to be the case. If that is true, there is a development in Jesus' thinking similar to the one expressed in Paul.

The answer to the problem disturbing the Thessalonians, which
Jesus also had to deal with in the *logion* under discussion, is important
for the question of salvation history since time goes on even for the
dead[1] in the course of the divine plan of salvation.

We cannot go in detail into the question of where the citation of this
saying of Jesus in I Thess. 4.15 begins and where it ends. (J. Jeremias,
Unknown Sayings of Jesus, 1957, p. 64, thinks that a genuine saying of Jesus

---

[1] This is also the opinion in Rev. 6.10 where the souls of the martyrs cry out
from under the altar, 'How long . . .?'

begins in v. 16. It appears to me quite possible that it is only in v. 15 or is already in v. 15—the problem remains the same.) J. A. T. Robinson, *Jesus and His Coming*, 1957, p. 25, cannot regard it as genuine because of C. H. Dodd's thesis. I cannot see why G. Bornkamm (*op. cit.*, p. 119) does not consider the possibility that this *logion* is genuine. He regards it with M. Dibelius (*An die Thessalonicher, HNT* 1925 *ad loc.*) as a 'prophetic oracle'.

The fact that Christians died at all was probably felt as a problem when the first instances of death occurred in the Church, as Ph. Menoud rightly emphasizes ('Le mort d'Ananias et de Saphira', *Mélanges Goguel, Aux sources de la tradition chrétienne*, 1950, pp. 146ff.). A text such as I Cor. 11.30 indicates that, according to the original notion, there really ought not to be any more sickness after Christ's resurrection. But this is a problem of the resurrection faith, not of the delay of the *parousia*. Therefore, W. Michaelis ('Kennen die Synoptiker eine Parusieverzögerung,' *Synoptische Studien A. Wikenhauser dargebracht*, 1954) probably unnecessarily disputes Menoud's thesis in order to argue against G. Bornkamm's interpretation.

We shall not linger over the countless attempts at a reinterpretation of the *logion* in Mark 9.1 from Clement of Alexandria to C. H. Dodd. They represent attempts to avoid the scandal that Jesus predicted the end for the time of his generation. Especially popular are the attempts which find the preliminary events before the end and not the end referred to in the words, 'until they see the kingdom of God coming in power': i.e., the transfiguration,[1] or the resurrection and ascension.[2] To refer the sayings to Pentecost,[3] or to the preaching of the gospel in the Church,[4] or to the destruction of Jerusalem is also a popular solution.[5] Dodd gives a special interpretation. It is not dictated by an effort to get around the offence of the unfulfilled prophecy of Jesus, but it is meant to mitigate the futurity of eschatological events in accord with Dodd's general view. By emphasizing the Greek perfect ἐληλυθυῖαν, Dodd translates, 'until

[1] Clement of Alexandria (*Excerpta Theodoti*), Chrysostom, Theophylact, and Enthymus.

[2] K. Barth, 'Auslegung von Mt. 28, 16–20' (*Basler Missionsmagazin*, 1945, pp. 5f.). It is possible (in fact even probable) that the early Church which preserved the saying understood it in this way.

[3] G. Wohlenberg, *Das Evangelium des Markus* (*Zahn-Kommentar zum NT*), 1910, pp. 240f.

[4] M. J. Lagrange, *L'évangile selon S. Luc*, 1942, *ad loc.*

[5] This is also considered by M. J. Lagrange, *ibid.* This hypothesis contains a kernel of truth to the extent that this event is expected as a part of the eschatological drama. But Jesus did not consider the destruction of the temple as *the* event of the end. See below pp. 224f., 227f., and above pp. 164f.

they have seen (found out) that the Kingdom of God has come in power'. He stresses the words 'in power' and refers them generally to Christ's exaltation.[1] Even though this interpretation is not impossible grammatically,[2] the verb 'to see' here must be thought of as meaning 'to see as eyewitnesses', followed by the Kingdom of God as object in the accusative.

The inference appears to me unavoidable that Jesus actually predicted in this saying that some of those hearing him then would experience the 'final' coming of the Kingdom. It is of equal importance that he assumes here that some of them, indeed, most of them, will have died.[3]

The second *logion* which attests in a similar way Jesus' expectation that the end was imminent is *Mark 13.30* and parallels: 'Truly, I say to you, this generation will not pass away before all these things take place.' In the three Synoptics it stands in the so-called Synoptic apocalypse, but it must surely be interpreted as a separate *logion*. Therefore all attempts to relate the words 'all these things', ταῦτα πάντα, only to one event or another mentioned in the apocalypse as it now stands are hardly correct. Particularly popular is the limiting of the saying to the capture of Jerusalem;[4] but we can hardly think that Jesus did not link this event, which he certainly predicted, with further eschatological events.[5]

The attempt, quite interesting in itself, to remove any expectation of a near end from the saying on the basis of the first clause, 'This

[1] A similar explanation is given by J. A. Baird, *The Justice of God in the Teaching of Jesus*, 1963, pp. 142ff.

[2] But see J. Y. Campbell, *Expository Times*, 1936/1937, pp. 93f., and J. M. Creed, *ibid.*, pp. 184f.

[3] W. Michaelis (*Der Herr verzieht nicht die Verheissung*, 1942, pp. 36f.) makes much too far-fetched an attempt at reinterpreting the first clause. Because of the position of ὧδε in Codex B, here he would translate this word with 'thus', and 'standing' would mean 'to stand firm' as opposed to 'fall', as in many Pauline passages. G. Wohlenberg (*op. cit.*, p. 239) thinks Jesus is speaking of those who stand in contrast to those who sit, a very improbable and almost humorous interpretation.

[4] Favouring this view is A. Feuillet in his article, 'Le Discourse de Jésus sur la Ruine du Temple', *Revue Biblique*, 1948, pp. 481ff., and 1949, pp. 61ff. Also V. Taylor, *The Gospel according to St. Mark*, 1952. Similarly A. Vögtle, 'Exegetische Erwägungen über das Wissen und Selbstbewusstsein Jesu', in *Gott in Welt, Festgabe K. Rahner*, 1964, pp. 642f.

[5] H. Conzelmann, *The Theology of St. Luke*, 1961, p. 120, stresses that Luke says only πάντα instead of ταῦτα πάντα, and that in this way the whole realization of the divine plan of salvation was included in this *logion* for the first time by the evangelist. E. Grässer (*op. cit.*, p. 130 n. 2) rightly concedes that Conzelmann places too much weight on Luke's omission of ταῦτα.

generation will not pass away', is hardly tenable. It is denied that γενεά here has the chronological meaning of 'generation' in two ways: The γενεά is sometimes related to the 'Jewish people'. This is the interpretation given by Schniewind,[1] and in this way he can understand the *logion* in the sense of Romans 9–11 which says the Jewish people will be preserved to the end. Then again, the γενεά is related to 'this corrupt generation', and the resultant meaning is that the corrupted nature of men will ensure until the last day.[2] But even though this meaning of the word γενεά is attested, it is still not the usual one. The word has primarily a temporal significance (e.g., Mark 8.12 and parallels; Matt. 11.16 and parallel; Matt. 23.36 and parallel), especially when connected with the demonstrative pronoun, where it translates the Hebrew *haddōr hazzeh*.[3]

The inference seems to me unavoidable that Jesus made a statement here very similar to the one in Mark 9.1: the Kingdom of God will come before all who belong to the living generation have died. The two sayings are closely connected with each other.[4] Here again the meaning cannot be, *'no one* belonging to this generation will die before the *parousia'*. In Mark 9.1 it is pointed out even more clearly than here that most will have died.

There is just as little reason for doubting that this saying is from Jesus as in the case of Mark 9.1. Those who deny the authenticity of Mark 9.1 are, of course, compelled to regard this, too, as a 'community formation' because of the close relationship of the two *logia*, although if they started with Mark 13.30 by itself and did not have the τίνες in Mark 9.1, interpreters would hardly have come to see in it a 'word of comfort due to the delay of the *parousia'*.[5]

---

[1] *Das Evangelium des Markus (NTD*, 1933, p. 167). So also F. Busch, *Zum Verständnis der synoptischen Eschatologie, Mk. 13 neu untersucht*, 1938, pp. 133f.

[2] So argues W. Michaelis, *Der Herr verzieht nicht die Verheissung*, 1942, pp. 30ff.

[3] See F. Büchsel, 'γενεά' in *TWNT* I, p. 661. So also B. Rigaux, 'La seconde venue de Jésus', *La venue du Messie, Rech. Sc. bibl.*, 1962, p. 197, and G. R. Beasley-Murray, *A Commentary on Mark 13*, 1957, pp. 99f.

[4] R. Bultmann, *History of the Synoptic Tradition*, p. 123, rightly sees this. He even views this *logion* as a variant to Mark 9.1. J. A. T. Robinson, *Jesus and His Coming*, 1957, p. 92, rightly points to the parallel construction of the three *logia*, Mark 9.1, Mark 13.30, and Matt. 10.23, but in accordance with his view he interprets all three in such a way that their chronological reference is secondary and has taken the place of a statement concerning the disciples' situation.

[5] Characteristically, Bultmann does not start from Mark 13.30, but from Mark 9.1, and E. Grässer, *op. cit.*, p. 130, must concede that 'in itself the verse (Mark 13.30) does not contain anything contradictory to Jesus' message'. Nevertheless, he still uses the same interpretative key, the delay of the *parousia* which the Church experienced, to answer the question of how this *logion*, too, arose.

The third *logion*, Matt. 10.23, is distinguished from the other two by the fact that the coming of the Kingdom of God (the 'Son of Man') is not linked to the living generation in a general way, but precisely, to a task of the disciples now being performed which will still be unfulfilled at the time of the *parousia*—the mission in Palestine: 'You will not have gone through all the towns in Israel before the Son of Man comes.' A great deal has been written about this saying. It is the basis for Albert Schweitzer's whole construction,[1] quite generally rejected by New Testament scholars today.[2] According to Schweitzer, Jesus expected the end to come during his lifetime while the disciples were on their way. Their return (Mark 6.30ff.) led to a great disappointment and caused Jesus to think the Kingdom of God would appear only with his death. But this thesis, uninformed by what we have learned from form criticism, is bound too much to the context in Matt. 10 and rests upon an arbitrary connection with Mark 6.30 where in any case nothing is said of a disappointment.

Nevertheless, this interpretation pays heed to the temporal limitation in the *logion*. The temporality of this *logion* is again eliminated by means of various interpretations. So J. Schniewind,[3] who is followed in the main by Michaelis,[4] advocates an interpretation analogous to the one for Mark 13.30: the mission among the Jews spoken of here is not limited to Jesus' lifetime nor to the generation of the disciples. Instead, it is merely said that the mission to the Jews, however long it may last, will be continued up to the last day. Nothing is said about the point in time when the Kingdom of God will come. Here again the idea of Romans 9–11 is present. But if this were really the meaning of the *logion*, the stress would have to lie on the idea that Israel's conversion will only take place at the end, whereas apparently our *logion* wishes to emphasize the 'already' when it says οὐ μὴ τελέσητε . . .

On the other hand, the attempt has been made to relate the οὐ μὴ τελέσητε not to the missionary proclamation, but to the possibility of flight—'you will always find cities into which you can flee'.[5] This

---

[1] See above p. 30.
[2] See H. Schuster, 'Die konsequente Eschatologie in der Interpretation des Neuen Testaments kritisch betrachtet', *ZNW*, 1956, pp. 1ff.
[3] *Das Evangelium nach Matthäus*, *NTD*, 1937, p. 131.
[4] *Op. cit.*, p. 63.
[5] So R. Schnackenburg, *Gottes Herrschaft und Reich*, 1959, pp. 142f.

interpretation can make a case from the context, of course, but is hard to reconcile with the meaning of οὐ τελέσητε.[1]

Along with the interpretations that seek to overcome the time limitation by pointing out that the length of time is unspecified in the first clause, there are attempts here, as in the case of Mark 13.30, to interpret the final clause in such a way that the 'coming of the Son of Man' does not represent the end. These interpretations which attempt to see the *parousia* not in a single act, but in various events preceding the end,[2] contradict too much the meaning the words 'coming of the Son of Man' otherwise have.

It does not surprise us that the authenticity of this *logion* is contested by some, but it is one of the few eschatological sayings Bultmann accepts as genuine.[3] However, Wellhausen and after him Grässer among others regard it as a secondary composition, as a saying aimed at stirring up the Church to carry out the mission courageously despite all the difficulties.[4]

Actually, there is no serious reason to be adduced which would justify declaring the *logion* to be inauthentic. Once again, the fact that a *logion* accords with a tendency of the early Church is not sufficient reason.

We cannot say with certainty from this whether Jesus reckoned with a short duration of time before the end in the period after his death. All three sayings (Mark 9.1; 13.30; Matt. 10.23) do agree, however, that he expected the Kingdom of God would come while at least some belonging to his generation were alive.

Does this really mean that the time remaining has no more significance for Jesus? It is only with this question that we must deal. For this reason we must, however, ask what caused Jesus to reckon

---

[1] See W. G. Kümmel, 'Die Naherwartung in der Verkündigung Jesu', in *Zeit und Geschichte. Dankesgabe für R. Bultmann*, 1964, pp. 41f.

[2] The collective interpretation of the term 'Son of Man' to refer to God's people has better support. J. W. Bowman, *The Religion of Maturity*, 1948, pp. 254f., argues in this fashion. In that case, the saying would envisage the origin of the Church. Although this usage of the term 'Son of Man', which goes back to the Book of Daniel, is not out of place with Jesus (see above p. 201), the passage does not at all suggest this interpretation.

[3] R. Bultmann, *The History of the Synoptic Tradition*, 1963, pp. 152ff., and *Theology of the New Testament*, 1952, p. 30.

[4] When a person is committed to 'realized eschatology', the saying is regarded as rewritten (J. A. T. Robinson, *Jesus and His Coming*, 1957, pp. 91f.), or as inauthentic (T. F. Glasson, *The Second Advent*, ²1947, pp. 103ff.). E. Stauffer, *New Testament Theology*, 1955, n. 267, and A. N. Wilder, *Eschatology and Ethics in the Teaching of Jesus*, ²1950, are also inclined to think it is inauthentic.

with so short a time and to express this opinion from time to time to his disciples.

I am not forcibly making these three statements innocuous when I say that their meaning within Jesus' total eschatological preaching does not consist in their fixing a date, although that is doubtless implicit in them.[1] They must be placed in the context of the rest of his statements about the coming end—about not knowing the hour ('. . . not even the Son!'), the suddenness of the end, the necessity of being wakeful, and *above all* they must be seen in line with his basing of the nearness of the end upon the *anticipation* of the end *already realized in his person*. For this reason we are not entitled to deny that the predictions come from Jesus, but they must be regarded as having secondary importance.

The endeavour to distinguish Jesus' central teachings from those derived from them ought not to be condemned in itself; the fault is the arbitrariness with which the criterion for this distinction is reached. According to all that we have found up to this point, the plan which God fulfils in time is important and an object of revelation for Jesus. In accord with everything he said about the authority of God in setting the date for the coming of the Kingdom, his limitation of the time remaining cannot have the importance that is attributed to it. It cannot entitle us to make an enthusiastic visionary of Jesus, for whom the time remaining has no significance. On the contrary, this time, despite its brevity, has its special meaning in salvation history. Time in terms of a date becomes unimportant for Jesus; but not time as a meaningful course of God's saving plan in successive stages.

If we bear in mind that the important thing is the way Jesus' eschatology rests on events in the present associated with his own consciousness of himself, then we may even say that the substance of his eschatology is indeed the temporal concept of the end, but not the precise declaration of when the end will come, as we occasionally find it in the sayings we have examined. If, as I believe I have shown in the case of Jesus' expectation of a near end, the most important thing is the founding of this expectation upon the 'already', then the essential thing is not the actual determining of a date, but

[1] I would especially ask the pupils of Bultmann to refrain from their unjust insinuation that ecclesiastical and apologetic reasons bring me to this judgment. If I allowed myself to be persuaded by such considerations, I 'could have made my explanation of these three *logia* easier for myself. I am making this request of the *pupils* of Bultmann, for I know that Bultmann himself does not impute such apologetic tendencies to me.

the fact that time has made a mighty leap towards its end in the person of Jesus, that we have entered the final phase of this aeon, and that now the end can come at any time.

It is fashionable to argue these days that there is a complete break between the salvation-historical conception of the later Church and Jesus' eschatology, which is allegedly dissociated from salvation history. It is customary for the advocates of this thesis to say that when the date of the end no longer posed a problem because all the weight was placed on the time of the Church in the present, upon the 'already', this development amounted to a complete *novum*, the so-called 'early Catholic' conception. Actually, we discover that the 'already' is so important for Jesus that his limitation of the time remaining to his own generation must not be over-emphasized. More-over, we have found that the question of the date belongs to those elements *which have undergone corrections in connection with the divine saving process again and again in the development of all biblical salvation history*, without the total salvation-historical view being altered.

It is almost beyond question that Paul did not always hold the same opinion about the question of the date of the *parousia*.[1] Theoretically it is not out of the question (as Albert Schweitzer believes, albeit in a way that is exegetically questionable) that the message of the incarnate Lord (whose ignorance of the date is expressed in Mark 13.32—'nor the Son') in this item of secondary importance went through a development in relation to the saving event which he himself accomplished. (See what is said above on I Thess. 4.15 and Mark 9.1.) This cannot, of course, be proved with certainty. The Epistle to the Hebrews (see my *Christology of the New Testament*, 1959, pp. 93ff.) assumes that during his incarnation, Jesus passed through a human development without which, of course, his humanity would not be complete.

If it is correct that Jesus was conscious of having to carry out the role of the *ebed Yahweh*,[2] then from the point of view of the 'historical Jesus' the death he foresaw for himself was to be at least the *decisive* future event, even though it does not coincide with the point in time when the end comes.[3] Hence, Jesus' agreement with the later Church at this central point is much more important than his difference with the Church, thinking as he did that the end would come within the lifetime of his own generation. Thus this abbreviated

---

[1] Cf. L. Goppelt, *Die apostolische und nachapostolische Zeit*, 1955ff., pp. A 93–94.
[2] See above pp. 107f., 199, n. 2, and my *Christology of the New Testament*, pp. 51ff.
[3] On this point see below pp. 227f.

perspective in Jesus is explained by his consciousness that in this respect, too, the *foundation* of his eschatological expectation is the essential and abiding factor.

At any rate, the continual demand of Jesus for constant vigilance shows that his primary concern was for his generation to prepare itself in the right way for the end. Therefore on occasions he imparts to his disciples his conviction that several or a few of them would yet experience the end. The essential thing for him was that they should take seriously the matter of always being prepared. Psychologically speaking, there is probably not the same stimulus for being ready if the end is expected within the present generation as there is if one reckons on a quite indefinite duration. But for *salvation history*, the crucial thing is knowing that the end can come at any time, since the final phase is ushered in with the decisive event that has occurred.

Jesus' urgent admonition to vigilance also shows that he attributed a *special significance in the saving event* to his generation within the brief time still remaining to it. Not only had he himself to fulfil his mission in this extremely important time, but the whole generation living in his time had an eminently significant task to carry out in the history of salvation. Hence the constitution of the circle of disciples, the 'people of the Holy One', identified in Daniel with the Son of Man.[1] *It is to the Messiah that the Messianic group belongs.*[2] Of course, this group is not yet the subsequent Church; but the members of Jesus' generation, as long as they are still alive, brief as the time before the end measured out to them is, not only have their definite place in the saving event, but are the 'salt of the earth' (Matt. 5.13). How can anyone then designate the time that still remains as a dark interval? How can anyone say that Jesus did not think of this time as belonging to salvation history? Jesus' limiting of this period, attested in the three *logia* we have dealt with, does not in any way justify our excluding an intermediate period in salvation history from Jesus' eschatological thinking. Thus, although for Jesus this period is restricted in contrast to the eschatology of the later Church, it is the natural beginning of the further development of a salvation-historical perspective.

What has been said here about Jesus' interest in the time still remaining in salvation history must now be demonstrated from his ethical instructions to the disciples.

[1] See above p. 201.
[2] F. J. Leenhardt, *Le Sacrement de la S. Cène*, 1948.

If Jesus imparted instructions to his disciples for their life in the world, then these presuppose a time in which the instructions are to be observed. It cannot then be insignificant for salvation that there is such a time. Certainly the consideration, important for later salvation history, that the lives and activities of the apostles are fundamental to subsequent generations, is one lying outside the horizon of Jesus' message. But this distinction does not entitle us to regard the time during which the disciples had to prove themselves and to preach the gospel as unimportant for salvation. The starting point for the early Christian conception of the role of the apostolate is given by Jesus in the fact that it is the task of the disciples to proclaim the gospel before the end in the twofold way of living up to their commitment and of preaching the message. The question as to the length of the time before the end plays a subordinate role, despite the distinction between Jesus' statements and those of the later Church. The relationship between Jesus and the later Church becomes apparent when Jesus preaches to the disciples that this time, as the final phase before the end, is relatively short, but that a time still remains to them during which they must fulfil a particular task. This means that even in the matter of ethics the temporal tension in Jesus' preaching is analogous to the message of the later Church. Jesus' ethics is indeed interim ethics, as Schweitzer says; his ethics are in fact related to an interval, a time of tension. But that does not mean that they can only be valid so long as one believes in the restriction of the interval to the generation of Jesus. They can also find application during a time prolonged over centuries without the temporal character of this period as an interval being given up and existentially dissolved. It is apparent that Jesus' ethics do not lend themselves to religious fanaticism.

This confirms everything we have said about Jesus' eschatology. Again and again people have marvelled that wisdom teachings are to be found in Jesus that do not stand directly in relation to the immediate nearness of the end.[1] Again, it is too easy a solution when one seeks to exclude this whole portion of Jesus' teachings as later compositions of the Church. In reality they, too, stand under the message that the Kingdom of God is at hand. Yet this must not be interpreted as a feverish message leaving no place for ethics proper. Both sides must be remembered: the Kingdom is already here in

[1] A. N. Wilder has wrestled with this problem in his book *Eschatology and Ethics in the Teaching of Jesus*, [2]1950.

Christ, and the Kingdom is coming. If we take both aspects into account, we are left with the two motives characteristic of Jesus' ethics: *decision* and *testing*. Everything Bultmann says about decision is right, provided a salvation-historical 'now' is put in place of 'always' (standing in decision). This 'now' includes the testing in the present which is the time of salvation. For determining the ethical significance of our time, it is important to know that it is an interval between 'already' and 'not yet'.

Whether we assume, as is at any rate possible,[1] that Jesus foresaw the preaching to the Gentiles in the brief period after his death, or whether he thought only of the further preaching to Israel, it is certain that *proclamation* is the ethical significance of the interval in view of the imminent end and the immediate past. That is the salvation-historical significance of the time of decision in which the disciples stand, or (if we want to use the term) of their 'existential' mission. That, too, is the *connecting link* between the brief interval in the perspective of Jesus and of the primitive Church on the one hand, and the prolonged interval of the later Church on the other.

Jesus is no fanatic. His ethical instructions show that despite his conviction about the near end, without any eschatological fever, without reckoning the day and hour, he calmly accepts the time yet remaining as time established in the will of God.

There must therefore be room for the disciples' own individual testing in terms of their sanctification. This testing is preaching, in view of the coming Kingdom. Here is the situation of the servant who has to prove himself in the short period before the master comes. Certainly this time is short, and certainly Jesus nowhere *speculates* about aligning it with a long history of salvation. This is the case only in the early Church, where the experiences of Easter and receiving the Spirit, not primarily the delay of the *parousia*, will bring about a completed salvation-historical perspective. It remains true that for Jesus as well it is the time in which the disciples enter into *Jesus' own* preaching.

Jesus' ethics is determined by the meaning of this interval. The nearness of the end makes the decision all the more serious, but the ethics itself gets its content from the tension of the interval in salvation history between 'already' and 'not yet'. So interim ethics does not at all mean an ethics that would not be applicable for a *prolonged* time. The essential thing is only that extended time is also

[1] D. Bosch, *Die Heidenmission in der Zukunftsschau Jesu*, 1959.

conceived as an end time and as an interval. Knowing the seriousness of the hour does not depend in Jesus' teachings upon the limitation of the interval to his own generation.

Jesus reckons on this interval as a matter of course without reflecting about it. This, however, is not an indication that the interval is insignificant for him. It shows instead his conviction that this time is willed by God. The well-known saying spoken by Jesus at his anointing in Bethany underlines this fact: 'You always have the poor with you . . . but you will not always have me' (Mark 14.7).[1] The stress is, of course, on the final clause here: 'you will not always have me'. The matter of fact way in which it is presumed that the disciples will always have the poor among them indicates that this frame of reference in which the poor still exist will continue even beyond Jesus' death which is foreseen in this passage.

The *logion* in Mark 14.7 does not contradict Jesus' notion that the Kingdom of God is still coming within his generation. But it does permit us to go a step further and clearly see that the Kingdom will only come *after his death*, even though it is coming very soon. This fact is not without significance, for it shows that the interval is already determined as one lying *between Jesus' death and the end*. In this respect a line is drawn from Jesus' message to the later scheme of salvation history, even though the difference in the length of time envisaged before the end—limited here, unlimited there—must not be overlooked.

Are there other *logia* of Jesus that confirm that he reckoned on a duration of time beyond his death? With Kümmel[2] we would like to answer this question in the affirmative. We have seen[3] that it is actually probable, judging from the expectation of the three sayings Mark 9.1, Mark 13.30, and Matt. 10.23, predicting the end in the time of Jesus' own generation, and almost certain from Mark 9.1 ($\tau\iota\nu\epsilon\varsigma$), that most persons belonging to Jesus' generation will have died and only a few will still be alive. This situation presupposes that the end will come *some time after Jesus' death*.

The saying concerning fasting must be mentioned here (Mark 2.18ff. and parallels), where the distinction is made between the time of the present as the time of the bridegroom and a time when he is taken from the disciples. We recall, furthermore, the predictions

[1] Against W. G. Kümmel, *op. cit.*, pp. 86f.
[2] See W. G. Kümmel, *Promise and Fulfilment*, pp. 64ff.
[3] See above pp. 212ff.

of persecutions that must be related primarily to the time after Jesus'
death.[1] Here in particular we return to the words about the temple.
Certainly Jesus predicted the destruction of the temple, and there is
no doubt that it amounted to an important event for him. The
saying, 'For if they do this when the wood is green, what will happen
when it is dry?' (Luke 23.31) implies the prediction of the destruction of Jerusalem. If Jesus, who rejects Zealotry, is crucified as a
Zealot, what will happen when the Romans go against the real
Zealots?[2] Here Jesus separates in time the destruction of Jerusalem
from his own death. The destruction of Jerusalem must therefore fall
in the time *after* his death.[3] Although the prediction of the destruction
of the temple is an element from late Jewish apocalyptic, it must be
evaluated in the same way as the so-called political predictions of the
Old Testament prophets. Looking from an event of his time, Jesus
makes statements about the future. That does not mean that this
event does not belong to the actual eschatological events. Nevertheless, it is not a part of the final act[4] of these events, belonging instead
to the brief space of time between the resurrection and the *parousia*.

If the destruction of Jerusalem takes place in this brief span of
time,[5] there are naturally important consequences for Jesus' prediction that he would build a temple not made with hands. Nothing
would then stand in the way of interpreting this saying to relate to
the new people of God. Then Jesus' prediction in the much-discussed
passage at Matt. 16.18 that he will build a *Q^ehal* may not be termed
'inauthentic' as casually as was done before the epoch introduced
by Kattenbusch and K. L. Schmidt,[6] and even today by the Bultmann school among others.[7] The people of God must enter into
Jesus' own task in this brief interval. The idea of a Messianic people
of God is most closely related to the self-consciousness of Jesus. To

[1] Naturally these sayings, too, are often dismissed as 'community formations'
one and all. Even if experiences in the early Church could figure as predictions
'*ex eventu*', there is still no reason whatever why Jesus should not have predicted
that the disciples following him would suffer and be persecuted in the time after
his life.

[2] O. Cullmann, *The State in the New Testament*, pp. 47ff.

[3] See the old tradition that has been preserved independently in Luke 21.20–24.

[4] Against W. G. Kümmel, see below pp. 228f. and above p. 114.

[5] See C. H. Dodd, 'The Fall of Jerusalem and the Abomination of Desolation',
in *Journal of Roman Studies*, 1947, pp. 47ff.

[6] W. G. Kümmel prefers this view in *Kirchenbegriff und Geschichtsbewusstsein in
der Urgemeinde und bei Jesus* (*Symb. Biblicae Upsalienses*, H. 1, 1943). He seems to me
to be as inconsistent as ever here.

[7] O. Cullmann, *Peter: Disciple, Apostle, Martyr*, ²1962, pp. 163ff.

the Messiah belongs the Messianic community which prepares the way for the end time. Certainly in these matters we must not imagine a 'time of the Church' hundreds of years long. For Jesus, the time of the Church would be one limited to a *brief* interval.

Decidedly indicative of such an interval is the saying in Matt. 12.41ff. about the Ninevites who will rise at the judgment 'with this generation' and judge it, and about the Queen of the South who will rise 'with this generation' and judge it. The presupposition here is the same as in Mark 9.1, and probably in Mark 13.30, that the majority of the members of this generation will have died.

One final text ought still to be mentioned, the saying before the high priest: 'You will see the Son of man sitting at the right hand of Power, and coming with the clouds of heaven' (Mark 14.62). As the coming on the clouds is mentioned here *after* the 'sitting at the right hand', an interval is distinguished from the end, an 'already' from the 'not yet'.

T. F. Glasson (*The Second Advent. The Origin of the New Testament Doctrine*, ²1947, pp. 17ff.; 63ff.) and J. A. T. Robinson (*Jesus and His Coming*, 1957, pp. 43ff.) raise an important objection against this application of Jesus' statement. In Jesus' answer two citations of the Old Testament are united. One is from Ps. 110 about the priest-king sitting at the right hand of power, and the other is from Dan. 7.13 about the coming of the Son of Man. It is significant that by his first citation before the high priest Jesus refers to what is going to happen in heaven. So far as the second is concerned, Glasson and Robinson affirm that in Dan. 7.13 the Son of Man does not come to earth at all, but to God, to the 'Ancient of Days'. Consequently, not the *parousia*, but Jesus' exaltation is meant here. The objection does not deserve to be flippantly brushed aside. I have always simply taken this text as indicating that Jesus thought there would be an interval. I confess that Glasson and Robinson's objection has impressed me and that I do not believe I may use the text without referring to this objection. In any case, their point must be taken more seriously than the assertion that this answer simply rests upon a later christological combination as we find it in credal form, where first of all the exaltation and then the *parousia* are spoken of (so E. Grässer, *op. cit.*, pp. 172ff.[1]). If I am unconvinced by Glasson and Robinson, it is because they cannot satisfactorily explain the remarkable placing of Ps. 110 *before* Dan. 7.13. Why

---

[1] To his further argument against the authenticity of this saying, that the whole scene of the session before the Sanhedrin is unhistorical, one may reply that only the character of the session, with its passing of a juristic sentence, is incorrect, and not the session itself. See O. Cullmann, *The State in the New Testament*, pp. 41ff.

is the sitting at the right hand of Power mentioned before the coming of the Son of Man if the latter means nothing more than his exaltation to God? J. A. T. Robinson (*Jesus and His Coming*, p. 45, n. 2) mentions the difficulty, but he does not solve it with the statement that originally 'parallel' statements were involved. Then, too, the claim that ἀπ' ἄρτι was originally in Mark does not seem to me to be demonstrated.

But in particular the question must be asked, did not the coming of the Son of Man on the clouds in Dan. 7.13 *have to* become a 'return' as soon as Jesus applied the prediction to himself as one 'already having come', who also ascribes the *eschatological* role of the Son of Man to himself? In that case, *must* not the passage from Daniel about the coming on the clouds become a coming from God's side to earth? Everything here, of course, depends upon whether Jesus regarded himself as the *future* Son of Man or not. If we do not eliminate the *logia* relevant to this idea as secondary compositions, Jesus must have regarded his role at the end as parallel to his first coming. Then the coming on the clouds becomes a coming to the earth. One fails to see why this reinterpretation of the passage from Daniel had to be undertaken for the first time by the Church, and not by Jesus himself. The necessity of doing this existed for him just as it did for the Church. The fact that the statement in Daniel was reinterpreted to mean Jesus' return at a very early stage, namely in I Thess. 4.15ff., appears to me to be best explained if this interpretation goes back to Jesus himself.[1] Furthermore if, as we believe together with J. Jeremias (*Unknown Sayings of Jesus*, 1957, pp. 64ff.; see above p. 212), Paul is using a saying of Jesus in I Thess. 4.15, then the interpretation of Mark 14.62 is certain from the outset. Acts 1.11 connects Dan. 7.13f. (cf. the cloud) with the exaltation *and* the return.

But even apart from this passage, the idea that Jesus thought of a continuation of the interval beyond his death, as we have seen, can hardly be doubted.[2] Jesus in effect ascribed to this interval a role in salvation history as the Messianic time of salvation, even though he did not articulate this theologically. Significant as his own death was to him for the eschatological saving process, he nevertheless separated it by a brief span of time from the actual end. According to Albert Schweitzer, after Jesus had given up his original conviction that the

[1] Interesting though J. A. T. Robinson's reference to Acts 3 is, it still seems to me to be a very hypothetical explanation for the origin of this belief.

[2] W. G. Kümmel, *Promise and Fulfilment*, p. 77, notes Jesus' saying at the Last Supper (Mark 14.25) that he will not drink of the wine until he drinks it anew in the Kingdom of God. In these words Kümmel sees an indication that Jesus did not expect the Kingdom of God to come in the *immediate* future. In view of the thesis that we both share, I must say that it is unfortunate I have to confess I do not understand why he says this.

Kingdom would come during his lifetime, he postponed the end to the moment of his death. This hypothesis is not tenable, and contains only a kernel of truth, namely, that Jesus gave a decisive significance to his own death in the eschatological process of salvation,[1] and that it thus represents a crucial stage chronologically.

In an earlier work ('The Return of Christ', *The Early Church*, pp. 141ff.) I have even considered the possibility whether Jesus thought simultaneously of his death as the decisive event *and* of his *parousia* in the three passages discussed above. It was not my opinion that he equated his death with the end, but that he did see in his own death the event crucial for the coming of the Kingdom of God. I should like to stress this distinction even more strongly today.

Now I do share Kümmel's conception that Jesus reckoned with a brief interval between his death and the end on the basis of the passages we have just treated. But I would like at least to take into account various theses, even apart from Albert Schweitzer's, which associate the resurrection and the end very closely in Jesus' expectation. In contrast to Kümmel,[2] I should like to stress the material (*sachlich*) connection of the two events and the material (*sachlich*) relationship of Jesus' death to the end.[3] It does not follow, however, that his death and the *parousia* coincide temporally. At this point Kümmel is right. The *logion* he thinks genuine in Luke 17.25,[4] stating that the Son of Man must first suffer much, confirms this thought, but refers nevertheless not to a chronological, but to a material (*sachlich*) precondition for the end.

The expressions and arguments for the thesis that Jesus expected the end at the moment of his death are different among the scholars who have represented this opinion from time to time. E. Lohmeyer (*Galiläa and Jerusalem*, 1936, pp. 10ff., and *Das Evangelium des Markus*, 1937, p. 356)

[1] If my understanding of what happened at the baptism is correct, then Jesus came to this realization through John at the baptism. Cf. *The Christology of the New Testament*, pp. 66ff.

[2] He says that these theses are totally untenable.

[3] Kümmel cannot acknowledge such a relationship, since according to him Jesus did not regard himself as the *ebed Yahweh*. However, I fail to find any valid counter-argument in Kümmel. In the Synoptic sayings of Jesus, the allusions to be found to Isa. 53 are always obscure. From the standpoint of form criticism this fact confirms rather than refutes the notion that Jesus thought of himself as the *ebed Yahweh*.

[4] M. Black ('The Son of Man in the Teaching of Jesus', *Expository Times* 1948/49, p. 35) and M. Goguel (*La Vie de Jésus*, 1932, pp. 373f.) have shown its great age.

refers as Schweitzer does to Jesus' predictions that he will go before the disciples to Galilee (Mark 14.28; 16.7), meaning by that the *parousia*. Others, such as J. Jeremias (*Jesus als Weltvollender*, 1930, pp. 38f.), refer to Jesus' saying that he will rebuild the temple after three days. See also C. K. Barrett, *The Holy Spirit and the Gospel Tradition*, 1947, p. 155.

C. H. Dodd and his school think that Jesus expected the events associated with his death and resurrection to come immediately after them. But these events have no further, independent significance, since for Jesus the Kingdom of God is already fully realized, and since a *parousia* and a cosmic turn of aeons no longer have any place. Because for Dodd and his pupils there is no longer any real intrusion into the course of further events to bring about the consummations, neither can there be any actual interval in salvation history.

We can in fact assume that Jesus expected an interval only if we see the eschatological saving process divided into various phases in his thinking, so that the decisive future event was his death as the crowning of his earthly work. Nevertheless, the completion of the saving process will be ushered in by a cosmic turn of aeons, which Jesus expected, along with the whole of Jewish apocalypticism. Yet he expected it in such a way that he attributed a decisive role to his own person because of his self-consciousness. If Jesus regarded the two events of his death and his return as the crucial stages in the eschatological events, temporally near yet separate, then a meaningful time span between his death and return must exist, even though it is a short one. Then a distinction must be made within the final event between ultimate events introduced by his *parousia* and penultimate events which constitute the brief intermediate period. The commission given to the disciples to carry out after Jesus' death belongs to these events.

I hope to establish exegetically at some time the distinction between ultimate and penultimate events in detail. This distinction is essentially dependent upon one's judgment of the disputed Synoptic apocalypse, which poses many literary problems, and its parts. Yet it is not entirely dependent upon that either, for it may be shown that apart from this apocalypse there are clear *logia* indirectly presupposing cosmic upheavals, and that the new factor in Jesus' eschatology here is the way in which they are connected with his earthly life.[1]

---

[1] For instance, Mark 8.38; Mark 14.62 and parallels; Mark 13.30 (as an individual saying that has been attached to the apocalyptic passage).

In no case may modern disinclination for such descriptions influence our judgment.

An exaggerated fear of attributing to Jesus statements dealing with final cosmic events can be found in the exegetical and theological writings of the English-speaking world in particular. It is not by accident that the thesis of 'realized eschatology' is advocated with special emphasis by Anglo-Saxon theologians. In the opposing camp we find Albert Schweitzer, for whom Jesus, on the contrary, lived entirely among apocalyptic ideas. Today, even where futuristic eschatology is not represented in Schweitzerian fashion, there is an anxious concern to remove from Jesus' message all the descriptions of eschatological events that do not fall within the framework of history. This endeavour we note even in the works of J. W. Bowman, who, incidentally, deserves credit for having advanced the salvation-historical interpretation of the New Testament in America. The more careful attention paid to apocalyptic in recent works by pupils of Bultmann[1] should consistently be extended to Jesus as well. This would have consequences for the interpretation of Mark 13 and parallels.

If, as I believe, there is a penultimate and an ultimate act within the events of the end in Jesus' thought, the first ushered in by his death and resurrection, and the second by his *parousia*, the line to the later salvation-historical perspective becomes clear. Again we do not want to overlook the fact that for Jesus, in contrast with the later salvation-historical perspectives, the two acts lie very close to one another in time. Therefore, an exact, chronological division of the events with which Mark 13 deals into those that will yet take place in the framework of history and those that will occur in connection with cosmic upheavals is impossible. However, the notion of two final acts separated by the *parousia* must be maintained in principle.

How are the events to be characterized which primarily fall in the first act, that is, in the interval that lasts beyond Jesus' death and takes place before the final act begins, according to the *logia* dealt with above pertaining to this segment of time? They are related to the salvation-historical significance of the whole interval to which, of course, Jesus' life and death also belong. The events of the interval include the anticipation of the end and the preaching of the gospel. A third event is added in view of the 'not yet'—persecution. What is later designated pictorially as 'the birth pangs of the end' now comes into operation. All this is already present in Jesus' earthly life, and his death itself is the decisive manifestation of these pangs. In Jesus'

[1] See above pp. 59f.

perspective, his earthly life and his death belong to the interval and form a unity with that brief span of time which begins after his death.

Everything happening in Jesus' life reaches a climax in the brief segment of time between his death and the end, and is intensified. This applies to both the anticipation of the end and the experience of suffering. The 'already' obtains more than ever now that the decisive saving act is accomplished. But for that very reason, everything is increasingly concentrated on the 'not yet'. Now things happen which have never happened 'from the beginning of the world' until now (Mark 13.19; Dan. 12.1; Joel 2.2). To the interval belong both the positive anticipation of the glorious eschatological state and the terrible things that must happen in order that the saving process shall not remain an anticipation, but come to its completion.

We conclude that in Jesus' preaching the present which extends beyond his death is *already the end*. But this does not in any way justify asserting that Jesus is the end of all salvation history. *The end time is, on the contrary, understood as belonging completely to salvation history, since each of its periods, short as they may be, has its own significance and is distinguished from others.* A final aspect should now confirm this fact.

D. THE ESCHATOLOGICAL PRESENT AS A FULFILMENT OF THE SALVATION-HISTORICAL PAST

Jesus' understanding of the brief intermediary period as belonging to salvation history is also implied in the connection of the intermediary period with the past in his preaching. The past of salvation history is not in any way dispensed with for Jesus by the eschatological time that has dawned. Nor in this respect is Jesus the end of salvation history. The past remains 'actual' for him in a real sense, as is the case in every salvation-historical perspective. Without the continual 'presentation' of the past, the eschatological orientation of the present is unintelligible. The very important concept of *fulfilment* necessitates a constant retrogressive relationship with the past of salvation history. The latter is *not* purely a past. It must constantly give meaning to the present so that the present finds its significance and fulfils its task in salvation history. Only the 'presentation' of the past of salvation history makes possible the eschatological understanding of the present. Therefore, Jesus does not think merely in a 'punctual' way.

To affirm the salvation-historical orientation of Jesus' thinking, it would be sufficient to refer to a single, but central point: his self-consciousness. Of this we have already spoken,[1] and we cannot avoid briefly returning to the matter again. I have already said that the decision about the genuineness of the *logia* to be considered here has weightier consequences than the decision on any other group of Synoptic *logia* of Jesus. Therefore, the methodological remarks I made about 'authentic' and 'inauthentic' *logia* are to be taken especially to heart in the case of these sayings. Jesus' teachings must appear in an entirely different light if Jesus was convinced that he had to carry out the role of the coming Son of Man and also that of the Suffering Servant of God in accord with the divine plan. *If* he had such a 'self-consciousness', not a single part of his preaching can be unaffected by it. But the answer to the question whether Jesus thought in terms of salvation history or not is dependent upon one's attitude towards Jesus' self-consciousness. Anyone who refuses to credit Jesus with such a consciousness in any form, the consciousness of fulfilling the function implicit in each Jewish honorific title, must also reject Jesus' relationship to salvation history. Again, anyone who denies that Jesus based his message on salvation history must dispute that he applied any Jewish titles of honour to himself. Hence, it is no accident that the Bultmann school declares itself against the notion that Jesus thought of himself as the Son of Man and the *ebed Yahweh* and at the same time against the salvation-historical basis of his message.

I am not going to repeat the arguments here that caused me to explain differently from the Bultmann school the evidence which it adduces by appealing to Wrede as its chief witness.[2] Nor shall I again examine the crucial Son of Man and *ebed Yahweh logia* relating to Jesus' own person which for form-critical reasons I cannot regard as secondary compositions. In addition, I have referred to Jesus' condemnation as a Zealot (cf. the inscription on the cross) as historical evidence for my claim, and to his authority to forgive sins as theological evidence.

If Jesus was convinced that this was his divine mission, then it is implied that he *deliberately included himself within salvation history*. I have stated that all salvation history continually developed in relation to new events and new revelations.[3] We have also seen that each new

---

[1] See above pp. 107ff. and pp. 193.
[2] See O. Cullmann, *The State in the New Testament*, pp. 17f.
[3] See above pp. 122f., also pp. 89, 116f.

prophetic revelation about events is regarded as a *part* of salvation history. This is particularly true in the case of Jesus' self-consciousness and self-revelation. At the same time, something unique takes place in this case, since Jesus regards himself as the *fulfilment* of the whole salvation history that has gone before. This new revelation is most closely associated with his self-consciousness, but his self-consciousness rests upon the divine revelation which has been imparted to him in connection with decisive events: the blind see, the lame walk, and so on (Matt. 11.5). These events, which fulfil salvation history, relate to his person. The Old Testament prophets also brought forth revelations about events of their times, and with their messages they aligned themselves with salvation history. But Jesus must include even his own person in salvation history. He is the event himself, together with everything he does and proclaims.

Therefore Jesus' self-consciousness cannot be designated as something secondary in the early Church's faith in Christ's Messiahship, which is what Bultmann does. To believe in Christ's Messiahship means to believe that he regarded himself as the Son of Man and *ebed Yahweh* and proclaimed himself to be such in his message. With this self-revelation he integrates his person and work into salvation history. So in Jesus, because of his new prophetic revelation, salvation history developed further in continuity with the salvation history of the Old Testament and Judaism.

The Parable of the Wicked Husbandmen (Mark 12.1–12), where the tenants mistreat all those sent by the owner of the vineyard and kill his son whom he finally sends, contains the idea, which is otherwise presupposed everywhere in Jesus' self-consciousness, that he is the fulfilment of Old Testament prophecy. This idea is part and parcel of salvation history.

To be sure, in the oral tradition the parable underwent transformations which are indicated by the differences between the forms in Mark, Matthew, and Luke (see the details in J. Jeremias, *The Parables of Jesus*, 1963, pp. 70ff.). It is also correct that when the plural occurs, 'the servants' (Matthew), instead of the one servant (in Mark and Luke), it should be regarded as an approach to an interpretation of these earlier messengers as the prophets. But it is not obvious that this interpretation of the one servant, or the servants, as God's earlier messengers, the prophets, must be totally rejected. (Thus C. H. Dodd and J. Jeremias attempt to give the parable a completely different point—the handing over of the Kingdom to the poor.) Who is to be thought of here if not the prophets?

(So W. Michaelis, *Die Gleichnisse Jesu*, ³1955, p. 21, rightly asks.) To regard the parable with W. G. Kümmel ('Das Gleichnis von den bösen Weingärtnern Mk. 12, 1–9', *Aux sources de la tradition chrétienne. Mélanges M. Goguel*, 1950, pp. 120ff.) as inauthentic on account of the designation 'son' is not enough because Jesus could have referred to himself by the figure of the son even though he did not have the *title* '*Son of God*' in mind. The parable simply describes a messenger standing closer to the owner than the servants. The reference to Jesus is clear in any case.

In Jesus' conviction the Kingdom of God does not come, of course, through continuous development, but suddenly from God's side. But it does not culminate a meaningless history, but a planned, divine process, even though the process is characterized by human sin and disaster. The message of the nearness and suddenness of the Kingdom of God does not abolish salvation history, but embraces it. Both contingency and continuity belong to the essence of all salvation history, as we have seen.

The continuity between Jesus' message and the salvation history of the Old Testament is already implicit in the extensive role which the liberation from sin plays for Jesus—from the call, 'Repent', on through the forgiveness of sins, which he himself performs with authority[1] in connection with his struggle with the demons, up to his assuming the role of *ebed Yahweh*. The whole Old Testament salvation history has its start in human sin and is the *history of the liberation of man from sin*. For this very reason, Jesus ought not to be set in opposition to salvation history.

All the Gospels make a connection between Jesus and John the Baptist. Certainly the writer of the Gospel of John often speaks through the mouth of Jesus about this relationship. But Jesus surely expressed himself on the subject too. If it is correct that his first disciples were disciples of John, then it is understandable why at every turn he meets the question of how this relationship is to be defined. In whatever form Jesus' saying about the Baptist originally appeared, either in the form of Matt. 11.13, 'All the prophets and the law prophesied until John', or, as seems more probable to me, in the form of Luke 16.16, 'The Law and the prophets were until John', the fact remains that John the Baptist is included in salvation history.[2] The associated saying about the 'men of violence', which should in the most probable interpretation be referred to the

[1] See above p. 197.
[2] See J. Daniélou, *Jean Baptiste, témoin de l'agneau*, 1964.

Zealots,[1] introduces a new epoch with the Baptist, and here Jesus sees himself and his time as being set in the decisive place within God's saving plan. Furthermore, Jesus' acceptance of the efforts of the disciples to determine his own relationship to John the Baptist and his identification of John with Elijah (Matt. 11.14; Mark 9.12) show that such references to the past not only take over Jewish thought forms, but also have a significance in locating the position of the present in salvation history.[2]

When Jesus in Mark 10.2ff. and Matt. 19.3ff. separates the original commandment of God which was 'from the beginning' from what Moses afterwards wrote on the question of divorce because of men's 'hardness of heart', he is interpreting the Law, too, in terms of salvation history. Again, he sees the further development of the Law in his own radical fulfilment of it in terms of salvation history: '. . . it was said to the men of old . . . but I say to you.'

We have already seen in the Parable of the Wicked Husbandmen that the killing of the prophets belongs to salvation history.[3] Although Jesus does not expressly draw a line to his death, that is still presupposed when he cries out, 'Jerusalem, Jerusalem, killing the prophets and stoning those who are sent to you! How often would I have gathered your children together.' Then the prediction follows, 'Behold your house is forsaken' (Matt. 23.37 and parallel). In connection with the 'shedding of righteous blood', Jesus speaks of the blood of Abel the righteous to the blood of Zechariah and the son of Barachiah (Matt. 23.35 and parallel). These are not just superficial allusions to the Old Testament. The election of the people of Israel remains the basis of salvation history for Jesus as well. For this reason, the disciples must limit their missionary activity to the lost sheep of the house of Israel (Matt. 10.5). Even where Jesus, speaking from his experiences of the present in a threat, says in a genuine prophetic way that the sons of the Kingdom will be thrown out and the outsiders will be admitted (Matt. 8.11f.; 12.41f.; 21.43;

---

[1] See O. Cullmann, *The State in the New Testament*, pp. 20ff.

[2] H. Conzelmann, *ZTK*, 1957, p. 292, speaks of Mark 9.11ff. in the paragraph entitled 'Die synoptische Tradition'. Here, he says, there is no 'interpretation of history being sketched'; the direct eschatological interpretation remains 'limited to the Baptist and Jesus'. But we have already seen (see above pp. 127ff.) that it is quite characteristic of sketches of salvation history that they do not always present a total perspective.

[3] On this Jewish motif see H. J. Schoeps, 'Die jüdischen Prophetenmorde' in *Aus frühchristlicher Zeit. Religionsgeschichtliche Untersuchungen*, 1950, pp. 126ff.

23.31f.), the thought of election remains the point of departure. Paul will fasten on to this in his imposing view of salvation history in Romans 9–11.

Jesus knows that salvation history is fulfilled in his own life, and that therefore every day and hour in the carrying out of his work are foreordained in the divine plan of salvation, and continue after him: 'Tell that fox (Herod), "Behold, I cast out demons and perform cures today and tomorrow, and the third day I finish my course. Nevertheless I must go on my way today and tomorrow and the day following . . .' (Luke 13.32f.). Then in Gethsemane: 'The hour has come' (Mark 14.41). Jesus' estimate of his own life as a part of salvation history is carried much further in the Gospel of John and is one of the chief themes of the Gospel.[1] In this assessment of his life, Jesus is conscious of the fact that what occurs during his earthly existence means salvation for men. He knows that not only his death, but his public ministry,[2] and the sequence of events of which he is instigator, occupy a decisive place in salvation history. The Gospel writers understood this, since they limit the expression εὐαγγέλιον to the narrating of the life of Jesus. Theoretically, they could have designated every literary form containing the Christian message as a εὐαγγέλιον.[3] Jesus himself knows that the decisive stages of his life run according to the same plan of God by which the history of Israel has run, but in this case the history of *one* man is involved, in which the former history finds its fulfilment in a crucial way.

From whatever vantage point we view Jesus' message, we come to the conclusion that salvation history is more for him than just an external thought-form taken over from Judaism. It is most deeply connected with his self-consciousness and his prophetic view of the events of the present at whose mid-point he himself stands. Granted he did not divide salvation history into periods, as was done later,

---

[1] See below pp. 270ff.

[2] In 'Die Geschichte Jesu Christi in Kerygma und Historie. Ein Beitrag zum Gespräch mit R. Bultmann', in *Sophia und Historie*, 1963, pp. 340ff. F. Lieb rightly says: 'Therefore the cross of Christ must obtain its saving significance not only through a preview of the resurrection event which is inseparable from it, or even through the experience at Pentecost, but also through looking in retrospect at past history and the special character of the man who died on this cross . . . Only the inclusion of the whole history of Jesus in the Gospel of John gives the complete gospel. That is the historical Jesus, who either at his birth or at his baptism begins the story of his first appearance on earth and his preaching which encounters so much resistance . . .' (p. 349).

[3] See above p. 84.

and his thinking contains a number of points of departure for a complete salvation-historical perspective. Nevertheless, salvation history not only means as much to him as to the Christians of the Early Church—it means more. He is at the same time the one who puts into operation the decisive events in the divine plan, and the one who proclaims the revelation about these events and their central place in the total plan of God. His view comprises past, future, and present. To interpret the events coming to pass through him and in his presence means for him as for the prophets to *align* them with salvation history, but in such a way that his revelation and work become the high-point of all salvation history, the fulfilment of the history of Israel.

To use Pascal's words, the God of Jesus is not the God of the philosophers, but the God of Abraham, Isaac, and Jacob (Mark 12.26). But this means that he is the God of salvation history.[1]

2. PRIMITIVE CHRISTIANITY: THE EXTENSION OF THE INTERMEDIATE PERIOD

(Its Influence on the Development of Salvation History Leading to Luke and the Later New Testament Writers)

If we were to proceed in strictly chronological fashion, we would have to speak about Paul before we dealt with the completed salvation-historical perspective as we encounter it, for instance, in the Lucan writings. But there were events that brought the Church to include the extension of the intermediate period in its salvation-historical perspective which took place in the time before Paul—in the time of the earliest Church. These events have determined the whole further development of salvation history in the same way as in times past prophetic revelation about new events has led to the advancing clarification and correction of the *kerygma* of the Bible already extant. At first, the Kingdom of God was reckoned to be

---

[1] This is probably the meaning of Yahweh's self-revelation usually translated with 'I am who I am' (Ex. 3.14). T. Boman in his book *Hebrew Thought Compared with Greek*, 1960, pp. 27ff., shows that the Hebrew *hayah* means 'to effect' rather than 'to be'. So Yahweh says, 'I act, as the one who acts, i.e. in salvation history; I am the God of salvation history.' Cf. G. v. Rad, *Old Testament Theology* I, 1962, pp. 180ff.

very near. But after Easter and especially after Pentecost, time underwent an extension in the sense that after the new experiences of the Holy Spirit in the Church, a heightened significance was given to the 'already', to the 'present', which always had its definite place in salvation history, even for Jesus. Thus, the expectation that the Kingdom would come within the generation then alive was progressively pushed into the background.

We shall see that this process was in no way a conscious one; nor did it come about primarily through reflection, as some are inclined to imagine. Instead, it unfolded gradually in connection with events experienced daily. Without bringing on an actual crisis, this development came quite naturally in such a way that the limiting of the interval to the lifetime of some living in that generation was dropped, and the indefiniteness of its duration was finally taken with unqualified seriousness.

It will not do, therefore, to speak of an extended time being found for the first time in Luke. In the approaches of the other Gospels, and in Paul, and before that in the early Church, the interval is extended by comparison with its length in Jesus' message, even though it is still limited. In this respect the school of Albert Schweitzer is right in thinking that a progressive development took place quite early. It is only in explaining the motives behind this development that I basically depart from the Schweitzer and Bultmann schools.

Particularly since the article by Vielhauer,[1] and also since Käsemann's[2] recent article carrying the discussion further, the Bultmann school usually concentrates on the confrontation between Paul on the one hand and Luke and the rest of the so-called 'early Catholic' writings on the other. Thus the difference between them is deepened from the outset.

In reality, the time after Jesus' death is characterized *as a whole* by the fact that salvation-historical thinking develops progressively in the interpretation of new events. Luke's work expresses most vividly the final point in the development of this interpretation and abandons any chronological limitation of the intermediate period. Luke deliberately attaches an indefinite duration to the period, and consistently carries through a division of salvation history into periods on the basis of an interpretative reflection, as Conzelmann has shown. But the *constant* of the whole process of salvation, as

---

[1] See above pp. 46f.
[2] 'Paulus und der Frühkatholizismus', *ZTK*, 1963, pp. 75ff.

always, is not affected by this further development. Here again we find constant and contingency lying side by side.

It should be clear from the preceding chapter that an actual break between Jesus' conception of salvation and that of the Church could not in any case arise over the question of the *length* of the interval. We lingered as long as we did on our description of Jesus' eschatological message to show that its futuristic character cannot be given up. Still, according to the Gospels, his limitation of the time of the Kingdom's coming to within his own generation must be regarded as something of secondary importance since everything depends upon the reason why the Kingdom is near: we have already entered the end time, but the end is still to come.

To be sure, the further development does concern the question of the duration of the interval. We do not wish to minimize the differences that arise here in any way by stating they do not amount to a break or that they are of secondary importance in the over-all perspective of salvation. No doubt a new psychological atmosphere was created when the end was no longer necessarily expected within the lifetime of the generation of the first Christians. Jesus had reckoned on a brief duration for the interval, and had regarded it as the framework willed by God in which all his instructions were to be carried out. He had therefore implicitly given it a significance as the time of preaching and testing. He and the Church during its earliest period were still not interested in extending the external forms of the framework of this intermediate period. The interest in organizing the Church develops in the same measure as it is felt meaningful to have such an organized Church for the longer duration of the interval. Jesus, of course, gave precise organizational instructions for his circle of disciples and their missionary activity, and it is not as if the short duration of the intermediate period made him spurn every form of organization. Paul recalls that God is a God of order (I Cor. 14.33), although by his time the limited period of the interval has already been widened. The fact remains that a development in salvation history is seen here which is correlated with the progressive extension of the interval, and that the longer the duration, the greater is the need of fixed forms.

Everything that has been said about the consequences of extending the intermediate period remains true. On the other hand, it is not true that the *salvation-historical conception as such has thereby changed, or that one can only speak of the history of salvation when the length of the interval is no longer limited to any known duration* (as for instance in Luke), whereas before this the limitation of the interval implicitly excluded all salvation history. This assertion would only be true if salvation history and history were identical, but we have seen[1] that despite all the points of contact between the two, salvation history is different from history, showing quite characteristic features of its own, chiefly the linking of constant and contingency. More room is left for contingency when the duration becomes indefinite, but at the same time the limitation of the end is actually fixed in the revealed plan of God.

The idea of a salvation-historical perspective has not changed with the extension of the interval. At the same time the fact remains that the salvation history of Israel is funnelled into the end time, and that the end time is divided into two parts: an interval when the past is fulfilled and the end is anticipated, and an actual end. In this sense, salvation history was always implicitly divided into periods, even for Jesus.

Neither the conviction that with Christ the end time is ushered in nor the intensity of the hope in the consummation yet to come necessarily had to undergo a diminution with the changed psychological atmosphere. If it is true that Jesus' own expectation was anchored in a faith in the 'already', then this hope had to remain alive so long as the 'already' was actually conceived as a part of salvation history, and in this way the tension with the 'not yet' was maintained. As a consequence of the changed atmosphere, the temptation not to take one's decision seriously and to drop the salvation-historical aspect of the 'already', so that eschatological expectation was degraded to a mere appendage of salvation history, was, of course, a strong one.

It must be granted that this danger became greater in the changed situation. It is also true that in the completed conception of salvation history found, for instance, in Luke, there is a *tendency* to conceive of the interval still as an end time, but no longer to regard it as the first stage of the end time, placing it instead as an independent period between past salvation history and the end itself. But these are only dangers and temptations which already existed apart from any extension of time (hence Jesus' continual call for wakefulness) and now have become greater. To keep my well-used comparison: the danger became greater that no one would believe any longer that the

[1] See above Part III, Chapter 2: 'New Testament Salvation History and History.'

decisive battle had already been fought, that time had made a mighty leap forward, that we already stand in the final phase (however long it may last), and that anticipations of the end already exist. But it is not correct that Luke has already succumbed to this danger, and that the interval was no longer the end time for him. Despite everything that must be said about the difference between his and Paul's concept of the Spirit, the eschatological notion of the Spirit is still common to both—the Spirit is an anticipation of the end. The crucial conviction that not only the real mid-point of time, but the last temporal phase before the unknown time of the end has been attained in Jesus, is maintained by Luke. This dividing of salvation history into periods was already done by Jesus. What is new in Luke is that he reflects about the periods of salvation history. A really new development that actually distorts the original conception comes in later with the elimination of the idea, fundamental to Jesus' eschatology, that we have entered the final phase of time.

The indefiniteness of the duration of this final time is at least foreshadowed in Jesus' stress that neither day nor hour is known, and that the coming of the Kingdom of God will be a sudden one. This indefiniteness, of course, undergoes an extension right from the beginning of the post-Easter period which it did not have for Jesus. Nevertheless, in the whole debate over whether there is a break or a development between Jesus and the early Church, it must not be forgotten that the statement about *not knowing* the hour *belongs* to the eschatological message of Jesus himself.[1]

But how was the extension of time arrived at in the Church's reflections about salvation history? Is it really true that it rests solely upon the *negative* fact that the Kingdom of God did *not* come, upon a disappointment, a serious crisis and a reflection attached to it, which tried to find an intellectual solution of the resultant 'tormenting problem'? All these questions are answered by the Bultmann school in the affirmative, often following the lead of Albert Schweitzer in the answers given, a remarkable fact from the dogmatic standpoint. The delay of the *parousia* is said to have been the one great problem distressing early Christianity until it finally found the emancipating, makeshift solution of salvation history, which, however, distorted the core of Jesus' message. Within salvation history, the interval of indefinite duration was regarded as sufficient fulfilment in itself, and

---

[1] See above pp. 204ff.

the question of the future coming of the Kingdom accordingly became completely irrelevant. Today, traces of the Church's endless efforts to get rid of this one problem are found in a great number of sayings attributed to Jesus, and countless transformations (particularly, new interpretations) of sayings of Jesus are attributed to this problem.

If this view were correct, we would not in fact have a normal further development of the beginnings of the salvation-historical perspective, but a conception of the history of salvation as a makeshift solution to the problem raised by the failure of the *parousia* to arrive. In referring to new events and positive revelations about these events, we have already indicated that the changes in the *kerygma* implicit in extending the interval are to be explained quite differently.

First of all, we must stress the hypothetical character of all constructions which have only the delay of the *parousia* in view. In the New Testament we actually find only two passages that clearly speak of a *problem* created by the delay of the *parousia*. Both are in the latest portions of the New Testament. First is the indirect reference in II Peter 3.3f. where the 'scoffers' are mentioned who say that everything remains the same as before. Second is the even more indirect allusion in the chapter added to the Gospel of John (21.23) where apparently the death of a disciple was sensed as a problem because of a *logion* causing the assumption that the disciple would still be alive at the *parousia*. It is a narrow basis if the whole Synoptic tradition is judged from these two passages.

On the other hand, in view of this situation, it is methodologically questionable to construct the delay of the *parousia* as a problem for the Church from the sayings handed down as having come from Jesus. It is, of course, possible to assume *a priori* that early Christianity had to regard as a problem the fact that the Kingdom of God did not come within the generation living at Jesus' time, contrary to his assumption. It appears to me worth noting that instead of the disappointment *one would expect* in the New Testament writings, we hear and see very little of any disappointment, even though the delay became an established fact.[1] More of it ought to be discernible in the *Epistles*. Does not the true problem posed by the delayed *parousia* lie in this fact?

[1] On this point see O. Cullmann, 'Das wahre durch die ausgebliebene Parusie gestellte neutestamentliche Problem', *TZ*, 1947, pp. 177ff. See also the rejoinder, 'Zur Diskussion des Problems der ausgebliebenen Parusie', *TZ*, 1947, pp. 428ff.

How does it happen that in the first century, despite the delay of the Kingdom of God, and although the expectation that the end was imminent progressively recedes in its original form, the hope loses none of its intensity? The answer to this question comes of and by itself. If the failure of the *parousia* to come did not call forth a crisis, it was because in Jesus' eschatology the *basis* for belief in the coming *parousia* was regarded as the main thing, the *basis* in the 'already'. The basis of Jesus' hope, namely, the belief that with his first appearance the decisive event had already occurred, did not totter. On the contrary, this belief had now become even more unshakable because it was now founded on new *events* which the disciples and the early Church experienced. In place of the 'already' of Jesus' miracles of healing, the victory over Satan, and the forgiveness of sins, there now came the 'already' of the events which the disciples interpreted by revelation as Jesus' resurrection and the works of the Spirit in the Church. In the presence of these events it became certain to the disciples that the decisive act in the development of the divine saving plan had indeed already occurred, and that with their missionary activity they themselves stood in the continuation of this saving plan.

However one evaluates what happened at Easter, it is certain that the first Christians at the time saw appearances of the Christ, and at the same time the interpretation of these events was revealed to them: he is indeed risen! That means that death is vanquished! If death could not hold fast to this *one man*, then the decisive breach in its power has already been made, even though men still die. Dying no longer has the same meaning as before. Death is no longer all-powerful. What else does this mean than that 'the Kingdom of God has already dawned, although men still die'? In this light, the revealed understanding of Jesus' death now became clear to the disciples. Jesus had already proclaimed this understanding in discreet references to the *ebed Yahweh*, but the disciples had not understood him (Mark 8.32f.). The work of Jesus, which was manifest before in his healing of the sick and forgiveness of sins as an emancipation of men from the power of sin and death, now reached its culmination—it was concluded. Thus, despite the still valid 'not yet', the 'already' naturally attained a stronger emphasis than in the time of the incarnate Lord, though even at that time 'the blind saw, the lame walked . . .' If time marches on despite everything, it is clear that the salvation-historical meaning of this interval now emerges in a very special way. The extension of time was not therefore primarily experienced as something negative, as a disappointment, but *as something highly positive*.

The second great event that permitted the early Church to experience the extension of time positively was that of the concrete working of the Holy Spirit which expressed itself in various forms: speaking in tongues, healings, the resolution to renounce property, and others as well. The Holy Spirit was already predicted in Judaism for the end by Joel—then the Spirit would take hold of *all*, large and small (Acts 2.17ff.). Therefore Paul calls the Holy Spirit an 'earnest'. It is what is already realized of the Kingdom of God.

These events anticipating the end were so overwhelming that the delay of the Kingdom of God could not at all become a 'tormenting problem'. The disciples experienced daily, in an almost uninterrupted sequence of events, the fact that the Kingdom of God had already dawned, even though it was not yet realized in its consummation. They felt at the same time that a task was thereby placed before them through which they themselves were involved in the events of the end—the task of proclaiming the gospel in the whole world as instruments of the continuation of God's saving plan before the end. At the same time they found that the interval was lasting longer than Jesus, and they themselves at the start, had believed it would. But so long as the manifestations of the Spirit and the conviction of their own, eschatological, missionary task were alive, they were not at all fully conscious that something was not yet fulfilled. The 'already' put the 'not yet' in the shade.

So we may not think that the Christians sat down disappointed and wondered how they could explain why Jesus predicted the end for the time of his generation when this had not yet happened.[1] The inclusion of the extended interval in the history of salvation was not a theological invention, not a 'makeshift solution'. It was not primarily *a solution of a problem* at all, but an *interpretation* of new events, something that had always existed in the development of the Bible's salvation history. It was not a disappointment, nor reflection over a disappointment, but joy over those events and the revelation imparted to the disciples that the events anticipated the end, which led to the thought that the interval would last longer, and which is fundamental to the inclusion of this extended interval in salvation

[1] Even H. J. Schoeps in *Paulus*, 1959, p. 123, thinks: '. . . the fact that history continues on its course . . . set in motion the whole theological brain-work of the first generations of Christians.'

history. The Holy Spirit was not invented as a substitute for the *parousia*, but was experienced as a reality.

Theological reflection begins, of course, in New Testament times, but only at a late stage, and it may be granted that when it occurs the delay of the *parousia* is secondarily felt to be a problem. But it is certainly not the primary item in this process of thinking. The beginning of the process is not theological reflection at all, but occasional events in which the first Christians saw a revelation concerning the Kingdom of God. We have found that, *mutatis mutandis*, the salvation-historical perspective of the Old Testament developed in precisely this fashion. The *new* revelation which the apostles, the first Christians, received concerned, on the one hand, Christ's resurrection, and, on the other hand, the various manifestations of the Spirit. The more persistently the events of Easter and Pentecost were repeated in the Church, the more confident the conviction became that the end could come at any subsequent time, whether early or late, and was no longer bound to a limitation of the interval.

In the discussion of this explanation of the inclusion of an extended intermediate period in salvation history, a remarkable argument emerges from the Bultmann school: it is said to amount to a deviation into a province of pious considerations! As if the inclusion of those events interpreted as resurrection and the manifestations of the Spirit in the Church did not rest upon historical fact, whatever our own judgment of what happened may be! Is not the failure to observe these events, on the contrary, a lack of historical insight into the actual situation in the Church?

Although this whole development actually began at Easter, long before Luke composed his two-volume work, it must be granted, as Conzelmann has shown, that Luke worked out a complete salvation-historical perspective for the first time in which the main accent is now on the interval, the time of the Holy Spirit, the apostles, the Church. This shift of accent is, of course, related to the fact that time is now extended. But it is not correct that the end is no longer taken seriously by Luke. The Holy Spirit is still understood as an element of the end time (Acts 2.17). What is right in Conzelmann's interpretation is that Luke does not just present portions of a salvation-historical perspective as they are characteristically found in the rest of the New Testament, but consistently draws out of the lines of salvation history in consciously reflecting about the 'periods' in salvation history. I would agree with many observations Conzelmann makes in his comparative confrontation of the Synoptics with Luke. Furthermore, we are indebted to him for valuable insights, even though a schematism driven too far often misleads him into claiming for Luke alone what in reality he has in common with the other Synoptics[1] and Paul as well.

However, Conzelmann's total evaluation seems to me to suffer on the one hand from an exaggerated contrasting of Luke and Jesus and on the other from a schematic classification of the New Testament writings. He proceeds from the assumption that no trace of a salvation-historical perspective is to be found in Jesus and that his message must be interpreted existentially. Then he follows the division of New Testament writings usual in the Bultmann school, according to which salvation history is foreign to Jesus, Paul and the Gospel of John, while the so-called Deutero-Pauline letters and others belong with Luke to the 'early Catholic' books, in other words, to those oriented toward a history of salvation.

In the first place, it must be recalled that *throughout* the first century the attitude of the Christians, including Luke, was not *basically* different from that of Jesus, despite the one great difference that the interval for Luke was no longer reckoned in a matter of a few decades as it was for Jesus. The faith that the decisive event had already occurred and was being manifested in the present was the foundation for their firm hope in the consummation, exactly as it was for Jesus. In both cases the crucial thing is that the coming of the Kingdom of God is expected *because* the act decisive for this coming has already transpired. We have seen that joy, not fanaticism, underlies Jesus' eschatology: the blind already see, the lame already walk, Satan has already fallen from heaven. Quite analogously, and yet in a further development in salvation history, these things are said in the early Church: Christ is already risen from the dead; death is vanquished (one may appreciate what such an assertion must have meant for the *whole* thinking of the first Christians!), the element of the Kingdom of God in the *eschaton*, the Holy Spirit, is already there as earnest; Christ is present in the Church; therefore the Kingdom *will* come.

Wherever this faith that the decisive act has already occurred recedes, and therefore the faith that the end time is ushered in is also dropped, either the hope in the future is displaced, or a regres-

---

[1] The value of E. Grässer's book lies in showing this.

sion into a cramped reckoning on date occurs. As soon as the 'already' is no longer thought of in the closest connection with the 'not yet', that is, as an anticipation of an end which is still to come, then a relapse to a Jewish level follows where the *tension*, which is the *specific peculiarity of the New Testament*, does not exist. Only then must the failure of the Kingdom of God to come be a problem.

It seems to me to be an *anachronism* to shift this situation into the first century. Therefore I cannot agree with Conzelmann on the second point, the position he assigns to the Gospel of Luke within the writings of early Christianity. The contrasting of Paul and Luke as carried out before Conzelmann in Vielhauer's article certainly brings out some correct insights, but this comparison would gain in value if it were detached from the questionable existential interpretation of Paul's letters which asserts that there is no salvation history for Paul. The differences between Paul and Luke actually go back to the fact that in the course of accepting an extended time into salvation history, Luke shows a conscious theological *reflection* about this development. But that is not the difference between the existential and salvation-historical conceptions of salvation.

Within the incipient Church history, it later happened that the whole interval was no longer reckoned as part of the end time. Then the biblical insight was lost that with Christ the end was ushered in in a temporal sense. At that point the interval actually ceased being an interval; it ceased to be characterized by the *tension* between 'already' and 'not yet'. *This, and not the extension of time, was the decisive turning-point.* For here the conception basic to the whole New Testament was given up, which stands or falls with the tension implicit in the thought that we have entered into the end time because it is already anticipated, and yet is *only* anticipated.

This attitude is, of course, characteristic of later Catholic conceptions in which the concept of the Church suffers from the fact that the 'tension' no longer exists.[1] However, Protestant theology has in the same way dropped this salvation-historical tension to a marked degree.

Here, and only here, I think, does the last farewell to the total biblical view lie. If here and there within the New Testament ap-

---

[1] Fundamentally, this tension was the main topic discussed by the delegates and the non-Catholic observers in the conversations about the Schema *De Ecclesia* organized by the Vatican Secretariat for Christian Unity during the first half of the second session of the Second Vatican Council.

proaches are made in this direction, only *after* New Testament times does the development ignorant of the *temporal tension* begin. There are, of course, differences among the various books of the New Testament on the subject of the *nearness of the end*, but none over the *tension*, and this is of crucial importance.

Therefore, I think the introduction of the category of 'early Catholicism' as a principle for classifying the New Testament writings was an unhappy one.[1] The traditional distinction between early Christianity and the ancient Church, between New Testament times and post-biblical times, seems to me to be as justified now as it was before, even though a really certain date for the separation between the two cannot be given.[2] *The inmost essence of the New Testament messages is lost, not with the abandonment of the idea of a near end, but with the abandonment of the tension of salvation history.*

A further, though related, point is that we understand the relationship between Paul and Luke differently from the Bultmann school, and we cannot make Luke responsible for the great apostasy from Paul.[3] Luke and the other writers (chiefly the Pastorals) referred to as 'early Catholic' have in common with the letters generally regarded as genuinely Pauline both a common salvation-historical basis for the temporal tension and also a development towards the inclusion of an extended time in place of a brief interval. The differences which are evident, for instance, in the construction of the Church's organization[4] are related to this progressive extension, and not to the basic salvation-historical conception itself.

Our understanding of the Gospel of John must be distinguished from that of the Bultmann school even more radically. It is in this Gospel, if anywhere, that the extension of time is taken seriously. It is here, if anywhere, that the extended interval is an object for the contemplation of a salvation-historical approach. We shall need to show where the difference between Luke's treatment of salvation history and that of the Gospel of John lies.

[1] In his article (*ZTK*, 1963), E. Käsemann recalls that he himself used the expression in this way for the first time.

[2] The otherwise interesting discussion between H. Küng and E. Käsemann on the question of early Catholicism therefore does not seem to me to rest upon a proper basis, when the expectation of a near end is introduced as a criterion.

[3] U. Wilckens in *Offenbarung als Geschichte*, p. 77, reacts against this judgment.

[4] See E. Käsemann's article (*ZTK*, 1963) in which he finds points of contact with the 'early Catholic' conception in the authentic Pauline letters, but views this conception with the Bultmann school as a *novum* introduced by abandoning the expectation of an imminent end.

So we must now raise the question of the relation of Paul and the Gospel of John to salvation history.

3. PAUL AND SALVATION HISTORY

This book was planned years ago, independently of the present discussions. If I had written it then, it certainly would not have occurred to me to ask in a chapter devoted to the apostle Paul whether he thought along the lines of salvation history. I would have limited myself to depicting his salvation-historical perspective, because the preliminary question, whether his theology is oriented towards salvation history, would have seemed to me just as superfluous as the question whether the orientation of the Old Testament is towards salvation history.[1] I am of this opinion even today, but I must now go into the opposite thesis of recent works, and I shall try to do justice to its kernel of truth. Let me anticipate my answer: certainly the emphasis, so strongly advanced in the works of the Bultmann school on the 'now of the decision', as it is found, for instance, in II Cor. 6.2 and in other passages, is very important for Paul. But not only does it not conflict with a salvation-historical attitude—it is subordinate to one. We can even say that Paul's faith in salvation history creates at every moment a basis for the existential decision, for which there is ample room.

To confirm this view, we shall inquire whether the characteristics typical both of the origin and the portrayal of all salvation history are to be found in a crucial place in Paul's theology. *That* Paul speaks of salvation history cannot be very well disputed and is hardly disputed. The advocates of the thesis that Paul's thinking is not basically salvation-historical say that salvation history is only a remnant from Paul's Jewish past. The problem must, accordingly, narrow down to whether salvation history constitutes the kernel of Pauline theology. At the same time, in line with what is said in the previous chapter, we must not limit ourselves to the partial question of the idea of a near end and an extension of the interval, as has often happened in the works of the last few years, whenever Pauline theology is contrasted with the salvation-historical theology of Luke.

[1] W. Wrede, *Paulus*, [2]1907, p. 68: 'Salvation history is the content of his faith.'

Paul takes over the Old Testament, and no one will deny that it occupies a central place in his thinking. The Marcionite interpretation of Paul is represented in its radical form by no serious scholar. But we still encounter Marcionism in a very refined form in current interpretation of Paul. The acceptance of the Old Testament by Paul is either judged as a framework dominated by the thinking of the day, or it is regarded as the apostle's intention to take his leave of Israel's salvation history as such, to demonstrate its secular character, to 'desacralize' it.[1]

We do not wish to oversimplify the matter by viewing our problem as already solved because Paul recognizes the Old Testament as authoritative. What was said above[2] about the necessary distinction between typological, or even allegorical, use of the Old Testament on the one hand, and its salvation-historical use on the other, must be recalled.[3] Allegorical exegesis, which is found only in a very few passages in Paul, has nothing to do with salvation history. On the contrary, it often serves to eliminate salvation history. The drawing of typological parallels is much closer to salvation history, and often the latter forms the background for the former, for typology may be linked with the scheme of promise and fulfilment. But typology lacks the element of development, the element of a link between events in salvation history individually separated. To be sure, in each instance *all* the individual connecting links need not be recounted, for we have seen[4] that from time to time the salvation-historical relationship is produced on the occasion of a concrete question. Individual connecting links can remain unheeded and can be passed over, for they may not be directly relevant to the actual problem being considered at the moment. But for an actual salvation-historical perspective it is fundamental that there should not only be a visible parallel between the facts adduced, but also an historical unfolding of a divine plan, at least in the background. The instances given above,[5] where the apostle answers basic, concrete questions of a theological kind from the insights of salvation history, make clear that this is the case. We shall return to the connection with the past,

[1] So G. Klein, 'Röm. 4 und die Idee der Heilsgeschichte', *EvT*, 1963, pp. 424ff.

[2] See above pp. 132ff.

[3] See also C. Dietzfelbinger, 'Paulus und das Alte Testament', *TEx*, 1961, and E. Ellis, *Paul's Use of the Old Testament*, 1957.

[4] See above pp. 128ff.

[5] See above pp. 129ff.

i.e., with Israel. But first of all, the main point to be shown is that Paul's salvation-historical perspective came about in the exact way characteristic of all biblical salvation history in its development.

The *kerygma* Paul received is that of the early Church. In it, the cross and the Easter appearances were interpreted in the same way as the decisive divine events within the whole salvation history from the creation to the end. An interpretative revelation is now imparted to Paul in connection with a new event to which he is a witness.[1] This happens in relation to the salvation-historical *kerygma* that has been handed down to him and which is clarified in this way and developed further.

The new event for Paul concerns primarily himself. On the road to Damascus he saw and heard Christ, and this appearance was bound up for him very closely at the same time with its interpretation, the '*apokalypsis*' (Gal. 1.12), with the apostolic commission to preach the gospel to the Gentiles. This event, however, did not just concern the apostle personally; in a special way it affected the whole meaning of the interval so that it became the time for the proclamation of the gospel to the Gentiles. Paul himself understood it in this way. First, before the end, 'the gospel must be preached to all the Gentiles'.[2] That is why there is an intermediate period. That is why time continues, though the decisive event has already occurred in Christ's death and resurrection. The call of Paul was in no way merely a general call to be a servant of Christ, but very precisely to preach the gospel of Christ to the Gentiles. Christ's appearance to Paul was a highly significant event in the development of salvation history. It meant Paul's inclusion in the saving process as the apostle to the Gentiles in this very definite moment between Christ's resurrection and the end.

The call to preach to the Gentiles is not just a commission; along with it comes a revelation concerning God's saving plan. In the exe-

---

[1] G. Schrenk, *Studien zu Paulus* (*ATANT*, 1954), p. 58 n. 23, accurately describes Paul's view of history in its positive and negative relationship to 'empirical history'. The reason why he rejects the term 'salvation history' is not quite clear, but it is probably related to the way it was used by the old salvation-historical dogmaticians. See above pp. 74f. Incidentally, his whole article, 'Die Geschichtsanschauung des Paulus auf dem Hintergrund seines Zeitalters' (*op. cit.*, pp. 49ff.) is well worth reading.

[2] See O. Cullmann, 'Le caractère eschatologique du devoir missionnaire et de la conscience apostolique de Saint Paul. Étude sur le κατέχων (—ον) de II Thess. 2, 6–7' (*RHPR*, 1936, pp. 210–45); this article will appear in German in my collected works.

cution of God's plan, inaugurated with the election of Israel, the gospel must now pass over to the Gentiles. That is the new factor, and yet the divine plan abides, as Rom. 11 shows—hence, the link of constant and contingency.

Paul is at the same time the one who carries out this further development of the saving plan and who is the revealer of it. Both are indicated in the event on the road to Damascus.

In the further course of happenings, the effective missionary successes in the Gentile world shape the new events which determine Paul's theological elaboration of salvation history. What he offers in Rom. 9–11 is a salvation-historical interpretation of events in the mission field. Through Israel's unbelief, the full number of Gentiles. comes in. Thus the path leads through Israel. The constant, which is the divine plan with the chosen people as its object, still remains; but God is carrying it out in an unforeseen way in the context of historical contingency until at last all Israel will be saved.[1] Thus, Paul sees a revelation of the plan of salvation which discloses the meaning of the interval, not only in the missionary commission imparted, but also in his successes on the mission field. This becomes clear from Gal. 1. The details of this important chapter show the significance of the office of apostle in salvation history—an apostle is an immediate eyewitness to Christ's resurrection, but now Paul in particular is the witness for the Gentiles. For those who believe in Christ, conversion means inclusion in God's saving plan in history. However, it means this for Paul in a special way, since he is the one who reveals and carries out this divine plan.

[1] H. J. Schoeps, *Paulus*, 1959, devotes a whole chapter in his book, pp. 231ff., to the problem of 'The Apostle Paul's Conception of Salvation History', and directs his attention here especially to Rom. 9–11, where he is only able to see a 'circumstantial speculation', an 'arbitrary typologizing of the history of Israel applied to the developing Church', 'much fantasy' (p. 258), 'a logic contrary to history (even though it is consistent)'. The author interestingly refers (pp. 259ff.) to a completely different solution to the problem which is presented in the Pseudo-Clementine writings: the same divine revelation is found in Moses and Jesus. In Moses, God made a covenant with the Jews, and in Jesus he made a covenant with the Gentiles. Schoeps develops this theory with a personal and inner interest, and sees in it the solution of the question of the relationship between Israel and the Christian Church which is so real today (pp. 273f.). Interesting as it is, it still seems impossible to me to call it 'salvation-historical', as Schoeps does. It is based upon the doctrine of the recurring 'true prophet', and is quite different from salvation history. Indeed, one must even say that only in contrast to this Jewish-Christian theory can we really understand the salvation-historical orientation of Rom. 9–11.

Paul expressly describes as an '*apokalypsis*' the way that he received the εὐαγγέλιον on the road to Damascus—δι' ἀποκαλύψεως (Gal. 1.12). For him, this act of revelation from now on belongs essentially to the history of salvation. Therefore he sees the whole history of salvation in the light of the present preaching to the Gentiles.[1] He is called to this preaching in the saving revelation already given to him. The great salvation-historical perspective of Rom. 9–11 is not in any way isolated; it permeates all the apostle's thinking and acting.[2] The 'mystery' of the οἰκονομία, which we have heard of in the passages in Colossians and Ephesians cited above,[3] relates to the apostle's office as a concrete commission to preach to the Gentiles, and thus in Rom. 11.25 the 'mystery' is related as well to the problem of Jews and Gentiles.

Because of the *revelation* of the ultimate saving plan that has been imparted to him, right at the end of the discussion of salvation history in Rom. 9–11, and thus after he has disclosed the 'mystery', Paul cries out in joy, 'O the depth of the riches and wisdom and know-ledge of God! How unsearchable are his judgments and how in-scrutable his ways' (11.33). That is, the depth of the *divine* σοφία cannot be fathomed by human σοφία. This is directly related to salva-tion history.[4] It can only be an object of revelation. We must compare what Paul exclaims here about the depth of the σοφία with what he says in I Cor. 1.18ff. about human σοφία (or the σοφία of this world). The depth of this divine σοφία that Paul discloses in Rom. 9–11 by virtue of the ἀποκάλυψις imparted to him is 'foolishness' for the Greeks. How is a history, and *such* a history, supposed to be salvation for them? Furthermore, it is a scandal for the Jews. They are not offended by the historical character of salvation, but they cannot conceive that what is new in Christ, precisely in the contingently historical event of the cross, is already supposed to be realized, although the consummation is still to come. They cannot conceive that the decisive act should have occurred historically in so mean and scandalous a fashion, and that still the Messiah does not reign

---

[1] J. Munck shows this in his book *Paul and the Salvation of Mankind*, 1959. See above p. 53.

[2] On Rom. 9–11 see especially J. Munck, *Christus und Israel. Zur Auslegung von Röm. 9–11*, 1956.

[3] See above pp. 75ff., 118.

[4] R. Bultmann, *Theology of the New Testament*, vol. II, 1955, p. 129, also connects the insights of Rom. 9–11 with this σοφία, though he defines this σοφία as 'fantasy and speculative thinking'.

visibly. For the Greeks, all salvation history is foolishness. On the other hand, for the Jews salvation history, as Paul and early Christianity see it, with Christ at the mid-point, is a scandal. We can apply everything that is said in I Cor. 1.18ff. about the cross, the centre of all salvation history, to salvation history itself. It is θεοῦ σοφία. Thus it is not accessible to philosophical thinking, the σοφία τοῦ κόσμου, nor to rabbinic thinking. It rests upon the ἀποκάλυψις Paul has received and communicated to us in such a way that the revealer is included, as always, in the event. In his efforts to explain this κήρυγμα for modern understanding, the modern exegete must be on his guard not to remove the μωρία which lies at its heart.

The seriousness with which Bultmann struggles to make the gospel understandable to modern man demands our respect. But I cannot help thinking that the price he has paid to the philosophy dominant today (for how long?) is too high. Is the existential reinterpretation of eschatology still a 'scandal and foolishness'? To be sure, Bultmann stresses emphatically that the *kerygma* determines our existence in that it places us in the world as 'desecularized' beings and makes a 'new creation' of us by our new self-understanding as we apply the Pauline antithesis, 'as dying, and behold we live' (II Cor. 6.9). This Bultmann shows particularly in his article, 'Das Befremdliche des christlichen Glaubens' (*ZTK*, 1958, p. 185). Here, as elsewhere in his works on demythologizing, whenever he places in the foreground the '*Geschichtlichkeit*' (in the existential sense) of the cross which becomes an address to us, he seems to approach the strangeness of the Pauline gospel. However, it is not the cross as an atoning death, but the cross as a means towards the understanding of our existence that is the important thing for Bultmann. For Paul, however, the foolishness lies precisely in the fact that in Christ God has vanquished sin and death by this saving drama apart from us and before our believing. I only ask, would the Greeks on Mars' Hill have had to laugh about 'desecularization' as they did about Paul's speech telling of a future event resting upon the resurrection of one man from the dead?

What is the picture of salvation history that Paul works out in this way? We have already said that for him, as well as for the Church following Easter, the present time of the interval is extended, and that he stands in this development that funnels into Luke's view, although it begins before him. A development is seen here in the fact that even within the Pauline letters themselves there appear to be traces of ideas proving that the apostle sometimes expected to belong to those still living at the time of the *parousia* (I Thess. 4.15ff.; I Cor.

15.51ff.) and sometimes reckoned with the possibility of dying before that moment arrives (II Cor. 5.1ff.).[1]

In any case, even for him 'the time is short' (I Cor. 7.29). Despite this brevity, however, the interval for him is an utterly indispensable part in God's saving plan, the meaning of which may not be lessened in terms of the 'end of history'. Albert Schweitzer is right when in his book *The Mysticism of Paul the Apostle* he regards this interval as the main characteristic in Paul's thought. In accord with his thesis of Paul's eschatological mysticism, he describes being in this time as 'being in Christ', and thereby he certainly takes account of one side of the Pauline conception. But it corresponds still better with the apostle's intention if we define this, 'being' *functionally*, in relation to the origin of Paul's view, that is, as being determined by the fact that in God's plan the gospel must be preached in this time, and that we must be tested in this way. Rom. 9–11 indicates that the interval has its quite necessary place in God's saving plan. How otherwise should this plan be fulfilled if there were no interval as a time of salvation when the fullness of the Gentiles enters in, and ultimately unbelieving Israel is converted? These events are already events of the end time, although they are not the end. Paul has the tremendously heightened consciousness of standing in this interval as an apostle: 'For necessity is laid upon me. Woe to me if I do not preach the gospel!' (I Cor. 9.16). Hence the haste with which he travels through the ancient world in order to preach the gospel to it, always seeking new τόποι. Despite its relatively short duration, this interval is therefore not the end of salvation history—it *is* salvation history.

Every decision is for Paul a decision 'now', and I stress repeatedly that 'now' plays a great role in the New Testament. However, this 'now' may not be adduced against a salvation-historical conception of the interval. Among the Pauline letters, II Cor. 6.2 must be referred to in particular. This certainly speaks of a decision in the present moment, 'now'. But this 'now' is the 'now' of salvation history and the νῦν may not be demythologized as though it had nothing to do with salvation history. I cannot agree with the position that seeks to place the continuity of the divine plan and the disconnected, punctual 'now' side by side in Paul,[2] for it fails to see rightly how in Paul

[1] On this point see L. Goppelt, *Die apostolische und nachapostolische Zeit*, 1955, pp. A. 93–94.

[2] Thus E. Dinkler, 'Earliest Christianity', in *The Idea of History in the Ancient Near East*, 1955, p. 181, and E. Schweizer, 'Der Kirchenbegriff im Evangelium und den Briefen des Johannes', in *Sammlung Neotestamentica*, 1963, pp. 254ff.

the vertical and the horizontal are linked together. The punctual 'now' of the free decision plays a great role, but it is not *co*ordinated with salvation history, but *sub*ordinated to it. Paul finds himself (II Cor. 6.2) right at the point where in the execution of his plan God brought in the 'welcome time' by reconciling the world to himself through Christ (II Cor. 5.18). Just at this point in time the apostle received his precise calling, his 'ministry of reconciliation' (5.18), and therefore must show himself as a 'servant of God' on this 'day of salvation', through all the tribulations which he enumerates.

The apostle is thinking primarily of himself as the one who in these tribulations stands at a particular point in salvation history. But the 'now' is also a 'now' of decision for his readers. For them, the 'now' means that they shall not have received in vain the grace to stand in this time. The 'now' is 'now' because there is a 'before' and an 'after' in the divine plan, not only in relation to the individual person, but also in relation to the whole of mankind and even the whole of creation, and because the individual may include himself in such a process. A 'now' so conceived, leaving ample room for individual decisions, gives a totally different impulse for acting from a disconnected 'now' that can be tantamount to 'always' and 'in every moment'. It is the joyous certainty of becoming a fellow-worker in a definite divine plan in a very special way.

The tension between 'already' and 'not yet', which we have said in the chapter on Jesus to be the main characteristic of what is called 'eschatology', now stands in the foreground in Paul and forms the most important connecting link in salvation history between him and Jesus. Paul's whole theology is dominated by this tension—his conception of the Holy Spirit, the Church, the sacraments, and his ethics. In no way does this tension merely relate to the existence of the individual. It relates to the whole salvation history of the interval which is the basis and presupposition of all existence.

If Hellenistic influences made themselves felt in Paul's belief in the Holy Spirit, its roots are not in Hellenism. This is chiefly shown by the Pauline expressions by which the Spirit is designated: ἀρραβών (II Cor. 1.22; 5.5; Eph. 1.14) and ἀπαρχή (Rom. 8.23). They should really be sufficient to show the Spirit's fundamental relationship to salvation history. If there are any special salvation-historical terms at all, here they are. The eighth chapter of Romans contains a doctrine of the Holy Spirit which is unintelligible without salvation history. The whole argument is meant to demonstrate that the Spirit shows us to be 'heirs'—an eschatological concept which is through and through characteristic of salvation history—in expectation of the 'coming glory' (Rom. 8.18). The work of the Spirit for Paul is still characterized by the tension between this 'already' and 'not yet'. The 'not yet' is expressed in the 'groaning' of the Spirit. When the Spirit seeks to push through the limits of our imperfect organs which share in the σάρξ, the result is the 'unspeakable' groans that witness to our waiting for the freedom from all corruptibility. Whenever he tries to speak through us in his own language, the result is speaking in tongues, which is at the same time the future, angelic language (I Cor. 13.1), and yet represents a groaning because of the 'not yet'. At the same time he bears witness to the coming glory and the sufferings of the present age and attests that the latter are nothing in the light of the former. We are already seized by the Spirit, and therefore we are waiting still.

We are waiting, and the creation is waiting as well. How much Paul sees the whole process in terms of salvation history is nowhere better shown than in the fact we have already referred to[1], that he includes the cosmic process in salvation history. In Rom. 8.20 we find a clear reference to the fall by which Adam involved the whole creation in his disobedience, and now the creation is subject, with Adam, to perishability. The participation of creation in salvation history is not just made manifest in the primeval fall of creation under the power of death and in its eschatological emancipation with the 'children of God'. It even goes so far that in the present time of the interval creation now groans with us, since because of the 'already' of redemption in Christ the creation waits with us (Rom. 8.19ff.). So the present period also stands in the time of the Holy Spirit—a very bold thought indeed.

The Church as the body of Christ and as the people of God is the locus from which the Holy Spirit carries out his work on earth. He is at work above all *in* the Church. Therefore for the Church, too, the tension is extraordinarily important. When Paul says that the Church is the body of Christ, that is, his resurrection body, it is the highest thing that he can ever say. The anticipation of the Kingdom of God thus appears so complete that the identification of the Church with the Kingdom of God on earth, a position which later ecclesiology threatens to approach, could seem justified. Yet the statement that Christ is the 'head of the Church' refers to a continuing tension,

[1] See pp. 130, 146.

even here. In fact, the two metaphors of Christ as the body of the Church and Christ as the head of the Church are impossible side by side.

The impossibility of placing both Church and Christ side by side by making the two identical, and the impossibility of placing both in opposition only indicates that, on the one hand, the Church is the most perfect anticipation of the end, and on the other, that it is still composed of sinful members. Hence the apparently contradictory statements contained in the Pauline indicatives and the imperatives so closely connected with them—we are already holy, and yet we are to pursue holiness continuously. 'You have received the Spirit' and 'Walk in the Spirit' (Gal. 5.16). Without the tension, it would be impossible to see how the imperative has any sense at all beside that indicative. Nowhere is this more clearly expressed than in the two parts of Romans, ch. 6: vv. 1–11 contain the indicative, and vv. 12–19 contain the imperative.[1]

The apostle does not forget for a moment that sin still prevails in the Church created and possessed by the Spirit. All his letters reckon with this reality. It is not as if Paul represents the 'enthusiastic' standpoint that the Church of Christ is in effect a community of sinless people, whereas Luke by his alleged early Catholic salvation history placed the reality of sin for the first time alongside the absolutizing of the Church, thus creating the tension of the interval. On the contrary, it may be shown that Luke instead has a tendency to mitigate the imperfections of the Church, particularly the differences between Jewish and Gentile Christians, although he does not suppress the fact that the Church was not perfect even at the start, as the case of Ananias and Sapphira shows, and also the murmuring of the Hellenists against the Hebrews, which, of course, could not exist in a perfect Church.

If, however, the tension has fundamental significance for Paul's concept of the Church, this means that the Church is always a salvation historical entity, defined by the salvation-historical significance of the present interval. It may be shown that the discussion between Catholics and Protestants about the Church actually has as its topic the way the Church's participation in the tension within salvation history is to be judged.

The Catholic Church, of course, also concedes this tension, and this was clearly expressed in the discussions of the Second Session of the Second

[1] G. Bornkamm, *Das Ende des Gesetzes. Paulusstudien*, 1952, pp. 34ff., sees the connection in the 'hiddenness of the new life'.

Vatican Council on the schema, *De Ecclesia.* Yet the tendency exists on the Catholic side to stress the 'already', the anticipation of the Kingdom of God, more strongly than the 'not yet'. So far as the question of ethical holiness is concerned, the tension is completely accepted. But it is for all intents and purposes given up in relation to the infallibility of the Church's teaching office. In Paul there is only one point where the 'not yet' appears to be abolished—the Lord's Supper (see below pp. 259f.).

The apostle's whole ethics can only be understood as an ethics of tension. Many controversies about apparently contradictory statements of Paul on questions of ethics, whether individual ethics, or the relation of the Church to the world, primarily the state, could be avoided if one started from the basis of this ethics in the tension between 'already' and 'not yet'. This can be verified in all the concrete questions dealt with in Paul's letters. This basic principle of ethics finds its most perfect expression in the statement in I Cor. 7.29–31: '. . . let those who have wives live as though they had none, and those who mourn as though they were not mourning, and those who rejoice as though they were not rejoicing, and those who buy as though they had no goods, and those who deal with the world as though they had no dealings with it', for 'the time is short', and yet Paul knows that we still must live within this aeon. The fact remains that the members of the Church *still* have wives, *still* mourn, *still* rejoice, *still* buy.

Here, of course, the stress is more on the 'already', as in Jesus, inasmuch as the new and unheard of thing is present here, and the tension is already 'relaxed' to the extent that death and sin are already vanquished. Hence the joyous outcry in II Cor. 5.17: 'Therefore, if any one is in Christ, he is a new creature; the old has passed away, behold the new has come.' If such a saying is interpreted any other way than salvation-historically (for instance in terms of desecularization), it is emptied of its meaning.

The 'already' is shown particularly clearly in *baptism* and *the Lord's Supper.* The indicatives of the 'already' are directly bound to baptism.[1] In baptism we are incorporated into salvation history at the place in which we find ourselves. At present we participate in the whole history of salvation—in the past now fulfilled, and the future now anticipated. Both must be noted. This is true also in the case of the Lord's Supper.

---

[1] T. Suss stresses this in 'La doctrine du baptême' in *Positions luthériennes*, 1963, pp. 199ff., without thinking in terms of a tension.

For this reason the *sacraments* for Paul *only have meaning within salvation history*, in which one looks backwards and forwards from the present, and in this way the present is understood as an interval. The sacraments would have no meaning if the interval, short as it may be for Paul, were not an object of salvation-historical interest. The sacraments realize the 'already' as they make the past present and anticipate what is coming.

The importance of the sacraments in Paul rests upon the fact that, apart from their orientation towards the anticipated end, they are related to past events which become present—Christ's cross and resurrection. They are distinguished from all mysteries by being linked not with myths, but with once-for-all events. It was Paul's great theological achievement that he did not just retain the eschatological reference of the sacraments characteristic of early Christianity but also established a theological basis for both baptism and the Lord's Supper quite consistently in the events of Jesus' death and resurrection.

Thus in speaking of the *Lord's Supper*, to correct too exclusive an emphasis upon the joyful character of the breaking of the bread, he must call to mind that in these celebrations we are proclaiming Christ's death (I Cor. 11.26). Yet *both* aspects are expressed—looking backwards and forwards. At the same time, in looking forwards he also retains the 'not yet': 'You proclaim the Lord's death until he comes' (I Cor. 11.26). The 'already' of the Lord's Supper is perhaps nowhere stressed more emphatically than in vv. 29ff. in the same chapter where Paul writes that the believer's participation in the bread and cup is a participation in the body and blood of the crucified and resurrected Lord, and that actually the sacrament ought to make all sickness, which is a special manifestation of death, and even death itself, impossible. But, on the other hand, the apostle knows only too well that the σάρξ is still at work in the Christian Church. Thus the Galatians, who had received the Spirit by Paul's preaching (Gal. 3.1ff.), still allow themselves to be agitated. All the apostle's letters testify that he knows the powers of sin (I Cor. 5.1ff.), which is still at work in the Church, even though it shares in salvation through baptism and the Lord's Supper. He also knows that there can be no completely 'worthy' eating of Christ's body (I Cor. 11.27), that even in the Church there is still sickness and death, although participation in Christ's body in the Lord's Supper already lets the members of the Church share in the resurrection. The Church is the body of

Christ, but its members are still sinners, even though they are already freed from sin. Precisely because during the Lord's Supper the 'already' is realized in an especially evident way by virtue of the 'presentation' of the past and by the anticipation of the future, the 'not yet' is felt especially painfully by Paul in I Cor. 11.30.

The 'already' of baptism at the same time points forward towards the end and backwards towards the decisive event on the cross in such a way that both are very closely bound up in the eschatological 'already'. The perspective tends to be more towards the future as one receives the gift of the Spirit and is incorporated into the body of Christ (I Cor. 12.13), whereas with the stress upon the forgiveness of sins it is backwards towards the event on the cross. However, the past and future of salvation history also come together in baptism during the present intermediate period in salvation history.

John's baptism merely points forward and is associated only with that part of salvation history which is coming later, and therefore does not bring about any 'already'. As a baptism for the forgiveness of sins, it cannot yet be dependent upon a particular event like Christian baptism, which has been accomplished as a general baptism by Christ himself on the cross. For John the Baptist, the tension does not yet exist in the same way, since what is yet to come is neither anticipated in the giving of the Spirit, nor has the decisive act already been fulfilled in the past. But for Paul, the tension between 'already' and 'not yet', between indicative and imperative, is shown precisely in baptism, as Rom. 6 makes clear.

In the New Testament there is a salvation history of baptism itself, with the following stages: circumcision as a seal[1] of the old

---

[1] E. Dinkler has shown that the term σφραγίς in Judaism and subsequently in Christian baptismal terminology presupposes a well-known practice in the history of religion which assigned a certain sign to members of a given cult; see 'Jesu Wort vom Kreuztragen', *Neutestamentliche Studien für R. Bultmann*, 1954, pp. 110ff.; 'Zur Geschichte des Kreuzsymbols', *ZTK*, 1951, pp. 162ff.; 'Die Taufterminologie in 2. Kor. 1, 21f.', *Neotestamentica et Patristica, Festschrift O. Cullmann*, 1962, pp. 183ff. This does not contradict Paul's conception, in which circumcision is the seal of the old covenant. Its significance as a seal of the righteousness of faith (Rom. 4.11) became apparent only as Paul's interpretation of circumcision was informed by Christ. G. Klein (article cited, p. 433) thinks that Paul had two conceptions of circumcision. One was a soteriological notion concerning only Abraham himself, and not those circumcised during the Old Testament period after Abraham. The other conception was that circumcision was valid after Abraham's time and related merely to an 'ethnographic fact'. But this double notion of circumcision is not attested in Paul. Circumcision is displaced by baptism because through Christ's death salvation history has passed from the old to the new and

covenant, John's baptism with water for the forgiveness of sins in view of the future covenant, the cross of Jesus as accomplishing a general baptism for the many, and the reinstatement of baptism by water in early Christianity for the forgiveness of sins and the giving of the Spirit. The two latter both relate to Christ's death and resurrection. This series of elements is thought through theologically for the first time in Paul.

The error of the Judaizers who retained circumcision despite baptism consists in giving up salvation history. They do not see that there is already fulfilment in baptism, that it is therefore impossible to keep requiring circumcision along with baptism into Christ's death. By their very holding to circumcision it is evident that they are not thinking in terms of salvation history. It is not enough simply to emphasize what is Jewish in order to take salvation history seriously. Paul's struggle with circumcision is ultimately a struggle for the recognition of salvation history, for the recognition that baptism follows circumcision, and that the new covenant with the new seal in Jesus' death follows the old covenant with the old seal. Because the Judaizers are not thinking in terms of salvation history, they do not take the 'already' of baptism seriously. They wish to place the seal of the old covenant beside that of the new, as though their commitment under the covenant had not been placed on a new basis by the decisive event on Christ's cross.

On the other hand, Paul would have resisted Marcionism if he had known it, for it destroyed salvation history in another way by not seeing the new covenant as the fulfilment of the old. Only in continuity with covenant thinking does baptism have meaning as a sign of the covenant. In Rom. 2.25f., Rom. 4, and Gal. 3–4 the confrontation of the old covenant with the new stands behind Paul's whole argument, but in such a way that in the salvation-historical perspective the old is abolished by the new divine event, and yet the new covenant is still seen in *continuity* with the old. The value of the

---

eschatological covenant. But seen in the light of Christ, all circumcision in the old covenant ought to be what it was for Abraham the patriarch. Wherever this has not been so, it is on account of human unfaithfulness. This unfaithfulness also belongs in the saving process. For Paul the line of salvation passes through the Israel κατὰ σάρκα to Christ. Only after Christ does Abraham's offspring, seen in terms of faith, expand to include the multitude of believers. This line of descent reckoned on the basis of faith was already in effect at the birth of Isaac. Rom. 9–11 shows that the divine plan of salvation, the vicarious election of Israel κατὰ σάρκα, is nevertheless still in view.

old sign, therefore, does not decrease in the light of the new, but increases in the significance that was attached to it in the old covenant. Only because Israel has already transgressed the Law within the old covenant has 'circumcision become uncircumcision' for it (Rom. 2.25). We must always remember that Paul sometimes had circumcision in the old covenant in mind and sometimes circumcision in the new. Within the old covenant it was only because of the unfaithfulness of Israel—*which also belongs to salvation history*—that circumcision has become ineffective. Because salvation history has progressed because of Israel's unfaithfulness, 'and because Christ established this new covenant in his death, and because baptism assimilates those believing in Christ into this death, circumcision is abolished in this new covenant.

A relationship between circumcision and baptism is, of course, made explicit only in Col. 2.11f. But in the long passages about salvation history just mentioned in Gal. 3–4 and Rom. 4, it also stands in the background. The discussion in Gal. 3–4 begins with Abraham without mentioning circumcision, but it ends with baptism (Gal. 3.21). In between lies the act performed by Christ, which is the basis for baptism.

It is not as if circumcision within the old covenant were represented as meaningless in the light of the Christ event and the whole Old Testament history were 'profaned' by Paul, so that he was stripping off its character as salvation history.[1] Rather, the meaning of circumcision, on the one hand, is elucidated by baptism into Christ, and, on the other hand, the meaning of baptism is recognized for the first time in connection with the whole salvation history as it is depicted in Gal. 3–4. Salvation history forms a whole that as such remains ever present. It is not rabbinic exegesis that is manifested in the passages of Gal. 3–4 and Rom. 4, even if here and there the *method* is rabbinic. Instead, for Paul past history has an eminently important meaning. In this whole section it is the deep knowledge of God's saving plan in history which makes past history present for him. Anyone who does not feel the joy of the apostle over the revelation of God's saving plan in history in this discussion has scarcely grasped what is said.

The intention of Paul's many references back to the history of Israel, even when the thought of circumcision and baptism does not prevail, is not to show that salvation history is done away with.

[1] Cf. G. Klein, the article cited.

On the contrary, Paul wants to illuminate the constant in the past by beginning with new events which amount, of course, to an onward development behind which one may not go, and in this way Paul tried to understand the present as the time of fulfilment.

That the past is never simply past is shown everywhere in Paul's theology of salvation history. The past is seen as salvation history in the light of the present, but the present cannot be recognized at all as salvation history without the *positive* 'presentation' of the past. I emphasize that this 'presentation' is a *positive* one, that is, one revealing the saving plan of God developing in history. This 'presentation' does not serve to show just the 'not yet' in the past, consequently proving the past to be subsequently irrelevant so far as salvation history is concerned. Instead, the 'presentation' shows the 'already' existing in the past in so far as the past reveals the plan of God. The 'already' of the present is recognized in connection with the 'already' of the past, and therefore the 'already' of the past remains very real along with everything in salvation history that has been left behind. Because a divine plan links past, present, and future, although the 'old has passed away and the new has come', the past remains real, *everlasting, and unrelinquishable*. That is what stands behind all Paul's numerous discussions of salvation history, and therefore these discussions must not be wrongly taken as a vestige of rabbinicism.

We spoke earlier of the excerpts of salvation history[1] which Paul gives us as a result of present problems which confront him. It is true in almost every case that when Paul refers back to Israel's salvation history, he is not just citing illustrations from the past. Rather, it is always important to him to show, on the one hand, that in Christ salvation history goes onward and is fulfilled, and yet on the other hand, that the constant element in Old Testament salvation history, which can be seen as pointing to Christ, gives Israel's salvation history its *abiding* validity, so that Christ's work cannot be properly understood without it. Thus, it is not merely a case of an understanding resting upon a rabbinic exegetical principle, but actually of the recognition of a profound coherence *in salvation history*.

In Gal. 3 and Rom. 4, Abraham is considered not merely as a 'paradigm' of a believer,[2] but as the progenitor of Israel the elect

---

[1] See above pp. 127ff.
[2] Even G. Klein, *art. cit.*, p. 434, concedes this. But he nevertheless sees the Pauline significance of Abraham, which extends beyond that of an example,

people, and primarily as the progenitor of Israel κατὰ σάρκα. However, from the outset this election of Israel κατὰ σάρκα has the believers in view, since the factor responsible for Abraham's establishing a lineage at the birth of Isaac (which was a miraculous birth actually contrary to the σάρξ) was not the fleshly element, but Abraham's faith in the miracle. In view of his age and the infertility of Sarah, this faith was already a faith in a miracle of resurrection, as Rom. 4.17 clearly indicates. The Israel κατὰ σάρκα remains the point of departure and course of salvation history. Israel also remains in view as the chosen people after Christ's ministry. In Christ, Israel expands to become the company of believers, and it forms the transition to the Church made up of Jews and Gentiles. The meaning of the mission and the whole interval is best disclosed when the principle of election, that is, the salvation-historical basis of the whole biblical history of the Old Testament, is constantly kept in mind. It is highly significant that the universalism in Rom. 9–11 that encompasses the whole Gentile world still remains bound up with Israel's election and does not contradict God's saving plan in history.

The history of election, that is, of the reduction from the many to one, Christ, and then of the extension from the one to the many, to the Church and to humanity, constantly presupposes the unfaithfulness of Israel. *There is an unfaithfulness that belongs in and with salvation history*. What I call the movement of salvation history, namely, the reduction from the many to the one and thence again to the many, is not a construction, but is obviously at the bottom of the discussion in Gal. 3–4.

---

quite differently: Abraham is no longer the progenitor of Israel according to the flesh. Actually, the important factor for Paul in the story of Abraham is that because of the miraculous birth of Isaac which rested upon Abraham's faith, Abraham became the father of a people which expanded from Israel κατὰ σάρκα to the multitude of believers. Paul wants to show that both epochs, one from Abraham to Christ, and the other commencing with Christ, go back to Abraham. Circumcision was significant for the whole period between Abraham and Christ; but what was intended in circumcision, because it was thwarted by Israel's unfaithfulness, only became a reality in Christ, and then after Christ in baptism. The period between Abraham and Christ is not included in a positive way in the view of salvation history in Rom. 4. On this point one may agree with Klein. But the negative assessment which says of this period that it was 'desacralized', or it 'should be removed from salvation history', is never hinted at in Rom. 4, and in effect is precluded by Paul's other discussions on history. Since the Law was added as a promise because of transgressions (Gal. 3.19), it still retains its significance in salvation history (Gal. 3.21). The basis for discussing Rom. 4 seems to me too narrow when this passage is interpreted apart from other Pauline passages.

How salvation history permeates the whole process is shown by the way in which the concept of the κληρονόμος, the heir, is connected with that of the νήπιος, the minor, in Gal. 4.1ff. Both concepts, the κληρονόμος and the νήπιος, are decidedly oriented towards salvation history. The concept of the heir indicates the constant of the divine plan; that of the minor shows the contingency. Both categories will be dissolved in Christ at the point in time fixed by the Father (προθεσμία), in the sonship which becomes apparent in the possession of the Spirit and gains expression in the prayer *Abba* (Gal. 4.6ff.).

The Law given four hundred and thirty years after the promise (Gal. 3.17) is mentioned not just for the negative intention of showing that the Law cannot destroy the promise. Paul poses the question of the meaning of the Law in salvation history—it was added because of transgressions (Gal. 3.19). In the same way, in Rom. 5.20ff. it is said of the Law's 'slipping in between' (a concept presupposing a salvation history) that by sin's taking the upper hand, the consequence is the even greater abundance of grace. Not that the Law is sinful in itself; but associated with human sin, which determines the whole salvation history, the law does have this effect. In itself it is holy, just, and good (Rom. 7.12).[1]

Rom. 5.13f. also shows how much everything is seen within the framework of the divine plan: 'Sin indeed was in the world before the law was given, but sin is not counted where there is no law. Yet death reigned from Adam to Moses.'

The whole salvation history as Paul interpreted it is understandable both as constant and as contingency only if we keep in mind that the constant, God's saving plan, is again and again thwarted *by the sin of man*, the disobedience that consists in man's putting himself in the place of God. Man, therefore, takes the stance opposite to faith and thus rebels against the divine plan of salvation. The sin of man, which stands at the beginning of all salvation history, now belongs in the further development of that history and conditions it. That is the meaning of Rom. 1–2, so difficult to understand in its content.

These chapters show that right from the beginning salvation history has all men, Jews and Gentiles, in view and therefore keeps them in view until the end. The primeval revelation in the creation was intended to bring about faith. However, man put himself in the

---

[1] What was said above pp. 125f. about the 'fluctuating line' applies here.

place of the creator and did not take up a stance of faith. He thought that he was able to deal with the self-revealing creator as some kind of object of knowledge instead of responding to his revelation through worship and glorifying him (Rom. 1.21). This original sin of unbelief determined the further development of salvation history—God's wrath and his grace in Christ's work.[1] The revelation which the Jews received in the Law likewise expected the response of faith, but the Jews made themselves guilty of exactly the same sin against this special revelation. Neither did they take up a stance in faith, which would have been the only response possible if they were to succeed in fulfilling the Law. Instead, for their own part they, too, confused creator and creature, not in theory, but in practice, by believing they were able of their own power to perform the works of the Law. Thus the wrath of God was 'revealed' (Rom. 1.18) against all unruliness.

All God's provisions for salvation, his revelation in the works of creation, and his revelation in the Law, theoretically could have led men to salvation if the Jews and Gentiles had responded to them in faith. Because this was not the case, the crucial saving drama in Christ had to come (Rom. 3.21ff.). This drama is related to the sin of the Gentiles and Jews in a twofold way: first, by God's revealing himself in the cross of Jesus, that is, in a work in which we ourselves have so little part that we can appropriate it neither through human knowing nor through human acting, but only through faith; second, by God's assimilating into his atoning work in Christ the original sin of Gentiles and Jews committed against his *earlier* revelations.[2]

This whole view of the past is dictated neither by a rabbinic enslavement to the Scripture nor even by an historical interest in our sense of the term. Neither of these would have had any living, dynamic relationship to salvation, nor would they have become an existential address. Rather, Paul shows by this view how he in his own time stands within a process, no single part of which is unimportant for the present. *This* history is not a 'field of ruins'. Salvation history is currently real for the apostle, and this is shown above all in the exuberance and joy with which he, the apostle, and with him the churches of Christ, share in this movement of salvation history (Rom. 11.33ff.). The beginning and end of this movement is revealed

---

[1] Cf. K. Barth, *Church Dogmatics* IV.1, pp. 358–513; IV.2, pp. 378–498; IV.3, pp. 368–478.

[2] See what is said above p. 124 on the inclusion of sin in salvation history.

to them. Nevertheless, this revelation leaves ample room for free, personal decision since it allows the general direction of salvation with which the apostle and the Church align themselves in their decision of faith to be clearly recognized, but leaves to every individual the task of defining the path of this direction more closely.

Furthermore, the future of salvation history, eschatology, is not forgotten either. Therefore the various elements in the revelation of salvation history are all inseparably bound up and are realized in the present in each of the apostle's decisions. The whole past has reached its high-point in the eschatological event which has already occurred in Christ's death and resurrection. This past, together with its high-point, indicates the movement of all salvation history, but a revelation concerning the consummation yet to come is indispensable for illuminating the way. Such a revelation in Paul does not serve to satisfy a curiosity about 'last things'. Instead, what he says about the transformation of our bodies has been revealed to him as one of the mysteries of salvation history (I Cor. 15.51) in the same way as all his knowledge of salvation history has come to him (Rom. 11.25). The theme of his eschatology is human sin and death, their being overcome by Christ. Even though the entry of all the Gentiles into salvation and the final entry of Israel will take place in the framework which today we call historical, this entry will occur on the same level of liberation from sin and death as the larger process related to the whole creation, which from the beginning has been implicated in the history of mankind (Rom. 8.19ff.).

That is what for Paul is yet to come: the resurrection power of the Holy Spirit who is already mightily at work, must at the final appearance of Christ (who is soon to come) take hold of the creation as well, including our mortal bodies which belong to the creation. The saving process aims at this goal so that sin and death will disappear completely and only life will remain.

It would be to mistake the necessary connection of the final events with the whole salvation history as interpreted by Paul if one sought to rob eschatology of its temporal character and say, for instance, that these things will occur for each man immediately upon his own death. To understand Paul's interpretation of the saving plan in its historical coherence, one dare not forsake its basis in the salvation history on which his whole theology stands nor take recourse in a reinterpretation which places the whole Pauline salvation history in question. As we have seen, it is Paul's opinion that by participation in Christ's resurrection body in the Lord's Supper our bodies are already transformed (I Cor. 11.29ff.). But Paul knows that the σάρξ still prevails, and he must watch as the members of the Church die before the *parousia*. His whole eschatological expectation would be unintelligible if we were to think that the dead who now sleep and are with Christ already possess their spiritual bodies. Perhaps they do find themselves closer now to Christ than during the time when they were yet bound to the σάρξ, but they still exist in time, they still wait for the consummation when their bodies will be awakened by the living power of the Spirit.[1] The discussion in I Thess. 4.15 about those alive and dead at the time of the *parousia*, as well as that in I Cor. 15.54, would have no sense if this were not Paul's opinion.

4. THE GOSPEL OF JOHN AND SALVATION HISTORY

According to the dominant view, the Gospel of John undertook a demythologizing of the kernel of eschatology, presumably to be understood existentially, in a direction opposite to salvation history. Bultmann justifies his demythologizing programme by arguing that within the New Testament itself there is a book, this book, in which demythologizing has been consistently carried out. What the exegete must strive to do with Jesus and Paul—to explain the core of their messages—has been done by the Gospel of John itself. Thus we no longer find here any futuristic eschatology or any salvation history.

No one will deny that John's Gospel, the Epistles of John, and perhaps the work most closely related to them, the Epistle to the Hebrews, represent a theological type different from the rest of the New Testament writings—different both from the Synoptics and from Paul. We cannot deal with this question here in detail;[2] we can only throw light on it from the particular vantage point of our concern here.

---

[1] See O. Cullmann, *The Immortality of the Soul or the Resurrection of the Dead?*, 1958.

[2] On this see my article, 'Le scoperte recenti e l'enigma del Vangelo di Giovanni', *Studi e Materiali di Storia delle Religioni*, Rome, 1958, pp. 3ff.; 165ff. The article appears in a briefer form as, 'L'opposition contre le Temple de Jérusalem, motif commun de la théologie johannique et du monde ambiant', *NTS*, 1958–59, pp. 157ff.

I shall say right at the start that the eschatological view of the Johannine writings is different from that of the other New Testament documents to the extent that the 'already' is much more strongly emphasized than the 'not yet'. Thus the 'relaxation' that we have noted everywhere in the background of the tension[1] comes much more into the foreground than elsewhere—more even than in Luke. This is because the christocentric orientation present everywhere in the New Testament is most consistently carried out here, for we have seen that in the person of Christ the tension is already suspended. That the tension is not present at all in the Gospel of John can only be asserted if the whole salvation-historical orientation which we are about to describe is denied.

Without a doubt, the longer extension of the present period is not treated in John's Gospel in the way it is in Jesus, the Synoptics, or Paul. The extended interval appears in John just as prominently as in Luke.

But is it correct that John differs radically from Luke in the fact that he renounces any salvation-historical perspective, depicting instead in pure form the essential eschatological kernel (to be interpreted existentially) which is already present in Jesus and Paul, but not yet demythologized? In his commentary on John, Bultmann tries to carry out this conception with a grand consistency. What actually appears to justify his existential understanding of this Gospel is the necessity of decision, so strongly advanced in Johannine theology. On this point, Bultmann has in fact picked up an important concern of the Gospel writer. But I dispute whether for John this decision has no place in the salvation-historical perspective. On the contrary, the situation of decision in John appears to me to be totally founded on salvation history. We are reminded that for Bultmann decision is an 'always standing in decision'. This 'always' does not appear to me to describe the decision properly. Instead of 'always standing in decision', I would say here, as for every other stratum of the New Testament, 'standing in decision because of my involvement in a divine saving plan encompassing worlds and times'. Just as Bultmann finds his view of the whole New Testament justified by the Gospel of John, so, too, I find the view I am here presenting substantiated in the same Gospel.

It may seem paradoxical when I assert that in the Gospel of John

[1] See above pp. 176, 184, 259.

salvation history is not only present, but *stressed*. I would like to demonstrate this at the following points:[1] 1. the appraisal of the historical life of Jesus as the centre of all history; 2. the relationship of the life of Jesus to the Church of the present; 3. the relationship of the life of Jesus to the past of salvation history, going as far back as creation; 4. the relationship of the life of Jesus to eschatology.

A. THE LIFE OF THE INCARNATE CHRIST AS THE CENTRE OF ALL HAPPENING

It is worth noting that the Gospel writer presents his theology in the form of a *life* of Jesus. A wrong interpretation of his work often stems from not heeding this fact. He could, of course, have offered his theology in another literary form, but here it is not simply a question of the formal acceptance of a type of literature common among early Christians. Rather, the evangelist is convinced that the historical life of Jesus is the *centre* of the whole saving process of God, as well as being the centre of all God's revelation. No New Testament writer was so serious about this as he. The Gospel seeks to tell not of God's being, but of his revelatory activity, and particularly of the mid-point of this activity. Therefore, after the statement that the Logos, God's self-communication, was in the beginning with God and was God (namely, God in so far as he reveals himself[2]), he passes immediately to God's activity, from the imperfect to the aorist: 'All things were made through the Logos . . .' (John 1.3). But the important thing for the evangelist is that God's self-communication, his saving activity, has its mid-point in the historical life of the man Jesus of Nazareth. The prologue is not a foreign element, but a real introduction to the life of Jesus. It we can speak and must speak anywhere of a 'mid-point of time', the centre and climax which gives history a meaning,[3] it is in the Gospel of John, and not just in Luke. All revelation, all God's acting, is disclosed from this mid-point. If the subject of this action at the decisive climax in history is the incarnate Lord, Jesus of Nazareth, if in him God has revealed his inmost essence, his *doxa* (John 1.14), then *he* must be the vehicle of all God's

---

[1] On what follows see my presidential address delivered at the meeting of the S.N.T.S. at Louvain in 1964: 'L'évangile johannique et l'histoire du Salut', *NTS*, 1965, pp. 111ff.

[2] Rightly seen by R. Bultmann, *Johanneskommentar*, 1941, p. 17.

[3] See above p. 176.

acting in relation to the world. The life of Jesus of Nazaret his not just any event in which God *also* reveals himself; rather it is *the* event in which he ultimately communicates himself to the world and in which he has redeemed the world. In this life the *whole history of salvation*, past and future, *is summed up vertically*, and yet this life is *incorporated into a horizontal line*. The meaning of the prologue is this connection of the life of Jesus with every divine event which has gone before, its relation to the rejection of the Logos by the ἴδιοι (John 1.11), and its reference backwards as far as creation. That is why the evangelist prefaces the account of the events and sayings of Jesus of Nazareth with this prologue. Right from the start he indicates the place of the life of Jesus in salvation history, namely, at the decisive climax of everything, including the cosmic process.

The work of the incarnate Lord begins with his baptism, and this work itself is salvation history in the temporal course of narrated events. It would amount to a complete misunderstanding of the evangelist's intention if the events of Christ's life were conceived of only as a *framework* which served him more or less as a pretext for expounding his theology. For the writer, history has far more value than that of a 'cipher'. Nor does it merely serve the pedagogical purpose of directing a claim at our understanding of existence. Instead, God's saving plan is fulfilled in the temporal events of the life of Jesus. The writer, of course, sees more in the divine events of this life than just what happened there and then. But the 'more' is not metaphysical truth nor truth about our existence separate from any divine, ontic events. Rather it is the *link of what happened earlier in salvation history with what occurs* in the present time of the Church and furthermore, with the history of Israel. Thus he sees the historical life of the incarnate Jesus in a unity with the life of the exalted Christ in his Church, representing both together in one perspective— not, of course, in the manner of Luke, who writes a Gospel as the first volume and the Acts of the Apostles as the second volume of the same work.[1] He draws out the line from each distinct event in the life of the incarnate Lord, who appeared at the centre of history, to the work of the exalted or pre-existent Christ. This perspective is conditioned wholly by salvation history. If the Lord who was incarnate and is now exalted is the subject of this one life of Jesus, the stress then falls on the central place of the events of this life. Thus, the

---

[1] Which is also a 'Gospel' in its totality; cf. E. Trocmé, *op. cit.*, pp. 41ff.

speech of the historical Jesus passes almost imperceptibly into the message of the exalted Christ, as we find, for instance, in the discussion with Nicodemus (John 3.3–21), where Jesus speaks in the past tense of him who *has* ascended into heaven (John 3.13). Yet the distinction in principle between the periods of salvation history is fundamental to this perspective, as can be clearly seen from the farewell discourses.

What we have described as constitutive of all prophetic views of history is therefore particularly true in this case: the interpretation is supplied simultaneously with the narration of the life of Jesus.[1] Here the interpretation is decidely a salvation-historical one, for the lines are drawn from the events of the life of Jesus to other events in salvation history which are illuminated in this way, chiefly to the Christ event occurring in the Church, but also backwards, to episodes in the Old Testament. The works of the historical Jesus are pointers to the 'greater works' which are accomplished in the Church by the believers, 'for Jesus goes to the Father' (John 14.12).

This interpretation is possible only in the Spirit. As always, revelation is the basis for knowledge of salvation history. The writer himself explains *how* he arrived at this view. In this regard, the farewell discourses contain the key to understanding the whole Gospel: 'The Holy Spirit, whom the Father will send in my name, he will teach you all things, and *bring to your remembrance* all that I have said to you' (John 14.26); 'I have yet many things to say to you, but you cannot understand them now. When the Spirit of truth comes, *he* will guide you into all the truth' (John 16.12). The writer expressly attributes his salvation-historical understanding of the life of Jesus to the Spirit, who in this way has called to mind and explained the events of the life of Jesus and his sayings. In this respect, the writer stands totally in the tradition of the prophetic thinking of salvation history as we have sketched it. John's salvation-historical interpretation of all the events of the life of Jesus is the work of the Spirit, though not in the sense that it occurred to the evangelist in all its ramifications in a sudden *apokalypsis*, like the one Paul speaks of in Gal. 1.15 or like those imparted to some Old Testament prophets as well. This new understanding ultimately rests upon an immediate experience of the exalted Lord and goes back to the experience of the Easter event. This is the basis for the evangelist's conscious-

[1] See above pp. 88ff., 97ff.

ness of being directly illuminated by the Spirit, of having reflected about the life of Jesus, and of having reached the view of the events which he presents to us in his Gospel.

What is true of all Jesus' disciples because of their being mediators of the tradition is even more pronounced in the case of the author of the Fourth Gospel.[1] He has to record the facts about Jesus and his sayings and at the same time, now, in the light of the resurrection experience and illumination by the Paraclete, he has to communicate the interpretation of those facts, the *kerygma* which Jesus himself had revealed, and which the disciples did not understand at the time. Hence in the whole Gospel of John, both aspects, the eyewitness and the interpretation of faith, are emphasized in their necessary *connection* and in their *distinction*: εἶδεν καὶ ἐπίστευσεν (John 20.8). This is the explanation of the use of expressions which have a double meaning, stating the visibly concrete *and* at the same time suggesting its interpretation.[2] The verb θεάομαι itself refers to the claim which the writer makes for his Gospel—that it rests at the same time both on eyewitness and spiritual vision. This juxtaposition of εἶδεν and ἐπίστευσεν seems to me to speak for the *distinction* between event and its appropriation in faith, so inadmissible among the advocates of existential exegesis.[3] Behind both, the transmission of facts and sayings on the one hand, and the communication of their interpretation on the other hand, stands the exalted Lord as the real instigator of the whole apostolic tradition.[4]

The 'remembering' spoken of by the evangelist[5] is thus 'remembering' the once-for-all event, but on the other hand it is the knowledge of the connection of this event with the past events of the Old Testament and with the coming events in the Church of Christ. In various passages of the Gospel the writer expressly notes that this link was disclosed to the disciples only after Christ was risen, that is, after the Paraclete had been at work (John 7.39). At the end of the story of the cleansing of the temple (John 2.22), the writer expressly

---

[1] See above pp. 102ff., 104f.

[2] See O. Cullmann, 'Der johanneische Gebrauch doppeldeutiger Ausdrücke als Schlüssel zum Verständnis des vierten Evangeliums', *TZ*, 1948, pp. 360ff., and 'Εἶδεν καὶ ἐπίστευσεν', *Aux sources de la tradition chrétienne* (*Mélanges M. Goguel*), pp. 52ff.

[3] See above p. 69.

[4] O. Cullmann, 'The Tradition', in *The Early Church*, pp. 59ff.

[5] Cf. the article by N. A. Dahl, 'Anamnesis, Mémoire et Commémoration dans le christianisme primitif', *Studia theologica*, 1947.

says the disciples 'only remembered' *after* the resurrection of the Lord that he spoke the saying to them about destroying and rebuilding the temple, meaning by that the body of Christ (v. 21). In 12.16 the evangelist again observes pointedly that the disciples did not at first understand the relationship of the entry into Jerusalem to the Old Testament prophecy: 'His disciples did not understand at first; but when Jesus was glorified, then they remembered that this had been written of him and had been done to him.' During the foot washing, Peter was told that only later would he find out what Jesus was doing at the time (13.7). The disciples' later 'remembering' is as Jesus intended it to be in his farewell speech: 'But I have said these things to you, that when the hour comes you may remember that I told you of them' (16.4). Again in 20.9 the evangelist refers to the recognition of the Old Testament witness to Jesus' resurrection which only came later.

Thus the link of the facts of Jesus' life with salvation history dawned on the evangelist some considerable time after they happened. The Gospel differs somewhat from the prophetic view of salvation history in that the lines are not drawn from present events backwards—in this case, from the events in the Church. On the contrary, here the writer takes his standpoint in retrospect *in the life of Jesus*. Hence the expression 'to remember'. He draws out the lines from every deed and saying of Jesus, but in such a way that, in the manner in which he tells the life of Jesus, these lines become visible without his having to point expressly to them each time, as he does in the passage cited above.

I do not oppose the Bultmannian conception with precisely the contrary notion simply out of a love of paradoxical assertions. I do it as the result of many years' study of the Gospel of John which I shall set down shortly in a detailed commentary. It is the aim of this Gospel to depict the connection of Jesus' life with the life of the risen Christ in his Church, seeing both at the same time. Such a view is, of course, distinct in its form of expression from the usual presentation of salvation history—for instance, that of Luke. But even here the basis and aim are decidedly salvation-historical. Hellenistic ideas, which probably go back to a Hellenistic Judaism,[1] are certainly present in John's Gospel; however, they are subordinate to this aim. If the writer wrote a Gospel radically different from all Gnostic

[1] See my article mentioned above on p. 268 n. 2.

Gospels despite this Hellenism, it is because of his purpose of describing the life of Jesus as salvation history.[1]

If this is his aim, we understand better how the historical life of Jesus *is taken very seriously in its course in time.* That is particularly clear from John 7.1ff. Here it becomes clear that the whole saving process is dependent upon the events of this life. That is the significance of Jesus' words in 7.6: 'My time (καιρός) has not come, but your time is always here.' This is his answer to his brothers' urging him to go up to the feast at Jerusalem at a point in time which Jesus knows not to be the point determined for his suffering and dying. 'Go to the feast yourselves; I am not going up to the feast' (John 7.8). Jesus is aware of carrying out his work according to a *divine plan* which is very definitely fixed. We have found this thought in the Synoptic Gospels as well, although it is only alluded to there. Compare the saying in Luke 13.32: 'I cast out demons and perform cures today and tomorrow, and the third day I finish my course.' In the Fourth Gospel the thought prevails that Jesus' καιροί are the salvation-historical καιροί of God, that is, precisely the ones which God in his authority has *selected* in advance in order that salvation history shall unfold its central events at these specific points in time. We are reminded that this selectivity belongs to the essence of salvation history.[2] Jesus is executing God's plan; and he is so inextricably bound up with the saving events of God that he knows exactly the events in which God will carry out his saving plan through him, Jesus. Here nothing is by chance; everything is the saving plan of God. Jesus himself knows the καιροί of the salvation history that he must carry out. His remark to his brothers, 'Your time is always here' (John 7.6), does not mean that their καιρός is singled out by God in the same way as the καιρός of Jesus, the *kairos* of the central saving occurrence. Their unbelief (v. 5) consists in the fact that they do not recognize that Jesus, unlike them, is bound to this *kairos.* The brothers, too, stand in the saving process, but not as though they were carrying through the history of salvation by their activity at every moment. They may go up to Jerusalem. Salvation for the whole world will not be dependent upon *their* stay in Jerusalem.

[1] The aim of the Gospel (to demonstrate Jesus' Messiahship to Judaism in the Diaspora) stated recently as the key to understanding the Gospel by L. van Hartingsveld, *Die Eschatologie des Johannesevangeliums,* 1962, pp. 3f., following the lead of W. C. van Unnik and J. A. T. Robinson, seems to me to be secondary to the aim stated above, even though this interpretation does maintain a correct aspect.

[2] See above pp. 154ff.

In his commentary, pp. 220f., Bultmann, in line with his conception, understands this saying quite differently, thinking it has the existentialist sense that we should all be in the same situation as Jesus. The saying does refer to a decision, but to *Jesus'* decision for the divine saving plan in which every καιρός of his earthly activity is firmly set. E. Fuchs ('The Quest of the Historical Jesus', *Studies of the Historical Jesus*, 1964, pp. 11ff.) stresses strongly that we must live the decision of Jesus after him. In the Gospel of John that can be true, however, only because first of all Jesus' decision in the course of salvation history is totally different from ours. Against this background we must, of course, also decide by accepting Jesus' decision in faith.

The unexpected mention of the ὧραι in the Gospel of John which recurs often and seems by itself strange and entirely superfluous ('it was about such-and-such an hour'), has the same intention of reminding us that salvation proceeds within the framework of time whose Lord is God, and that within this time God has singled out the hours that bring salvation.

But the central hour towards which everything even within the life of Jesus tends is the hour of his death. It must not occur a single minute earlier than the point fixed for it. Therefore, in the situation of John 7.1ff., Jesus must not go up to Jerusalem as his brothers want him to. In the Synoptics, from a certain moment on we encounter the recurring stereotype predictions of Jesus' suffering. In John's Gospel the reference to the 'hour' that has not yet come stresses much more Jesus' link with the divine saving plan. Starting with 2.4, 'The hour has not yet come', the Gospel leads up to 12.23, 'The hour *has* come'.

From this one hour the other hours of Jesus' activity in salvation history receive their unique significance. It is not as though the other events reported of the life of Jesus did not also have their saving meaning.[1] Each healing performed on a sick person is, according to John, precisely predetermined in God's saving plan. In 9.2, the disciples ask Jesus whether it was the man born blind or his parents who sinned. Jesus' answer is in the negative: 'Neither the blind man nor his parents', and in the positive: 'That the works of God might be made manifest in him. We must work the works . . . while it is day.' In other words, in order that Jesus might encounter the man *born* blind in this specific moment, at this specific place, and be able

[1] Thus rightly F. Lieb, 'Die Geschichte Jesu Christi in Kerygma und Historie. Ein Beitrag zum Gespräch mit R. Bultmann', in the volume *Sophia und Historie*, 1962, p. 349. See the citation above p. 235 n. 2.

to accomplish the miracle of healing, this man had to be born blind! Unless salvation-historical thinking in John's Gospel is taken seriously, such an answer must be offensive. The necessity for Jesus to keep exactly to the divine 'schedule' in order to carry out what he must accomplish within his earthly life is emphasized even more often. 'We must work the works of him who sent me, while it is day' (9.4). In the same way, in 11.9 Jesus says, 'Are there not twelve hours in the day? If any one walks in the day, he does not stumble . . .' Just as the blind man must be born blind in order that Christ can heal him, very similarly Lazarus must die in order that Christ can raise him, and Jesus rejoices that he did not arrive in Bethany at the right time, since otherwise Lazarus would have been healed and accordingly would not have been raised from the dead (John 11.15). But Jesus was to perform a miracle in raising a dead person at this point in time. Again, without an understanding of salvation history, this statement would inevitably be repulsive.

The salvation-historical perspective of the life of Jesus perhaps finds its strongest expression in 5.17, in Jesus' justification for transgressing the commandment of the Sabbath.[1] Compared with the Synoptic sayings on the Sabbath, we find here a new, christological basis: 'My Father is working still, and I am working.' Particularly important are the words ἕως ἄρτι. They include the contemplation of a time when the Father will work no more, when the 'Sabbath rest', of which the Epistle to the Hebrews speaks, will have come. In other words, a time will come when God's saving activity will have reached its end. It is the time spoken of only on the outermost fringes of the New Testament. The whole content of the New Testament (and of the Old as well) is God's acting, not his being.[2] Now in the life of Jesus we stand in the centre of the divine saving *activity*. Here there is no more rest for Jesus the Logos than for the Father with whom he is completely one in his activity. Here he must heal the lame man on this Sabbath.[3]

[1] Cf. O. Cullmann, 'Sabbat und Sonntag nach dem Johannesevangelium. ῞Εως ἄρτι, Joh. 5, 17', in *In memoriam Ernst Lohmeyer*, 1951, pp. 127ff. Cf. also W. Rordorf, *Der Sonntag. Geschichte des Ruhe- und Gottesdiensttages im ältesten Christentum*, 1962, pp. 46ff. ET, 1967.

[2] See above pp. 177f.

[3] Could it be that in Mark 2.28 there are two totally different *logia* which have been linked together, one of which should be regarded as the conclusion of the preceding verses and translated, 'therefore *man* is Lord of the Sabbath', while the other should actually be related to the Son of Man, to Jesus, and understood in the sense of John 5.17?

The Jews say in 18.32: 'It is not lawful for us to put any man to death', and the evangelist notes here, 'This was to fulfil the word which Jesus had spoken to show by what death he was to die.' The whole trial of Jesus had to proceed so that Jesus would not be executed by the Jews, but by the Romans, and hence would be killed by the Roman method, that is, by crucifixion, and not by stoning. This was because Jesus had to die on the cross—he had to be 'lifted up' on the cross (3.14; 12.32). By using a word with a double meaning,[1] the evangelist thinks again of the connection between being lifted up on the cross and his exaltation to the Father. Everything in this life and death was predetermined in God's saving plan.

Even the geographical framework of this life is precisely predetermined. So the evangelist notes *why* Jesus had to go to Galilee or to Judea for this or that work (cf. 4.43f.). He mentions in particular in the introduction to the story of his encounter with the woman of Samaria that to depart from Judea to go to Galilee he *had* to pass through Samaria (4.4). This ἔδει not only refers to the topographical necessity, but at the same time to the fact that Jesus had to encounter the woman of Samaria exactly at this time and on this day, there at Jacob's well, to lay the groundwork for the mission which was so important for salvation history.

Thus, according to the Fourth Gospel, because Jesus' work is decisive for the salvation of mankind, it was accomplished not just at any time, but precisely in the time of the first century determined in God's saving plan, at very definite hours.

The line now leads from this brief space of time to the time of the Church, so that *in each event and in each saying during the historical life of Jesus* its effect in the activity of the exalted Lord in the early Church is announced, and because of the Spirit-given perspective the evangelist can write a life of Jesus that is at the same time a life of the Church of the exalted Christ. This leads us to the second pronounced salvation-historical interest of this Gospel.

B. THE RELATIONSHIP OF THE LIFE OF JESUS TO THE ACTION OF THE EXALTED ONE IN HIS CHURCH

The word 'Church' does not, of course, occur in John's Gospel, and yet John is the real Gospel of the Church. In my book *Early Christian*

---

[1] See above p. 273.

Worship,[1] I have shown how the writer draws the lines from the various episodes in the life of Jesus to the worship of the Church during his own lifetime. Thus the Christ present in the Church's worship is announced in the life of the incarnate Lord.

The question of the temple cult occupies the evangelist right from the beginning. This problem of the early Church is now pursued backward into the life of Jesus. One of the main Johannine leitmotifs is that *Christ appears in place of the temple*.[2] The *shekina*, the δόξα of God, is no longer bound to the temple, but has freed itself from it and is made visible in the incarnate Lord. 'We have seen his δόξα' (1.14). This is already stressed in the prologue. The verb ἐσκήνωσεν in v. 14 is chosen because the word σκηνή, tabernacle, is contained in it, and because it is associated with *shekina* phonetically.[3] God's presence is no longer bound to a place at all, nor to an object like the movable tabernacle, but to the person of the incarnate Logos. John 1.51 says, 'You will see heaven opened, and the angels of God ascending and descending upon the Son of Man', and the reference is clearly made to Jacob's dream in Gen. 28.12. Here again, the basic thought is that the connection with the locus of the cult at Bethel is abolished—the bridge between heaven and earth from now on is the Son of Man. Hence the line is drawn here from the incarnate to the exalted Lord. We find the same, heightened interest in this subject expressed in John's placing the story of the cleansing of the temple at the beginning of Jesus' ministry (2.13ff.), when in reality it occurred at the end of Jesus' life. John continues the same line of thought by relating the temple to Christ's body (2.21). Again, in the discussion with the Samaritan woman, worship in Spirit and in truth is contrasted with the temple cult (4.20ff.). John 12.41, with a clear reference to Isaiah's vision in the temple (Isa. 6), says that it was the glory of Christ that the prophet saw there.

Because the temple is displaced by Christ, baptism and the Lord's Supper, in which Christ himself is now acting in his Church, both play great roles in John's Gospel. *They are related to episodes occurring during the life of Jesus*. That is why the account of the cleansing of the

---

[1] Fourth edition of the German *Urchristentum und Gottesdienst*, 1962; the English edition appeared in 1953.

[2] I have indicated the Johannine relationship to Stephen and the Hellenists in my article, 'L'opposition contre le Temple de Jérusalem, motif commun de la théologie johannique et du monde ambiant', *NTS*, 1959, pp. 8ff.; 39ff.

[3] Cf. C. F. Burney, *The Aramaic Origin of the Fourth Gospel*, 1922, p. 35, and R. Reitzenstein and H. H. Schaeder, *Studien zum antiken Synkretismus*, 1926, p. 318.

temple stands between that of the marriage at Cana, where the Lord's Supper is alluded to, and the discussion with Nicodemus, which revolves around baptism. I cannot repeat here all the argumentation that I applied to the whole Gospel in the work mentioned above and which finds its confirmation in the First Epistle of John.

In his commentary Bultmann must, of course, deny that the Gospel of John has this interest in the sacraments, since it contradicts his understanding of John. Consequently, he must exclude the words ὕδατος καί in John 3.5 and the whole passage 6.51b–58 as interpolations (so also G. Bornkamm, 'Die eucharistische Rede im Johannesevangelium', *ZNW*, 1956, pp. 161ff., and E. Lohse, 'Wort und Sakrament im Johannesevangelium', *NTS*, 1960–1, pp. 117ff., among others; but E. Ruckstuhl, *Die literarische Einheit des Johannesevangeliums*, 1951, pp. 169ff.; P. Borgen, 'The Unity of Discourse in John 6', *ANW*, 1959, pp. 277f.; H. Schürmann, 'Joh. 6, 51c, ein Schlüssel zur grossen johanneischen Brotrede', *Bibl. Ztschrft.*, 1958, pp. 245ff., and W. G. Kümmel, *Introduction to the New Testament*. 1966, p. 150, argue that these verses belonged to the original text. My thesis, earlier represented by A. Schweitzer, has especially been contested by W. Michaelis. Anyone who thinks that for the evangelist the sacraments were done away with, as Bultmann does, must then explain why in the Johannine epistles, which are at least related to the Gospel, the sacraments, at any rate baptism, play such an important part.

The Gospel of John does not, of course, report the institution of the Lord's Supper, which must surely have been known to the author. The important thing for him is to show that the whole work of Jesus stands in relation to the life of the Church. Therefore he speaks indirectly of the Lord's Supper in telling of the other works of the incarnate Logos, above all in the Feeding of the Five Thousand (John 6.1ff.), but in other passages as well, such as the Marriage at Cana (2.1ff.). In the same way, other events of the life of Jesus are intended to depict its relationship to baptism as performed in the Church. The lancing of Jesus' side (19.34) refers to both baptism *and* the Lord's Supper.

Although interest in worship during the present seems to me to predominate in John's Gospel, this is not at all the only expression of the life of the early Church that the evangelist traces back to the life of Jesus. Above all, a line is drawn to the *missionary activity* of the Church. In this activity, too, the exalted Christ, identical with the incarnate Lord, is at work. The fourth chapter is concerned with the question of the origin of all missions, which the evangelist sees in the missionary activity of the ἄλλοι (4.38)—probably the 'Hellenists' of the early Church. I have tried to show elsewhere[1] that the Gospel of John is interested in a very special way in these 'Hellenists' of Acts, these bold missionaries of the early Church.

After the martydom of Stephen, the Hellenists were driven out of Jerusalem, because of their radical rejection of the temple, whereas the Twelve, who apparently did *not* share their radicalism, could remain there (Acts 8.1). The Hellenists then turned to Samaria, the land of a syncretism whose adherents were closely related to Judaism, but who also rejected the temple at Jerusalem, not because of a spiritualistic conception like that of the Hellenists in Acts, but in favour of their own sanctuary on Mt. Gerizim. We can understand why the Hellenists proceeded to Samaria with their message of the God bound neither to the temple nor to any location (cf. Stephen's speech, Acts 7.2–53). Here for the first time the gospel was preached to non-Jews. The mission in Samaria, whose inhabitants belonged to a half-Jewish, half-pagan religion, formed the proper transition to the mission in the pagan world. Hence the prominence attached to the Samaritan mission.

The Gospel of John recognizes this and finds the basis for this mission in Jesus' encounter with the Samaritan woman. But the Gospel also recognizes that the credit for this missionary work goes to those first Hellenistic missionaries, anonymous with the exception of Phillip. The book of Acts allows us to surmise that these missionaries were apparently regarded as not entirely suitable in Jerusalem. Thus the apostles John and Peter were subsequently sent from Jerusalem, and had to lay their hands on the Samaritans already converted by the Hellenists (Acts 8.14ff.). We must keep these events in mind when we read the Johannine narration of Jesus' encounter with the Samaritan woman. The fourth evangelist certainly wished to indicate the line of connection between this encounter and the founding of the mission in Samaria, and therefore of all Christian missions. The symbolic expressions borrowed from farming in the second part of the chapter (4.35ff.), sowing and harvesting, belong to the language of early Christian mission. The transition from the preaching of the gospel among the Jews to the mission among the Samaritans was not a self-evident thing. On the contrary, it was very problematic, especially since the saying of Jesus in Matt. 10.5 had been preserved, 'Enter no town of the Samaritans.' John's Gospel wishes to balance this saying with the account of Jesus' encounter with the Samaritan woman to show that the mission of the primitive Church in Samaria was intended by Jesus. While Jesus is still

[1] 'La Samarie et les origines de la mission chrétienne. Qui sont les ἄλλοι de Jean 4, 38?' in *Annuaire 1953–54 de l'École pratique des Hautes Études, Section des Sciences religieuses*, Paris, 1953, pp. 3ff., ET in *The Early Church*, pp. 185ff.

speaking with the disciples, the Samaritans, informed by the women, come to the well (v. 30), and their coming causes Jesus to say to his disciples that the fields are already white for the harvest (v. 35). These words are very typical of the salvation-historical perspective of John's Gospel. The mission field is meant. Jesus points to the Samaritans who stream to him from the city. He himself has scattered the seed there at Jacob's well. He, the sower, stands behind the mission in Samaria—'sower and reaper may rejoice together' (v. 36). So it will be in the early Church. Although it is the disciples who will do the harvesting when the actual missionary work in Samaria begins, Jesus, nevertheless, stands behind them, for *he* has sent them (ἐγώ v. 38). But standing *between* the disciples who harvest and Jesus who sows, according to v. 38, are the ἄλλοι who have worked and into whose work the disciples have entered. If my hypothesis is correct (and I see no other explanation for the ἄλλοι), this refers to the Hellenists, who are, of course, the true founders of the mission in Samaria. It was into their work that the apostles from Jerusalem entered (Acts 8.14).

The interest of the Gospel of John in the occurrence at Jacob's well is therefore clear. It connects the life of Jesus with the mission work in this half-Jewish land and with mission in general, since the basis for all Christian mission is laid here. From there the preaching of the gospel passes to the pagans, the 'Greeks'.

The evangelist also finds this important expansion in salvation history anticipated during Jesus' life in the account given in 12.20ff., where we hear of the Greeks who would see Jesus. There Jesus points out the necessity of his dying first (v. 24). Then in his exaltation (to the cross and to the Father)[1] he will draw all men to himself (John 12.32). The actual mission to the Gentiles presupposes Jesus' death and exaltation. That is the *typical*, *salvation-historical* thought with which the evangelist is concerned. Again, as in Chapter 4, he uses the image of the seed and the fruit to describe the mission: 'Unless a grain of wheat . . . dies, it remains alone; but if it dies, it bears much fruit' (v. 24). In accord with the Johannine theology, Jesus in his person is himself the seed from which the conversion of the Gentiles issues as fruit—but Jesus as the crucified and glorified. So here, in the answer which he gives to the longing of the Greeks to see him, Jesus draws out the connection between his life and death on the one hand, and the events happening in the Church's mission on the other.

In the chapter on the Good Shepherd, the focus is on the Gentiles

---

[1] On the double meaning of the verb ὑφωθῆναι see above p. 278.

again: 'And I have other sheep, that are not of this fold; I must bring them also, and they will heed my voice. So there shall be one flock, one shepherd' (10.16). Furthermore, other believers are referred to in 11.52 and 17.20. It is no accident that these references to the Gentile mission also stand in a context stressing very emphatically that in the course of salvation history the Good Shepherd, who freely gives his life for the sheep, must die. The problem of the 'Church composed of Jews and Gentiles' is also a Johannine problem. It occupies the writer in the prologue even where it is stated that the Logos came to his 'own', and his 'own' did not receive him. Since the thought of the 'true Israel' also emerges later in the Gospel, we should probably think of the Jews here.[1]

The extension of the life of Jesus into the time of the founding of the Church is the aim pursued by the fourth evangelist. But he does not add a second volume on the life of Jesus the exalted Lord as Luke does in his 'Acts of the Apostles', which followed a first, the 'life of Jesus who appeared in the flesh'. Instead, he presents salvation history in his characteristic perspective of the life of Jesus. The Johannine words, 'the hour is coming and now is', are not only characteristic of the eschatological tension found in the Fourth Gospel; they also represent the author's view of both the life of Jesus and the life of Christ seen together in his Church. In 4.23 the words refer to worshipping in spirit and in truth, which means worship in the Church.

The farewell discourses in 14–17 show that the chief concern of the evangelist in connection with salvation history is to connect the life of Jesus with the Church. The interpretation of the whole Gospel should start with these discourses. But it would be wrong to want to limit the evangelist's interest in salvation history to this one view. John's total perspective includes the history of Israel too.

C. THE RELATIONSHIP OF THE LIFE OF JESUS TO THE SALVATION HISTORY OF THE PAST

The knowledge that the believers in Christ are the true Israel, this salvation-historical 'self-understanding', is in no way merely Pauline. It is also Johannine. The thought which is probably alluded to as early as the prologue that '. . . his own received him not. But to all

[1] See C. H. Dodd, *The Interpretation of the Fourth Gospel*, 1953, pp. 270 and 272.

who received him, who believed in his name, he gave power to become children of God' (John 1.11-12) is one of the Johannine motives
permeating the whole Gospel. Hence the numerous references to
Moses and Abraham and the constant citing of the Old Testament.
The testimony of the 'Israelite in whom there is no guile' says not
only, 'You are the Son of God', but also, 'You are the King of Israel'
(1.49). The intensive use of the Old Testament by John ought to
preclude speaking of an elimination of salvation history in this
Gospel.[1] A comparison of John 8.33ff. with Gal. 3.6ff. and particularly Gal. 4.21ff. shows that, despite all the differences between the
two documents, the evangelist agrees with Paul to the extent that his
thinking is oriented towards salvation history. The 'offspring of
Abraham' is also the leitmotif in the passage in John. Despite their
protest that they have not been born of fornication, according to
John 8.41 the unbelieving Jews are not the offspring of Abraham.
They do not have God, but the devil as their father, for the devil is
a murderer and liar 'from the beginning' (8.44). Here a line is
drawn from the devil in the paradise story, who initiated men into
death by a lie, then to Cain's fratricide, and thence to the unbelieving
Jews who murder Jesus. The conclusion for the evangelist is that the
unbelieving Jews are not 'the offspring of Abraham', for Abraham's
offspring do the works of Abraham, and not those of the murderer.
Paul does not go so far as to term the unbelieving Jews 'sons of the
devil', but for him the Jews are by principle of descent the offspring
of Ishmael, for whom everything depends upon the σάρξ. For the
offspring who look back to the miracle of faith at the time of Isaac's
birth, however, faith is the decisive factor. The relation of Abraham
to faith does not appear in John 8.44ff., but his relation to Christ is
drawn out at the end of the chapter.

Hence we hear in v. 56 that Abraham rejoiced, looking to the day
of Jesus. Gen. 17.17, as it was interpreted by rabbinic exegesis, is
referred to here. At the same time it is interesting that the chronological sequence of salvation history is not given up, but is instead
bound up with the Johannine notion that Christ was at work in
salvation history throughout the past, in his pre-existence. Abraham
saw Jesus' day, and Jesus saw Abraham. Isaiah also saw Christ's
glory (John 12.41). The vision of Isaiah in the temple (Isa. 6.1ff.)
is referred to here. The men of the old covenant had their roles to

[1] See F. M. Braun, *Jean le Théologien II. Les grandes traditions d'Israël. L'accord
des Écritures d'après le quatrième Évangile*, 1964.

play in salvation history during *their* time, and yet, because of their prophetic gift, they saw the connection of periods, just as the evangelist himself sees this connection from his standpoint at the decsive mid-point.

In the light of the above, we cannot conclude that salvation history is abolished in the Gospel of John. It is characteristic of salvation history in the New Testament that, on the one hand, *the various epochs follow one another, but, on the other hand, that all are bound together among themselves by their orientation towards Christ, the mid-point of salvation history, who supplies this history with its meaning and sums up the epochs of salvation history in himself.*

The recognition that this is the centre of all history and the emphasis upon the connection of the central saving revelation in Jesus of Nazareth with the *whole* saving revelation of God necessarily includes faith in the pre-existence of Jesus. The same Logos-Christ, who in Jesus of Nazareth has become flesh, must have existed right from the beginning of salvation history.

The duality between the chronological sequence of epochs and the abrogating of this sequence by Christ's pre-existence is nowhere more forcefully expressed than in the connection made in John's Gospel between Jesus and John the Baptist. The Gospel of John has in common with the Synoptic tradition the fact that the role of John the Baptist is recognized as belonging *chronologically* to *salvation history* —the Baptist has come *before* Christ as a witness to him. The connection of the life of the incarnate Lord with the past of salvation history leads through the Baptist. This fact cannot be shaken. Whether he is the forerunner, as in the Synoptics, or the witness, as in the Gospel of John, at any rate part of his task in salvation history is that he must precede Jesus. This is an element germane to *all* the Gospel tradition. Therefore the Johannine prologue, which speaks of the pre-existent Logos having participated in creation, includes the historical level where John the Baptist comes *before* Christ 'for testimony'.[1]

Only after this salvation-historical background has been established do the Baptist's words in 1.15 demonstrate the fact that 'he who comes after' him 'was before' him. That had to be emphasized over against the Baptist's disciples who, of course, are attacked in these first chapters and are refuted by the Baptist himself. This is a further

[1] "O ὀπίσω μου ἐρχόμενος', in *Coniectanea Neotestamenica XI, in honorem A. Fridrichsen,* 1948, pp. 26ff.; ET in *The Early Church,* pp. 177ff.

concern of the early Church which is dealt with through the life of Jesus. It is a polemic against heretics,[1] who are attacked indirectly, just as the first of all heresies, Docetism, was. But this emphasis on Jesus' pre-existence is important quite apart from polemics. The further role assigned to John in the narrative following the prologue shows that the evangelist has not forgotten for one moment what must be said about the chronological sequence of events. If the relation between Jesus and the Baptist were not seen in this chronological light, the evangelist would have stated only the negative part about the Baptist—which is also found in his Gospel—namely, what he is not (not the light, not the Christ). He would not have expressed what is to be said positively about John; he can do so because he knows that Jesus is the bearer of the salvation history with which John the Baptist is aligned as *witness*.

Moses also retains his role in salvation history, but at the same time this role is seen in the light of Christ the fulfiller. So we already hear in the prologue, 'For the law was given through Moses; grace and truth came through Jesus Christ' (John 1.17). Philip says to Nathanael (1.45), 'We have found him of whom Moses in the law and also the prophets wrote.' Again and again Moses is spoken of, 'Who wrote of me' (5.46). The lifting up of the serpent is referred to typologically (3.14). The connection with salvation history is even more pronounced when the manna that could not give eternal life to the fathers in the wilderness is alluded to in a passage referring to the Eucharist which Christ brings to the Church. On the other hand, however, the Law given by Moses (7.19) and circumcision (7.22) were already divine gifts.

Only in a few passages like John 3.14 is the use of the Old Testament typological rather than salvation-historical. This fact should remind us that even typology is founded upon salvation history, and that the divisions between typology and salvation history are in flux. In any case, we are not dealing with an allegorizing interpretation that does away with the historical element, nor does the use of the Old Testament rest upon a simple, mechanical application of hermeneutical principles.

Often the Old Testament passage intended is not expressly cited.

---

[1] See H. H. Schaeder, 'Der "Mensch" im Prolog des 4. Evangeliums' (R. Reitzenstein—H. H. Schaeder, *Studien zum antiken Synkretismus*, 1926) pp. 306ff. The question can remain open whether the prologue is an adaptation of a hymn to John the Baptist widespread among the Baptist's circles.

In all the passages where Jesus' atoning death is alluded to—in the witness of the Baptist to the Lamb of God that bears the sin of the world (1.29, 36),[1] or in the saying about the voluntary death of the Good Shepherd (10.17)—the thought of Isa. 53 surely stands in the background.

We have already spoken above of the salvation-historical notion that Christ has come to displace the temple. In Christ the *shekina* of God is now visible. The connection with heaven is no longer made through the locus of the cult, but through the Son of Man on whom the angels descend. In him heaven is opened (John 1.51). Here, as in the passage about the manna, a connection is seen forwards to the worship of the Church, and backwards, to the old covenant which has been fulfilled.

As in the Epistle to the Hebrews, the assertion that the old covenant has been dissolved is associated everywhere in the Gospel with the recognition of Israel's role in salvation history. Therefore, although he rejects the cult in the temple at Jerusalem as well as that on Mt. Gerizim, Jesus says to the Samaritan women, 'salvation comes from the Jews' (4.22). This does not, as Bultmann thinks,[2] in any way stand in contradiction to the extremely sharp saying in 8.41ff., where the Jews are termed sons of the devil. The latter passage obviously concerns unbelieving Jews, and the salvation-historical mission of Israel is no more discarded with this judgment than in Paul's assertion that the unbelieving Jews are sons of Hagar. The Johannine saying to the Samaritan woman may not therefore arbitrarily be excluded as a gloss, as by Bultmann and W. Bauer.[3] On the contrary, it sets down the evangelist's conviction as it may be followed through the whole Gospel.

Since Jesus is the centre of the whole saving process, the line must be extended back from John and the people of Israel into primeval history, and so the writer's view in retrospect concerns primeval history as well. Christ's place as mediator of creation, spoken of at the beginning of the prologue, is mentioned often. This extension of salvation history follows automatically from the recognition that the life of Jesus is the decisive, saving revelation of God. The Logos, who afterwards became flesh, is the bearer of all God's saving communica-

---

[1] See O. Cullmann, *Baptism in the New Testament*, pp. 19f.
[2] Cf. Bultmann's commentary on John, *ad loc.*, p. 139.
[3] Against Bultmann, see C. K. Barrett, *The Gospel According to St John*, 1955, *ad loc.*

tion, even at the beginning: everything has been made through him (John 1.3).

In other New Testament writings the role of Christ as the mediator of creation is also stressed, but the christological association of creation and redemption is nowhere so close as in the Gospel of John. In the Old Testament, primeval history precedes the history of Israel, but in the New Testament, primeval history is not put before history proper. To be sure, the creation is narrated anew, but now wholly in the light of the incarnate Lord, whose life story is told as the centre of all salvation history. This new creation story is not only the first chapter of salvation history, but is actually the 'prologue' or 'overture' anticipating the main motif of the Gospel. This main motif is what I refer to as the *overall view* of the life of Jesus, linked with all the past and future epochs of salvation history.

The account of the new creation begins exactly like that of the Old Testament—$\dot{\epsilon}\nu\dot{\alpha}\rho\chi\hat{\eta}=$ b^{e}reshith. Although late Jewish and Hellenistic speculations about the 'Word' or 'Wisdom' as hypostases of God must be adduced to interpret the passage, nevertheless it is clear that the first thought is of God's work spoken at the beginning, 'Let there be light', especially since the 'Word' of v. 4 onward is identified with 'life' and 'light'. At the same time it is a significant fact that the evangelist, even in these speculative statements (which perhaps were really *only* speculative in a source that he has taken over), does not forget for a moment that he is speaking of the Lord who became flesh, whose words and deeds constitute the content of his book.

John's salvation-historical view of the connection between the life of Jesus and primeval history is carried out in a consummate way, but not in such a way as to do away with the distinction between epochs. Although the writer of the First Epistle of John narrates no life of Jesus, he says in the same way that the witnesses who saw and heard the historical Jesus in the most direct way report what 'was from the very beginning', $\dot{\alpha}\pi$' $\dot{\alpha}\rho\chi\hat{\eta}s$.

Having established that the Gospel of John has connected the central events of Jesus' life with all the rest of the periods in salvation history, we would be more than surprised if this salvation-historical perspective took into account only the history of the Church, the history of Israel, and creation, while excluding the history of the end time. This leads us to the final point.

D. THE RELATIONSHIP OF THE LIFE OF JESUS
TO THE HISTORY OF THE END TIME

The Bultmann school emphatically represents temporal eschatology as irreconcilable with Johannine thinking. In the case of eschatology, it is made clear how the Gospel of John has freed the kernel of Jesus' existential *kerygma* and has detached it from all salvation-historical 'mythology'. This question of eschatology in John cannot in fact be answered without dealing with the rest of salvation history, just as throughout the New Testament eschatology can be spoken of only in connection with salvation history. For this reason, we have first discussed here the role of the life of the historical Jesus in salvation history, then the connection which it has with the history of the early Church, and finally its relationship to Old Testament history. At the same time, we have in each case emphasized the characteristic *total view*, which *at the same time* allows the *distinction* of periods and their *concentration* in Christ to be clarified. The fact that the periods are summed up in Christ must not lead one to overlook the distinction between them that is still retained.

It seems to me that the widespread notion that the Gospel of John wanted to eliminate temporal eschatology by forcefully emphasizing sayings concerning the present is responsible for the fact that this total perspective is not generally recognized as the aim of the Johannine portrayal of the life of Jesus. The way in which the writer fused things that happened later on in the life of the Church with episodes in the life of Jesus does not mean he had no interest in what was occurring in the life of the Church. By the same token, just because he emphasized the eschatology 'realized' in the life of Jesus, it does not mean that he wanted to eliminate all eschatology not yet realized. Just as the words at 4.23 on true worship, 'the hour is coming and now is', have in mind both the time when the incarnate Lord is present and the time of the Church, so the similar sounding words relating to judgment and resurrection mean *at the same time* the present *and* the future, including the eschatological future extending beyond the time of the Church.

As we have mentioned at the beginning of this chapter, it is certain that the 'already' of the present, the realization which has taken place before now, is more strongly emphasized than in the Synoptics. But the tension is here also. We, of course, know why the 'relaxation' of the tension is more apparent here, why the 'already' stands in the foreground more dominantly. It is because the whole perspective of the Gospel puts the historical life of Jesus in its place as the decisive mid-point of history more emphatically than any other Gospel does. Thus the thought found in the Synoptics as well[1] that the Kingdom of God is already *anticipated* in the presence of the person of Jesus is more consistently carried out in the Gospel of John. The anticipation of the end in Christ is because the person of Christ, in whom the whole redemptive process is summed up, stands so much in the foreground of this Gospel.

In comparison with Jesus and Paul, the interval is extended here just as it is in Luke. As in Luke, so here also a longer time of the Paraclete and of the Church is reckoned with. But it would be wrong to think that it is no longer viewed as an interval. On the contrary, all the instructions of the farewell discourses about the time of the Church only become understandable with the background of a futuristic eschatology, and in the statements of 11.25f. one can even see a reference to the fate of the dead during the interval.

When we feel that the impressive emphasis on the end time being *now* (cf. I John 2.18, 'Children, it is the last hour') is intended in the *temporal* sense, we are in harmony with the Fourth Gospel's basic, overall conception. But in this case the statements about the present only have meaning if they include the presupposition that what *has* happened now in the Lord who has appeared in the flesh *will* take place at the end. In the preceding paragraphs we have produced evidence that the Gospel of John is oriented toward the history of salvation in a twofold way: It sees the whole history of salvation as summed up in the life of Jesus, and it connects his life with this history. If this interpretation of the Gospel is correct, no further discussion is required to show that in the Johannine relationship of present to future the future is not to be thought to be utterly swallowed up by the present.

I have deliberately avoided introducing the numerous passages which without doubt reckon with future events and an end that is still to come (5.28; 6.39, 40, 44, 54; 11.24; 12.48). Bultmann views them all without exception as interpolations. Theoretically, the possibility that they are interpolations can be entertained, although there are neither textual nor literary grounds for doing so. But the question, much discussed in recent times, whether the writer of John

---

[1] See above pp. 193ff.

really eliminated temporal eschatology or not[1] cannot in any case be answered simply by the passages in question.[2] This is, incidentally, the attitude of more recent works, chiefly that of L. van Hartingsveld, with whom I essentially agree, except in the case of the purpose he ascribes to the Gospel.[3] For the details, I refer to his comments. But the main consideration for me here has been to treat the problem in relation to the role of the *total* salvation history in the Gospel of John, especially since the Bultmann school thinks it necessary to exclude both eschatology and salvation history in general from the Gospel.

[1] Cf. R. Bultmann, 'Die Eschatologie des Johannesevangeliums', *Zwischen den Zeiten*, 1928, pp. 4ff.; now in *Glauben und Verstehen* I, pp. 134ff.; *Das Evangelium des Johannes*, 1950; *Die Theologie des Neuen Testaments*, [3]1958; ET vol. I, 1952, vol. II, 1955; G. Stählin, 'Zum Problem der johanneischen Eschatologie', *ZNW*, 1934, pp. 225ff.; D. E. Holwerda, *The Holy Spirit and Eschatology in the Gospel of John*, 1959; W. F. Howard, *The Fourth Gospel in Recent Criticism and Interpretation*, [4]1955; B. Aebert, *Die Eschatologie des Johannes-Evangeliums, eine systematische Untersuchung auf Grund seiner religionsgeschichtlichen Voraussetzungen*, 1936; A. Corell, *Consummatum est, Eschatology and Church in the Gospel of St John*, 1958; C. H. Dodd, *The Interpretation of the Fourth Gospel*, 1953; P. W. Meijer, *The Eschatology of the Fourth Gospel, a Study in Early Christian Reinterpretation* (dissertation Union Theol. Seminary, New York 1955); E. Stauffer, 'Agnostos Christos, Joh. 2, 24, und die Eschatologie des vierten Evangeliums', *The Background of the New Testament and its Eschatology*, 1956, pp. 281ff.; 'Messias oder Menschensohn', *NovT*, 1956, pp. 81ff.; *The Theology of the New Testament*, 1955; P. Ricca, *Die Eschatologie des 4. Evangeliums* (a Basel University dissertation, 1964, as yet unpublished); T. Müller, *Das Heilsgeschehen im Johannesevangelium. Eine exegetische Studie und zugleich Versuch einer Antwort an R. Bultmann*, 1961.

[2] These passages are defended as original by W. G. Kümmel in his revision of Feine and Behm's *Introduction to the New Testament*, 1966, pp. 149f., and also by others such as E. Ruckstuhl, *op. cit.*, pp. 159ff., and S. Schulz, *Untersuchungen zur Menschensohn-Christologie im Johannesevangelium*, 1957, pp. 109ff.

[3] See above p. 275 n. 1.

V

A SURVEY OF SYSTEMATIC THEOLOGY AND THE HISTORY OF DOGMA: SALVATION HISTORY AND THE POST-BIBLICAL PERIOD

SO FAR, WE have deliberately limited ourselves to the exegetical-historical question, that is, to the New Testament. The problem that has occupied us is, however, constituted in such a way that it leads directly into the dogmatic question, whether salvation history continues, or stops at the end of New Testament times. Indeed, one can even say the dogmatic question is also a New Testament problem. Without trying to offer here an outline of a dogmatics or an ethics of salvation history, which of course ought to be written some day, we wish to indicate at least some of the main lines which issue from the conclusions reached by our New Testament study. The questions with which we must deal here are the following: (1) In what way is salvation history concluded with the end of the apostolic age, and in what way does it continue? What do the answers to these two questions mean for the problem of the canon and for the problem of the relationship between Scripture and tradition? (2) If we can speak in a certain sense of a continuation of salvation history, how can we know where and when salvation history occurs in the post-biblical period? (3) What is the significance of the worship of the Christian Church for the presentation of salvation history in our time? (4) How are *our* faith and *our* endeavours in theology and in the Church related to salvation history? (5) How can an ethics be constructed upon salvation history?

1. THE LIMITATION AND CONTINUATION
OF SALVATION HISTORY

(*Canon, Scripture, and Tradition*)

We could simplify the answer to the question whether salvation history continues on in post-biblical time simply by answering it in the affirmative, referring to the fact that according to the New Testament itself the eschatological events are yet to come, and that we therefore stand in the midst of a stream of salvation history that starts in the biblical period and according to the biblical witness itself will find its consummation only at the end. This way of handling the question is in no way wrong, and it must actually be taken into serious consideration. But it is incomplete, and does not do justice to the complexity of the problem. According to the New Testament, we find ourselves in an intermediate stage between two poles, the poles of the biblical period and the end time. The question is only whether this intermediate stage as such belongs to salvation history, or whether it represents a great gap in the divine process, or even whether the problem is complex at all.

We have found[1] that although all history stands in some sort of relationship to the saving process, there are larger and smaller gaps in salvation history in the *narrower* sense when one compares this process with the whole of history. It is not as if the chronology of salvation history were simply identical with the chronology of history in general. Is it possible, then, that the whole post-biblical period of church history up to the dawn of the end time represents such a gap, in which salvation history in the narrower sense is absent? In view of the situation of tension, this is hardly possible. Because the high-point of the saving process is already attained in Christ, and the consummation is still to come, there can be no vacuum before the end. Instead, what has happened in Christ must now unfold in the direction of the consummation.

This is all the more so since the start of the *interval* separating Christ's resurrection from the end falls into the apostolic period in which the New Testament books arose. The fact that the interval, to which our whole 'time of the Church' belongs, *began* within 'biblical' time is very important for the question we are dealing with

---

[1] See above pp. 154ff.

here. It would be simply inexplicable that a sudden interruption lasting up to the end should enter into this period which, according to the New Testament itself, represents a unity as a preparation for the end.

Still, in the New Testament we do find just such an abrupt break. Nowhere is it more evident than at the end of Acts, which concludes with Paul's preaching in Rome (28.31). How is the limitation by the apostolic age and at the same time the continuation of salvation history to be explained? Let me anticipate the answer to this question: *Salvation history itself continues, but only as the unfolding of the Christ event. However, the revelation of the divine plan presented through event and interpretation, according to which salvation history has developed and will continue to develop up to the end, is concluded.* The question how far new knowledge effected by the Holy Spirit is still possible will occupy us in Chapter Four.

Both the limitation *and* the continuation of salvation history are well founded within the biblical salvation history itself. Its limitation amounts to the fixing of the canon. It seems to me impossible to justify the canon apart from salvation history and it is not by accident that its justification is inevitably questioned whenever salvation history is rejected. But the usual attempts to establish the dogmatic necessity of the canon seem insufficient to me, for they do not see how the canon is necessarily anchored in the inmost essence of the Bible itself, that is, in salvation history. It is not as though with the fixing of the canon a foreign element was imposed on the books of the Bible which was absent in its various writings. On the contrary, I would like to show here that both the idea of a canon and the manner of its realization are *a crucial part* of the salvation history of the Bible.

The interpretation which Karl Barth impressively represents is indeed valuable and correct. Barth says that the canon originated in such a way that the books accepted into it forced themselves upon the Church. But this does not explain the *idea* of a canon as such. I myself have tried to show in another way in 'The Tradition', *The Early Church*, 1956, pp. 57ff., the necessity which the Church felt when it subjected itself to a norm in the awareness that the transmission of a tradition faithful to the truth could no longer be automatically guaranteed. I still maintain this position from the particular standpoint taken in that work. However, it is still not sufficient, for it likewise does not derive the *inner* necessity of the canon *from the Bible itself.*

When I speak of the canon I mean, of course, here as in my earlier work, the conception of the *idea* of a canon, not its final and actual fixing, which extendes over centuries.

Why did the Bible's salvation history have to find its normal issue in the fixing of the canon? To answer this question we need only refer back to everything said in the present work. The first thing to be considered here is that *all* salvation history, the past as well as the future or eschatological, has found its climax and recapitulation in the life, death, and resurrection of Jesus. What is still to come is the unfolding and the consummation of what is already there in Jesus Christ. If the temporality of salvation history is taken seriously, *the history of the revelation* of the saving plan[1] must stand as concluded with this event that took place in the first century in our scheme of reckoning time. The process itself continues on, of course, and develops. New saving events enter it. But not only are we in no position to say with certainty where this is the case, but the onward development can only unfold what has appeared in the previous development leading to Christ. We have described above[2] how by the election of a minority the movement of salvation history progresses in constant reduction to the One, and how from this high-point the path leads from the One back again to the many, to humanity, to creation. Throughout, the principle of being represented by the One remains in force. The direction of the 'return route', which commences in the New Testament, is therefore already revealed in the path leading up to Christ. This path was decisive, and thus the demarcation of its total extension belongs in the canon as the *terminus of the path itself*.

A further essential feature of all biblical salvation history issues directly into the notion that so far as revelation is concerned, salvation history has reached its conclusion. We have always stressed the important fact that the revealers themselves belong to salvation history as eyewitnesses of new events and as interpreters of these events which they linked with the preceding interpretations. We have seen that both belong together—ϵἶδϵν καὶ ἐπίστϵυσϵν (John 20.8). Therefore it was again a crucial moment in salvation history when the generation of the eyewitnesses to those central events died out. From now on there will be further witnesses of those events and their unfolding in

[1] This history also belongs, of course, to salvation history; see above pp. 89ff.
[2] See above pp. 160ff., 263ff.

subsequent history, there will be theologians who continue the interpretation; but no longer can there be any witnesses who are at the same time eyewitnesses *to the central decisive events*. The eyewitness of the apostles is very important within the New Testament. Even Paul had to have seen the risen Lord bodily (I Cor. 9.1). Because the apostles themselves belong in salvation history as eyewitnesses and interpreters, the New Testament goes beyond the time of the life of Jesus to the point when these eyewitnesses have died.[1]

No one can understand the origin of the canon without taking this New Testament idea of eyewitness into account. The discussion between Catholics and Protestants on Scripture and tradition suffers from the fact that the full significance of the fact that the idea of a canon is founded on the concept of the apostles' eyewitness is not recognized. Here again, a direct line leads from the fundamental New Testament notion to the canon. At the same time it must be noted that the apostles' eyewitness is more important than that of all the other biblical witnesses because it relates to the decisive events and in this way indirectly *guarantees the revelations of all the previous witnesses*.

The faith that the interpretation of events at any one time rests upon a revelation through the Holy Spirit also belongs to the biblical development of all salvation history. The final interpretation implicitly present in the canon also presupposes this faith. This interpretation extends to all the books united in the canon. Moreover, the whole Church is to be regarded as the mediator of this revelation.

The interpretation that came with the setting up of the canon in itself marks the *end of all the preceding history of interpretation*. Indeed, we can and must say that the factor which from the beginning, even in the Old Testament, bound together events and their interpretations and new interpretations calls for a *total interpretation* which concludes the whole process of interpretation. This we are offered in the canon. The canon represents the end of the process of revelation and interpretation. We have seen that one can speak of a kind of chain in which each new event together with its interpretation attaches to the earlier interpretations of previous events and in this connection interprets them anew. The final new interpretation of the whole comes through a realization that the time of salvation goes on,

[1] This also includes eyewitnesses of the events occurring during the apostolic period which, of course, cannot be demarcated by specific dates. But with the exception of the person who wrote II Peter, all the writers of the New Testament books lived during a period to which this specification may be applied.

but that with the deaths of the apostles the crucial time of revelation is past. It is contained in the idea of the canon itself in that the New Testament is associated with the Old Testament on one and the same level. Thus, both Testaments together receive a unified interpretation on the basis of the saving events of the New Testament. This fusing of both Testaments means nothing less than that here the idea of salvation history is finally *raised to its position as the principle of the whole Bible*.

At the same time I emphasize again that I am not speaking of 'final' as though I were overlooking the fact that the final *number* of books belonging to this canon was accepted only gradually. I am speaking of *the* point in time when the writings of the New Testament were placed in principle on the level with the Old Testament.

If the view propounded in the present work is correct, the meaning of the canon is that here, as always in the previous history of interpretation, the constant factor is retained. This factor is the development of the salvation history according to a divine plan. But at the same time a clarifying new interpretation ensues, as has always happened before. The thing that is new in this concluding new interpretation is the fact that not just individual excerpts of salvation history are presented, as was the case earlier, but that now, through the *collection together* of the various books of the Bible, the whole history of salvation must be taken into account in understanding any one of the books of the Bible.[1] When we wish to interpret some affirmation coming from early Christianity not merely as an isolated phenomenon, but as an actual *biblical text*, as a part belonging to a totality, we must call upon salvation history as a hermeneutical key, for it is the factor binding all the biblical texts together.

Thus the canon is, on the one hand, a product of the basic thought of the whole Bible, and, on the other hand, it is the principle of unity in the Bible consistently carrying through what encompasses the whole.

In recent times there has been much discussion about what constitutes the unity of the Bible, or what must be regarded as the norm in the Bible ('the canon in the canon').[2] The problem is not new; it

---

[1] H. Diem also stressed this, starting from other premises, of course.

[2] See the discussion between E. Käsemann, 'Begründet der neutestamentliche Kanon die Einheit der Kirche?', *EvT*, 1951–52, pp. 13ff., and H. Diem, *Theologie als kirchliche Wissenschaft*, Bd. II, ²1957 (the chapter entitled 'Dogmatik. Ihr Weg

was implied in the criterion set up by Luther—only '*was Christum treibet*' (what directs towards Christ) is according to Scripture. Each period in Church history has made a selection among the motifs of the Bible based on its favourite ideas. For Erasmus and the Enlightenment the Sermon on the Mount stood in the centre. According to Käsemann most recently it is justification by faith. Any selection of a criterion is bound to be subjective and arbitrary. If we take seriously at all the thought of a canon comprising both Testaments, then we must say that it can only be salvation history which constitutes the unity of Scripture, not because of a pet theological idea and not because of a selection, but because only it can include all these books. I simply do not see any other biblical notion which makes a link between all the books of the Bible such as the fixing of the canon sought to express.

The demand to be 'honest' in the area of Christian thought is raised with special emphasis today. Among other things the question must also be raised whether in all honesty we may really lay the Bible upon our altars if we reject what makes the collection of these books in particular into the 'Bible', namely, salvation history. Luther's principle ('*was Christum treibet*') must not be entirely rejected. But it needs to be supplemented so that the work of the incarnate Christ on the cross and in the resurrection is the orientation, mid-point, and summing up of a whole process leading up to him and proceeding from him, so that the incarnate Lord is the crucified and risen mediator and revealer of that process. Otherwise, we are in danger of limiting '*was Christum treibet*' to what 'claims' us, and we are back again to selection. It could then happen that we do not know what to do, for instance, with the Apocalypse of John.

Before the canon was fixed, it was always new events that led to new interpretations. In the final new interpretation implied by the idea of the canon, we have two basic facts noted by early Christianity as it drew near the end of its primitive phase: (1) the fact of the extension of time which we have spoken of, that is, the fact that the interval can last for a period of uncertain length; (2) the fact that the generation of the eyewitnesses of the decisive events had died out.

---

zwischen Historismus und Existentialismus', pp. 196ff.), and the position taken by H. Küng in 'Der Frühkatholizismus im Neuen Testament als kontroverstheologisches Problem', *Tübinger Theol. Quartalschr.*, 1962, pp. 385ff., as well as E. Käsemann's answer, 'Paulus und der Frühkatholizismus', *ZTK*, 1963, pp. 75ff.

These two facts required a norm that could determine the essence and activity of the Church in the time thereafter.

The question whether salvation history continues is therefore settled by Protestant theology in too simple a manner when it is answered in the negative with an appeal to the principle of Scripture. But its complexity is also overlooked if it is simply answered in the affirmative in such a way that no distinction exists between, on the one hand, the salvation history of the Bible which comes to a climax in the events of Jesus Christ, and on the other, the events during the time of the Church. We pose this question as sharply as possible. Above all we must make a clear separation between the *continuation* of salvation history as such and our *knowledge* about it. To what extent is the development of salvation history during the biblical period different from its development in our time? To what extent is *our knowledge* about *our* time different from the knowledge we possess about biblical time?

We have in fact already answered the first question. The distinction consists in the fact that in the Bible the whole saving process tends towards the work of the Lord who appeared in the flesh, while in post-biblical time the whole saving process issues from him, as is symbolically indicated in our scheme of reckoning time, with its years numerically decreasing as they approach Christ and increasing after Christ. Since the high-point has already been attained, there is now merely an *unfolding* of what has been reached. Before this high-point was attained, salvation history was building up to a climax, although in *God's plan* even the events in the Old Testament already contained the whole process in themselves. On the other hand, there is a considerable analogy between our situation and the pre-Christian situation inasmuch as the post-biblical process, like the pre-Christian one, tends toward a final point, namely, the eschatological consummation. The aim, of course, is already anticipated at the start; but the tendency toward the goal of the process is still the common factor in both cases.

But the crucial distinction has to do not with the saving process before and after Christ himself, but with our *knowledge* about it. We know precisely in what way the saving process developed in biblical times. We know about the relationships between this process and ancient history, for we possess the Bible. On the other hand, the Bible tells us about our present time only the fact that it continues, and the direction in which it continues; we are not told the individual events and interpretations in which it is developed. Only apocalyptic and sectarian movements read such *detailed data* out of the Bible by a highly questionable exegesis.

At present salvation history is being developed further in a way *hidden* to us. Whereas we know precisely the past events and their prophetic interpretations resting on revelation, we can never say with certainty, so far as *our* present is concerned, where God is now extending his salvation history in its unfolding and interpretation. The Bible makes us certain that there are new saving events today in which the end is indicated in a special way. But we refuse to fix the date of the end by interpreting the events of the present, a practice rejected in the Bible. Moreover, because of our basic conviction, we do not presume either to ascribe the authority of revelation possessed by the biblical events to events in our time or to contemporary interpretations of Christian truth. We must leave questions such as whether this or that event of our time is a sign of the end, or whether in this or that post-biblical preacher of the gospel we see a prophet speaking, or whether in this event or in this man God is actually unfolding his salvation history in a special way, to God alone to answer.

By and large, J. Daniélou stands very close to my understanding of salvation history; he has, however, raised the objection[1] that for me the men of the old covenant are given preference over the men of the present day if we cannot reach any absolute degree of certainty (such as the Catholic Church sees guaranteed in establishing authentic tradition by its infallible teaching office). According to Daniélou, now that Christ has already died and been raised, it is inconceivable that we should today be in a position less advantageous than that of the old covenant. But here again we must first of all remember the necessary distinction between the process that actually unfolded at the time of the old covenant and our knowledge about it. For *us*, thanks to the canon, the Old Testament events have authoritative worth and to that extent what we know about the saving process and the saving revelation of the Old Testament is a norm, while no event and no interpretation of the *post*-biblical period can be a norm. It we believe in the canon as the final interepration, we know when and where salvation occurred in the time of the Old Testament. This we do not know in our own time. But our knowledge in the former case and our ignorance in the latter do not imply that we are at a disadvantage with regard to the old covenant. The prophets of the Old Testament had the

---

[1] For the first time in writing in his 'Réponse à Oscar Cullmann', *Dieu vivant* No. 24, pp. 112ff.

consciousness of being direct bearers of revelation. But does not this consciousness also exist in the post-biblical period? The distinction between the time of the Old Testament and post-biblical time does not have to do with the reality of such a saving process and such testimony, but with the normative character bestowed in the canon by Christ on the facts reported in the Old Testament. The history that was moving towards Christ is *concluded*, and that is not the case for the post-biblical time proceeding from him and moving toward the end. Therefore it cannot be said that we are in a less favourable position than that of the men of the old covenant. On the contrary, we have the advantage over them of not only possessing Scriptures about past events as they did, but also of having the canon as our norm. To appraise our time salvation-historically, not only do we have the Spirit who comes to the aid of our weakness as they did, but we also have the canon. The most important item is that this norm contains not only the revelations of the old covenant, but also the attestation to the *decisive* events wrought by Christ which give the preceding events their legitimacy. That the Bible is given to the Church is itself an event of salvation history (even though it is not a dateable one) which determines our present.

Our norm does not, of course, permit us to designate events of the present as saving events with the same certainty we have in regard to biblical events. But this state of affairs is inherent in the special character of the present period of salvation history. Individual events of the present cannot be identified as saving events on biblical grounds with final certainty. The interval of time in which we live is not yet concluded. Because it is not concluded, there can be no canon that narrates the individual events of the interval, just as there could not be a canon before Christ because that whole period was not yet concluded. In theory there can only be a canon for the present interval, telling what individual events in the present belong to salvation history, once the end has come, and only from the perspective of the final consummation, just as our canon covering the biblical period could be set up only in retrospect after the fulfilment in Christ.

It is part of our situation in the interval, characterized by the tension between 'already' and 'not yet', that we have already the biblical canon which lets us know precisely in which direction salvation history runs. By this canon and with the aid of the Holy Spirit we are in a position to interpret properly the revelation of the signs of our time, despite the fact that we can speak only of a hidden continuation of salvation history.

We know that the Holy Spirit at work in the Church of Christ as he was at work in the biblical revelation of salvation leads us 'into all truth', and allows us to recognize the 'living tradition' of which Y. Congar speaks so impressively.[1] We know that he helps us in the interpretation of Scripture which is performed in the context of the Church and with the means of scholarship given to us by God. We know that he aids us in recognizing with the light that we have where salvation history is being unfolded—in this or that event of secular history or Church history, in this or that witness of faith given by a member of Church, or in this or that resolution of a council. We may even be so bold as to attempt to write a Church history in relation to the secular history of post-biblical time as 'salvation history'. But it would be rash to place such an undertaking on the same level with the canon. That would amount to the surrender of precisely what we have recognized as decisive for the time from Christ onward, the principle of the tension between 'already' and 'not yet'. The 'already' is supplied with the Holy Spirit who is at work for all in the Church of Christ and with the possession of the Bible, and the 'not yet' is supplied in what we now see only 'in a mirror dimly' (I Cor. 13.12).

The ecumenical dialogue between Catholics and Protestants, particularly on the issue of 'Scripture and tradition',[2] will be especially fruitful if it is carried out with the question of the continuation of salvation history as a common basis for discussion. As a start for a discussion, I would like to point out that there seem to me to be two inferences that follow from the New Testament:

(1) It must not happen that a biblical principle too mechanically conceived leads Protestants into denying that the New Testament itself reckons on a continuation of salvation history as a development towards the end, which proceeds from the Christ event and leads into the events of the Eschaton, *whose first phase is still the object of the New Testament canon.* If the end of the apostolic age meant an interruption in salvation history until the events of the end time, the present historical process would no longer be located on the same historical level as that of the Bible. Wherever this notion prevails, the way is open to interpreting the Bible for the present generation otherwise than in terms of salvation history. The 'already' is then given a

---

[1] See his book *La Tradition et la vie de l'Église,* 1963.

[2] For literature on the problem of 'Scripture and Tradition', see G. Pedersen's bibliography covering the years 1930–62 in *Schrift und Tradition,* put out by the *Kommission für Glaube und Kirchenverfassung des Ökumenischen Rates der Kirchen,* 1963, pp. 157ff.

different character from that which it has in the New Testament. But then the whole *dynamics* by which we understand ourselves in the Church today, as persons who have been placed in the mighty stream of a saving process, is lost. It is through this dynamics that profound interrelations with so-called secular events are disclosed; and if one accepts such an interruption in salvation history, the mighty impulse initiated by faith to lead us not only through these interrelations, but forward in the same stream, is lost.

(2) The canonization of the Bible as a norm marks a conclusion to the biblical period of salvation history and at the same time is a part of this history, growing out of it organically, as we have seen. On the other hand, this same canonization of the Bible stands at the beginning of the post-biblical period as a point of departure for another stage of salvation history; it therefore supplies a salvation-historical norm for all interpretation in the present. Since our period has not yet reached its conclusion, there cannot be any other norm of authority equal to the canon. No infallible teaching office, whether it be in the person of the Pope, or in a council, or in the collaboration of both, can take a place equal to the apostles' once-for-all eye-witness to the decisive events of Christ's death and resurrection in the Bible—not even as the interpretation of the Bible.

In the Church we find the help of the Holy Spirit; we possess the Bible, and with it goes the teaching office (not, however, infallible) as the common concern of the Church with the Spirit of truth. *With all this we find ourselves on the level of the biblical salvation history.* Salvation history takes its norm from salvation history. But I would raise the question whether by introducing an *infallible* teaching office as a norm for the present alongside the Bible and the Holy Spirit we introduce an authority of revelation alien to the process found in the Bible—an institution. Certainly the teaching office and the Church as an institution are parts of salvation history. But if the teaching office is credited with infallibility, is not the interval changed in its salvation-historical structure inasmuch as the 'not yet' gives way at this point? Does not a static element thereby enter into our interpretation, an element foreign to the salvation-historical character of our time? Is there not then a danger to the great continuity which we have found up till now in biblical salvation history and beyond it? Does not the danger of a rigidity threaten the dynamic of salvation history which is intended to continue in the present? Despite the final uncertainty, is not this dynamic better preserved if, in our interpretation of post-biblical time, in complete trust in the Holy Spirit, we allow the 'not yet' to stand beside the 'already' on the level of knowledge as well—in other words, if we believe that the Holy Spirit plays his part in our interpretation of the Bible, even though mistakes are not precluded from the Church's exegesis? Is not our position in salvation history manifest in our unqualified participation in the tension between a *real* 'already' and a *real* 'not yet'?

The denial of the continuation of salvation history by the Protestant side, and the Catholic association of salvation history with an institution which in its claim to infallibility has not, like the canon, developed from the biblical salvation history itself, amount to two opposing positions. In contrast to the opposing Protestant conception, the Catholic notion maintains the forceful impulse of the certainty of standing today mid-stream in the process unfolding according to God's plan. This same certainty determined the whole life of the early Church. On the other hand, it shares something of the Protestant denial of the continuity of salvation history by introducing an infallible office of authority which jeopardizes the continuity of the present period with the past. Precisely because of this continuity, the biblical salvation history ought to remain in its exclusiveness as the only norm, but, on the other hand, the present period ought to be recognized in the light of this norm as the unfolding of salvation history. How this is to take place we shall show in what follows.

2. SALVATION HISTORY AS A NORM FOR PRESENT HAPPENING

If we are really in the stream of salvation history which is characterized not only by contingency, but above all by the constant of the divine plan summed up in the Christ event, then in the Bible we have the norm uniquely adequate for application to our time. With this norm in hand we can at least attempt to establish where and how the saving process is unfolded. If the present period actually belongs to salvation history, then all the elements of the constant of salvation history must be discernible in this period, even though the details of how salvation history continues remain hidden for the present.

The *beginning* of the period in salvation history in which we live, the segment between Christ's resurrection and the end, *is already integrated into this norm as the time of the apostles*. The importance of this fact can hardly be overemphasized. The time between Christ's resurrection and the end forms a whole. Both the time of the apostles spoken of in the Bible and the post-biblical time of the Church in which we live amount to an interval. The only difference between the biblical stage at the beginning and its continuation consists in the fact that the eyewitnesses of the decisive events, who were still alive at the beginning, are dead today, and we therefore give our witness, so to speak, second hand. *All the rest* of the essential features of the interval which are discernible during the time of the apostles therefore have validity for our time too. Because of this fact we have the possibility of measuring our time by quite *concrete* events in salvation history during the apostolic age and of recognizing the signs of these events in the present period. Although nothing is said in the Bible about the individual events of the post-biblical interval, the characterization of the apostolic age contained in the Bible still allows us to set up guide-lines by which the unfolding of the saving process is recognizable.

It is therefore necessary that we *recapitulate* briefly the elements which according to the New Testament provide the special meaning of the *interval* within salvation history. First of all, the tension between 'already' and 'not yet' is peculiar to the interval. It offers us the key to understanding the whole period. The two great gifts of salvation history, the Holy Spirit and the Church, which in Christ are granted to this period, and which allow salvation to become a present reality, as well as the obligation imposed on us during this time, point to that tension.

The *Spirit* is the 'already'. He indicates that the end time has already begun. He is *the* element of the end time. 'In the last days' (Acts 2.17), what Joel prophesied is happening, namely, the Holy Spirit is no longer the gift entrusted exclusively to a few prophets. Instead, everyone in the Church, great and small, becomes a prophet gifted with the Spirit. Because the Holy Spirit supplies the basis of the end time, he is called ἀρραβών and ἀπαρχή. He is the power of the *resurrection*, the great adversary of sin and death, and he will also recreate our bodies (Rom. 8.11). This future power is already at work. That is the meaning of our time in salvation history, the 'already'. Yet the same Spirit causes us to groan, or better, he groans in us. Sin and death still exist, and the Spirit is still enclosed within the limits of our fleshly existence. He seeks a divine language befitting him, an 'angel language' (I Cor. 13.1), but he comes up against our imperfect human organs, and thus the result is merely the 'groaning' of speaking in tongues. But of course we know even in this instance that the tension still existing is already relaxed in Christ.

The same is to be said of the other gift, the Church. Our time is the time of the Holy Spirit, and it is the time of the Church. The Church also—indeed, particularly—shares in the tension of 'already' and 'not yet'. It is the great divine gift on earth—the body of Christ himself. At the same time, the New Testament writers know that this body is composed of men who are still sinful. Nowhere is the chasm between what *already* is (the body of Christ) and what *still* is (sin) more painfully felt than in the Church. In no New Testament book does this tension go unheeded. The letters of Paul are full of references to the miraculous work of the Holy Spirit and at the same time to the sad facts which attest that the Church is not the Kingdom of God. In the same way, the Book of Acts does not conceal the fact that even at the beginning there was not a perfect Church. We hear of the sins of Ananias and Sapphira, of the grumbling of the Hellenists, of a dispute between Paul and Barnabas. Certainly Paul and Acts view the lingering of coarse sins 'against the Holy Spirit' in the Church, such as incest (I Cor. 5.1ff) and the sin of Ananias and Sapphira (Acts 5.1–11), as irreconcilable with the essence of the Church, yet the reality of sin is discerned daily in the Church.

The future dialogue between Catholics and Protestants should concentrate upon the tension to be found in the Church. All of our differences can be traced back to our respective understandings of this relationship of tension. The Protestants find that the Catholics fail to heed the 'not yet', as it is exemplified in the Catholic doctrine of the infallible teaching office. The Catholics, on the contrary, find that we Protestants do not take the 'already' seriously, that we therefore overlook the fact that in Christ and in his Church the tension is already set aside.

Furthermore, the *christological aspect* is extraordinarily important for a salvation-historical understanding of our time. Christ has died and is risen, and at the end he will return. Is his function completely interrupted in the interval in which we find ourselves? What does the New Testament teach on this point? Christ rules over his Church and over the world. Thus, it is the primary aim of John's Gospel to show that the same Christ who appeared on earth in the flesh remains linked with his own in the present. 'I will not leave you orphans' (John 14.18). That is the leitmotif of the farewell discourses. In the earliest brief confessions of faith, the first Christians proclaim the invisible but actual kingship of Christ which is visible only to faith—Κύριος Χριστός! We must consider what this meant. The later and more developed creeds express Christ's lordship with the word of Ps. 110: 'He sits at the right hand of God, all powers are subject to him.'[1] It is no accident that no Old Testament text was cited more

---

[1] O. Cullmann, *The Earliest Christian Confessions*, Chapter IV.

often by the first Christians than this. It expresses precisely what has been revealed about the relationship of christology to the present. The words of the psalm explain, in fact, the manner in which Christ's victory is unfolded within the plan of divine events.

All the confessional formulas summing up the early Church's faith particularly emphasize the victory Christ has won over the invisible powers. I refer merely to Phil. 2.9f.: God has highly exalted him, and has given him the name that is above every name, the name of God himself (κύριος—adonai)! To this name every knee of the invisible powers bends. They are the same powers as those who stand behind the earthly governments. But again it is clear here that the present time is the time of the tension between 'already' and 'not yet'. These powers are already subject to Christ, and yet they must be subjected to Christ once again at the end of the ages.

Christ invisibly governs the Church and the world. I usually represent this lordship graphically by means of two concentric circles. The smaller circle is the Church, the greater one the world. The common centre is Christ. From the smaller circle, the Church, the body of Christ, he governs the world.

What differentiates the lordship of Christ over the world from his lordship over the Church? The world does not know that it is ruled by Christ, for his lordship is, of course, invisible. It is visible only to faith. The Church is the fellowship of those who through faith know that Christ is the Lord. They have no privilege in regard to salvation, since salvation, of course, encompasses the whole world. Their privilege consists uniquely and solely in the fact that they are *aware* of their status as members of the Kingdom of Christ, and are to witness that we are saved through Christ. All this we must remember when we use the Bible as the norm for assessing our period in terms of salvation history. All these distinguishing marks, valid for the biblical time of the apostles, are valid for the whole period in which we stand.

Thus, we are also in the fortunate situation of being informed by the New Testament about the special *task* which confronts us precisely at this time. Why does time still continue at all? Why did not the end come with the resurrection? Because the New Testament answer to this question comprises the meaning of the interval, at the same time it places our precise task before us. This task is contained in the Synoptic apocalypse (Matt. 24.14; Mark 13.10): 'This gospel of the kingdom will be preached throughout the whole world . . . and then the end will come.' Therefore, as we have already mentioned, Paul always seeks new places to preach: 'Woe to me if I do not preach the gospel (I Cor. 9.17).' Along with other commentators, I think it probable that in Rev. 6.2 the first rider does not, like the others, depict an apocalyptic 'plague', but the victorious proclamation before the end comes. In Acts 1.6 the disciples ask the risen Lord, 'Will you at this time restore the Kingdom to Israel?' The Lord answers, 'It is not for you to know the day or hour . . . but you will receive the Holy Spirit, and he will enable you to preach the gospel . . . to the ends of the earth.' The meaning of the continuation of salvation history therefore consists in *preaching*, in the witness that we give before the world through our preaching and our lives. The Church's task consists in this proclamation to the world.

Each individual's task corresponds with this. We shall come back to this when we briefly indicate the guide-lines of ethics which follow from our position in the interval.

It was necessary here briefly to give a summary of the most important aspects of the salvation-historical perspective of the Bible which have already been spoken of often. The way in which we apply these aspects to our time quite obviously depends upon our description of them.[1] This is so only because the present period belongs to the great stream of salvation history, whose mid-point is the saving process of the Bible in which special significance is attached to the events which began with the activity of the apostles after Christ's death and resurrection. When our preachers construct their sermons starting from texts of the Old and New Testaments, and when 'biblical history' is taught in our Christian education, we are giving recognition to the fact that the past stands in the closest relationship with our present and therefore is not just past.[2] For this reason, a really biblical foundation for dogmatics is possible on the basis of the salvation-historical understanding of the Bible.

At this point we shall not return to the question whether we need a teaching office alongside the Bible to identify the progress of salvation history. The necessity of a teaching office must certainly be affirmed. But to ascribe infallibility to it seems to us to be irreconcilable with the tension between 'already' and 'not yet'. The progress

---

[1] Thus, K. Barth could directly apply to our times in 'The Christian Community and the Civil Community', *Against the Stream*, 1954, what I said about the relationship between Christ's lordship over the world and over the Church in *Königsherrschaft Christi und Kirche im Neuen Testament*, 1941, ³1950 (ET in *The Early Church*, pp. 105ff.), *Christengemeinde und Burgergemeinde*, 1949.

[2] K. G. Steck, *op. cit.*, p. 57, thinks that the thought of the so-called 'theologians of salvation history' is merely based on an 'assurance' of God's activity. His opinion overlooks the biblical foundation of salvation-historical theology, the only basis that this theology has. What is crucial for salvation-historical theology is the relationship to the present. The idea that the need for 'assurance' is the motivation leading to a salvation-historical theology is ruled out not only by the fact that by no means everything is predictable in the biblical saving process, but also by the fact that in the present, salvation history unfolds in a hidden way. See above p. 278f.

of salvation history in the world, as for instance in political events, cannot be defined by the Church's teaching office with absolute certainty. Still, this progress continues in political events that quite obviously lie within the Bible's perspective and are to enter into salvation history more and more during the interval. In the same way, in the case of events in the history of the Church itself, an identification of the saving process with this or that event also remains impossible. This is also true for the unfolding interpretation of these events. Church history is not simply salvation history, and the history of dogma is not simply interpretation resting upon divine revelation. However, Church history is the place where we seek the unfolding of the saving process, and the history of dogma and theology is the place where we seek the unfolding of the salvation-historical interpretation in constant contact with the events of the Bible. A norm that sets itself between us and these biblical events runs the risk of interrupting the *living* stream. For this reason, when other norms endanger the connection with these events, a return to the biblical salvation history again and again becomes necessary—in Catholicism as in Protestantism. The norm cannot be set up by the Church of our time. The Church is given it in the Bible.

The Bible teaches us to understand the 'signs' of our times. Everything happening in our time, which is already the end time, is an omen of the end. At this point, so-called 'secular' history comes under our consideration. The Bible shows us how even in pre-Christian times lines lead from secular history to salvation history. Christian faith sees Christ's lordship over the world as already having begun, and from this faith much closer relationships between general history and salvation history may be drawn. Here the final entry of all history into salvation history is announced. We do not therefore think it necessary that a government be Christian if it is to fulfil its task rightly. Christ can make use of a non-Christian government to carry out his lordship not only in a negative way (as Pilate belongs to salvation history), but positively, in the terms of Rom. 13 which, of course, relate to a pagan state. So long as the non-Christian government remains within the limits fixed for it and does not transgress them by, for instance, requiring the 'Κύριος Καῖσαρ', it can carry out the divine saving plan *without knowing it*. For this there are precise norms in the New Testament, both for the pagan government standing in Christ's service (Rom. 13), and for the government that becomes demonic (Rev. 13.1ff.).

Certainly we dare not fall into the venture of the sects which use the Bible to calculate dates ('day and hour'), thereby placing the ultimate secrecy of the divine plan of salvation at man's own disposal. We know from the Bible the direction in which salvation history is moving. With great caution we may therefore dare to term isolated instances the signs of salvation history in a special way. We may see Antichrist at work in a dictator in whom the demonic erupts openly in a self-deified government, as is described so forcefully in Rev. 13. But we shall never venture to say, even in this case, that this is now *the* Antichrist.

We pay heed both to the positive saving work and the demonic counter-attacks when we judge current events from the special vantage point of salvation history. As members of the Church we must put the newspaper beside the Bible and, more particularly, the Bible beside the newspaper. To argue, 'Politics does not belong in the pulpit', may certainly be justified if politics is being promoted for politics' sake, or if the Church is usurping some kind of political power which is not its domain. But a salvation-historical judgment on the events of our time is part of preaching, of the witnessing in which the meaning and task of our time consists. In its preaching the Church may not allow any limitation to be imposed upon itself under the pretext of a slogan, for that would amount to failure to heed the universalism which is of the essence of all the saving process.

We have seen that from the beginning all salvation history is universally oriented. The 'return route' leads to the Church composed of Jews and pagans, and then to the whole world. Even after Christ's resurrection, salvation history still rests upon the principle of election. But now more than ever election does not mean simply the limiting of salvation to the elect, but election for the special mission of proclaiming salvation to the world. That is the path of all salvation history—*universalism as its goal, concentration as the means of its realization.* In this, the way is opened even to the non-Christian, or better said, extra-biblical religions, for Jewish religion, of course, belongs to salvation history in the *narrower sense*. To use another illustration,[1] the little caravan marches on, and gradually from both sides further groups join it.

[1] Remarkably enough this illustration was not used for the first time by a theologian, but by a layman. A reporter for one of the daily newspapers in Rome used it in covering a lecture I gave during the second session of the Vatican Council.

Here, of course, one must warn against a misunderstanding which ought to be precluded by biblical salvation history. Although the biblical revelation supplies the general movement with the direction and goal mentioned above, it would be a mistake to think that the development is running in a straight line. Sin, apart from which all salvation history is totally unintelligible, stands at the beginning of salvation history and determines its further development. In mysterious ways God can make use of human sin to carry out his plan. It is precisely this revelation that fills Paul with deep reverence before the divine wisdom and its ways. Hence the exceedingly important section in Rom. 9–11 is especially illuminating as a norm for our knowledge of the present saving process. From this passage, we understand that even today the Jews remain the elect people, and that they have a permanent role to play in salvation history. According to Paul, God made use of their unbelief in order to include the Gentiles in salvation history. The Gentiles were grafted on to the Jewish tree, but the foundation is still this Jewish tree, and at the end even Israel 'according to the flesh' will be converted.

This passage gives us the key for understanding many of the events of our time. Is it not a fact that the Jewish people have been preserved in a miraculous way, despite all the persecutions they have endured, a sign that by their very existence they are witnessing to salvation history, and that in the *eschaton* God will lead the elect people to their consummation?[1] Only with reference to salvation history is it understandable that Judaism, as opposed to other non-Christian religions, belongs to salvation history not only in the narrower sense, but in the wider sense as well.[2]

God has not revealed to us in detail how in mysterious ways even during the present period he will bring salvation out of human sin. But the passage mentioned above, to which we can add others from the New Testament and especially from the Old Testament, contains a valuable clue, and is well suited to guard us against the misunderstanding that failures contradict the onward progress of salvation history. It also reminds us that the progress of salvation history cannot be determined quantitatively nor by the numbers of those con-

---

[1] K. Barth has made a well-known remark that the continued existence of the people Israel up to the present is the only 'natural' proof for the existence of God.

[2] The failure of some of the delegates at the Second Vatican Council to understand the special place of the Jewish people is due to their failure to understand salvation history in general.

verted. On the contrary, we find in the biblical references to the end time the conviction that the eschatological entry of the nations into salvation history stands side by side with the other idea of the increase of sin, regardless of how their chronological relationship is to be exactly defined.

The biblical revelation of how God brings forth salvation out of human sin contains a tremendous lesson for the present period, which ought to exclude all discouragement because of failures. Paul has shown that human responsibility for sin is in no way diminished by this (Rom. 3.3ff.). The knowledge that God in his authority may use sin for salvation may in no case excuse us from resisting sin.

Again, starting from these considerations, and with every necessary precaution and the reservations made above, we can attempt to see the hand of God even *in all the divisions of Christianity*, though we do bear a heavy responsibility for having used the Spirit's greatest gift of manifesting itself in diverse ways as an inducement for creating divisions.[1] The question which side bears the greater sin is not under discussion here. But in the light of the biblical salvation history, we can ask whether these divisions may not have gained a meaning in themselves in salvation history. Are they not a constant, spiritual incitement to renewal? Is this not a 'detour' in salvation history like the detour via Israel's unbelief, which does not lose sight of the final goal that 'all may be one' (John 17.21)? Is not the desire for reform, so powerfully at work today in the Catholic Church, a sign that salvation history is continuing, and that God is at work in our divisions?

In a similar way, our confrontation with the *non-Christian world* may be thought of as an element in the divine plan of salvation. We have already said that the existence of non-Christians in no way means that they are at a disadvantage with regard to salvation; but their existence ought to be an inducement to the Church to proclaim to them that we are redeemed in Christ. The election of the Church only means that we are entrusted with the fulfilment of this task, not that we have any advantage over non-Christians in regard to salvation. This task of preaching is also clearly prescribed for the Church of the present time. What meaning this ought to have for the indivi-

---

[1] A conception of the divisions of Christianity oriented toward salvation history, though differently and more positively, can also be seen in J. L. Leuba's *L'institution et l'événement*, 1950 (also in German translation).

dual and his ethical 'decision' will be briefly sketched in our last chapter. But we have yet to speak of another form of the actualization of salvation history.

3. SALVATION HISTORY AND WORSHIP

Within the limits stated in the previous chapter, while taking its norm strictly from the Bible, the proclamation of the Church today must point to God's rule and the unfolding of his saving plan in relation to the events of our time. But alongside this form of the 'presentation' of salvation history, an event which in fact actualizes the past and future of salvation history takes place in the Church, in worship, in the liturgy.[1] Here in a direct way the past and future of salvation history become present, and nowhere does the central role attached to salvation history appear more evident than in this highly significant fact that the *whole worship* of the Christian Church, like Jewish worship, is oriented towards salvation history. Here again we can only repeat that a remarkable hiatus between practice and theory arises as soon as the salvation-historical basis is given up in theory. In that case the 'Church year' can no longer be significant, and in all honesty it is better to give it up. What meaning have Advent, Christmas, Holy Week, Easter and Pentecost if they do not continually allow us to experience anew and in the present the *development* of the saving process in the past in connection with its further development in the present? The fact that the saving events wrought in Christ are to be thought of not only punctually, but in their relationship to salvation history, is nowhere more strongly expressed than in liturgy. The Church year originated, of course, in post-biblical times. But the liturgical presentation of the past and future of salvation history is *already present in the salvation history of the Bible*.

Even within the province of the Old Testament and Judaism, ancient feasts, originally having an agrarian character, are historicized. Hence the old Passover feast, originally associated with farming, is connected with the Exodus from Egypt, and this once-for-all event now becomes present each year. The same thing happens with other feasts. The harvest feast becomes a feast of the giving of the

---

[1] On the following see, among others, C. Vagaggini, *Theologie der Liturgie,* 1959; J. J. von Allmen, *Prophétisme sacramentel,* 1964.

Law at Sinai. It is interesting to see how the developing salvation history seizes upon these feasts in the new covenant and connects them with the central Christ event—at Easter the death and resurrection of Christ are made present, at Pentecost the pouring out of the Holy Spirit upon the Church.[1] Later, this historicizing takes hold of pagan feasts which originally had a totally unhistorical character. The festival of the sun, the '*sol invictus*', is thus connected with the celebration of Christ's birth.[2] Sunday observance goes back, of course, to the earliest period of the Church, and each week it serves to make present the central event of the whole saving process—the resurrection of Christ. But later on it is connected with the pagan astral significance of the day[3] in such a way that, as in the case of the celebration of Christmas, the relationship to the sun is completely subordinate to the meaning which the day derived from salvation history.

Incidentally, even where the liturgy is related to creation in the Old Testament, it stands in the closest relationship with salvation history in contrast to the liturgical use of creation myths in pagan religions. This accords with what was said above[4] about the historicizing of myth.[5]

It may be shown, and has rightly been shown by Old Testament scholars, how the critical events of Israel's history—Exodus, Sinai, the entry into the land of Canaan—were used liturgically. Scholars usually emphasize in this connection that the narratives about the historical events were fixed for the first time in the liturgy. The liturgy is therefore thought of as the *Sitz im Leben* of the respective narratives. The correct element in this view is that the narratives as such received their formation in the liturgy. It is also correct that individual features of the narratives owe their origins to worship. It would, however, be the exaggeration of a correct observation if the historical fact were regarded as an invention created for the first time by the liturgy, for the process was really circular. The event itself gives the impulse for its liturgical presentation. The latter gives

---

[1] Would it not be meaningful and in accord with salvation history to let the facts of Christian salvation history stand in the foreground in Christian worship, while at the same time not allowing the pre-Christian, salvation-historical significance behind these facts to go unmentioned?

[2] See O. Cullmann, 'The Origin of Christmas', in *The Early Church*, pp. 17ff.

[3] See W. Rordorf, *Der Sonntag*, 1962, pp. 213ff., 280ff. (ET, 1967).

[4] See above pp. 139ff.

[5] Cf. R. Prenter, 'Worship and Creation', *Studia Liturgica*, 1963, pp. 82ff.

the impulse for the literary fixation of the event. The narrative accounts of the event are in turn influenced in such a way that liturgical elements are also taken up in historicized form.

What transpired in the liturgy was set down in literary form in the Psalms, and they are especially related to the saving events of Israel's history.[1] Here we really see what salvation history meant for the life of the Israelites and what it can mean. Anyone who today asserts that salvation history is interesting only for the knowledge of the past ought to learn better from the Psalms. The thankfulness expressed in them for the great saving events is deeply felt and does not just arise from liturgical rhetoric. The fact that salvation history is infinitely more than a theological concept finds confirmation here. Here is where the heart of all the biblical life in faith actually beats. This thankfulness of faith for the divine saving events is also basic to the whole New Testament. It is expressed not only in the spontaneous, prayerful outcry of Rom. 11.33f., often quoted in this work, which the apostle is forced to make in view of his insight into the salvation-historical revelation about the way of the gospel, but in all the doxological formulas that Paul and the writers of the other New Testament books have derived from the Church's liturgy or have shaped themselves. Certainly salvation history can degenerate into a rigid theological theory. But wherever it enlivens worship, as in Israel and the early Church, and indeed creates a new cultic form, its entire dynamic becomes apparent.

All the worship that we hear about in the Bible makes the past and future present. This is true even for Jewish worship. However, since New Testament salvation history is essentially characterized by the *tension* between 'already' and 'not yet', between fulfilment of the past and expectation of the consummation, in the Christian Church the correspondence between the theme of salvation history and its realization in worship is complete. The fulfilment of the past and the expectation of the consummation are experienced in Christian worship as present realities. We have often referred to the fact that the tension is already abolished in Christ, although for us it still continues. This relaxation of tension in Christ becomes visible in early Christian worship, for there Christ is present at the same time as the crucified and resurrected Lord and as the coming Messiah.

Because Christ's presence becomes a reality in the fellowship meal,

[1] See the work which has just appeared, H. Zirker, *Die kultische Vergegenwärtigung der Vergangenheit in den Psalmen*, 1964.

early Christian worship, except for missionary services, is unthinkable without the breaking of bread.[1] In the early Christian Eucharist, the Last Supper of the incarnate Christ, the Passover meals of the resurrected Lord and the Messianic feast of the coming Christ all become present at once. The crucial phases of salvation history are in this way all bound up with one another. Wherever Christ himself is present today, his salvation-historical activity becomes visible in all its extension.

Of course one can make a valid distinction between the presentation of the past and the repetition of the past. The ἐφ' ἅπαξ, the once-for-all character of the various Christ events of salvation history, may not be given up. The misinterpretation that Christ is crucified anew each time the Eucharist is celebrated must be avoided. Catholic doctrine in fact attempts to escape this conclusion, and the over-simplified objections of Protestantism which do not heed this effort are really unjustified. Nevertheless, the question must be raised whether the sacrificial theory of Catholicism does not further such a misunderstanding, *in practice* coming dangerously close to the thought of a repetition.

The problem of the relationship between ἐφ' ἅπαξ and the presentation of the past is ultimately that of salvation history itself, for which the complex relationship between the constant plan of God and its historical development is characteristic. It is the problem of the relationship between the vertical and the horizontal. We have often referred to this relationship in other contexts. We encounter it in a particular way in the Gospel of John. On the one hand, this Gospel presents a view in which the christological periods are so enmeshed that their distinctions in Christ hardly appear visible any more. On the other hand, the unique character of the life of Jesus is so strongly emphasized that the once-for-all-ness of the phases in salvation history grows out of the life of Christ. The manner in which they are summed up in Christ brings the development of salvation history particularly to light.

This intertwining is shown in what happens in the Church's worship. The whole Christ, including the crucified Lord, is experienced in the Eucharist, but as the Eucharist is celebrated today *after* his death and *after* his resurrection, it can only be the exalted Lord at the right hand of God who is present. The christological activity

[1] O. Cullmann, *Early Christian Worship*, pp. 16ff., 27ff.

has reached the stage which the first Christians describe with the words of Ps. 110 as 'Christ's sitting at the right hand of God'. This stage they also express in their confessions with the formula Κύριος Χριστός. If what transpires in worship gives us a survey of the Christ event in its whole extension in salvation history, including the cross, it nevertheless must not be forgotten that our worship today does not escape from the context of the salvation-historical development *in which we find ourselves now.*

Is this aspect sufficiently heeded in the Catholic mass and in the Protestant celebrations of the Lord's Supper? Not quite, I am afraid. That is why it is so important to me in this matter of the Eucharist to refer to the meals of the first Easter during which the *resurrected Lord* appeared to his own. Certainly, when they came together to break bread in early times, the Christians looked back to these meals and not simply to the Last Supper of the incarnate one. Indeed, the thought of these meals probably overshadowed the meal on the eve of the crucifixion, and this explains the gladness in Acts 2.46.

In this sacramental event, the connection with the full Christ becomes visible, that is, with the incarnate Lord, who was with his disciples at the last meal, and the coming Lord, who will lie at the table with his own in the Messianic feast as a sign of his complete and inner relationship with them. This link with the history of salvation is already indicated in the words of institution referring to the wine that Jesus 'will drink anew'. In I Cor. 11.26 Paul also alludes to the eschatological consummation of the 'not yet' when he says 'until he comes'.

It befits the institution of the Lord's Supper that the death of Christ is made present in a special way among the Christ events of salvation history. Although its 'once-for-all-ness' must not be jeopardized by the thought of a repetition, we must still refer here to the present, real experience of the past in the *anamnesis*,[1] just as the Johannine 'remembering'[2] is more than a mere reminding oneself of a past fact.

The anchoring of the Eucharist in salvation history nowhere finds a more adequate expression than in the prayer '*Maranatha*'. From *Did.* 14 and I Cor. 16.22 we see that it was actually a eucharistic prayer. The Church prays for Christ's presence in the midst of the fellowship of the Lord's table. But the Church prays in the same

---

[1] See F. Leenhardt, *Ceci est mon corps*, 1955.   [2] See above p. 273.

prayer for his final coming to the Messianic banquet, and it bases its faith on the certain answer to this prayer in the fellowship of the apostles with the Christ who appeared to them while they were sitting at the table at Easter. The same salvation-historical relationship finds expression in the weekly celebration of Sunday. Sunday as the Day of the Lord (ἡμέρα τοῦ κυρίου) refers backwards to the resurrection of Christ and forwards to the eschatological 'Day of the Lord', which in the Old Testament is the *yom Yahweh* (LXX = ἡμέρα τοῦ κυρίου).

Hence the important thing for John's Gospel, in contrast to the Synoptics, is not to show merely the relationship of the Eucharist to its institution. A much wider aspect of the Christ event is illuminated by the Eucharist—the whole life of the incarnate Christ. Several events in the life of Jesus as it is depicted by this Gospel point to the Christ present in the Eucharist—above all, the Feeding of the Five Thousand in chapter 6, and very probably the miracle at Cana in Chapter 2 and other episodes.[1] Thus the Eucharist depicts the whole 'historical Jesus'.

The miracle of the manna points beyond the life of Jesus, primarily, of course, to show the incompleteness of this miracle in comparison with the true miracle of the bread in the Eucharist (Ch. 6).[2]

Even baptism, too, is related to events in the life of Jesus in the Gospel of John.[3] Paul relates baptism to the events of salvation history in the old covenant—specifically, the Exodus. The symbolic baptismal sketches in the catacombs prove that the relationship of baptism to salvation history was more than a piece of playful ingenuity for the early Church, and that this relationship was actually experienced as a present reality in the ceremony of baptism.

The salvation-historical relationship of worship forwards, to eschatology is indirectly confirmed by the Apocalypse.[4] Up to now we have found that all worship signifies an anticipation of the end. In worship the end becomes present. Thus the writer can make use of symbols derived from early Christian worship to depict the eschato-

---

[1] See O. Cullmann, *Early Christian Worship*, pp. 66ff., 93ff.

[2] If it is correct that the whole life of Jesus in the Gospel of John is oriented towards the liturgy of the Jewish feasts (see A. Guilding, *The Fourth Gospel and Jewish Worship*, 1960), then the relationship between worship and salvation history is all the more firmly embedded in the Gospel of John.

[3] See O. Cullmann, *Early Christian Worship*, pp. 59ff.

[4] *Ibid.*, p. 7, and P. Prigent's *Apocalypse et Liturgie* (*Cahiers théologiques*).

logical drama which is in the last resort indescribable. Against the background of the conviction that what occurs in worship already realizes the end now, these symbols clamoured to be used. Only they can approach what a description of the eschatological events wishes to express. Thus the trumpet, the instrument of Jewish worship, had long ago become an eschatological instrument that would announce the coming of the point in time determined by God in his authority. We must not forget that according to Rev. 1.10 the seer has his vision 'on the day of the Lord', the day when the Christians experience the resurrection of Christ in worship. In Rev. 3.20 ('Behold, I stand at the door and knock; if any one hears my voice and opens the door, I will come in to him and eat with him and he with me') the thought of a union with Christ at the end stands in the foreground. The use of the traditional symbol of the Messianic feast within the Apocalypse is, nevertheless, inspired by the Church's meal at worship. The whole book could and should be explained in the light of early Christian worship.

Jewish and Christian worship are essentially unintelligible without salvation history. Just as Jewish and Christian theology are robbed of their substance if salvation history is eliminated from them, as was attempted in Gnostic syncretism, so Jewish and Christian worship cease to have what distinguishes them from the worship of the rest of the religions of antiquity when they lose their relationship to the once-for-all events and the eschatological event bound up with them, and use myths instead to symbolize the meaning of worship.

4. SALVATION HISTORY, FAITH AND EXEGESIS

We have attempted to describe what the biblical witnesses say about *their* faith in the saving events and *their* new interpretations of the *kerygma* of salvation history. As we speak of *our* taking up their faith in this salvation history and of *our* new interpretations which we call 'theology', we must at the same time consider both what links us with those witnesses, and what separates us from them.

First of all, however, we must reject the false notion that our separation from the biblical witnesses has been caused by the progress of modern science, so that today we cannot believe in salvation history because our world-view has changed. We must see clearly at the start that the most recent discoveries about nuclear energy, for instance, in no way make faith in salvation history more difficult than it was for men during the days of early Christianity. This faith was just as difficult for men at that time and for the philosophers of that age as it is for us, even though their philosophy was different from that of our age. What Luke reports (Acts 17.16ff., even if Lucan theology has coloured the passage) about the reaction of the Athenians to Paul's message corresponds exactly to the situation in which the gospel was preached. The philosophers could only laugh at a faith in which the resurrection 'of one man' from the dead was connected with the eschatological judgment of the whole world. The scandal of the cross and resurrection as the centre of all history was 'foolishness' then as it is today. The scandal for the philosophers of the first century was not a salvation by way of becoming 'desecularized', but salvation in connection with history, just as it is for the philosophers of our time. We must have the courage to retain what Paul termed a scandal in all its strangeness, as the object of faith preached to us as it was to the men of the first century, not robbing it of precisely what made it a scandal from the beginning. Only the elements which really are associated with a bygone world-view, or are merely an outmoded form of expression, may and must be stripped away as an exterior garb. Now I cannot say that the claim that an ontic process having its mid-point in the cross and resurrection of Jesus means salvation, and that this mid-point is also the mid-point of all revelation and history, is a mere form of expression, and does not have anything to do with the world-view and progress of science. That is precisely what makes the scandal a true scandal.[1] If this element is removed, there is no longer any scandal. In that case the 'Athenians' of antiquity and of the modern age need laugh no more. The people on Mars Hill would certainly not have laughed at salvation as desecularization.

We have something in common with the witnesses who wrote the New Testament in the object of our faith being a scandal. The scandal that I cannot be the instigator of my salvation finds its strongest expression in the salvation history which God has ordained by his free choice. The scandal of the cross, that is, of the high-point of salvation history, is the scandal of my complete incapacity to bring

---

[1] This is the very point where Bultmann and his school as a rule speak of a 'false' scandal.

about my own salvation. It must not happen that by appealing to the act and decision of faith which I perform, I myself become the starting point for the saving process—even in the 'hermeneutical' I-Thou relationship. Granted my act of faith and my decision are indispensable. But whenever they, as an encounter, become independent of any previous ontic event, I again stand in the foreground of the saving process. Therefore a separation *must* be made between an objective event and its subjective appropriation.

The basis for this separation between an objective event on the one hand, and my faith in it and my decision on the other, is not an 'unconscious', antiquated philosophy of the separation between object and subject, outdated by existentialism, as the theologians influenced by Heidegger assert. It is the plain and simple New Testament concept of faith as it is developed especially clearly in Paul. *The act of faith itself requires this distinction.* Faith means that in humility I turn away from myself and look only to the radiant light of an event in which I am totally uninvolved, so that I can only fall down in worship before him who has brought about this event (Rom. 1.21). As I humbly turn away from myself and look to the event, I appropriate the event in faith. Faith means excluding myself and thus including myself. *So I gain my self-understanding when I am not observing my self-understanding.* Therein lies the paradox of New Testament faith.

At the centre of his whole theology, Paul regarded the separation between a divine event brought about independently of my faith and the acknowledging of this event in believing humility, worship, and thankfulness as belonging to the essence of faith itself. No one is prevented from calling this separation a (false) 'philosophy'. Here I can only see in it a primary *theological* concern of Paul which has nothing to do with philosophical 'conceptuality'.

I could and should cite all of Paul's letters here. But on this point one need only read the first three chapters of Romans, where it is said that man has committed the original sin of human pride in response to the revelation of God both in the creation and in the Law, placing creator and creature on the same level by not venturing out into the attitude of faith in acknowledging his own impotence. The revelation in creation could have led to faith, and thus to the knowledge of God, if man had disregarded from the start any knowledge that he thought he had. The revelation in the Law could likewise have led to faith, and thus to sanctification, if man had renounced any fulfilment of God's will by his own ability. Because of this double original sin, a new saving drama has become necessary now, νυνί (Rom. 3.21), one that at the same time takes into account the sin of pride committed by man. This saving drama in Christ is of such a quality that it now finally becomes apparent that we can respond neither with our knowledge nor with our behaviour, but only with our turning away from ourselves in faith, looking to an *event* that has been accomplished by someone else without our help and without our faith. It is essential to this saving drama that it involves a divine, ontic event (Rom. 3.21ff.) linked with preceding events including human rebellion through original sin. Faith's only possible reaction to this saving drama must include the recognition that the event as such is decisive for my salvation, and not just the moment of my faith. What would Paul, or for that matter Luther, to whom some like to appeal in justifying their preoccupation with the act of faith, have said to detaching the act of faith from the ontic event? Is it really admissible in such an important question to claim that, by means of Heidegger's conceptuality, one understands Paul better than he understood himself, and Luther better than he understood himself?

If I now attempt to show that faith in salvation history so understood is possible even today, I do not mean to circumvent the scandal in yet another way, for without this scandal whatever faith there may be is unrelated to faith in the biblical sense.

Faith presupposes hearing, says Paul (Rom. 10.14ff.). We have seen above that this hearing can be done by anyone, even those who are not led to faith. But at least one must attempt not to shut off the possibility of a proper hearing by excluding from the questions one poses any connection of one's self-understanding with a coherent salvation history. What must be required here for scholarly reasons[1] is now theologically important as well, for obedient listening to the story of an event completely foreign to us ought to lead us to faith in what is revealed as the meaning of this event by the New Testament witnesses—that it has happened for us because it happened *without* us. Next, of course, we come to an address and a decision of faith. The address says, 'This history foreign to you took place, is taking place, and will take place for your sake.' The decision says, 'We purposely align ourselves with this history foreign to us.' Just as we

---

[1] See above pp. 70ff.

belong in a natural way to the particular history of the people among
whom we are born, so we know that *we belong now to this restricted
history of salvation* in which God is at work in Christ in a special way
to direct all history.

We come to faith when we are so overwhelmed by salvation
history as such that we cannot help regarding ourselves as included
in it, and we must therefore consciously align ourselves with it. This
experience of being overwhelmed involves two factors—the facts
communicated *and* the interpretative revelation about these facts.
We have emphasized from the start that both belong to salvation
history itself—the fact and its interpretation by the biblical witnesses. Faith is therefore also a faith in the witnesses, or rather in
their function in salvation history. Faith intrudes upon us as we hear
the witness, although we see the human weakness and imperfection
of the witnesses themselves. *We* cannot be eyewitnesses any more. But
to be *witnesses* ourselves we must believe in their witness. This looks
like dead 'faith in authority'. But the biblical witnesses, the prophets
and apostles, are so closely bound up with the salvation history revealed to them that their witness as such can become an object of
a true and living faith in their mission the basis of which lies in the
mission of the bearer of revelation, Christ. We have seen that the
biblical witnesses too believe in the witness of their predecessors, so
that the new facts and their interpretation are connected with the
salvation history of the past. We find ourselves in this same situation,
but now vis-à-vis the *whole* salvation history of the Bible.

The role of the Bible in our Church cannot be justified without
this faith in the function of the biblical witnesses in salvation history
which, as we have seen, leads to the canon.[1] These witnesses belong
in the sphere of history, like the events of salvation history to which
they testify and which they interpret by the revelation imparted to
them. Therefore, it is possible for us in our modest place to align
ourselves with this saving process that took place independently of
us, placing ourselves beside the biblical witnesses, while at the same
time maintaining the immeasurable distance that separates us from
them. In this way the scandal of a connected history appears to faith
as a divine means for bringing about salvation.

The fact that an address and decision in faith follow presupposes,
of course, that we are aware of sin and its consequences because of

1 See above p. 116.

which this whole salvation history has come to pass. The need for such a point of contact implicit in our human existence is undisputed, but the indissoluble bond between our sin and our redemption from it in the salvation history which is proclaimed in the Bible is given neither by our human existence nor by some kind of *Vorverständnis*. This is the scandal that claims me in the realm of faith. What addresses me and leads me to a decision is not the question intrinsic in my consciousness of sin nor an answer given at the level of my self-understanding. Rather, it is the fact that sin and death, like redemption and life, appear in full reality only *on a totally different level*, namely, the level of a connected history (and therefore not in a punctual history in the existential sense).

Not only does original sin stand at the beginning of salvation history as the starting point for this history which rests upon the election of a minority, but human sin constantly rebels against the saving plan. God can, however, make use of human sin to carry out his plan. Hence the juxtaposition of the divine plan and historical contingency (Gal. 3.19; Rom. 5.20).

We would misunderstand this decisive role we have attributed to human sin in the course of salvation history if we were still to see in reference to salvation history a secondary objectification and historicization of something that happens to us psychologically or existentially. Although Paul maintains our responsibility for our sin, in his view our sinning is nevertheless dependent upon a sinful act of our human ancestors, in other words, upon an *event*. That is the meaning of Rom. 5.12ff. Just as in our sin and its consequences we are dependent upon a sin committed before us and stand in the solidarity of the history of sinful mankind and its consequence, death, so we are dependent upon another's act of grace for our justification leading us to life. The conviction of predestination issues from this faith, and from this faith issues the decision to align our existence with this saving process.

We know that the saving process in the present merely takes further what has already happened independently of us. Here it is proper to distinguish clearly the prophets and apostles from all the later witnesses with whom we identify ourselves in our faith. Nevertheless, if our faith is indeed oriented toward the faith of the biblical witnesses, both our faith and theirs will share the vivid awareness *of finding ourselves in a stream of salvation history* as it is revealed to us in the Bible. Our solidarity with this history then becomes infinitely more significant to us than our solidarity with any other history, such as the history of our own nation.

Anyone who cannot summon up any understanding of salvation history and can see only static thinking in it ought to reflect whether the extraordinary impulse that propelled the gospel in the first century did not stem from the Christian certainty of standing in this narrow but so uniquely active current to which the decisive Christ events belong, and to which, furthermore, the history of the people of the old covenant belongs. For the first Christians to attempt to provide a connection between themselves and the Old Testament was not an 'unheard-of philological farce over the Old Testament';[1] it was more than academic biblicism, and was more than mere apologetic. It was the expression of a joyful consciousness of belonging to this same history.

Why should this consciousness of faith be impossible today? Certainly not because of the advance of science. Why should we not be able to believe that we stand in the development of this history and, with the biblical witnesses, are actually bringing about this historical development? Even the knowledge of our own sin cannot exclude such a consciousness, for we know that alongside the 'already' the 'not yet' still remains in effect.

Is not salvation history an element of a present reality which is always advancing and never exhausted, quite different from any mere doctrine, however lofty it may be, laid down in the holy scriptures of other religions?[2] The Bible owes its lasting significance for the present to the fact that it points beyond itself to the post-biblical present as the norm of an unfinished history. The faith that we stand in this history implies above all that we are situated in the development of the decisive events wrought in Christ. Christ is so near to us because he has appeared at the high-point of God's saving drama in history, and has clearly shown that he has already been at work in salvation history as the pre-existent Christ, and that he continues working as the exalted Lord in the period of salvation history with which we may align ourselves in faith.

The work of Christ can be regarded as the return of all history back to salvation history. We are tempted to forget that Christ became history at the same time he became man. The debate over

---

[1] See above p. 87.

[2] One could also discuss salvation history and Islam. But that would extend beyond the limits of this work.

'substance' in the history of dogma was indeed necessary, but it pushed this aspect of the New Testament too much into the background. We could alter the patristic doctrine that Christ became man so that man might become God into *Christ became history so that all history might become salvation history*. In that case, the statement that Christ humiliated himself for us takes on an especially concrete character. To be linked with him in faith, we do not need to leave our level or wait for momentary epiphanies; we must make a decision for salvation history on our level of history.

Faith in salvation history and its unfolding in the present now means that we, like the biblical witnesses, are obliged to make constant *new interpretations*. For the ministers of the Church charged with the commission of proclaiming the gospel, this new interpretation is called preaching. For those charged with doctrine, it is called exegesis and (as an extension of exegesis) theology. The task of the preacher and exegete is to interpret the past and future of salvation history in *relation to its present development in our time. Thus, all our theological work belongs to the development of salvation history*.

Despite the analogy of our task to that of the biblical witnesses, we must again be careful not to identify the two. In contrast to them, we are witnesses only in a secondary way. We are reminded that the prophets and the apostles always reinterpreted the *kerygma* of salvation history handed down to them in the light of new events. Since, however, salvation history has already reached its high-point for us, we are no longer concerned with new events leading the divine saving drama to its high-point, but only with the development of drama towards its end. Here we must pay heed to everything we have said above about the *development* of salvation history in our time. We can never point with certainty to the present events in which salvation history in the narrower sense is being developed, but the salvation history in the Bible does offer us guide-lines here.

It teaches us above all that the locus from which this development proceeds is the Church. Thus, it is primarily on the basis of experiences in the Church that the preacher and the exegete must attempt their new interpretations. This sounds, of course, very unscholarly and 'pietistic', and since I have tried here to do justice through the New Testament concept of faith to a concern for objectivity which is in such bad taste these days, this 'hermeneutical' demand might appear surprising. But I have always indicated that one has to have the faith of the writers of the New Testament for a deeper understanding of the message of salvation history in the New Testament. This is only possible within the Church, for the faith of the New Testament writers cannot be separated from their membership of the Church. There is no 'self-understanding' of individual existence in the New Testament which ignores the Church.

The Church is the place where all the writings of the New Testament arose, where all the new interpretations of salvation history dawned on the New Testament writers. Hence it is entirely justified and even necessary, from the point of view of scholarship, to take into account one's participation in the life of the present Church as an important aid to interpretation in the second of the exegetical phases which we have distinguished.[1] If, in accord with our knowledge of form criticism, we regard the early Christian Church as the legitimate place of origin of the interpretation of Jesus' life and message, then, despite the great chronological distance, we must not exclude the life of the Church of today from our understanding of the New Testament writings.

Furthermore, this or that event of world affairs in the present, which the Bible allows us to see with cautious reservation as an event of salvation history, may for its own part serve to illuminate the biblical salvation history in a kind of circular procedure.[2] However, it is in any case less dangerous to keep to the events happening in the life of the present Church. Here again caution is, of course, necessary, and I must repeat everything that I have said above[3] about a concern for objectivity and the requirement that we should not begin with *our own* question.

But a reservation must be made in these matters even about the present Church. There is a continuity in the life of the Church of Christ from its beginnings up to today. Yet we must take into account not only continuity and legitimate development onwards, but also sources of error. Therefore we cannot view the teaching office of the Church as infallible. If the entry of the present life of the Church into our consideration is not to become a source of error, then it must go hand in hand with an endeavour to describe the faith of the

[1] I have shown elsewhere that these do not have to be two phases in strict succession; see 'Les problèmes posés par la méthode exégétique de Karl Barth', *RHPR*, 1928, pp. 70ff.

[2] Thus at the time of National Socialism, certain descriptions of the self-deifying state ('the beast from the abyss') found in the Apocalypse of John became remarkably understandable.

[3] See above p. 68.

early Church in the saving process while deliberately disregarding the present Church (and our existential questions), by the use of philological, literary, historical, and archaeological aids. If we wish to share the faith of the first Christians as we stand in the context of the Church's life, we must submit ourselves to the constant control of these scholarly aids and be ready to give up ideas and associations that seem important to us whenever such things do not stand up under this control.

The use of modern scholarly aids distinguishes the new interpretations of present-day exegetes from the new interpretations of all the biblical witnesses. The requirement that these aids be used for biblical exegesis does not only stem from a postulate of the study of all documents belonging to the past; it also has a theological basis— a basis in salvation history. We have tried to show in this whole book that the content of the biblical message is made up of events and their interpretations. Furthermore, we have indicated that we can emulate the biblical witnesses' act of faith in the events interpreted only if we are confronted with the *event* to which they were eyewitnesses and which they interpreted for us. To be sure, the aids of scholarship do not put us in a position to ascertain the naked events of biblical history with certainty. But is there not an element of salvation-historical development in the fact that in the post-biblical period, when there are no longer eyewitnesses to the decisive events, these aids are granted to us which, at least within the confines of human knowledge, place us before these events which have provided the initiative for their own interpretations, which in turn make the claim that these events have occurred for our salvation? This is important for all new interpretations we make today.

5. SALVATION HISTORY AND ETHICS

The success of existentialism is partly explained by the fact that it presents an ethics which is neither static nor nomistic, and which therefore places a great demand upon us. But at this crucial point it is evident that it would be false to see existentialism and salvation history standing in opposition to one another, as though only a static ethics could go hand in hand with salvation history. On the contrary, an ethics anchored in salvation history recognizes very clearly the concrete situation of existence. This is where a point of contact between existentialism and salvation-historical theology should be noted. Furthermore, salvation history is in a position to protect existentialist ethics from a danger which is not necessarily inherent in it, but which somehow continually threatens it—the danger of an antinomian nihilism. At the same time salvation history can also maintain the dynamic character of existentialist ethics.

In this final chapter I am merely trying to point out how salvation history can continue in the post-biblical period in the specific case of ethical conduct. I cannot elaborate an ethics of salvation history or even give the outline for one. However, such an ethics ought to be written some day.[1] In order not to trespass too much beyond the limits within which I have confined myself in this book, I shall limit myself to sketching briefly the basic lines of a salvation-historical ethics as I see it.

Salvation history is realized in Christian conduct. Salvation history as summed up in Christ becomes concentrated in ethical decision ($\delta o \kappa \iota \mu \acute{a} \zeta \epsilon \iota \nu$) at *one* point in which the Christ event becomes visible in its total, temporal extension. At the moment when existence is integrated into the saving event, the vertical and horizontal lines of salvation intersect. The punctual and the linear, existence and salvation history, meet. At this juncture salvation-historical theology and existentialism make contact. Here (but only here!) one could speak of a 'salvation-historical existentialism'. This is a direct and proper conclusion from the preceding discussion.

In the Bible, an ethical imperative always follows from an (or the!) *indicative*. However, because the central concern in the Old and New Testament is salvation history, and therefore because the biblical indicative *is a self-developing and self-unfolding salvation history*, an ethics rooted in it cannot be static or nomistic, nor can it be antinomian like 'situation ethics'. All the characteristics of salvation history found in the Bible in general and in the New Testament in particular, as we have described them here, must be rediscovered in the ethics of the New Testament. We are therefore looking for the intertwining of God's plan with the contingency of historical develop-

[1] There have been several attempts to solve *individual* problems by recourse to salvation history. But to my knowledge a comprehensive 'salvation-historical ethics' is still to be written. Among the well-known textbooks on ethics, some (for instance the works of N. H. Søe, H. van Oyen, and others) come close to my understanding, even though in their totality they have not been the products of thinking along the lines of salvation history.

ment, the intertwining of the vertical with the horizontal, which is so important in all salvation history.

The connection of the commandment with the saving event is quite obvious even in the Old Testament. The combination permeates the whole Old Testament like a leitmotif: 'You have seen . . . therefore do . . .' It is no different in the New Testament. Ethics has its foundation, on the one hand, in the decisive Christ event at the mid-point in history and, on the other hand, in its christological development. One may recall the sixth chapter of Romans. The first part indicates the relationship between baptism and the event accomplished once-for-all in Christ's death and resurrection. In the second part, the imperative (what we *ought* to be) follows this indicative (what we already *are*) very forcefully. Col. 3.1–3 also links the great Christ events very closely with the life of the Christian: 'If then you have been raised with Christ, seek the things that are above, where Christ is, seated at the right hand of God. Set your minds on things that are above, not on things that are on earth. For you have died, and your life is hid with Christ in God.' An *imitatio Christi* rightly understood and oriented towards the New Testament is founded on salvation history.

As soon as a person takes his ethical norm from biblical salvation history, it becomes apparent that the accusation, constantly repeated in a quite tiresome way, that salvation history allows no room for decision, is without foundation. If one does make a decision anchored in salvation history, it is not left floating in the air. It is only through salvation history that decision takes on the very concrete character that existentialism demands, and ceases being simply decision for decision. Decision for Christ is not vague decision for what is not at my disposal, for desecularization, for the 'wholly other'. Decision for Christ places me into a very definite context which is conditioned by salvation history past and future. In this context a very definite task must be fulfilled, the guide-lines of which (for the present period of salvation history) are stated in the Bible.[1] Wherever 'what is not at my disposal' is seen merely in terms of '*punctual* history', and is no longer anchored in salvation history, ethics loses the concrete specification attached to it in the Bible, and is in this way in danger of lapsing again into general principles. Yet that is what every ethics based on existentialism actually seeks to guard against.

The contingency which together with the constant constitutes all

---

[1] See above pp. 304ff.

biblical salvation history shows that neither God's saving plan itself nor our knowledge of this plan excludes free decision. The importance of the fact that in the Bible the ethical norm is a history becomes evident here. A norm that is history cannot be static. The free decision to align ourselves with the events in the Bible opens to us a *variety* of tasks and modes of life among which we must make a *choice* in our specific case and our concrete situation. This variety is related to the variety of gifts given by the Spirit, and the variety of gifts is conditioned by the variety of tasks, or 'ministries', furnished in turn by the plan and development of salvation history. This decision to perform some special ministry is also in accordance with the resolution to align oneself with salvation history. Despite the knowledge of the divine plan, and even because of it, this decision is no less a decision. But at this point we must remember everything we said about the 'fluctuating' development of salvation history which includes detours. There have always been regressions. Human sin always rebelled against God's saving plan, and God always included sin in the subsequent execution of his plan. We have seen that even in the post-biblical period, as salvation history develops, the development proceeds in this way. The 'linear' process must be seen in this way and only in this way, and I have never understood it otherwise. Therein lies the simultaneous relationship of ethical decision both to the divine plan and to the freedom of historical contingency. *Both* guarantee the concrete character of all decision. Because the biblical salvation history comprises both God's plan and historical contingency, salvation-historical ethics is more *concretely* oriented than any other ethics.

The juxtaposition of a constant plan with historical contingency characterizes the *relationship between a firm norm and the application of all New Testament ethics to situations*. The old Law remains. The New Testament does not bring any new law, but it does apply the old in the light of the fulfilment of all salvation history. Even in the Sermon on the Mount Jesus brings no new law, but shows how in each situation the old Law is to be fulfilled radically[1] in view of the Kingdom of God which is immeasurably closer. The antitheses found in the Sermon on the Mount and in the parables in their original form show this especially clearly. That Jesus himself proclaims the decisive 'but I say to you . . .', and thus becomes the fulfilment of the Law

[1] The lasting merit of R. Bultmann's little book on Jesus was in showing so clearly this demand for radical fulfilment.

in his own person,[1] agrees with the fact that in him all salvation history reaches its high-point. How much everything depends upon the inclusion of the Law *within the framework of the New Testament events* is shown by the profound saying of Jesus about the Sabbath that we know only from Manuscript D at Luke 6.5: 'On the same day, seeing someone working on the Sabbath, he said to him, "Man, if you know what you are doing you are blessed; but if you do not know, you are accursed and a transgressor of the Law".' Above all, one could refer to everything Paul says about conduct in very practical questions which must now be answered in the light of fulfilling the commandment of love (for instance, the question of buying and eating meat sacrificed to idols).[2]

Because salvation history *advances and undergoes development*, there are always new situations within the biblical salvation history. That is the reason why the old Law must always be applied anew, and why it is conditioned by the new indicatives of salvation history. But since the high-point of salvation history has been attained in Christ, decisive significance is attached to this *one* indicative, and it furnishes the basic principle for ethical application.

All this is applicable specifically in post-biblical times. Here again salvation history advances, and here again there are new events in salvation history, but they are now, as we have seen, the *development* of what has gone before. The ethical task here is more than ever application to the concrete situations of the present time, but application of a *norm*, which goes back to the Old Testament, is conditioned by the decisive Christ event, and is clarified for the present period by the characteristics of this period between Christ and the end, the period of preaching and of the Church.

The character of post-biblical time as an interval is normative for ethics. A. Schweitzer's position is correct to the extent that he describes Jesus' instructions for this interval as an '*Interimsethik*'. But Schweitzer stresses only the *negative* character of this interim, arguing that those instructions were exclusively applicable to the interim, which was originally thought to be of short duration, whereas in reality the positive side of this interim must be stressed, belonging as it does to salvation history. Although the extension of time has,

---

[1] See W. D. Davies, *The Setting of the Sermon on the Mount*, 1964, as well as the rest of his publications, which are so important for this problem.

[2] Cf. W. Schrage, *Die konkreten Einzelgebote in der paulinischen Paränese. Ein Beitrag zur neutestamentlichen Ethik*, 1961.

of course, ethical consequences[1] which may not be minimized, it is still true that the question of temporal extension does not *basically* change the ethical problem of the interval so long as we do not lose sight of the fact that the present period is an interval.

Ethical decisions are made harder, not easier for the Christian by this task of applying the old Law fulfilled in Christ to the situation created by new events. The difficulty stems from the fact that an ethics rooted in salvation history can only be an ethics which applies in every case to a concrete situation, but that it must at the same time be founded on a norm drawn from salvation history. Both descriptions fit New Testament ethics. The ethical judgment, the δοκιμάζειν which Paul repeatedly speaks of, expresses this precisely. A norm which is history cannot lead to a static ethics. On the other hand, historical contingency which takes place in the framework of a saving plan revealed by God cannot justify an arbitrary decision. Hence the complex relationship of the vertical to the horizontal is given expression in the sphere of ethics. Instead of being eliminated, the *'conscience'* finds its function in the δοκιμάζειν performed in the context of salvation history.

Because ethics is anchored in salvation history, we must take seriously the message that our time, regardless of its length, is an end time. The seriousness of the decision which Bultmann stresses so much is given an increased urgency in New Testament ethics by the temporal understanding of eschatology rejected by existentialism. This urgency is lost as soon as the temporal understanding is given up. I do not say that the seriousness or the urgency is lost in an 'always standing in decision', understood quite apart from salvation history. But at least it is not oriented in the same way as the call for 'wakefulness' contained in the Synoptic *logia* and parables.

Because the ethical δοκιμάζειν is rooted in the indicative describing the decisive Christ event, the *love* implicit in this indicative contains the principle that gives guidance for all ethical judgment in each concrete situation during the interval. ἀγάπη[2] as the principle for applying Christian ethics is anchored in terms of salvation history in the love God showed us in Christ as the decisive climax of all his saving activity. The practice of ἀγάπη is founded on this love and finds in it the possibility of unqualified realization, as is shown most clearly in the First Epistle of John.

[1] See below p. 337.
[2] See C. Spicq, *Agapé dans le Nouveau Testament*, 1-3, 1959ff.

Therefore ἀγάπη is linked also with the *Holy Spirit* who typifies *the period in which we live*. Paul shows this in an especially profound way in the important passage in Gal. 5.14ff. When every analogy of these statements with Hellenistic-Jewish parenaetic sources is considered, and their dependence upon them is taken into account, the remarks in this passage still surpass such literature because they are bound up with the Pauline *contrast* of σάρξ *and* πνεῦμα which is part and parcel of salvation history. The impossibility of loving our neighbour as we (who are driven by the σάρξ) love ourselves has already become possible through the πνεῦμα. Only the latter can offset the deadly power of the σάρξ, which is already vanquished by the πνεῦμα, and yet is still not vanquished. The σάρξ can only drive us to self-love, and this means to mutual destruction (v. 15). The *pneuma* must motivate us to love of neighbour. A *pneuma* that does not share itself with others, or create a constant relationship of give-and-take, is not *pneuma*.

Wherever the *pneuma* is at work, it creates fellowship through the love of our neighbour. Thus when Paul recounts the fruits of the flesh, he simply mentions expressions and consequences of self-love (vv. 19ff.). The fruits of the Spirit, however, are the fruits of the love which creates fellowship (v. 22).

In I Corinthians, the apostle himself applies the δοκιμάζειν to the various situations in the Church. He shows how, for example, the question of eating meat sacrificed to idols, or the question of speaking in tongues, may not be solved in a theoretical or arbitrary way, but only in a concrete instance on the basis of the indicative of love as revealed in salvation history. In Paulinism, the Law is not abolished as the formulation of the divine will. But its radical fulfilment is possible for the first time only through the *pneuma* which is received in faith and which impels us to love our neighbour. Paul's complex attitude towards the Law is conditioned by his total view of salvation history. The juxtaposition of God's constant plan with the historical contingency characteristic of all salvation history is very evident here. The Law retains its validity (Rom. 7.12, 'holy, just, and good') as a commandment. But since man does not commit himself to the humble attitude of faith with respect to the Law when he fails to acknowledge his incapacity to fulfil it with his own power, and perpetrates the original human sin of confusing creator and creature (Rom. 1.21ff.), it has become clear in the final saving drama of Christ which atones for this sin that only the deed of another can enable one to carry out the Law. This means in turn that I must receive the Spirit through faith in this deed, and that the Spirit enables me to fulfil the Law (Rom. 3.21ff.).

Thus the Law abides as a commandment, but everything that was superseded when the divine saving plan progressed from the saving drama of the old covenant to that of the new is abolished. Therefore circumcision, which had its validity as the seal of the old covenant and points in the direction of faith (Rom. 4), is abolished, since the Spirit is bestowed by baptism, the seal of the new covenant. Without taking salvation history into account, we would have to regard Paul's teaching on the Law as completely self-contradictory. The Law remains the formulation of the divine will (but not the means to carry it out), and yet at the same time it is abolished as far as some essential items commanded in the old covenant, such as sacrifice and circumcision, are concerned. This notion can be made intelligible only by salvation history. Paul resists the further practice of circumcision so vehemently because it does not acknowledge the saving plan revealed by God nor its progress from the saving drama of the old to that of the new covenant. This same advance on the other hand affects the new interpretation of the whole Law *by a single principle*, namely, the principle of radical love established in the indicative of the new drama of salvation performed in Christ.

In terms of ethics, the fact that the σάρξ is vanquished but not yet destroyed corresponds with the tension of 'already' and 'not yet' which we have claimed as the key to all salvation history. Related to the 'not yet' is the fact that not only the σάρξ, *but also the whole structure of this world* still continues to exist, and this, too, has important consequences for ethics. Our task consists in the fact that we must live within this divinely ordained structure which we know to be passing away, looking to the coming Kingdom. The dialectic of New Testament ethics rests upon the fact that we must acknowledge this structure as still existing by the will of God, we must work in and within it, we must constantly improve it, and yet we must not be absorbed into it. We may never regard it as our final goal, either positively, as if to set up an earthly Kingdom of God, or negatively, as if to destroy it through human means. Above all our striving stands the dictum, 'The form of this world is passing away' (I Cor. 7.31). Thus we have an obligation to the earthly government which belongs to this structure. Even as a pagan government it is a part of Christ's lordship without knowing it, and as those who do know this fact we must assist the state. Paul speaks of the government in this way in Rom. 13.1ff. But even towards such a 'good' government our attitude remains critical. We know that it cannot become an ultimate value for us (I Cor. 6.1ff.). We give it its due without seeing in it an end in itself. Instead, we keep in mind the narrow line of salvation history which it will join when God ushers in the end time. On this basis we seek to judge and aid it in fulfilling its mission. If it hinders us in giving to God what belongs to God (Rev. 13), we shall resist without working to bring about its destruction in the name of Christ. The idea of a crusade is foreign to the New Testament, for it is irreconcilable with the tension between 'already' and 'not yet'.[1]

We see, of course, in the case of our obligation towards the *state* how difficult and complex ethical decision is because of this tension. Thus Paul's positive statements on the state in Rom. 13 relate to the same pagan government of Rome as do those in Chapter 13 of the Apocalypse. Paul would surely have approved the latter's remarks in the context about the deification of the state (the worship of the emperor, the 'beast out of the abyss'). Any interim ethics as an ethics for the interval must therefore be formulated in each case by the norms mentioned above. The ethical δοκιμάζειν is the great gift of the Spirit which we need in order to apply rightly the norms given us.

The same is true of all the so-called *cultural values* which the divinely ordained structure of this world offers us. We seek to evaluate them according to our knowledge of the *kairos* in salvation history and to bring them into harmony with it without destroying their secular structure, which is no more to be condemned as such than the structure of the pagan state. But after we have evaluated them we must also write an ultimate question mark after them.

The important inference that Paul draws from the 'brevity of the time' in I Cor. 7.29, that those who are married should live as though they were not, those who mourn as though they were not mourning, those who rejoice as though they were not rejoicing, those who buy as though they had no goods, contains the guide-line for all ethics characterized by the 'already' and the 'not yet' of salvation history: ὡς μή. The stress here is on the 'not', of course. But there is *still* marriage, there is *still* mourning, there is *still* rejoicing, and there is *still* buying, all of which are taken into consideration in Paul's

---

[1] See O. Cullmann, *The State in the New Testament*, [2]1962.

ethical outlook, as is shown by the way he applies this ethical demand in all his letters.

We dare not detach these imperatives from their temporal context, for without the temporal context the imperatives are robbed of their basic Pauline orientation. They are found after the statement that the time 'is short'. Paul is not thinking here of centuries, and it is important for the ethical application of these instructions that the development of salvation history which already occurs in the New Testament includes the *extension* of time to an unspecified duration. There are, of course, ethical consequences stemming from the fact that we, in contrast to Paul, reckon with an *indefinite* duration of this world's structure. Interest in working in the 'structure' of this world, and the ethical obligation that goes with it, must naturally increase as we come to realize that many generations, and not just ours, must live within this structure. We must consider what great ethical importance there is in the question of whether this structure is in agreement with what we have recognized as the ethical injunction in the current situation. Nevertheless, we have seen that it is still important for the extended period that now as before it is an eschatological interval, and that with Christ the end has come nearer since we have entered the 'final' phase, however long it may last.

The consequence of knowing about this *kairos* (Rom. 13.11) is that we judge the structure God has intended both more positively and *at the same time* more negatively than when we merely contrast the 'world with the other-worldly'. We judge it more positively, to the extent that we accept this structure as still belonging to our time, as something God has willed, and more negatively, inasmuch as we know that it is condemned to disappear, and that the coming Kingdom is already breaking in.[1]

Our understanding, informed by salvation history, must prevent us from drawing two false inferences from the fact that God still intends this structure to exist. On the one hand, we must not allow ourselves to be misled into deriving our norms from this structure instead of from the narrow line of salvation; for these norms must indeed be applied to the structure. On the other hand, our knowing about the 'not yet', or even our knowing that human sin is included in God's saving plan, may in no case become a pretext for ethical compromises. Instead, all our acts must be inspired by the 'already'

[1] We are well aware that it is difficult to delineate what belongs to this 'structure', but we must attempt to do so.

of the end anticipated in Christ. The knowledge of the 'not yet', linked with the knowledge of this 'already', can have ethical influence only as it intensifies our consciousness of being fellow-workers in carrying out the saving plan in history. This is what characterizes our ethical decisions.

If this consciousness is really rooted in the revelation in salvation history which we have described, our failure to see success will evoke neither Pharisaic complacency nor despair in us. We know that God is carrying out his saving plan in our presence, although the details of his ways are hidden from us. We also know that we our-selves are fellow workers in God's plan, although the saving process and its consummation are not dependent upon us. This knowledge strengthens us in what we undertake so that we may work with confidence. It also gives us the dignity that lies in labouring on for the cause of God in faithfulness and endurance, without being per-suaded by success or dissuaded by failure. We place ourselves in the current of this narrow and yet forceful process, for we know that we are involved in it. It has often become fashionable these days to regard our ignorance of our 'whence' and 'whither' as the basis of the dignity of human existence. The knowledge of this process that we have tried to depict in the light of the New Testament certainly does not impair this dignity; on the contrary, it can give to our being depth and intensity, and to our deeds the dynamic and the joy to which the members of the early Church first gave witness. We have tried to show that the 'nevertheless' of faith and decision does not just find a place here—its only proper place *is* here.

We may sum up everything we have said about the basis of New Testament ethics in salvation history with the triad which appears several times in Paul (I Thess. 1.3; 5.8; I Cor. 13.13): faith in the Christ event past and present, hope in the saving event yet to come, love as the normative principle and realization of faith and hope. These three make salvation history past, present, and future real in the 'now' of ethical decision.

INDEX OF BIBLICAL REFERENCES

OLD TESTAMENT

NEW TESTAMENT

INDEX OF PROPER NAMES

INDEX OF SUBJECTS